Also by Michael Moss
Palace Coup

Salt Sugar Fat

salt sugar fat salt sugar fat salt sugar fat salt sugar fat salt sugar fat salt sugar fat salt sugar fat
salt sugar fat salt sugar fat salt sugar fat salt sugar fat salt sugar fat salt sugar fat salt sugar fat
salt sugar fat salt sugar fat salt sugar fat salt sugar fat salt sugar fat salt sugar fat salt sugar fat
salt sugar fat salt sugar fat salt sugar fat salt sugar fat salt sugar fat salt sugar fat salt sugar fat
salt sugar fat salt sugar fat salt sugar fat salt sugar fat salt sugar fat salt sugar fat salt sugar fat
salt sugar fat salt sugar fat salt sugar fat salt sugar fat salt sugar fat salt sugar fat salt sugar fat
salt sugar fat salt sugar fat salt sugar fat salt sugar fat salt sugar fat salt sugar fat salt sugar fat
salt sugar fat salt sugar fat salt sugar fat salt sugar fat salt sugar fat salt sugar fat salt sugar fat
salt sugar fat salt sugar fat salt sugar fat salt sugar fat salt sugar fat salt sugar fat salt sugar fat
salt sugar fat salt sugar fat salt sugar fat salt sugar fat salt sugar fat salt sugar fat salt sugar fat
salt sugar fat salt sugar fat salt sugar fat salt sugar fat salt sugar fat salt sugar fat salt sugar fat
salt sugar fat salt sugar fat salt sugar fat salt sugar fat salt sugar fat salt sugar fat salt sugar fat
salt sugar fat salt sugar fat salt sugar fat salt sugar fat salt sugar fat salt sugar fat salt sugar fat
salt sugar fat salt sugar fat salt sugar fat salt sugar fat salt sugar fat salt sugar fat salt sugar fat
salt sugar fat salt sugar fat salt sugar fat salt sugar fat salt sugar fat salt sugar fat salt sugar fat
salt sugar fat salt sugar fat salt sugar fat salt sugar fat salt sugar fat salt sugar fat salt sugar fat
salt sugar fat salt sugar fat salt sugar fat salt sugar fat salt sugar fat salt sugar fat salt sugar fat
salt sugar fat salt sugar fat salt sugar fat salt sugar fat salt sugar fat salt sugar fat salt sugar fat
salt sugar fat salt sugar fat salt sugar fat salt sugar fat salt sugar fat salt sugar fat salt sugar fat
salt sugar fat salt sugar fat salt sugar fat salt sugar fat salt sugar fat salt sugar fat salt sugar fat
salt sugar fat salt sugar fat salt sugar fat salt sugar fat salt sugar fat salt sugar fat salt sugar fat
salt sugar fat salt sugar fat salt sugar fat salt sugar fat salt sugar fat salt sugar fat salt sugar fat
salt sugar fat salt sugar fat salt sugar fat salt sugar fat salt sugar fat salt sugar fat salt sugar fat
salt sugar fat salt sugar fat salt sugar fat salt sugar fat salt sugar fat salt sugar fat salt sugar fat
salt sugar fat salt sugar fat salt sugar fat salt sugar fat salt sugar fat salt sugar fat salt sugar fat
salt sugar fat salt sugar fat salt sugar fat salt sugar fat salt sugar fat salt sugar fat salt sugar fat
salt sugar fat salt sugar fat salt sugar fat salt sugar fat salt sugar fat salt sugar fat salt sugar fat
salt sugar fat salt sugar fat salt sugar fat salt sugar fat salt sugar fat salt sugar fat salt sugar fat
salt sugar fat salt sugar fat salt sugar fat salt sugar fat salt sugar fat salt sugar fat salt sugar fat
salt sugar fat salt sugar fat salt sugar fat salt sugar fat salt sugar fat salt sugar fat salt sugar fat
salt sugar fat salt sugar fat salt sugar fat salt sugar fat salt sugar fat salt sugar fat salt sugar fat
salt sugar fat salt sugar fat salt sugar fat salt sugar fat salt sugar fat salt sugar fat salt sugar fat
salt sugar fat salt sugar fat salt sugar fat salt sugar fat salt sugar fat salt sugar fat salt sugar fat
salt sugar fat salt sugar fat salt sugar fat salt sugar fat salt sugar fat salt sugar fat salt sugar fat

Salt Sugar Fat

How the Food Giants Hooked Us

Michael Moss

Random House

New York

Published in the United States by Random House, an imprint of The Random House Publishing Group, a division of Random House, Inc., New York.

RANDOM HOUSE and colophon are registered trademarks of Random House, Inc.

Library of Congress Cataloging-in-Publication Data

Moss, Michael.
Salt, sugar, fat : how the food giants hooked us / Michael Moss.
p. cm.
ISBN 978-1-4000-6980-4—ISBN 978-0-679-60477-8 (ebook)
1. Nutrition—Economic aspects—United States.   2. Food habits—Economic aspects—United States.   3. Food industry and trade—United States.   I. Title.
RA784.M638 2013
613.2—dc23   2012033034

Printed in the United States of America on acid-free paper

www.atrandom.com

2 3 4 5 6 7 8 9

Book design by Diane Hobbing

For EVE, AREN, AND WILL,
my all and everythings

contents

part **three**
salt • sugar • fat

Minneapolis was having a blustery spring evening on April 8, 1999, when a long line of town cars and taxis pulled up to the office complex on South 6th Street and discharged their well-dressed passengers. These eleven men were the heads of America's largest food companies. Among them, they controlled seven hundred thousand employees and $280 billion in annual sales. And even before their sumptuous dinner was served, they would be charting a course for their industry for years to come.

There would be no reporters at this gathering. No minutes taken, no recordings made. Rivals any other day, the CEOs and company presidents had come together for a meeting that was as secretive as it was rare. On the agenda was one item: the emerging epidemic of obesity and how to deal with it.

Pillsbury was playing host at its corporate headquarters, two glass and steel towers perched on the eastern edge of downtown. The largest falls on the Mississippi River rumbled a few blocks away, near the historic brick and iron-roller mills that, generations before, had made this city the flour-grinding capital of the world. A noisy midwestern wind gusting to 45 miles an hour buffeted the towers as the executives boarded the elevators and made their way to the thirty-first floor.

A top official at Pillsbury, fifty-five-year-old James Behnke, greeted the men as they walked in. He was anxious but also confident about the plan that he and a few other food company executives had devised to engage the CEOs on America's growing weight problem. "We were very concerned, and rightfully so, that obesity was becoming a major issue," Behnke recalled. "People were starting to talk about sugar taxes, and there was a lot of pressure on food companies." As the executives took their seats, Behnke particularly worried about how they would respond to the evening's most delicate matter: the notion that they and their companies had played a central role in creating this health crisis. Getting the company chiefs in the same room to talk about anything, much less a sensitive issue like this, was a tricky business, so Behnke and his fellow organizers had scripted the meeting carefully, crafting a seating chart and honing the message to its barest essentials. "CEOs in the food industry are typically not technical guys, and they're uncomfortable going to meetings where technical people talk in technical terms about technical things," Behnke said. "They don't want to be embarrassed. They don't want to make commitments. They want to maintain their aloofness and autonomy."

Nestlé was in attendance, as were Kraft and Nabisco, General Mills and Procter & Gamble, Coca-Cola and Mars. The companies present were the dominant players in processed industrial food, fiercely aggressive competitors who, when not gathering in secret, were looking to bludgeon one another in the grocery store.

Just that year, the head of General Mills had muscled his company past Kellogg to become the country's largest cereal maker, hooking shoppers with a dazzling lineup of new products and flavors, sold at reduced prices to boost sales all the more. General Mills was dominating in the dairy aisle as well, showing the rest of the industry just how easy it was to influence America's eating habits. The company's Yoplait brand had already transformed traditional unsweetened breakfast yogurt into a dessert-like snack. It now had twice as much sugar per serving as Lucky Charms, the company's cloyingly sweet, marshmallow-filled cereal. And yet, because of yogurt's well-tended image as a wholesome, life-giving snack, sales of Yoplait were soaring, with annual revenue topping $500 million. Emboldened by the success, General Mills' development wing pushed even harder, inventing a yogurt that came in a squeezable tube—perfect for kids—eliminating the need for a spoon. They called it Go-Gurt, and rolled it out nationally in the weeks before the CEO meeting. (By year's end, it would hit $100 million in sales.)

So while the atmosphere at the meeting was cordial, the CEOs were hardly friends. Their stature was defined by their skill in fighting each other for what they called "stomach share," or the amount of digestive space that any one company's brand can grab from the competition. If they eyed one another suspiciously that evening, it was for good reason. By 2001, Pillsbury's chief would be gone and the 127-year-old company—with its cookies, biscuits, and toaster strudel—would be acquired by General Mills.

Two of the men at the meeting rose above the fray. They were here to represent the industry titans, Cargill and Tate & Lyle, whose role it was to supply the CEOs with the ingredients they relied on to win. These were no run-of-the-mill ingredients, either. These were the three pillars of processed food, the creators of crave, and each of the CEOs needed them in huge quantities to turn their products into hits. These were also the ingredients that, more than any other, were directly responsible for the obesity epidemic. Together, the two suppliers had the salt, which was processed in dozens of ways to maximize the jolt that taste buds would feel with the very first bite; they had the fats, which delivered the biggest loads of calories and worked more subtly in inducing people to overeat; and they had the sugar, whose raw power in exciting the brain made it perhaps the most formidable ingredient of all, dictating the formulations of products from one side of the grocery store to the other.

James Behnke was all too familiar with the power of salt, sugar, and fat, having spent twenty-six years at Pillsbury under six chief executive officers. A chemist by training with a doctoral degree in food science, he became the company's chief technical officer in 1979 and was instrumental in creating a long line of hit products, including microwavable popcorn. He deeply admired Pillsbury, its employees, and the warm image of its brand. But in recent years, he had seen the endearing, innocent image of the Pillsbury Doughboy replaced by news pictures of children too obese to play, suffering from diabetes and the earliest signs of hypertension and heart disease. He didn't blame himself for creating high-calorie foods that the public found irresistible. He and other food scientists took comfort in knowing that the grocery store icons they had invented in a more innocent era—the soda and chips and TV dinners—had been imagined as occasional fare. It was society that had changed, changed so dramatically that these snacks and convenience foods had become a daily—even hourly—habit, a staple of the American diet.

Behnke's perspective on his life's work, though, began to shift when he was made a special advisor to Pillsbury's chief executive in 1999. From his new perch, Behnke started to get a different view of what he called the "big tenets" of his industry—taste, convenience, and cost. He worried, especially, about the economics that drive companies to spend as little money as possible in making processed foods. "Cost was always there," he told me. "Companies had different names for it. Sometimes they were called PIPs, or profit improvement programs, or margin enhancements, or cost reduction. Whatever you want to call it, people are always looking for a less expensive way."

In the months leading up to the CEO meeting, Behnke was engaged in conversation with a group of food science experts who were painting an increasingly grim picture of the public's ability to cope with the industry's formulations. These discussions were sponsored by a food industry group, the International Life Sciences Institute, for which Behnke was the incoming president, and the topics—from the body's fragile controls on overeating to the hidden power of some processed foods to make people feel hungrier still—convinced Behnke and the other insiders who organized the meeting that an intervention was needed. It was time to warn the CEOs that their companies may have gone too far in creating and marketing products to maximize their allure.

The discussion took place in Pillsbury's auditorium. The executives took the first two rows of seats, just in front of the stage, which was raised slightly from the floor. The first speaker was a man named Michael Mudd, and he was not some white-coated researcher from the Pacific Northwest. He was from Chicago, one of the industry's own: a vice president of Kraft.

Routinely ranked at or near the top of the industry with tens of billions of dollars in annual sales, Kraft has a power lineup of more than fifty-five brands that can carry the consumer through an entire day, from breakfast to midnight snack. For breakfast, it has stuffed bagels in eight varieties, with fully cooked bacon you can store in the cupboard right next to Tang, its powdered drink you can substitute for real orange juice. For lunch it has hot dogs, mac and cheese, and a TV dinner–like tray of meat and cheese called Lunchables. For dinner, it has the Velveeta Cheesy Skillets dinner kit, Shake 'n Bake, and Stove Top Stuffing. And for snacking, it has the king of cookies, the Oreo, which, at 490 billion cookies sold since its introduction a century ago, holds the crown as the most popular cookie of all time. As Kraft's CEO, Bob Eckert, would tell a reporter later that year, his singular aim was to dominate the industry: "If I ask who's the undisputed leader of the food industry, you might say Kraft. Then again, you might say Nestlé, Kellogg, General Mills, Nabisco. There is a whole cadre of companies performing well, but nobody's really broken away from the pack. And that's what I'd like to see Kraft do."

Mudd had risen through Kraft's corporate affairs office to become a company spokesman and much more. He tracked how consumers viewed the company generally, watched for signs of trouble from regulators, and helped guide the company's rapid response to any significant threats, like the tempest that had arisen a few years earlier over trans fats. He was deeply attuned to public sentiment, a seasoned fixer highly skilled in dealing with critics. His insights had garnered so much respect that—at least in the view of other senior Kraft officials—Mudd became something of a consigliere to the company's chief executives, the adviser whose whisperings helped guide the boss's every move. As he stood on the stage that evening, the CEOs in the audience knew that it was in their interest to listen.

"I very much appreciate this opportunity to talk to you about childhood obesity and the growing challenge it presents for us all," Mudd began. "Let me say right at the start, this is not an easy subject. There are no easy answers—for what the public health community must do to bring this problem under control. Or for what the industry should do as others seek to hold it accountable for what has happened. But this much is clear: For those of us who've looked hard at this issue, whether they're public health professionals or staff specialists in your own companies, we feel sure that the one thing we shouldn't do is nothing."

As he spoke, Mudd clicked through a deck of slides—114 in all—that were projected on a large screen behind him. This would be straight-up, in-your-face talk, no sugar-coating on his part. The headlines and phrases and figures were nothing short of staggering.

More than half of American adults were now considered overweight, with nearly one-quarter of the population—40 million adults—carrying so many extra pounds that they were clinically defined as obese. Among children, the rates had more than doubled since 1980, the year when the fat line on the charts began angling up, and the number of kids considered obese had shot past 12 million. (It was still only 1999; the nation's obesity rates would climb much higher.)

"Massive social costs estimated as high as $40–$100 billion a year," announced one of Mudd's slides in bright, bold lettering.

Then came the specifics: diabetes, heart disease, hypertension, gallbladder disease, osteoarthritis, three types of cancer—breast, colon, and that of the uterus lining—all on the rise. To varying degrees, the executives were told, obesity was being cited as one of the causes for each of these health crises. To drive the point home, they were shown how to calculate obesity using the body mass index, a simple ratio of height to weight, and given a few moments to determine their own BMIs with the formula that flashed up on the screen. (On this count, most of the men in the room could rest easy. They had personal trainers, gym memberships, and enough nutritional awareness to avoid diets that were heavy in the foods they manufactured.)

Mudd then brought them back to the reality as experienced by their middle-class customers, who were spending their gym time working a second job to make ends meet and not thinking too hard about their own diets. The media were having a field day with these people, he said, churning out front-page stories on obesity and the industry's role in fostering overconsumption. Up on the screen, he played a snippet from a new PBS *Frontline* report called "Fat," which featured the chair of Harvard's Department of Nutrition, Walter Willett, pointing the finger directly at the food companies. "The transition of food to being an industrial product really has been a fundamental problem," Willett said. "First, the actual processing has stripped away the nutritional value of the food. Most of the grains have been converted to starches. We have sugar in concentrated form, and many of the fats have been concentrated and then, worst of all, hydrogenated, which creates trans-fatty acids with very adverse effects on health."

Food manufacturers were getting heat not only from powerful critics at Harvard, the federal Centers for Disease Control and Prevention, the American Heart Association, and the Cancer Society, Mudd said. They were now losing key allies. The secretary of agriculture, over whom the industry had long held sway, had recently called obesity a "national epidemic." And it didn't take much effort to see why the USDA chief felt compelled to bite the hand that feeds. The agency promoted healthy eating through its food pyramid, with grains at the base and far smaller quantities of sweets and fat squeezed into the top. Their companies, Mudd told the executives, were promoting the *opposite* habits. "If you mapped categories of food advertising, especially advertising to kids, against the Food Guide Pyramid, it would turn the pyramid on its head," he said. "We cannot pretend food isn't part of the obesity problem. No credible expert will attribute the rise in obesity solely to decreased physical activity."

He flashed another slide up on the screen. "What's driving the increase?" it asked. "Ubiquity of inexpensive, good-tasting, super-sized, energy-dense foods." In other words, the very foods on which these executives, along with their brethren in the fast food chains, had staked the success of their companies.

Having laid the blame for obesity at the feet of the CEOs, Mudd then did the unthinkable. He touched the third rail of the processed food industry, drawing a connection to the last thing in the world the CEOs wanted linked to their products: cigarettes. First came a quote from a Yale University professor of psychology and public health, Kelly Brownell, who had become an especially vocal proponent of the view that the processed food industry should be seen as a public health menace: "As a culture, we've become upset by the tobacco companies advertising to children, but we sit idly by while the food companies do the very same thing. And we could make a claim that the toll taken on the public health by a poor diet rivals that taken by tobacco."

Mudd then flashed a big yellow caution sign with the words, "SLIPPERY SLOPE," up on the screen. "If anyone in the food industry ever doubted there was a slippery slope out there, I imagine they are beginning to experience a distinct sliding sensation right about now," he said. "We all know that the food and tobacco situations are not the same," but the same trial lawyers who were flush with the spoils of tobacco litigation were now lurking, poised to strike the food industry as well. Moreover, the surgeon general—whose office had produced the landmark attack on cigarettes back in 1964—was preparing a report on obesity. In the hands of these lawyers and politicians, one aspect of the obesity crisis in particular would leave the food industry exposed: the public nature of overeating and its consequences. The sight of an overweight adult trudging down the grocery aisle or an overweight kid on the playground was galvanizing. "Obesity is an utterly visible problem," Mudd said. "As its prevalence increases, it will be obvious to all."

Then Mudd shifted gears. He stopped with the bad news and presented the plan he and the other industry insiders had devised to address the obesity problem. Merely getting the executives to acknowledge some culpability was an important first step, he knew, so his plan would start off with a small but crucial move. The industry, he said, should take up the obesity crisis and use the expertise of scientists—its own and others—to gain a much deeper understanding of what exactly was driving Americans to overeat. Once this was achieved, the effort could unfold on several fronts. To be sure, there would be no getting around the role that packaged foods and drinks play in overconsumption. Some industry officials had already begun discussing the power of foods to create cravings and to overwhelm the best intentions of dieters. To diminish these cravings, they would have to pull back on their use of salt, sugar, and fat, perhaps by imposing industry-wide limits—not on the meager-selling low-fat or low-sugar items that companies put on the grocery shelf for dieters, but on the big-selling, mainline products themselves, which had a huge effect on the nation's health. However, these three ingredients and their formulas were not the only tools the industry wielded to create the greatest possible allure for their products. The schemes they used to advertise and market their products were critical, too. In keeping with his desire to avoid alienating the executives entirely, Mudd emphasized this aspect of their trade. He proposed creating a "code to guide the nutritional aspects of food marketing, especially to children."

He also suggested that they begin promoting the role of exercise in controlling weight, since no one could expect to get trim—or stay that way—sitting on the couch. This could include public service announcements, he said, or a powerful, full-blown advertising campaign like that deployed by the Partnership for a Drug-Free America, in which tobacco and pharmaceutical industries had joined forces to produce iconic ads like the 1987 commercial that showed a man cracking an egg into a frying pan while saying, "This is your brain on drugs."

"I want to be very clear here," Mudd said in closing, and he underlined words in his written presentation to make sure he hit the right notes. "In saying that the obesity problem will take a long time to solve, or even by using the word 'solve,' we are not for a moment suggesting that this program or the food industry alone can possibly solve the problem. Or that *that's* the measure of success for this program. We *are* saying that the industry should make a sincere effort to be *part* of the solution. And that by doing so, we can help to defuse the criticism that's building against us. We don't have to singlehandedly *solve* the obesity problem in order to address the criticism. But we have to make a sincere effort to be *part* of the solution if we expect to avoid being demonized."

What happened next was not written down. But according to three participants, when Mudd stopped talking, all eyes turned to the one CEO whose recent exploits in the grocery store had awed the rest of the industry. His name was Stephen Sanger, and he was also the person—as head of General Mills—who had the most to lose when it came to dealing with obesity. His $2 billion lineup of sugary cereals, from Count Chocula to Lucky Charms, was now drawing more fire from consumer advocates than soda. Under his leadership, General Mills had transformed entire sections of the grocery store, capitalizing on society's hunger for faster, more convenient food. Sanger had been sitting front and center, in a seat that reflected his position atop the pecking order. Now he stood, his body tense, to address Michael Mudd, and he did so visibly upset.

Sanger began by reminding the group that consumers were "fickle," as were their ivory tower advocates. Their concerns about the health implications of packaged foods waxed and waned. Sometimes they worried about sugar, other times fat. But most often, he said, they bought what they liked, and they liked what tasted good. "Don't talk to me about nutrition," he said, taking on the voice of a typical consumer. "Talk to me about taste, and if this stuff tastes better, don't run around trying to sell stuff that doesn't taste good."

Besides, Sanger said, the industry had always managed to ride things out—the trans fats panic, for instance, or the desire for more whole grains—by making adjustments. In fact, the industry had not only weathered these squalls, it had acted responsibly, to the public *and* to its shareholders. To go further, to react to the critics, would jeopardize the sanctity of the recipes that had made his products so successful. General Mills would not pull back, Sanger said. He would push his people onward, and he urged his peers to do the same. Then he sat down.

Not everyone at the meeting shared Sanger's views. But his stance was so forceful, so persuasive and, yes, so comforting to the other executives that no one else sought to counter the position he voiced. Sanger's response effectively ended the meeting.

Years later, his words still stung. "What can I say," Behnke said. "It didn't work. These guys weren't as receptive as we thought they would be." Behnke chose his words slowly and deliberately, to paraphrase them as best he could. He wanted to be fair. "Sanger felt very strongly that, 'Look, we fortify our cereals. We are very concerned about nutrition. We've got a big range of products. You know, you tell me what you're interested in, and we've got a product that serves your needs. And so why should we adjust our sights and move the whole portfolio towards some lower calorie, lower sugar level, lower fat level kind of product line? There is no need to do that. We already have those alternatives. And we're selling all of those things. You guys are overreacting.'

"Sanger," Behnke added, "was trying to say, 'Look, we're not going to screw around with the company jewels here and change the formulations because a bunch of guys in white coats are worried about obesity.' "

And that was that. The executives got up and took the elevators to the 40th floor for dinner, where the talk was polite and insubstantial. Except for Kraft, all eleven of the major food manufacturers at the meeting spurned the idea of collectively down-formulating their products to ease their effects on Americans' health. They even largely ignored Mudd's request that they start fighting obesity by contributing to a modest $15 million fund for research and public education. "I don't think anything ever came of that as a group effort," recalls John Cady, who was president of the National Food Processors Association, one of two trade organizations at the dinner.

Instead, America's food companies charged into the new millennium. Publicly, there would be some overtures toward better nutrition, especially when it came to reducing salt in their products. General Mills—eight years later, after intense public pressure—even began lowering the sugar loads in its cereals and later announced, in 2009, that it would take another half a teaspoon of sugar out of the cereals it advertised to children, steps that some health advocates dismissed as late and disappointingly small. The reality was that behind the scenes, having resolved to ignore obesity, the CEOs and their companies picked up right where they had left off, using, in some cases, more salt, more sugar, and more fat to edge out the competition.

Even Kraft set aside its initiative to fight obesity and got caught up in this fervor in 2003 when Hershey began cutting into its share of the cookie aisle. Hershey was famous for its chocolates, but to expand its sales it introduced a new line of products that combined its chocolate with wafers to create chocolate cookies like its S'more product. The company's chocolate already had lots of fat, but the S'more took the allure to new heights by adding more sugar and salt to the mix. Each of these mega-rich cookies weighed less than two ounces and contained five teaspoons of sugar. Alarmed by this incursion, Kraft responded with force. Daryl Brewster, who ran the Nabisco division at the time, told me that Hershey's move "put us in one of those interesting squeezes that big companies can find themselves in. To be competitive, we've got to add fat." Its biggest seller, the Oreo, got a slew of rich, fat-laden variations, from Banana Split Creme Oreo to Triple Double Oreo to Oreo Fudge Sundae Creme. Kraft then went out and acquired its very own chocolate maker, Cadbury, one of the world's biggest confectionaries. It would use Cadbury's marketing arm to spread this new lineup to places like India, where, starting in 2011, the country's 1.2 billion people got hit by Oreo ads that caught them up on some of the American processed food industry's most compelling eating instructions: "Twist, Lick, Dunk."

As in slam dunk, for Kraft.

I was five months into the reporting and research for this book when I heard about the secret CEO meeting. I found it remarkable, first and foremost, for the insider admissions of guilt. This kind of frankness almost never happens in large corporations; it is tantamount to a bunch of mafia dons getting together to express remorse for breaking heads. But I was also struck by how prescient the organizers of the sit-down had been. Ten years after the meeting, concerns over obesity had not only continued, they had reached hurricane strength: from Washington, where Army generals testified publicly that eighteen-year-olds were getting too fat to recruit; to Philadelphia, where city officials banished TastyKake pastries—a hometown favorite—from school cafeterias in declaring an all-out war to help overweight kids; to Los Angeles, where doctors reported a rise in maternal deaths because excessive weight was increasingly hampering surgical needs in cesarean births. On both coasts and in between, there were too many millions of obese people to believe that they had all done themselves in, either by failing to exert enough willpower or because of some other personal flaw. Children had become especially vulnerable. Excessive weight among kids went from double to triple the rate it had been in 1980, when the trend began to surface. Diabetes was up, too, and not just in adults—doctors had begun spotting the early signs of this debilitating disease in young children. Even gout, an exceedingly painful and rare form of arthritis once dubbed "the rich's man's disease" for its associations with gluttony, now afflicted eight million Americans.

If the problem was much smaller in 1999, the opportunity to change course had never been greater. This was a time when we, as consumers, trusted more than we doubted. We didn't question, or understand, what we were putting into our bodies—at least not like we do today. At that point, the media still fawned over the release of every new food or drink designed to be handheld, for the road, convenient. "Slow food" was a complaint, not a social movement.

In some ways, the officials at Pillsbury and Kraft who organized the CEO meeting went even further than I was prepared to go, more than a decade later, in assessing the effects of their work, especially with their talk of cancer. Nutrition science is so notoriously mushy that blaming even a fraction of our cancer on processed foods requires a leap I am not comfortable making. Food studies don't have the rigor of the double-blind randomized trials that are the norm in drug company research, and blaming any single food product for our health troubles is particularly fraught. Yet here they were, linking their own products to a significant part of the country's health troubles, from diabetes to heart disease to cancer.

Their lack of reticence raised a tantalizing question: If industry officials were willing to go this far, this fast, in accepting responsibility, what else did they know that they were not saying publicly?

The lengths to which food companies will go in order to shield their operations from public view were already apparent to me from my own recent reporting odyssey, which had started in early 2009 in southwest Georgia, where an outbreak of salmonella in a decrepit peanut factory left eight people dead and an estimated nineteen thousand in forty-three states sick. It took a long, winding hunt for me to track down the secret inspection report that revealed one of the root causes: Food manufacturers like Kellogg had relied on a private inspector, paid by the factory, to vouch for the safety of the peanuts. The report the inspector wrote in visiting the factory shortly before the outbreak cited none of the obvious warning signs, like the rats and the leaky roof.

Later, in attempting to trace an *E. coli*–tainted shipment of hamburger that had made hundreds ill and paralyzed a twenty-two-year-old former dance teacher in Minnesota named Stephanie Smith, I found the federal government to be of little help. Not only that, the Department of Agriculture is actually complicit in the meat industry's secrecy. Citing competitive interests, the public agency refused my requests for the most basic facts, like which slaughterhouses had supplied the meat. I ultimately obtained the information from an industry insider, and the smoking-gun document—a detailed, second-by-second account of the hamburger production process called a "grinding log"—showed why the government is so protective of the industry it is supposed to be holding accountable. The burger that Stephanie ate, made by Cargill, had been an amalgam of various grades of meat from different parts of the cow and from multiple slaughterhouses as far away as Uruguay. The meat industry, with the blessing of the federal government, was avoiding steps that could make their products safer for consumers. The *E. coli* starts in the slaughterhouses, where feces tainted with the pathogen can contaminate the meat when the hides of cows are pulled off. Yet many of the biggest slaughterhouses would sell their meat only to hamburger makers like Cargill if they agreed *not* to test their meat for *E. coli* until it was mixed together with shipments from other slaughterhouses. This insulated the slaughterhouses from costly recalls when the pathogen was found in ground beef, but it also prevented government officials and the public from tracing the *E. coli* back to its source. When it comes to pathogens in the meat industry, ignorance is financial bliss.

Salt, sugar, and fat are an entirely different game. Not only are they not accidental contaminants like *E. coli*, the industry methodically studies and controls their use. The confidential industry records that came my way in the course of reporting this book show exactly how deliberate and calculating a matter this is. To make a new soda guaranteed to create a craving requires the high math of regression analysis and intricate charts to plot what industry insiders call the "bliss point," or the precise amount of sugar or fat or salt that will send consumers over the moon. At a laboratory in White Plains, New York, industry scientists who perform this alchemy walked me, step by step, through the process of engineering a new soda so that I could see the creation of bliss firsthand. To understand how the industry deploys fat in creating allure, I traveled to Madison, Wisconsin, home of Oscar Mayer and of the man who invented the prepackaged whole meals called Lunchables, a colossus among convenience foods that radically changed the eating habits of millions of American kids. He went into his cabinets to pull out the company records that weighed the pros and cons of using real pepperoni versus pepperoni flavor and described the allure of fat-laden meat and cheese in cuddly terms like "product delivery cues." Both fat and salt are at the heart of Frito-Lay's operations in Plano, Texas, and some of the company's favorite methods for manipulating these two ingredients were relayed to me by a former chief scientist there named Robert I-San Lin. These include a remarkable effort by company officials to reduce the ideal snack to a mathematical equation of taste and convenience—"$P = A_1T + A_2C + A_3U - B_1\$ - B_2H - B_3Q$," with the P standing for Purchase and the allure of fat and salt easily overcoming the H, or the public's health concerns.

I would find out that one of the most compelling, and unsettling, aspects of the role of salt, sugar, and fat in processed foods is the way the industry, in an effort to boost their power, has sought to alter their physical shape and structure. Scientists at Nestlé are currently fiddling with the distribution and shape of fat globules to affect their absorption rate and, as it's known in the industry, their "mouthfeel." At Cargill, the world's leading supplier of salt, scientists are altering the physical shape of salt, pulverizing it into a fine powder to hit the taste buds faster and harder, improving what the company calls its "flavor burst." Sugar is being altered in myriad ways as well. The sweetest component of simple sugar, fructose, has been crystallized into an additive that boosts the allure of foods. Scientists have also created enhancers that amplify the sweetness of sugar to two hundred times its natural strength.

Some of the physical reconfiguration of salt, sugar, and fat is couched as an effort to reduce the consumption of any one ingredient, as in low-fat or low-sugar products; a super salt, for instance, might mean that less salt is needed. But one facet of processed food is held sacrosanct by the industry. Any improvement to the nutritional profile of a product can in no way diminish its allure, and this has led to one of the industry's most devious moves: lowering one bad boy ingredient like fat while quietly adding more sugar to keep people hooked.

As powerful as they are, salt, sugar, and fat are just part of the industry's blueprint for shaping America's eating habits. Marketing is a full partner to the ingredients. Lunchables, for one, are a marketing powerhouse, specifically designed to exploit the guilt of working moms and the desire of kids for a little empowerment. These ready-to-eat meals typically include pieces of meat, cheese, crackers, and candy, allowing kids to assemble them in whatever combination they desire. Food marketers wield pinpoint psychological targeting, and they didn't disappoint on the Lunchables ads: The ads stressed that lunch was a time for them, not their parents.

The marketing side of processed food, it became clear in the research for this book, is also where the industry's hold on federal regulators is most evident. Federal officials do more than shield company records from public view. The biggest government watchdogs show no teeth when it comes to controlling the industry's excesses in promoting sugary, high-calorie fare, not only on TV but also in the full range of social media now used by the food industry in its pursuit of kids. Moreover, the government has grown so cozy with food manufacturers that some of the biggest industry coups would not have been possible without Washington's help. When consumers tried to improve their health by shifting to skim milk, Congress set up a scheme for the powerful dairy industry through which it has quietly turned all that unwanted, surplus fat into huge sales of cheese—not cheese to be eaten before or after dinner as a delicacy, but cheese that is slipped into our food as an alluring but unnecessary extra ingredient. The toll, thirty years later: The average American now consumes as much as thirty-three pounds of cheese a year.

The industry's pursuit of allure is extremely sophisticated, and it leaves nothing to chance. Some of the largest companies are now using brain scans to study how we react neurologically to certain foods, especially to sugar. They've discovered that the brain lights up for sugar the same way it does for cocaine, and this knowledge is useful, not only in formulating foods. The world's biggest ice cream maker, Unilever, for instance, parlayed its brain research into a brilliant marketing campaign that sells the eating of ice cream as a "scientifically proven" way to make ourselves happy.

The manufacturers of processed food have also benefited profoundly from a corner of the consumer goods market where shrewdness in marketing has no equal: the tobacco industry. This relationship began in 1985, when R. J. Reynolds bought Nabisco, and reached epic levels a few years later when the world's largest cigarette maker, Philip Morris, became the largest food company by acquiring the two largest food manufacturers, General Foods and Kraft. A trove of confidential tobacco industry records—81 million pages and growing—opened to public viewing by the states' legal settlement with the industry reveals that top officials at Philip Morris were guiding the food giants through their most critical moments, from rescuing products when sales foundered to devising a strategy for dealing with the public's mounting health concerns. In fact, the same year that the CEOs met to consider obesity, Philip Morris was undergoing its own strategic shift in how it discussed and handled the health aspects of nicotine. Bludgeoned by media attacks and the public's growing concern about smoking, the company privately warned and prepared its food executives to deal with similar bloody battles over the heart of their operations: namely, the salt, sugar, and fat.

"The tobacco wars are coming to everyone's neighborhood," one Philip Morris strategy paper warned back in the 1999. "For beer, we have evidence of rising anti-alcohol sentiment in the U.S. And for food, it is clear that the biotech issue, already so ripe in Europe, is spreading internationally. There are also the continuing issues of food safety and the health effects of certain food elements such as fat, salt and sugar."

To win these wars, the strategy paper continued, the company would have to explore and study its vulnerabilities and even open dialogues with its critics. "This means we have to engage. No more bunkers."

More and more, consumers have come to focus on these same three ingredients, whether out of concern for obesity and heart disease or simply a desire to eat food that is less processed and more real. There has been a commensurate push from elected officials too, from the White House to City Hall in New York, where salt, sugar, fat, and calories in processed foods have come under heightened criticism. The response from food manufacturers has been to give health-conscious consumers more of a choice by turning out better-for-you versions of their mainline products. The further they go down this path, however, the harder they bump up against two stark realities of their industry.

First, the food companies themselves are hooked on salt, sugar, and fat. Their relentless drive to achieve the greatest allure for the lowest possible cost has drawn them, inexorably, to these three ingredients time and time again. Sugar not only sweetens, it replaces more costly ingredients—like tomatoes in ketchup—to add bulk and texture. For little added expense, a variety of fats can be slipped into food formulas to stimulate overeating and improve mouthfeel. And salt, barely more expensive than water, has miraculous powers to boost the appeal of processed food.

The industry's dependence on these ingredients became starkly evident when three of the biggest food manufacturers let me in to observe their efforts to cut back on salt. Kellogg, for one, made me a saltless version of their mega-selling Cheez-Its, which normally I can keep eating forever. Without any salt, however, the crackers lost their magic. They felt like straw, chewed like cardboard, and had zero taste. The same thing happened with the soups and meats and breads that other manufacturers, including Campbell, attempted to make for me. Take more than a little salt, or sugar, or fat out of processed food, these experiments showed, and there is nothing left. Or, even worse, what is left are the inexorable consequences of food processing, repulsive tastes that are bitter, metallic, and astringent. The industry has boxed itself in.

The second obstacle the industry faces in exacting any real reforms is the relentless competition for space on the grocery shelf. When PepsiCo in 2010 launched a campaign to promote its line of better-for-you products, the first drop in sales prompted Wall Street to demand that the company return to promoting its core drinks and snacks: those with the most salt, sugar, and fat. At Coca-Cola, meanwhile, PepsiCo's move was immediately seized upon as an opportunity to gain ground by pumping more money and effort into doing the one thing they do best—selling soda.

"We are doubling down on soft drinks," Coke's executives boasted to Jeffrey Dunn, a former president of Coca-Cola North America and Latin America who left the company after trying, and failing, to instill some health consciousness at Coke. Dunn, who would share some of the soda industry's most closely held secrets with me, said that Coke's reaction was understandable, given the fierce competition, but indefensible in the context of surging obesity rates. "To me, that is like damn the torpedoes, full speed ahead. If they choose that path, they have to be accountable for the social costs of what they are doing."

In the end, that is what this book is about. It will show how the makers of processed foods have chosen, time and again, to double down on their efforts to dominate the American diet, gambling that consumers won't figure them out. It will show how they push ahead, despite their own misgivings. And it will hold them accountable for the social costs that keep climbing even as some of their own say, "Enough already."

Inevitably, the manufacturers of processed food argue that they have allowed us to become the people we want to be, fast and busy, no longer slaves to the stove. But in their hands, the salt, sugar, and fat they have used to propel this social transformation are not nutrients as much as weapons— weapons they deploy, certainly, to defeat their competitors but also to keep us coming back for more.

part one sugar

chapter one

"Exploiting the Biology of the Child"

The first thing to know about sugar is this: Our bodies are hard-wired for sweets.

Forget what we learned in school from that old diagram called the tongue map, the one that says our five main tastes are detected by five distinct parts of the tongue. That the back has a big zone for blasts of bitter, the sides grab the sour and the salty, and the tip of the tongue has that one single spot for sweet. The tongue map is wrong. As researchers would discover in the 1970s, its creators misinterpreted the work of a German graduate student that was published in 1901; his experiments showed only that we might taste a little more sweetness on the tip of the tongue. In truth, the entire mouth goes crazy for sugar, including the upper reaches known as the palate. There are special receptors for sweetness in every one of the mouth's ten thousand taste buds, and they are all hooked up, one way or another, to the parts of the brain known as the pleasure zones, where we get rewarded for stoking our bodies with energy. But our zeal doesn't stop there. Scientists are now finding taste receptors that light up for sugar all the way down our esophagus to our stomach and pancreas, and they appear to be intricately tied to our appetites.

The second thing to know about sugar: Food manufacturers are well aware of the tongue map folly, along with a whole lot more about why we crave sweets. They have on staff cadres of scientists who specialize in the senses, and the companies use their knowledge to put sugar to work for them in countless ways. Sugar not only makes the taste of food and drink irresistible. The industry has learned that it can also be used to pull off a string of manufacturing miracles, from donuts that fry up bigger to bread that won't go stale to cereal that is toasty-brown and fluffy. All of this has made sugar a go-to ingredient in processed foods. On average, we consume 71 pounds of caloric sweeteners each year. That's 22 teaspoons of sugar, per person, per day. The amount is almost equally split three ways, with the sugar derived from sugar cane, sugar beets, and the group of corn sweeteners that includes high-fructose corn syrup (with a little honey and syrup thrown into the mix).

That we love, and crave, sugar is hardly news. Whole books have been devoted to its romp through history, in which people overcame geography, strife, and overwhelming technical hurdles to feed their insatiable habit. The highlights start with Christopher Columbus, who brought sugar cane along on his second voyage to the New World, where it was planted in Spanish Santo Domingo, was eventually worked into granulated sugar by enslaved Africans, and, starting in 1516, was shipped back to Europe to meet the continent's surging appetite for the stuff. The next notable development came in 1807 when a British naval blockade of France cut off easy access to sugar cane crops, and entrepreneurs, racing to meet demand, figured out how to extract sugar from beets, which could be grown easily in temperate Europe. Cane and beets remained the two main sources of sugar until the 1970s, when rising prices spurred the invention of high-fructose corn syrup, which had two attributes that were attractive to the soda industry. One, it was cheap, effectively subsidized by the federal price supports for corn; and two, it was liquid, which meant that it could be pumped directly into food and drink. Over the next thirty years, our consumption of sugar-sweetened soda more than doubled to 40 gallons a year per person, and while this has tapered off since then, hitting 32 gallons in 2011, there has been a commensurate surge in other sweet drinks, like teas, sports ades, vitamin waters, and energy drinks. Their yearly consumption has nearly doubled in the past decade to 14 gallons a person.

Far less well known than the history of sugar, however, is the intense research that scientists have conducted into its allure, the biology and psychology of why we find it so irresistible.

For the longest time, the people who spent their careers studying nutrition could only guess at the extent to which people are attracted to sugar. They had a sense, but no proof, that sugar was so powerful it could compel us to eat more than we should and thus do harm to our health. That all changed in the late 1960s, when some lab rats in upstate New York got ahold of Froot Loops, the supersweet cereal made by Kellogg. The rats were fed the cereal by a graduate student named Anthony Sclafani who, at first, was just being nice to the animals in his care. But when Sclafani noticed how fast they gobbled it up, he decided to concoct a test to measure their zeal. Rats hate open spaces; even in cages, they tend to stick to the shadowy corners and sides. So Sclafani put a little of the cereal in the brightly lit, open center of their cages—normally an area to be avoided—to see what would happen. Sure enough, the rats overcame their instinctual fears and ran out in the open to gorge.

Their predilection for sweets became scientifically significant a few years later when Sclafani—who'd become an assistant professor of psychology at Brooklyn College—was trying to fatten some rats for a study. Their standard Purina Dog Chow wasn't doing the trick, even when Sclafani added lots of fats to the mix. The rats wouldn't eat enough to gain significant weight. So Sclafani, remembering the Froot Loops experiment, sent a graduate student out to a supermarket on Flatbush Avenue to buy some cookies and candies and other sugar-laden products. And the rats went bananas, they couldn't resist. They were particularly fond of sweetened condensed milk and chocolate bars. They ate so much over the course of a few weeks that they grew obese.

"Everyone who owns pet rats knows if you give them a cookie they will like that, but no one experimentally had given them all they want," Sclafani told me when I met him at his lab in Brooklyn, where he continues to use rodents in studying the psychology and brain mechanisms that underlie the desire for high-fat and high-sugar foods. When he did just that, when he gave his rats all they wanted, he saw their appetite for sugar in a new light. They loved it, and this craving completely overrode the biological brakes that should have been saying: Stop.

The details of Sclafani's experiment went into a 1976 paper that is revered by researchers as one of the first experimental proofs of food cravings. Since its publication, a whole body of research has been undertaken to link sugar to compulsive overeating. In Florida, researchers have conditioned rats to expect an electrical shock when they eat cheesecake, and still they lunge for it. Scientists at Princeton found that rats taken off a sugary diet will exhibit signs of withdrawal, such as chattering teeth. Still, these studies involve only rodents, which in the world of science are known to have a limited ability to predict human physiology and behavior.

What about people and Froot Loops?

For some answers to this question, and for most of the foundational science on how and why we are so attracted to sugar, the food industry has turned to a place called the Monell Chemical Senses Center in Philadelphia. It is located a few blocks west of the Amtrak station, in a bland five-story brick building easily overlooked in the architectural wasteland of the district known as University City—except for "Eddy," the giant sculpture that stands guarding the entrance. Eddy is a ten-foot-high fragment of a face, and he perfectly captures the obsessions of those inside: He is all nose and mouth.

Getting buzzed through the center's front door is like stepping into a clubhouse for PhDs. The scientists here hang out in the corridors to swap notions that lead to wild discoveries, like how cats are unable to taste sweets, or how the cough that results from sipping a high-quality olive oil is caused by an anti-inflammatory agent, which may prove to be yet another reason for nutritionists to love this oil so much. The researchers at Monell bustle to and from conference rooms and equipment-filled labs and peer through one-way mirrors at the children and adults who eat and drink their way through the center's many ongoing experiments. Over the last forty years, more than three hundred physiologists, chemists, neuroscientists, biologists, and geneticists have cycled through Monell to help decipher the mechanisms of taste and smell along with the complex psychology that underlies our love for food. They are among the world's foremost authorities on taste. In 2001, they identified the actual protein molecule, T1R3, that sits in the taste bud and detects sugar. More recently they have been tracking the sugar sensors that are spread throughout the digestive system, and they now suspect that these sensors are playing a variety of key roles in our metabolism. They have even solved one of the more enduring mysteries in food cravings: the marijuana-induced state known as "the munchies." This came about in 2009 when Robert Margolskee, a molecular biologist and associate director of the center, joined other scientists in discovering that the sweet taste receptors on the tongue get aroused by endocannabinoids—substances that are produced in the brain to increase our appetite. They are chemical sisters to THC, the active ingredient in marijuana, which may explain why smoking marijuana can trigger hunger pangs. "Our taste cells are turning out to be smarter than we thought, and more involved in regulating our appetites," Margolskee told me.

The stickiest subject at Monell, however, is not sugar. It's money. Taxpayers fund about half of the center's $17.5 million annual budget through federal grants, but much of the rest of its operation comes from the food industry, including the big manufacturers, as well as several tobacco companies. A large golden plaque in the lobby pays homage to PepsiCo, Coca-Cola, Kraft, Nestlé, Philip Morris, among others. It's an odd arrangement, for sure, one that evokes past efforts by the tobacco industry to buy "research" that put cigarettes in a favorable light. At Monell, the industry funding buys companies a privileged access to the center and its labs. They get exclusive first looks at the center's research, often as early as three years before the information goes public, and are also able to engage some of Monell's scientists to conduct special studies for their particular needs. But Monell prides itself on the integrity and independence of its scientists. Some of their work, in fact, is funded with monies from the lawsuits that states brought against the tobacco manufacturers.

"At Monell, scientists choose their research projects based solely on their own curiosity and interests and are deeply committed to the pursuit of fundamental knowledge," the center said in response to my questions about its financial structure. Indeed, as I would discover, though Monell receives industry funding, some of its scientists sound like consumer activists when they speak about the power their benefactors wield, especially when it comes to children.

This tension between the industry's excitement about the research at Monell and the center's own unease about the industry's practices dates back to some of the center's earliest research on our taste buds—based on age, sex, and race. Back in the 1970s, researchers at Monell discovered that kids and African Americans were particularly keen on foods that were salty and sweet. They gave solutions of varying sweetness and saltiness to a group of 140 adults and then to a group of 618 children aged nine to fifteen, and the kids were found to like the highest level of sweet and salty—even more than the adults. Twice as many kids as adults chose the sweetest and saltiest solutions. (This was the first scientific proof of what parents, watching their kids lunge for the sugar bowl at the breakfast table, already knew instinctively.) The difference among adults was less striking but still significant: More African Americans chose the sweetest and saltiest solutions.

One of Monell's sponsors, Frito-Lay, was particularly interested in the salt part of the study, since the company made most of its money on salty chips. Citing Monell's work in a 1980 internal memo, a Frito-Lay food scientist summed up the finding on kids and added, "Racial Effect: It has been shown that blacks (in particular, black adolescents) displayed the greatest preference for a high concentration of salt." The Monell scientist who did this groundbreaking study, however, raised another issue that reflected his anxiety about the food industry. Kids didn't just *like* sugar more than adults, this scientist, Lawrence Greene, pointed out in a paper published in 1975. Data showed they were actually consuming more of the stuff, and Greene suggested there might be a chicken-and-egg issue at play: Some of this craving for sugar may not be innate in kids but rather is the result of the massive amounts of sugar being added to processed foods. Scientists call this a learned behavior, and Greene was one of the first to suggest that the increasingly sweet American diet could be driving the desire for more sugar, which, he wrote, "may or may not correspond to optimum nutritional practices."

In other words, the sweeter the industry made its food, the sweeter kids liked their food to be.

I wanted to explore this idea a bit more deeply, so I spent some time with Julie Mennella, a biopsychologist who first came to Monell in 1988. In graduate school, she had studied maternal behavior in animals and realized that no one was examining the influence that food and flavors had on women who were mothers. She joined Monell to answer a set of unknowns about food. Do the flavors of the food you eat transmit to your milk? Do they transmit to amniotic fluid? Do babies develop likes and dislikes for foods even *before* they are born?

"One of the most fundamental mysteries is why we like the foods that we do," Mennella said. "The liking of sweet is part of the basic biology of a child. When you think of the taste system, it makes one of the most important decisions of all: whether to accept a food. And, once we do, to warn the digestive system of impending nutrients. The taste system is our gatekeeper and one of the research approaches has been to take a developmental route, to look from the beginning—and what you see is that children are living in different sensory worlds than you and I. As a group, they prefer much higher levels of sweet and salt, rejecting bitter more than we do. I would argue that part of the reason children like high levels of sweet and salt is a reflection of their basic biology."

Twenty-five years later, Mennella has gotten closer than any other scientist to one of the most compelling—and, to the food industry, financially important—aspects of the relationship kids have to sugar. In her most recent project, she tested 356 children, ages five to ten, who were brought to Monell to determine their "bliss point" for sugar. The bliss point is the precise amount of sweetness—no more, no less—that makes food and drink most enjoyable. She was finishing up this project in the fall of 2010 when she agreed to show me some of the methods she had developed. Before we got started, I did a little research on the term *bliss point* itself. Its origins are murky, having some roots in economic theory. In relation to sugar, however, the term appears to have been coined in the 1970s by a Boston mathematician named Joseph Balintfy, who used computer modeling to predict eating behavior. The concept has obsessed the food industry ever since.

Food technicians typically refer to the bliss point privately when they are perfecting the formulas for their products, from sodas to flavored potato chips, but oddly enough, the industry has also sought to use the bliss point in defending itself from criticism that it was jamming the grocery store with foods that create unhealthy cravings. In 1991, this view of the bliss point as a natural phenomenon took center stage at a gathering of one of the more unusual industry associations. Based in London, the group was called ARISE (Associates for Research into the Science of Enjoyment), and its sponsors included food and tobacco companies. ARISE saw its mission as mounting a "resistance to the 'Calvinistic' attacks on people who are obtaining pleasure without harming others." The meeting, held in Venice, Italy, started off with a British scientist who discussed what he called "moreishness," in which the early moments of eating—as in appetizers—were shown to be valuable in the pursuit of pleasure by actually making you hungrier still. Monell's own director, Gary Beauchamp, gave a presentation in which he detailed the varied responses that infants have to tastes. Children developed a taste for salt as early as four or five months, he told the assembled scientists, while their liking for sweet appears to be in place the moment they are born.

The next presenter was an Australian psychologist named Robert McBride, who captivated the audience with a presentation he called "The Bliss Point: Implication for Product Choice."

Food manufacturers need not fear the implication of pleasure in the word *bliss*, he began. After all, he said, who among us chooses food based on its nutritional status? People pick products off the grocery shelf based on how they expect them to taste and feel in their mouths, not to mention the signals of pleasure their brains will discharge as a reward for choosing the tastiest foods. "Nutrition is not foremost on people's mind when they choose their food," he said. "It's the taste, the flavor, the sensory satisfaction."

And when it comes to these attributes, none is more powerful—or more conducive to being framed by the bliss point—than the taste of sugar, he said. "Humans like sweetness, but how much sweetness? For all ingredients in food and drink, there is an optimum concentration at which the sensory pleasure is maximal. This optimum level is called the bliss point. The bliss point is a powerful phenomenon and dictates what we eat and drink more than we realize."

The only real challenge for companies when it comes to the bliss point is ensuring that their products hit this sweet spot dead on. Companies are not going to sell as much ketchup, Go-Gurt, or loaves of bread if they're not sweet enough. Or, put a different way, they will sell a lot more ketchup, Go-Gurt, and loaves of bread if they can determine the precise bliss point for sugar in each of those items.

McBride ended his presentation that day in Venice with words of encouragement for the food company attendees. With a little work, he said, the bliss point can be computed and totted up like so much protein or fiber or calcium in food. It may not be something that companies would want to put on their labels, like they do in boasting about a product's infusion with vitamins. But the bliss point was, nonetheless, just as real and important to their customers.

"Pleasure from food is not a diffuse concept," he said. "It can be measured just as the physical, chemical, and nutritional factors can be measured. With more concrete status, the capacity of food flavors to evoke pleasure may start to be regarded as a real, tangible property of products, along with their nutritional status."

Julie Mennella, the biopsychologist at Monell, agreed to show me how the bliss point is calculated. I returned to the center on a warm day in November, and she took me into a small tasting room, where we met our guinea pig: an adorable six-year-old girl named Tatyana Gray. Tatyana had brightly colored beads in her hair and a pink T-shirt that read "5-Cent Bubble Gum" across the front. The expression on her face was one of cool professionalism: This was a job she could handle.

"What's your favorite cereal in the whole world?" Mennella asked Tatyana, just for fun.

"My favorite cereal is . . . Cinnamon CRUNCH," Tatyana replied.

Tatyana sat at a small table, with little stuffed versions of Big Bird and Oscar the Grouch perched next to her. As a lab assistant started to assemble the food to be tested, Mennella explained that the protocol for this experiment had been derived from twenty years of trials and was designed to elicit a scientifically measurable response. "We are dealing with foods that are very well liked, and so we're going to ask the child which one they like *better*. The one they like better, they are going to give to Big Bird because they know he likes things that taste good. We're looking at a wide range of children, as young as three, and we don't want language to play a role here. The child doesn't have to say anything. They either point to the one they like, or in this case, they give it to Big Bird. It's meant to minimize the impact of language."

Why not just ask the kids straight out if they like it? I asked.

"It just doesn't work, especially for the young ones," she said. "You can give them everything and they will say yes or no. Though, in this context, it tends to be yes. Children are smart. They'll tell you what they think you want to hear."

We tested this notion out by asking Tatyana which she preferred: broccoli or the Philadelphia-made snack called the TastyKake.

"Broccoli," she said, ready for a pat on the head.

For our bliss point test, Mennella's assistant had whipped up a dozen vanilla puddings, each at a different level of sweetness. She started by putting two of the variations into small plastic cups and setting them in front of Tatyana. Tatyana tasted the one on the left, swallowed, and took a sip of water. Then she tasted the one on the right. She didn't speak, but she didn't have to. Her face lit up as her tongue pressed into the roof of her mouth, pushing the pudding into the thousands of receptors waiting for sweetness. Being an old hand at the test, she ignored the stuffed animals and simply pointed to the cup she preferred.

There was one problem with watching Tatyana work her way through the puddings, though. So much was going on in creating the bliss she felt that was invisible to us. Each little spoonful disappeared into her mouth, and we could see her facial expressions and, ultimately, her decision. But in between tasting and choosing, a whole chain of events was unfolding inside her body, starting with her taste buds, that was critical to understanding how and why she was so happy.

To better understand what, exactly, was going on, I turned to another Monell scientist, Danielle Reed, who had trained in psychology at Yale. Reed, when we met, was using quantitative genetics to examine how inheritance might affect the pleasure we derive from sensations like tasting sugar, but her research on the sweet taste has also focused on the mechanics. Reed was among the group at Monell who discovered T1R3, the sweet receptor protein. She told me that Tatyana's swoon for the sugar in the pudding begins with her saliva. After all, we don't call tasty food "mouthwatering" for nothing. The mere sight of a sugary treat will start the saliva flowing, which in turn primes the digestive system. "The sugar, or sweet molecule, dissolves in your saliva," Reed said. Our taste buds are not smooth little bumps like we might imagine, she explained. They have clumps of tiny, hair-like fronds that rise up from the bud, and it's these fronds, called microvilli, that hold the cell that detects and receives the taste. "And that sets off a series of chain reactions inside the cell. So that the taste receptor cell talks to its friends in the taste bud. There is a lot of microprocessing of that signal, and then eventually it decides that what is in your mouth is sweet, and it squirts out neurotransmitters onto the nerve, which then goes to the brain."

Like most everything that goes on inside the brain, what happens up there in relation to food is still being sorted out. But researchers are beginning to chart the pathway that sugar takes—which Reed described as more of a deliberate march. "There is a very orderly progress of pathways in the brain that people are just now starting to learn," she said. "It stops at the first relay station and moves forward and forward and it eventually ends up in the pleasure centers, like the orbital frontal cortex of the brain, and that's when you have the experience, 'Ahh, sweet.' The *good* aspect of sweet."

We don't even have to eat sugar to feel its allure. Pizza will do, or any other refined starch, which the body converts to sugar—starting right in the mouth, with an enzyme called amylase. "The faster the starch becomes sugar, the quicker our brain gets the reward for it," Reed said. "We like the highly refined things because they bring us immediate pleasure, associated with high sugar, but obviously there are consequences. It's sort of like if you drink alcohol really fast, you get drunk really fast. When you break down sugar really fast your body gets flooded with sugar more than it can handle, whereas with a whole grain it is more gradual and you can digest it in a more orderly fashion."

In the testing that Mennella conducted to calculate Tatyana's bliss point for sugar, the six-year-old worked her way through two dozen puddings, each prepared to a different level of sweetness. The puddings were presented to her in pairs, from which she would choose the one she liked more. Each of her choices dictated what pudding pair would come next, and slowly Tatyana moved toward the level of sweetness she preferred most of all. When Mennella got the results, it was plain to see that there was no way Tatyana would ever have fed Big Bird a twig of broccoli over a Krimpet, a Kreamie, or anything else from the TastyKake line. Tatyana's bliss point for the pudding was 24 percent sugar, twice the level of sweetness that most adults can handle in pudding. As far as children go, she was on the lower side; some go as high as 36 percent.

"What we find is that the foods that are targeted to children, the cereals and the beverages, they are way up," Mennella said. "Tatyana's favorite cereal is Cinnamon Crunch, and what we'll do, we'll measure the level of sweetness that the child prefers in the laboratory with a sucrose solution and it matches the sugar content of the most preferred cereal. There are individual differences, but as a group, in every culture that has been studied around the world, children prefer more intense sweetness than adults."

Beyond the basic biology, there are three other aspects of sugar that seem to make it attractive to children, Mennella said. One, the sweet taste is their signal for foods that are rich in energy, and since kids are growing so fast, their bodies crave foods that provide quick fuel. Two, as humans, we didn't evolve in an environment that had lots of intensely sweet foods, which probably heightens the excitement we feel when we eat sugar. And finally, sugar makes children feel good. "It's an analgesic," Mennella said. "It will reduce crying in a newborn baby. A young child can keep their hand in a cold water bath longer if a sweet taste is in their mouth."

These are huge, powerful concepts—concepts that are crucial to understanding why so much of the grocery store food is sweet, and why we feel so drawn to sugar. We need energy, and Cinnamon Crunch delivers it quickly. We've been intimate with sweet taste since we were born, and yet our ancestors had nothing as thrilling as Coke. Sugar will even make us feel better, and who doesn't want that?

Mennella has become convinced that our bliss point for sugar—and all foods, for that matter—is shaped by our earliest experiences. But as babies grow into youngsters, the opportunity for food companies to influence our taste grows as well. For Mennella, this is troubling. It's not that food companies are teaching children to like sweetness; rather, they are teaching children what foods should taste like. And increasingly, this curriculum has been all about sugar.

"What basic research and taste in children is shedding light on—and why the foods that they're making for children are so high in sugar and salt—is they are manipulating or exploiting the biology of the child," she said. "I think that anyone who makes a product for a child has to take responsibility because what they are doing is teaching the child the level of sweetness or saltiness the food should be.

"They're not just providing a source of calories for a child," she added. "They're impacting the *health* of that child."

This much is clear from the research at Monell: People love sugar, especially kids. And up to a certain point—the bliss point—the more sugar there is, the better.

We may not yet know all the twists and turns that sugar takes in racing from our mouths to our brains, but the end results are not in dispute. Sugar has few peers in its ability to create cravings, and as the public gradually came to understand this power, sugar turned into a political problem for the manufacturers of processed food—a problem for which they would turn, once again, to Monell for help.

The money that the big food companies give to Monell accords them one special privilege: These corporate sponsors can ask the center's scientists to conduct special studies just for them. A dozen times or so each year, companies bring vexing problems to Monell, like why the texture of starch is perceived so differently by people, or what causes the terrible aftertaste in infant formula, and Monell's scientists will put their PhD brains to work in solving these puzzles. In the 1980s, however, a group of Monell funders asked for help with a more pressing matter: They needed assistance in defending themselves from public attack.

Sugar was coming under heavy fire from several directions. The Food and Drug Administration had taken it up as part of an effort to examine the safety of all food additives. The report it commissioned didn't recommend regulatory action, but it did contain several warnings: Dental decay was rampant, sugar was possibly tied to heart disease, and consumers had all but lost control of its use. Getting rid of the sugar bowl at home would barely help to cut back on consumption, the report said, as more than two-thirds of the sugar in America's diet was now coming from processed foods.

At the same time, a select committee of U.S. senators—including George McGovern, Bob Dole, Walter Mondale, Ted Kennedy, and Hubert Humphrey—caused a stir by releasing the federal government's first official guideline on how Americans should shape their diet. The committee had started out looking at hunger and poverty but quickly turned its attention to heart disease and other illnesses that experts were linking to diet. "I testified that Americans should eat less food; less meat; less fat, particularly saturated fat; less cholesterol; less sugar; more unsaturated fat, fruits, vegetables and cereal products," an adviser to the Agriculture Department, Mark Hegsted, wrote in an account of the proceedings. On top of that, Michael Jacobson, an MIT-trained protégé of the consumer advocacy superstar Ralph Nader, was lighting a fire under the Federal Trade Commission. Jacobson's group, the Center for Science in the Public Interest, had gathered twelve thousand signatures from health professionals in urging the agency to ban the advertising of sugary foods on children's television.

The headlines from these and other attacks on the processed food industry had led to a surge in consumer awareness and concern. A federal survey found that three in four shoppers were reading and acting on the nutritional information provided on labels; half of these consumers said that they studied the labels to avoid certain additives, including salt, sugar, fats, and artificial colors. Even more troubling than that for the processed food industry, there was a growing public sentiment that its use of sugar, as well as colors, flavors, and other additives, was causing hyperactivity in children and overeating by adults. "It was coming from the general public, and there are always voices, activist voices, that say this is fact, that sugar causes over-activity," recalled Al Clausi, who retired in 1987 as a senior vice president and chief research officer for General Foods. "That was one of the folklore. That and flavors make you eat more of something that otherwise you wouldn't." With Clausi as the leader, officials from Kellogg and General Mills formed a group called the Flavor Benefits Committee, and they asked Monell to conduct research that would help quiet the nay-sayers, putting sugar and other food additives in a more favorable light by emphasizing their nutritional benefits.

Monell was an obvious choice for the industry. With limited funds from the government, the center had begun soliciting monies from food companies, keeping them apprised of research that would interest them. In a 1978 letter to Clausi, Monell's former director, Morley Kare, thanked General Foods for its latest check and suggested that center scientists conduct a seminar for product developers at the company. "We currently are emphasizing the growth of our program on taste and nutrition," Kare wrote. "A study with adolescents is being planned, focusing on their desire for high concentrations of sweeteners, saltiness and, evidently, the flavor and texture of fat."

By 1985, there were nine scientists at the center working on the industry's Flavor Benefits project, and some of their findings were things the industry could relish only in private. One discovery would have been a morale booster in food company labs where technicians had qualms about their employers' heavy reliance on sugar: Monell helped to establish that sugar is inherently loved by newborn babies. This enabled companies to argue, at least, that sugar was not something "artificial" they were thrusting upon an unsuspecting public. Rather, sugar was sinless, if not entirely wholesome. "Sweet was very important to us," Clausi said. "And when Monell found that of all the basic flavors, sweet is the only one a neonate shows a preference for, that said to us, 'Hey, there is something *natural* we are dealing with. This is not something we created out of whole cloth.'"

Monell, on behalf of the food manufacturers, also dug into the question of whether sugar causes people to overeat, and in this area the scientists made some troubling discoveries. For instance, it wasn't enough for food to have an attractive taste, they found. To be really enticing, these products had to be loaded with sugar and fat. Only these two ingredients, along with salt, seemed to have the power to excite the brain about eating. With this in mind, Monell turned to an item on the grocery shelf that was starting to have perhaps more impact on the American diet than anything else the food industry sold: soda, which people were starting to drink in unprecedented amounts.

Much of the work on soda at Monell was undertaken by one of the center's brightest scientists, Michael Tordoff, who had earned his doctoral degree at the University of California at Los Angeles in one of science's most challenging disciplines, a division of behavioral science called physiological psychology. (This is the field of research that looks at things like the role of the hippocampus in learning and memory.) Tordoff had already shown that he was capable of work that could open some interesting doors for the food industry. With a colleague, he invented a sweet compound dubbed Charmitrol, which could work in opposite ways, both of them potentially lucrative. The animal studies he performed indicated that the compound could cause people to eat larger amounts of food. Or, applied differently, it could cause them to eat less. "It made fat rats thin and thin rats fat," he told me. Two companies licensed the substance from Monell but turned up neurological hazards that nixed its commercial utility.

In turning to soda, Tordoff wanted to examine how soda might affect the appetite, and right off the bat he made a startling discovery. Sweetened drinks made his rats *more* hungry, not less. At first, this appeared to indict diet sodas, because he had used saccharine, the artificial sweetener, instead of sugar to sweeten the drinks. He got the same result when he used gum sweetened with saccharine. But then he turned to testing people, and this time he used regular soda made with high-fructose corn syrup.

In the fall of 1987, Tordoff recruited thirty people from nearby universities. They were all screened for obvious disqualifications—like if they were pregnant or dieting—and then they were put to work. Each week, for nine weeks, the thirty participants came to Monell to be questioned and weighed and were sent home with twenty-eight bottles of soda that had been specially crafted for this experiment by two of Monell's corporate sponsors, with instructions to keep careful track of what they drank. Experiments like this face a significant challenge: The scientists must rely on ordinary people to be very scientific, and people are people. They forget, they fudge, they obfuscate, all of which messes with the results. To boost their compliance—and forthrightness—the participants were told, "We could determine what you have eaten from analysis of urine samples," which was actually untrue in this trial, the published study noted.

Monell doled out five thousand bottles of the specially formulated sodas, in three distinct phases. "For three weeks we gave them nothing," Tordoff said. "Three weeks they got 40 ounces a day of diet soda. And for three weeks they got 40 ounces a day of regular soda." The diet soda turned out to be something of a wash, or at best a small help in losing weight. Men lost about a quarter pound when drinking the diet soda. For women, there was no statistically significant change.

The most significant finding came with the regular soda, which was sweetened with high-fructose corn syrup. With regular soda, both sexes gained weight: an average of nearly a pound and a half in just three weeks. At that rate, a person would put on 26 pounds in a year. "It might have been a big relief for the diet soda industry, but it was not good news for the makers of corn syrup," Tordoff said. (Or for table sugar, since most nutrition experts agree that when it comes to gaining weight, there appears to be little difference between sweeteners derived from corn and those drawn from cane or beets.)

This was one of the first studies to establish that sugary soda was likely a heavy contributor to obesity, which was just beginning to surge into the epidemic it is today. Until then, scientists had surmised this might be the case but lacked proof. Just like Brooklyn professor Sclafani's studies two decades earlier had shown that sugary foods would compel rats to overeat, Tordoff's experiment emboldened other scientists to look more closely at the effects that sweet drinks can have on one's appetite. Julie Mennella says that one of the big risks in letting children drink soda is that it leads them to expect—and want—more sweetness in all of their drinks. In her view, soda has moved the bliss point higher across the spectrum of drinks—from vitamin waters to sport ades—that is gaining popularity even as soda consumption begins to taper off. "There is no evidence that this is going to affect the level of sweetness they like in a pudding," she said. "But it teaches children that hey, when you drink a carbonated beverage, this is how sweet it should be."

Another of their colleagues at Monell, Karen Teff, has found signs that sweet drinks may be a Trojan horse when it comes to making people gain weight. Our bodies might not be able to identify the calories in sweet liquids as well as they can in solid foods. Such a blindness to soda and other caloric drinks would circumvent the natural controls that the body has in place to prevent excessive weight gain. In 2006, she conducted a study in which people received an infusion of glucose, and she then watched their response. The test lasted only forty-eight hours, but the results were striking: The subjects did not cut back on their eating at all. They just took in those extra glucose calories like they were invisible. "If these liquids do not activate the nervous system, they may not be recognized," Teff said.

More experimentation would need to be done for this notion to gain currency among nutritionists, but like Mennella, Teff is not shy about holding the food industry's feet to the fire. When it comes to sugar in drinks or solid food, their practice is to add more first and study later—if at all. "I'm still shocked at what goes on in this country," she told me. "Where every single food has some sweetened component that wasn't normally supposed to be sweetened. Honey wheat bread, honey mustard. Foods that were associated with non-sweet or that had slightly bitter components have now been made sweeter. There is absolutely no tolerance now for foods that are not sweet."

The research on sugar at Monell, it should be noted, is incomplete. Some of the most critical things about it remain a mystery, such as the precise parameters of its risk in heart disease and other health problems, or whether it deceives us in liquid form, or whether its many substitutes, from saccharine to the emerging plant-based sweetener stevia, will help us lose weight. The best guess today on the low-calorie sweeteners is that they can work only in a highly disciplined diet: Wolfing down two cupcakes after being restrained by drinking only diet sodas clearly won't help take the weight off.

One thing, however, has become perfectly clear in recent years. The overconsumption of sugar in solid foods or drinks has increasingly been tied to the obesity epidemic, which has only grown more dire. Overeating is now a global issue. In China, for the first time, the people who weigh too much now outnumber those who weigh too little. In France, where obesity has climbed from 8.5 percent to 14.5 percent since 1997, Nestlé has been enjoying great success in selling the Jenny Craig weight-loss program to the same Parisians who once sneered at Americans' proclivity to glom onto one diet fad after another. Mexico's obesity rate has tripled in the past three decades, leading to worries that it now has the fattest kids in the world, with fewer resources to do anything about it: Most schools in Mexico City lack both playgrounds and water fountains. The United States, however, remains the most obese country in the world. And where the rates of obesity appear to be reaching a plateau among adults at 35 percent, they are still climbing among the group that is the most vulnerable to the food industry's products: children. The most recent data, from 2006 to 2008, shows that obesity among kids aged six to eleven jumped from 15 to 20 percent.

And yet, for more than three decades, federal officials in Washington have exempted sugar from the recommended maximum limits that they set for the other two pillars of processed foods, salt and fat. Nor are manufacturers required to disclose how much sugar they add to their products: The amounts they cite include the sugar that occurs naturally in food. In 2009, the American Heart Association stepped in and issued a recommended limit for sugar. In a statement published in its scientific journal *Circulation*, the association declared, "High intakes of dietary sugars in the setting of a worldwide pandemic of obesity and cardiovascular disease have heightened concerns about the adverse effects of excessive consumption of sugars." The limits it recommended were even bolder. Noting that people were getting on average 22 teaspoons of added sugar a day, the association urged Americans to cut back. Moderately active women should get no more than 5 teaspoons of sugar—9 for sedentary, middle-aged men—in what nutritionists call "discretionary calories." These are the treats that people who are watching their weight can have once they meet their daily nutritional needs, and the association was not messing around. For women, the 5-teaspoon daily limit would mean having barely half of a 12-ounce can of Coke, or one Twinkie, or one-and-a-half Fig Newtons, or a half-cup of Jell-O. To be clear, those are connected by *or*, not *and*. Five teaspoons don't get you very far in the grocery store.

This time, however, food companies didn't need Monell's help to mount a vigorous defense. Their dependence on sugar by now ran so deep that representatives from every corner of the industry, from cookies to soda, attended a summit the AHA held in Washington in the spring of 2010 to discuss its proposal. One after another they made their case: It wasn't just taste that made their use of sugar invaluable. Sugar was critical to the entire manufacturing process. To lessen it would jeopardize the nation's supply of food.

The candy makers cited the bulk, texture, and crystallization that sugar gave them. The cereal makers added color, crisp, and crunch to the list of sugar's miracles. The bread makers conceded that they rely on every known form of the stuff in their factories—corn syrup, high-fructose corn syrup, dextrose, inverted syrup, malt, molasses, honey, and table sugar in three forms (granulated, powdered, and liquid). To drive their point home, the bakers cooked up special versions of their products using sugar substitutes, and they splashed pictures of the horrific results on the screen. The message was clear: Limit sugar, and you're left with a sad bunch of cookies, crackers, and breads that come out shrunken, pale, flat, or distended.

"Let's get practical," a food engineer from Israel told the group before launching into a chemistry lesson on a browning phenomenon called the Maillard reaction. Maillard is responsible for much of the pleasing caramel coloring in processed food, from quick breads to roasted meats, and

Maillard can't happen in many foods without a group of sugars that includes fructose.

Not to be outdone, a corn refiner's consultant wrapped up his presentation by suggesting the AHA's focus on sugar was misguided. If it really wanted to look at calories and the things in the American diet that made people gain weight, why pick on sugar when the bigger culprit may be fat?

"Certainly you can reformulate foods to reduce sugar and salt," this consultant, John White, told me later. "You can replace them with noncaloric sweeteners or synthetic fats. But the character of the product always changes, and you have to accept the tradeoff."

There would be no need for tradeoffs, however. The Heart Association's recommendation came and went, with little action by the industry to cut back. Sugar's value to food companies was only going up.

chapter two

"How Do You Get People to Crave?"

John Lennon couldn't find it in England, so he had cases of it shipped from New York to fuel the *Imagine* sessions. The Beach Boys, ZZ Top, and Cher took no chances either: They all stipulated in their contract riders that it be put in their dressing rooms when they toured. Hillary Clinton asked for it, too, when she traveled as First Lady, and ever after her hotel suites were dutifully stocked.

What they all wanted, and got, was Dr Pepper. Its unique taste, neither cola nor root beer, has won it a global cult following. Its most rabid devotees proudly call themselves Peppers, belong to a club called the 10-2-4—so named for one of the early advertising campaigns, which encouraged people to drink three Dr Peppers a day, at ten, two, and four o'clock—and make pilgrimages to Waco, Texas, where a pharmacist at Morrison's Old Corner Drug Store invented the drink in 1885. This kind of devotion afforded Dr Pepper a distant but comfortable third-place spot behind Coke and Pepsi, the giants of the soda aisle until 2001, when sudden changes in the marketing game in the soda aisle precipitated a crisis for Dr Pepper. The trouble began when a flood of spinoffs from Coca-Cola and Pepsi showed up on the shelves. Seemingly overnight, there were lemons and limes, vanillas and coffees, raspberries and oranges, whites and blues and clears—all vying for the shopper's attention. In grocery lingo, these new flavors and colors are known as "line extensions," and they're not meant to replace the original product. Rather, they're meant to bring buzz to the brand, and often they do this so well that people start eating or drinking more of the original product too.

In this case, Pepsi and Coke were using their line extensions to strengthen their hold on the soda aisle at a critical moment, just as American consumption was starting to peak. As Pepsi and Coke grew their sales with these new extensions, Dr Pepper began to slip from the third-place perch it had enjoyed for so long. In 2002, Coca-Cola sold 93 million cases more than the previous year, for a total of 4.5 billion cases in the United States alone. Pepsi was up a little bit too, with its 3.2 billion cases. By contrast, Dr Pepper was slumping, down 15 million cases to a total of 708 million, and soda industry watchers sounded a warning. "Dr Pepper—once an industry growth brand—lost volume and share," the trade journal *Beverage Digest* reported. The soda from Waco needed to turn things around.

Never in its 115-year history had Dr Pepper created a line extension, beyond a diet version. Given the cult following, the idea of tinkering with the soda's unique taste seemed dubious, even dangerous. But with sales declining and the soda aisle changing, Dr Pepper had to act. In 2002, it created its first-ever spinoff, which by any measure should have been a hit. The new flavor had a rich cherry taste, a bold red color, and a name, Red Fusion, that had been carefully chosen from a field of three hundred candidates. "If we are to re-establish Dr Pepper back to its historic growth rates, we have to add more excitement," the company's president, Jack Kilduff, said. Research showed that Red Fusion would even attract new customers to the brand. One particularly promising market, Kilduff pointed out, was the "rapidly growing Hispanic and African-American communities," where Dr Pepper had "lower brand development."

But the sales force never got a chance to explore these new markets. Red Fusion's failure wasn't the fault of the company's advertising crew. Rather, it was its taste. Consumers hated it, and diehard Peppers were aghast. "Dr Pepper is my all time favorite drink, so I was curious about the Red Fusion," a California mother of three wrote on a blog to warn other Peppers away. "It's disgusting. Gagging. Never again."

Stung by the rejection, the company regrouped and spent the next year developing and testing a different variation. This time, the company's technicians couldn't even get it past the taste testers. The hope for a new soda died before going into production.

In 2004, Dr Pepper decided to go outside the company for help. It turned to a man named Howard Moskowitz, whose success in delivering mega-sellers had turned him a food industry legend. Trained in mathematics and experimental psychology, Moskowitz runs a consulting firm in White Plains, New York, where he has established a long track record of triumphs in consumer goods, from credit cards to point-and-shoot cameras to computer games. Much of his success stems from his ability to group consumers into segments, with different emotional needs, and target them with precision. He boosted sales for the jewelry company Shaw's, for instance, by creating two versions of its brochure: one for people he categorized as optimists, the other for pessimists. The optimists got lines like, "I walk out of the store feeling great," while the pessimists got reassurance: "Jewelry with a classic look." As Moskowitz explained, "The importance here was not simply to identify these two different mindsets. Probably other methods might generate similar segments. Instead, Shaw's was interested in what *specific messaging* would drive purchase. That is, once we know the segments, we know what to say, how to say it, and who to say it to."

But Moskowitz's principal focus—and success—was in the processed food industry. The jewelry market, after all, is one thing; shelf space in American supermarkets is another. The largest stores carry as many as sixty thousand items. The competition is utterly fierce to win space from the store managers who lord over their aisles with one maxim: The most space goes to the biggest sellers. Supermarket real estate is so precious, in fact, that consumer scientists have conducted experiments in which they place devices on the heads of shoppers to track their eye movements as they roam the store, and the gleanings from these studies has helped define the pecking order on the shelf. Down low, by the shoppers' feet, not surprisingly, is death. Eye level is prime, especially toward the middle stretches of the aisle. The special displays at the ends of the aisle, called "caps," are the best of all.

The main point of generating product line extensions is to win more space on the shelf. Store managers will give only so much room to any one product, no matter how briskly it is selling. Adding new flavors and colors creates new products that get their own space, and the more likely shoppers are to see a brand, the more likely they are to buy it. In Dr Pepper's case, its space on the shelf was being devoured by Coke and Pepsi with all their new lemons and limes and vanillas.

There is another little-known aspect to marketing groceries that reflects this intense targeting of shoppers. The seemingly static, familiar nature of these stores is an illusion. Your supermarket today will not be the same store a month from now. To stand out in the crowd and excite the shopper, manufacturers constantly vary their mainline products, usually ever so slightly, with changes that range from packaging size to color to flavor to celebrity endorsements. Howard Moskowitz, however, doesn't fiddle with ad campaigns or packaging when it comes to his biggest food projects. He reworks the food itself, playing with the magical formulations of salt, sugar, and fat. For more than three decades, he has worked behind the scenes to stage dramatic rescues, turning losers into hits. Campbell Soup, General Foods, Kraft, and PepsiCo have all come to Moskowitz for help when their sales have flagged or a competitor has gained an edge. And his goal in each case has been to find the bliss point. Moskowitz searches for just the right amount of certain ingredients to generate the greatest appeal among consumers. Too little of this or too much of that might not ruin a product's taste or texture, but the shortcoming will be reflected in sales, where even tiny slippages can cause food company executives to lose their jobs. In the lingo of product developers, Moskowitz's stock in trade is known as "optimization," and he is not bashful in chronicling his deeds: "I've optimized soups," he told me. "I've optimized pizzas. I've optimized salad dressings and pickles. In this field, I'm a game changer."

Moskowitz knows his way around fats, and more recently he has been working with food manufacturers to perfect their use of salt. But he is at his best when working with sugar, which has no equal in creating appeal. It is with sugar that his technique is most effective. And he doesn't merely invent new sweetened products. Using high math and computations, he engineers them, with one goal in mind: to create the biggest crave. "People say, 'I crave chocolate,' " Moskowitz told me. "But why do we crave chocolate, or chips? And how do you get people to crave these and other foods?"

Conceptually, his technique is simple enough. Grocery products have lots of attributes that make them attractive, chief among them color, smell, packaging, and taste. In the craft called optimization, food engineers alter these variables ever so slightly in making dozens and dozens of new versions, each just a bit different from the next. These are not new products to sell. They are created with the sole intent of finding the most perfect variation, which is divined by putting all these experimental versions to the test. Ordinary consumers are paid to spend days sitting in rooms where they are presented with the many variations, which they touch, feel, sip, smell, swirl, and most of all taste. Their opinions are logged and dumped into a computer, which is where Moskowitz's training in high math comes in. The data is sifted and sorted through a statistical method called conjoint analysis, which determines what features in a product will be most attractive to consumers. Moskowitz likes to imagine that his computer is divided into silos, in which each of the attributes is stacked. But it's not simply a matter of comparing color 23 to color 24. In the most complicated projects, color 23 must be compared with syrup 11 and packaging 6, and on and on. Even in jobs where the only concern is taste and the variables are limited to the ingredients, endless charts and graphs will come spewing out of his computer. "I mix and match ingredients by this experimental design," he told me. "The mathematical model maps out the ingredients to the sensory perceptions these ingredients create, so I can just dial a new product. This is the engineering approach."

After four months of this work for Dr Pepper, in which he analyzed and then tested a slew of possible variations, Moskowitz and his team delivered the new Dr Pepper flavor. Dr Pepper, which for years had been trying to compete with Coke and Pepsi, finally had the hit it was looking for. It tasted of cherry and also of vanilla—hence the name, Cherry Vanilla Dr Pepper—and it hit stores in 2004. It proved so successful that the parent company, Cadbury Schweppes, couldn't resist selling the brand in 2008, along with Snapple and 7-Up. The Dr Pepper Snapple Group has since been valued in excess of $11 billion, a figure undoubtedly enhanced by Moskowitz's labors.

The Dr Pepper project was extraordinary in one other way. The company wasn't looking for new customers as much as it was trying to get its existing customers to buy more of its product, without regard to whether it was the original flavor or the Cherry Vanilla. Thus, the Moskowitz team's campaign was for nothing less than the hearts and minds of the most devoted Pepper fans. They devised sixty-one different formulations, varying the sugar flavorings ever so slightly with each incarnation. They rounded up tasters across the country, and sat them down to a series of 3,904 tastings. And once all that testing was done, Moskowitz then performed his high math, searching for the one thing the food industry covets more than anything else, the defining facet of consumer craving: the bliss point.

I met Howard Moskowitz on a crisp day in the spring of 2010 at the Harvard Club in midtown Manhattan. He is a large man in every sense of the word, tall with sandy gray hair, and the club's cushy chairs and refined breakfast menu suit him well. Moskowitz obtained his doctoral degree from Harvard in the late 1960s, adding a PhD in experimental psychology to his earlier focus in mathematics. In choosing a subject for his thesis, his professors gave him a choice between political polling and human taste, and for Moskowitz, the decision was easy. "I was young and thin, and had grown up in a kosher home," he explained. "At Harvard I was eating hamburgers, fried fish, fries." He went for the human taste. Back in the 1960s, so little was known about why people like the foods they do that Moskowitz focused on creating a scientific method by which researchers could study taste. He devised an experimental protocol in which he methodically created mixtures of sweet with salty, salty with bitter, and bitter with other flavors. He then walked around campus corralling guinea pigs, whom he paid fifty cents to taste the mixtures and tell him which ones they liked and which ones they did not.

When we first sat down, Moskowitz wanted to make it clear that, while he derived much of his income from large food companies, he was no industry sycophant. We started off talking about salt, which had become a hot-button issue for food manufacturers, who increasingly stood accused of oversalting their products to boost their allure. Manufacturers were failing to cope with the increasing health concerns about salt through no fault but their own, he told me. "They have a real fear of playing around with the products, and my own personal feeling is there is an intellectual laziness in the food industry. We talk a lot about taking salt out, but we don't want to do our homework." On the other hand, salt—with its long-term health issues—does not have the power of sugar in compelling the industry to act. Sugar is directly linked to body fat, and as a result, low-calorie sweeteners have opened up a huge market of people eager to look better by losing weight. "If all of a sudden people started demanding lower salt because low salt makes them look younger, this problem would be solved overnight," he said.

We also talked about the obesity crisis, and while he has some suggestions for how the industry could help curb obesity—applying more rigorous research to the problem, for example—he said he had no qualms about his own pioneering work on the bliss point or any of the other systems that helped food companies create the greatest amount of crave. "There's no moral issue for me," he said flatly. "I did the best science I could. I was struggling to survive and didn't have the luxury of being a moral creature. As a researcher, I was ahead of my time, and I had to take what I can get. Would I do it again? Yes, I would do it again. Did I do the right thing? If you were in my position, what would you have done?"

Moskowitz takes pride in the science he brought to food invention. As he told a gathering of food technicians in 2010, "The history of your field wasn't real science. There were no methods. There was no corpus of knowledge. Where did sensory research come from? It was a bunch of bench chemists asking why things taste good. And the market researcher was some hapless person trying to figure out whether the stuff would sell or not."

His path to mastering the bliss point began in earnest not at Harvard but a few months after graduation, sixteen miles from Cambridge, in the town of Natick, where the U.S. Army hired him to work in its research labs. The military has long been in a peculiar bind when it comes to food: how to get soldiers to eat *more* rations, not less, when they are out in the field, running operations. "The problem in the military is the same as in nursing homes," said Herb Meiselman, one of Moskowitz's former colleagues at the Army labs. "When you go into combat, you reduce your eating, and if you do that for too long, you lose body weight."

The soldier's basic food in the field is the pouch of dehydrated rations known as the MRE, which stands for "Meal, Ready to Eat," and the shelf life alone is an appetite killer. At Natick, the technicians laugh when civilian food makers complain about having to formulate their products to hold up in the grocery store for ninety days. Army rations must last for three years, in scorching heat. To address the body weight problem, the Army knew it would have to compete with the convenience foods that soldiers are accustomed to eating back home. "To get them to eat more, every year we're coming out with seven or eight new entrees to test, looking at the trends, what's popular in restaurants," said Jeannette Kennedy, the project officer for Natick's research on the MRE. "The beef patty did great at the beginning of the Iraq War but got taken out because it was not scoring well in field tests. So for 2012, we're doing more than simple hamburgers. It's Asian pepper steak and Mexican-style chicken stew."

Natick was just starting to experiment with the MRE in 1969 when it hired Moskowitz. One thing was quite clear when it came to these packaged meals. Soldiers gradually began to find them so boring that they would toss them away, half-eaten, and not get all the calories they needed. But what was causing this MRE fatigue was a mystery. "So I started asking soldiers how frequently they would like to eat this or that, trying to figure out which products they would find boring," he said. The answers he got were inconsistent. "They liked flavorful foods like turkey tetrazzini, but only at first; they quickly grew tired of them. On the other hand, mundane foods like white bread would never get them too excited, but they could eat lots and lots of it without feeling they'd had enough."

This contradiction would come to be known as "sensory-specific satiety." In lay terms, this is the tendency for big distinct flavors to overwhelm the brain, which responds by making you feel full, or satiated, really fast. Sensory-specific satiety not only helped shape the Army's mass production of MREs; it also became a guiding principle for the processed food industry. The biggest hits—be they Coca-Cola or Doritos or Kraft's Velveeta Cheesy Skillets dinner kits—owe their success to formulas that pique the taste buds enough to be alluring but don't have a distinct overriding single flavor that says to the brain: Enough already!

With the appetites of soldiers flattened by war, Moskowitz began to focus his research on the one ingredient that packs more allure than anything else: sugar. This was still the early 1970s, when scientists had little understanding of how sugar created such strong magnetism in food. Exploring the science of how sugar traveled from the taste buds to the brain to create cravings would require cutting-edge medical equipment, such as the full-body scanner known as the MRI, which would not be invented until 1977. Moskowitz, however, toiling in the drab, institutional Army labs at Natick, produced some of the first primitive studies on cravings for scientific journals with titles like "Taste Intensity as a Function of Stimulus

Concentration and Solvent Viscosity." Eventually, he hit a vein of research that, in years to come, would prove to be a rich strike for the manufacturers of processed foods.

Moskowitz initially set out to learn how to maximize the power of sugar in foods, conducting the same kind of taste tests he designed at Harvard. With the resulting data he created graphs that, he noticed, looked like an inverted U. They showed that our liking of food rose as the amount of sugar was increased, but only to a point; after that peak, adding more sugar was not only a waste, it *diminished* the allure of the food.

Moskowitz wasn't the first scientist to notice this phenomenon, but he takes credit for being the first to recognize its financial potential—an epiphany that came one afternoon in 1972, as a colleague looked over his work. This colleague, Joseph Balintfy, was a University of Massachusetts professor who was pioneering the use of computer modeling to create complex menus for hospitals and other institutions where large numbers of people had widely divergent nutritional needs and tastes. The Army labs had retained him to work on its menus. Balintfy was examining Moskowitz's graphs on sugar's allure one day when he pointed to the top of the upside-down U and said, "That's your bliss point."

"And I said, 'That's a great name,'" Moskowitz told me. "It's just so sexy. What are you going to call it, the 'optimum sensory liking'?"

It wasn't until the early 1980s that Moskowitz became a full-fledged industry star. By that time, he had married, and struggling to raise a family on his Army salary, he moved to White Plains, about twenty-five miles north of New York City. White Plains had become a magnet for some of the largest processed food manufacturers in the country, and shortly after arriving, Moskowitz started his own consulting business. The food giants were facing some of the toughest years in their history, transitioning from an era of smugness—in which almost everything they invented, from Hamburger

Helper to Pringles, was a surefire hit—to getting called on the carpet regularly for lackluster sales by their ultimate master: Wall Street.

The largest manufacturer of all, General Foods, had come to be seen as a plodding dinosaur that feared innovation and relied too heavily on old products, including coffee—which, at $2.5 billion, accounted for more than a quarter of its annual sales—and frozen vegetables. The company, plagued by bureaucracy, was notorious for moving slowly in response to marketplace trends. The thousand people who worked at its vast research and development operations on the banks of the Hudson River were churning out precious few hits. One financial analyst dubbed it "one of the great ho-hummers among giant food companies." In 1985, General Foods got a new lease on life when the tobacco giant Philip Morris acquired it for $5.75 billion, but that only intensified the pressure on the beleaguered food side executives. The tobacco company wasn't being philanthropic. Philip Morris wanted a return on that investment, and fires were soon lit within General Foods to get the profits up.

Howard Moskowitz had already been working on projects for General Foods for a number of years, helping the company develop winning formulas for its cereals and Jell-O, when the company called on him in 1986 to help with a more pressing crisis. Maxwell House, their flagship coffee brand, was losing badly to Folgers, and the coffee managers were at a loss about how to turn the tide. The problem was not marketing. It was far worse than that. A string of taste tests showed that people simply liked Folgers better. Pressed by their new bosses at Philip Morris, the General Food executives knew there was only one way out: They needed a new formula. Whatever beans and roasting process the company was using, it wasn't working. They needed to start over.

Instead of making a few different roasts and submitting them to a new panel of tasters, Moskowitz pored over the data from the tests that had been done. In these, and in subsequent tests, he made a key observation. The data showed that people had varied preferences for coffee that could be grouped into three different roasts, weak, medium, and strong. Each roast was considered equally perfect by their respective fans. This was a novel concept at the time. The American consumer was viewed as a singular target, uncomplicated by variation, and every food company making every grocery product was focused on finding the one perfect formulation. Moskowitz, in a bold stroke, convinced General Foods that it should be selling not one but all three of these roasts—a breakthrough that the executive in charge of fixing Maxwell House at the time, John Ruff, told me saved the brand. "We actually reversed a loss to a win against Folgers," he said.

If coffee had not one but three states of perfection, Moskowitz asked, what about the rest of the grocery store? Couldn't the same principle apply there? He wasn't envisioning the line extensions that companies later adopted to boost sales, using slight variations in color or taste or packaging to bring new consumer excitement to the main product; he imagined reworking the main products themselves, with the idea that consumers could be sorted into groups with distinct preferences. With that insight, Moskowitz's shop turned into the industry's miracle maker as food companies ditched their own in-house food technicians to retain his advice. Vlasic, the pickle maker, hired Moskowitz and came away with the finding that pickle lovers fell into three large groups whose preference for tartness ranged from weak to strong. Campbell, the soup manufacturer, brought him aboard to revamp its Prego spaghetti sauce, which was getting trounced by Ragu.

The brilliance of his work on Prego was memorialized in a 2004 presentation by the author Malcolm Gladwell at the TED Conference in Monterey, California, in which Gladwell called Moskowitz a "personal hero":

> After . . . months and months, he had a mountain of data about how the American people feel about spaghetti sauce. . . . Did he look for the most popular brand, variety of spaghetti sauce? No, . . . instead he looked at the data and he said, "Let's see if we can group all these different data points into clusters. Let's see if they congregate around certain ideas." And sure enough, if you sit

down and you analyze all this data on spaghetti sauce, you realize that all Americans fall into one of three groups. There are people who like their spaghetti sauce plain. There are people who like their spaghetti sauce spicy. And there are people who like it extra chunky. And of those three facts, the third one was the most significant, because at the time, in the early 1980s, if you went to a supermarket, you would not find extra chunky spaghetti sauce. And Prego turned to Howard, and they said, "Are you telling me that one third of Americans crave extra chunky spaghetti sauce, and yet no one is servicing their needs?" And he said, "Yes." And Prego then went back and completely reformulated their spaghetti sauce and came out with a line of extra chunky that immediately and completely took over the spaghetti sauce business in this country. And over the next ten years, they made $600 million off their line of extra chunky sauces. And everyone else in the industry looked at what Howard had done, and they said, "Oh my god, we've been thinking all wrong." And that's when you started to get seven different kinds of vinegar and fourteen different kinds of mustard and seventy-one different kinds of olive oil.

And then eventually even Ragu hired Howard, . . . and today [with Ragu] there are thirty-six in six varieties. Cheese. Light. Robusto. Rich and Hearty. Old World Traditional. Extra Chunky Garden. That's Howard's doing. That is Howard's gift to the American people. . . . He fundamentally changed the way the food industry thinks about making you happy.

Well, yes, and no. One thing Gladwell didn't mention is that the food industry already knew some things about making people happy—namely, sugar. The Prego sauces—whether cheesy, chunky, or light—have one feature in common: The largest ingredient, after tomatoes, is sugar. A mere half cup of Prego Traditional, for instance, has more than two teaspoons of sugar, as much as three Oreo cookies, a tube of Go-Gurt, or some of the Pepperidge Farm Apple Turnovers that Campbell also makes. It also delivers one-third of the salt recommended for a majority of American adults for an entire day. Some of the meat versions of Prego have even higher amounts of sugar and salt, along with nearly half a day's recommended limit for saturated fat. In making these sauces, Campbell supplied the ingredients, including the salt, sugar, and fat, while Moskowitz supplied the optimization technique and his deep knowledge of sugar. "More is not necessarily better," Moskowitz wrote in his own account of the Prego project. "As the sensory intensity (say, of sweetness) increases, consumers first say that they like the product more, but eventually, with a middle level of sweetness, consumers like the product the most (this is their optimum, or 'bliss,' point)."

In the food industry, finding the bliss point for sugar in dinner products like pasta sauce would soon become passé. Products for meals were relatively easy. People had to eat dinner, so pasta sauces merely had to be more exciting than the rival brand. Snack products, by contrast, were a much bigger challenge. They were expendable—in theory, at least—and therefore required the most powerful sensory drivers. As snacks moved toward the $90 billion market they are today and the pressure for profit rose on everything else in the grocery store, food manufacturers sought formulations that would do more than make people happy. They wanted formulations that would increase desire.

It was on this front that Howard Moskowitz made his most lasting mark, starting with an investigation he undertook in 2001 to determine the factors that drove people not merely to like their food but to eagerly snatch it up. The research was funded by the ingredient giant McCormick, and Moskowitz gave it a title that reflected the industry's drive to make people ecstatic about their food: "Crave It!"

He conducted the study with a New Jersey–based food development expert, Jacquelyn Beckley, and together they sought to identify exactly what it is about certain foods that takes us to this level of desire. They gathered consumer views on cheesecake, ice cream, chips, hamburgers, and pretzels—some thirty grocery icons in all. The resulting reams of data turned up results that not only serve as a guide for food manufacturers who want to know why cinnamon buns are so alluring; they also shed light on the very underpinnings of the obesity crisis. Because what Moskowitz found is that hunger is a poor driver of cravings. We rarely get in the situation where our body and brain are depleted of nutrients and are actually in need of replenishment. Rather, he discovered, we are driven to eat by other forces in our lives. Some of these are emotional needs, while others reflect the pillars of processed food: first and foremost taste, followed by aroma, appearance, and texture.

As disparate as these pillars may seem, one ingredient—sugar—can do it all.

Howard Moskowitz slid into a booth in a diner near his office in White Plains, where we had adjourned for lunch. We were joined by Michele Reisner, his vice president for research. The waitress suggested the Reuben sandwich, but all three of us thought better of that. I settled for the turkey club. Reisner ordered an egg-white omelet with multigrain toast. Moskowitz, who said he was watching his weight, asked for a plate of turkey breast with gravy on the side. I asked him for the particulars of his diet. "I try not to eat potatoes," he said. "I eat bread, but not too much. I try to eat healthfully. We have diabetes in the family."

I ordered three cans of Dr Pepper for the table, not wanting to miss the chance for a tasting with the man who had reversed the company's fortunes. But Moskowitz demurred. "I'm not a soda drinker," he said. "It's not good for your teeth." The waitress was on my side, however, and she brought out the regular Dr Pepper along with a brand-new flavor, Dr Pepper Cherry. Relenting, Moskowitz sipped some of each, grimaced, and searched his brain to explain the trouble that his taste buds were having. "I find it terrible, really," he said. "The cherry is overwhelming. A lot of stuff in there. Like something took. . . . Just awful." He was trying to describe what was making him so unhappy.

"Benzaldehyde," he said a few moments later. "It's common benzaldehyde, which gives it an almond and cherry flavor. This is not in the same class as Coke." Reisner took a few sips too and confessed that she only likes Coke, and the diet version at that. When I asked her what she thought of the taste, she simply shrugged.

Back in their office, after lunch, Reisner was blasé about their not being members of the Pepper cult. In fact, she said, the soda maker fully understood that the unique flavor of Dr Pepper was not to everyone's liking—if it was, it would be selling as well as Coke. It has a niche that it's trying to grow by degrees, or at least maintain, which is what Moskowitz was told when Cadbury asked for his help with Dr Pepper back in 2004. Its primary goal was not stealing customers from Pepsi or Coke. Rather, Cadbury wanted a flavor that would coax existing Dr Pepper fans into trying something new—and, with any luck, expand the reach of the brand. "This was basically, 'We've got our users, and we want to bring them into something else,' " Reisner told me as she booted up her laptop to retrieve the records of the campaign. She offered to walk me through it, showing me just what they did.

First, they put up flyers at grocery stores and placed ads to recruit ordinary people for taste tests, and then they screened the applicants for people who already loved Dr Pepper. "These were our users," Reisner said. In keeping with the company's desire to deepen its base in communities that had growing African American and Hispanic populations, the resulting group of 415 tasters were spread among four cities: Los Angeles, Dallas, Chicago, and Philadelphia. Half were male. Six in ten were Caucasian. Their ages ranged between eighteen and forty-nine.

Cadbury wanted its new flavor to have cherry and vanilla on top of the basic Dr Pepper taste. Thus, there were three main components to play with. A sweet cherry flavor, a sweet vanilla flavor, and a sweet syrup known as "Dr Pepper Flavoring" that rendered the basic Dr Pepper taste. The precise ingredients in the final component remains a secret. In all, Dr Pepper is said to have twenty-seven ingredients. But besides water, the main ingredient, first and foremost, is sugar.

Moskowitz would pull together all his studies at Harvard, along with his math and the things he learned about taste and allure in his research for the Army and his many food company clients. He conducted what he calls an optimization, which translates like this: selecting the best element from a set of available alternatives. "What I say is, let's base it on science," he said. "Let's make twenty or thirty or forty variations. When you do that, you'll see that we like some of the variations more and like others less. And you can build a mathematical model that shows you exactly the relation between what's under your control and how consumers respond. Bingo. You engineer the product."

Engineering Cherry Vanilla Dr Pepper was no easy feat. Finding the bliss point required the preparation of sixty-one distinct formulas—thirty-one for the regular version and thirty for diet. (They differed ever so slightly in their ratios of flavorings.) The formulas were then presented to the tasters, who had to be managed a bit to get the most accurate results. Now and then, someone chooses to lie, usually just to rush through the tasting. But Moskowitz's system is specifically designed to engage the tasters and convince them of the seriousness of the test. "We don't let them talk," Reisner said. "The rooms look professional, with nice computers. These are not junky places we have. The people are paid well, and the moderator will tell them there is no talking or discussing the products. They have to turn off their cell phones. They start to feel like their opinions count."

Starting on July 12, 2004, in Los Angeles, Dallas, Chicago, and Philadelphia, the Dr Pepper tasters began working through their samples, resting five minutes between each sip to restore their taste buds. After each sample, they answered a set of questions: How much did they like it overall? (0=hate; 100=love.) How strong is the taste? How do they feel about the taste? How would they describe the quality of this product? And perhaps most important of all: How likely would they be to purchase this product? (From "definitely would buy" to "definitely would not buy.") The scores were then added up. A score of 60 suggests the product will sell well.

Fourteen of Moskowitz's variations scored 61 or better, with two at 67 and two at a spectacular 70. Moreover, more than half of the panelists said that they would definitely buy the product, which in food marketing surveys is considered a terrific result.

The data that Moskowitz compiled in assessing the variations would outlive the cherry vanilla flavor itself. By evaluating consumer tastes so thoroughly, he had created a framework the soda maker could use to turn out a string of additional flavors that targeted specific groups of consumers. His data—compiled in a 135-page report for the soda maker, chock full of detailed charts and graphs—shows how people feel about a strong vanilla taste versus weak, various aspects of aroma, and the powerful sensory force that food scientists call "mouthfeel." This is the way a product interacts with the mouth, as defined more specifically by a host of related sensations, from dryness to gumminess to moisture release. These are terms more familiar to people in tasting wines, but the mouthfeel of soda and many other food items, especially those high in fat, is second only to the bliss point in its ability to predict how much craving a product will induce.

In addition to taste, the consumers were also tested on their response to color, which proved to be highly sensitive. Reisner clicked on page 92 of the report, which showed a bright blue line streaking across a graph that depicted their liking for the color. "When we increased the level of the Dr Pepper Flavoring, it gets darker and liking goes off," she said. The data can also cross-reference these preferences by age, gender, and race. The biggest surprise for most of Moskowitz's customers relates to the consumer's bliss point for sugar. The term *bliss point*, Moskowitz discovered, is actually a misnomer. It's not a single point at all. It's a range of points, which can be conceptualized like this: Take the graph that shows a bell curve, or an upside-down U; the top is actually a plateau with a range of points that will generate the same dose of pleasure. For Dr Pepper, the significance of this discovery is financial. Through the taste tests and mathematical modeling called optimization, Moskowitz found that Cadbury didn't have to use the version of its new soda with the most syrupy Dr Pepper Flavoring. The same level of bliss could be achieved by using a bit less flavoring in each twelve-ounce can.

Page 83 of the Moskowitz report puts this phenomenon into a handy graph, and I followed along in my own copy of the report as Reisner explained. A thin blue line represents the amount of Dr Pepper Flavoring needed to generate the maximum appeal, and the line is not straight. It arcs, just like the bliss point curve that Moskowitz studied thirty years earlier in his Army lab. And at the top of the arc, there is not a single sweet spot but instead, a sweet range. The potential savings is merely a few percentage points, and it won't mean much to individual consumers who are counting calories or grams of sugar. But for Dr Pepper, it adds up to colossal savings. The more soda it sells, the more money it can save by edging back on its key ingredient, the sugary Dr Pepper syrup, without losing the bliss.

"What we were able to do is show them that they could drop the Dr Pepper Flavoring, and that saves them money," Reisner told me. Instead of using 2 millimeters of the flavoring, for instance, they could use 1.69 millimeters and achieve the same effect. "That looks like nothing," Reisner said. "But it's a lot of money. A *lot* of money. Millions."

In the end, Cadbury not only made its fall 2004 deadline for launching the new flavor that Moskowitz optimized. The launch was deemed a resounding success. "Don't chug, people," the company warned fans on its website. "You'll want to savor this rich soda fountain goodness. So pull up a seat and enjoy a taste so flavorful it just goes on and on, and on. . . ."

By 2006, the company's CEO, Todd Stitzer, was crowing to investors that the new flavor was not only a big hit among Peppers, it was also bringing newcomers to the brand who had begun to expand the soda's reach from its heartland, the eleven southern states where more than half of the traditional Dr Pepper was being drunk by just 20 percent of the U.S. population. "We know that Dr Pepper's franchise with consumers is rooted in its unique bold taste," he told Wall Street analysts that year. "Cherry Vanilla Dr Pepper, launched in October 2004, builds on this heritage. The launch has surpassed ours and anybody's expectations." Cadbury was so enthused, he added, it would soon launch another new flavor called Berries and Creme, but he cautioned the analysts to be careful. Cadbury would be serving this flavor along with a newly released candy bar version of its classic Easter treat, the cream egg. For none of its products, it is safe to say, is the bliss point for sugar anything but maxed out.

"There will be some Berries and Creme at dinner tonight to wash down your cream egg bar," Stitzer said. "You'll have a sugar shock by the end of the evening."

chapter three

"Convenience with a Capital 'C' "

In the spring of 1946, Al Clausi was back home, living with his parents in Brooklyn, having just returned from the South Pacific, where he had been stationed during the war. He was trying to figure out what to do with the rest of his life. He was twenty-four, with an undergraduate degree in chemistry, and had applied to medical school at the Johns Hopkins University in Baltimore. He whiled away the weeks waiting to hear back from the school, waiting to get on with his career. One day, his father burst through the front door. He'd been down at the local American Legion hall, and he was holding a copy of its magazine, pointing to a help-wanted ad.

"He said to me, 'You're a chemist, aren't you? Here is this food company in New Jersey advertising for chemists.' And I said, 'What's a food company want with a chemist?' I had worked at an explosives plant in Niagara Falls, and I knew chemistry for petroleum, and chemistry for pharmaceuticals, but food? I took the job out of curiosity."

The company was General Foods, which had its headquarters on Park

Avenue in Manhattan. But Clausi wasn't headed to New York; he was assigned to an outpost in Hoboken, New Jersey. Clausi was given a desk in the research labs, which were housed in a small building on the waterfront. Nearby was the company's massive production plant—home to Maxwell House, whose iconic neon sign of a tilting coffee cup towered over the Hudson. His first assignment had nothing to do with food. At the time, General Foods had a laundry detergent called LaFrance Bluing Agent, famous for "bringing out the whiteness" in clothes, and Clausi was given the task of modernizing the soap. More specifically, he was asked to change its physical structure from flakes to a powder detergent. This would become the hallmark of Clausi's career, using chemistry to modernize consumer goods at a time when American consumption was being transformed with incredible speed. He was soon rewarded for his success on the soap with a promotion into the heart of General Food's operations, which made the goods that were poised to change faster than any other: Clausi was put to work reimagining the company's line of processed foods.

He was entering the business at an epic moment. The family-owned American grocery store was fast evolving into the supermarket, and food manufacturers were scrambling to fill the shelves with time-saving innovations that fed directly into the country's frenzy to modernize. The locus of this movement, in fact, resided within General Foods itself, where a rising star in the marketing division named Charles Mortimer had embraced this transformation early on, and with great fervor. He even coined the phrase "convenience foods," a phrase that would galvanize the industry for decades to come.

At the same time, a network of professional homemakers across the country were struggling to keep America's food simple and pure. These were the twenty-five thousand women who taught high school students how to shop and cook, and they promoted the ideal of home cooking with as much vigor as the food manufacturers were pushing the frozen, fast, and boxed. Among them was an unassuming South Carolina woman named Betty Dickson, who left her parents' farm for a teaching career in the early 1950s, just as Mortimer and Clausi were hitting their stride at

General Foods. For the next ten years, these three—the chemist, the marketer, and the teacher—would compete for the attention of shoppers across the country. Their efforts mirrored the push and pull in the country between convenience food that wasn't so healthy and healthy food that wasn't so convenient. And nowhere did this struggle for the nation's diet play out more fiercely than in the sugary products that Americans were now eating for breakfast, lunch, and dinner.

By the time the acceptance letter from Johns Hopkins arrived, it was too late: Al Clausi was having so much fun in Hoboken that he had come to see food as his calling in life. He was just twenty-six, but following his success on detergent, the company handed him a much different project. He led a small team of researchers charged with updating one of the company's icons, a mega-brand that epitomized American culture, but one that was also in grave danger of falling behind: Jell-O pudding. In those days, there was no such thing as instant pudding. The mix came in a box, but it took hours to prepare. "Pudding was a cornstarch-based product," Clausi told me. "You had to add it to water, disperse it, and bring the water to a boil. The problem was, as you brought the water to a boil, it would coagulate and get thick, so if you didn't stand there and keep stirring, it would stick to the bottom and burn. It was very demanding. You had to stay there over a stove, stirring this hot bubbling stuff to keep it from sticking. And once it got fully thickened—this took minutes and minutes—you would have to take it out of the sauce pan and put it in a pudding dish and that took another hour to get to room temperature. You wanted it cold, so you had to put that in the fridge to chill, another hour or two. So it might be ready at dinner if you started early in the afternoon."

Knocking an hour or two off that ordeal would give a competitor a decisive advantage, the General Foods executives realized. They asked Clausi to get there first by inventing an instant formula.

Some food creations happen in a flash. Most take months. This one took years. From 1947 to 1950, Clausi and his team cooked, ate, and breathed pudding. They tinkered with its chemical composition. They played with its physical structure. General Foods preferred using cornstarch as the base, but Clausi's crew looked at potatoes and every other starch they could find, including the sago palm, which Clausi tracked down himself after traveling, via prop plane, to Indonesia. Nothing worked. The problem was that, at the time, General Foods was staunchly committed to pure ingredients. Food additives such as boric acid, a preservative, and artificial dyes were showing up in more and more items on the grocery shelf, but General Foods knew that consumers had deep trepidations about these ingredients, especially those that were synthetic. Clausi's marching orders, then, had been quite strict: He was to create his instant pudding using only starch, sugar, and natural flavorings.

That all changed in the summer of 1949 when he returned from two weeks of fishing in the Catskills to find that all hell had broken loose. A competitor, National Brands, had filed for a patent on instant pudding by using not one synthetic but a blend of synthetics, including an orthophosphate that was usually added to drinking water supplies to prevent corrosion and controlled the acidity of foods; a pyrophosphate, which thickens foods; and water-soluble salts like calcium acetate, which extend shelf life. On his desk that first day back was an envelope marked "Open Immediately." Inside was National's patent application. And when he went to see his boss, the section head of desserts, Clausi was told that the rules had changed, public fears be damned. "He said, 'Marketing wants us to outdo the competition,' " Clausi told me. "That it was urgent. And when I asked if it still had to be 100 percent starch, he said, 'That's all out the window. Just come up with an instant pudding that can be made in thirty minutes.' Overnight, the constraints were removed. Now it was, do whatever you could to develop the pudding, and that opened the door. We studied National's patent and saw that it was using a chemical called acetate. Calcium acetate, a chemical that caused the milk to gel and that gave it the structure, so to speak, so it simulated the cooked pudding. However, it had a weakness: It kept on thickening. The chemical reaction didn't stop. It took fifteen minutes to get to an edible stage, and if you didn't consume it within five or ten minutes, it kept thickening until it got almost rubbery."

Clausi began spending a lot of time in the General Foods research library, studying the chemical composition of milk. After a few months of tinkering, he settled on using two different chemicals to simulate real cooking. One, a pyrophosphate, coagulated the milk, while the other, an orthophosphate, acted as an accelerator to hasten the thickening. They allowed him to develop an instant, no-cook pudding that was so much better, more stable and lasting. "Not only did it gel," Clausi said. "It would happen within five minutes, not fifteen minutes, which was what the competition was doing. And then it would stop. It wouldn't continue to get thicker and thicker and eventually end up like rubber. So overnight, we had a superior product with the Jell-O name, and we just took over." The National Brands version never made it into production. Clausi's formula became a bedrock hit for General Foods.

I first interviewed Clausi in the summer of 2010. We met at the office he keeps in Greenwich, Connecticut, an hour north of New York City, where he still works on various projects for the food industry. He was eighty-eight years old, with a full head of white hair and thick-framed reading glasses, which dangled from the neck of his short-sleeved shirt. By the door hung a copy of Patent No. 2,801,924, the instant pudding that had made him a legend at General Foods, and on the wall behind his desk was a gigantic wood-framed collage of some of the thousand women and men who worked for him at the company's research complex in nearby Tarrytown, New York. On a shelf opposite his desk was a toy replica of the trucks that delivered Tang, another of his iconic inventions. As we spoke, he moved easily through his four decades at General Foods, stopping now and then to dig through his collection of files that held speeches, planning documents, and other internal company records, which he kept in a couple of cardboard boxes. Food additives were a recurring theme.

The public, at times, would grow quite concerned about additives, Clausi said. Especially when a troubling incident made headlines, as it did in the early 1950s when several children were made sick by Halloween candy that contained excessive amounts of a dye called Orange Number 1. By 1960, companies had come to rely on so many additives to process, preserve, color, and otherwise treat their foods—there were fifteen hundred flavorings alone—that federal regulators moved to reconsider a host of additives they had previously approved. But one of the staunchest opponents to this move in Washington was none other than General Foods, the same company that had once put handcuffs on their young chemist Clausi, barring him from using any chemicals in pursuing an instant pudding. Executives there now belittled the federal decision to question these additives, calling it an overreach by bureaucrats. General Foods had come to embrace Clausi's view that the use of chemicals in foods was more than justified, as long as they were used safely. The improvements they made to processed foods were critical to the industry's mission, which wasn't just making money for the company's stockholders. America's population was surging, and the industry saw its role as nothing less than nurturing the masses by delivering food that was safe, easy to prepare, and affordable. This was a mission critical to America's success, and yet it stood to be compromised by watchdogs who overreacted to the isolated incidents in which the chemicals caused harm. "All the sensible people, whether they were from academia, government, industry, or even the public sector, knew that we needed these chemicals and wanted to be sure what we were using was controlled and used properly," Clausi said. Moreover, as additives go, the phosphates he used in creating instant pudding for the Jell-O brand have raised little concern among scientists. Only in large amounts do they appear to pose any kind of health risk, the Center for Science in the Public Interest, a consumer advocacy group, today agrees. (It has a chart that sorts more than 140 additives by their toxicity risk, and phosphates are categorized as safe.) In time, the public concern about the potential toxicity of chemical additives with long scientific names would be eclipsed by a more basic concern about three others with the simplest of names: salt, sugar, and fat.

Clausi would come to see his tussle with General Foods over chemical additives as an invaluable lesson, one that would guide him through the next forty years of food invention. The company's initial refusal to let him use chemicals had almost cost it dearly. No longer would he or the army of food technicians that he would soon lead at General Foods hold themselves to some antiquated notion of what was wholesome or proper in processed foods. "I learned something there which I always remembered," Clausi told me. "And that is, if you want innovation, tell me where you want to go, but don't tell me how I must get there."

On the marketing side of General Foods, however, where Charles Mortimer toiled before becoming the company's CEO, there was something else about Clausi's pudding that was firing these executives up, something much bigger than a few phosphates whose names they couldn't even pronounce. In their view, the patent that hung on his wall with the prosaic title "Pudding Composition and the Process of Producing the Same" had done even more than just beat the competition. It had shown how the use of an additive could tap into, and help shape, an entirely new way of thinking about food. The advertisements they created for the pudding captured their own excitement as well as that of the public. "Quick! Easy!" one ad said, depicting a placid and smiling mom in her sparkling kitchen as her two kids looked on. "New Busy-Day Dessert," said another. "You can make and serve it at the very last minute!"

Still, the additive they were excited about on the marketing side of General Foods wasn't phosphate or any other chemical. These wouldn't turn General Foods into the biggest and richest food company in the world. Rather, it was the artful way in which the pudding—an instant hit—was making life easier for consumers who were increasingly harried by modern life. When Mortimer emerged from the marketing side in the early 1950s to run the whole company, he would have a name for this phenomenon. He called it "convenience," and it wasn't just any old additive, he said in one of his speeches, this one to an industry group. "Serving the modern consumer has become a creative art, with convenience the super-additive that is changing the whole face of competitive business."

Instant pudding had made Clausi the company's go-to guy in a crisis, and it wasn't long before the young problem-solver had his chance to shine. In 1952, he was pulled out of Hoboken and sent to Battle Creek, Michigan, where the company's Post division was in dire need of help. After years of unbroken success, it found itself in a fight to the death over breakfast cereal. And no chemical additive would help this situation. It would require something more basic: lots of plain sugar and Mortimer's drive to create convenience.

From the late 1800s through the 1940s, the cereal sold by Post—along with those of the other big national brands—had been crisped and flaked and puffed but only modestly sweetened, if at all. Cereals were sold as healthy alternatives to what much of the country was eating for breakfast: spam, bacon, and sausage. Indeed, the physician who had invented the cereal flake, John Harvey Kellogg, was quite a stickler on sweets, running his cereal company from a sanitarium where he banned sugar altogether. That all changed, quite suddenly, in 1949, when Post became the first national brand to sell a sugar-coated cereal, which allowed the manufacturer, and not the parents, to control the amount of sugar that went into the cereal bowls of children. Post introduced a string of concoctions with names like Sugar Crisps, Krinkles, and Corn-Fetti, and kids everywhere went nuts.

Nothing in the cereal business stays exclusive for long, however, and soon Post's competitors had joined the fray. They brought their superior marketing skills to bear and quickly propelled their own sugary inventions past Post. General Mills came up with a trio of cereals called Sugar Jets, Trix, and Cocoa Puffs and turned out an endless stream of spinoffs that quickly captured huge swaths of the cereal aisle. Then, in 1951, Kellogg jumped to the front of the pack by unleashing a marketing force of nature known as Tony the Tiger, whom kids loved for his signature roar: "Sugar Frosted Flakes are GR-R-REAT!"

Pushed back to third place, General Foods decided to change the game. It dismissed the head of its cereal unit and brought the surviving executives to company headquarters in New York for some new marching orders. If they couldn't go head to head with Kellogg and General Mills on cereal, the executives were told, they would have to find something else to sell for breakfast. Something just as quick and easy and just as popular with the kids.

General Foods at the time wasn't so much a food company as it was a humongous shopping cart, which it was filling up with the biggest brands it could buy. It had started out humbly in 1895 selling a wheat cereal–based beverage called Postum, which, given the public's nascent interest in healthier eating, was advertised as having "a small portion of New Orleans Molasses." In 1929, the Postum company, which also sold Grape-Nuts cereal, bought a frozen-foods company whose name, General Foods, it adopted. With financial backing from Goldman Sachs, General Foods began to acquire a string of the most popular processed foods in America: Jell-O, Kool-Aid, Log Cabin Syrup, the whole retinue of Oscar Mayer processed meats, Entenmann's baked sweets, Hellmann's mayo, Maxwell House coffee, Birdseye frozen foods, and Minute Tapioca, the sweet pudding that gave rise to Minute Rice, the parboiled phenomenon. By 1985, when General Foods was purchased by Philip Morris, it had grown from an $18 million startup to a $9 billion industry leader. It had 56,000 employees, a research budget of $113 million, and hefty market shares in powdered soft drinks, cereals, coffee, lunch meats, hot dogs, and bacon.

General Foods was based in New York City until the early 1950s, when it moved its burgeoning portfolio from its cramped offices on Park Avenue to a fourteen-acre site in suburban White Plains, where it built an expansive, campus-like complex. Designed by the legendary architect Philip Johnson, even the parking lot was state-of-the-art, outfitted with a heated, covered walkway that said to the 1,200 employees: You are valued, and we are going places. One of the men arriving that day in 1956 from Battle Creek already had a pretty good idea he was valued. Al Clausi, now thirty-four, had become one of the youngest managers at General Foods, and he had fought valiantly to help put Post back on its feet.

By now, though, many cereal makers were not only adding sugar, they had made it their single biggest ingredient, pushing the levels past 50 percent. Post found it hard to improve on that, but Clausi gave the company an edge by tinkering with the way it looked. He invented the letter-shaped cereal Alpha-Bits, the idea for which occurred to him after dining on pasta one evening and realizing that cereal could also be made into interesting shapes, not just flakes. "We thought it would be attractive to kids," Clausi said. "Alpha-Bits was being sold on the merit of the shape and the fact that it was a combination of oat and corn cereal, not as a candy."*

The hardest part in that venture was not optimizing the cereal's sugar level but maneuvering around the bizarre way that cereals are made. Typically, the dough that forms the cereal is first extruded from oat flour and cornstarch and then shot by a cannon-like machine into a room-sized bin where a sudden drop in pressure causes the heated moisture in the dough to turn into steam, which cooks and puffs the dough into cereal. To retain the letter shapes as they flew across the room, however, Clausi had to formulate a combination of cooked and uncooked dough. Alpha-Bits inspired a whole slew of novel cereal shapes in the supermarket, starting with Post's own lineup of Honeycomb, Crispy Critters, and Waffle Crisp.

Clausi was proving himself to be expert at more than just chemistry. He was a gregarious man with great people skills. His outgoing nature made him something of an anomaly in an industry where the food technicians were prone to be introverts. Clausi moved easily between the laboratories, where the food chemists crafted their formulas, and the marketing offices, where the company aggressors, the sales executives, had a prickly view of the technologists who invented the company's products. Clausi assumed the role of mediator, especially later when consumers began placing greater demands on the industry, asking for more fiber or less fat. The marketing executives would demand instant changes from the food technologists, and Clausi would intervene and smooth things over. "They would drive the technologists crazy," he said. "They are instantaneous responders. When people want low fat, they immediately say to the technologists, 'Make *all* our products with low fat!' "

---

* Clausi recalled that Alpha-Bits had far less sugar than the sweetest cereals. But by 1983, it was named among the company's most sugary cereals in a consumer lawsuit, and ten years later, when companies had begun disclosing the salt, sugar, and fat content on their labels, *Consumer Reports* listed the sugar load in one version, Marshmallow Alpha-Bits, at 49 percent.

As good as he was, Clausi didn't yet have the grand vision for what food inventors like himself could really achieve, vis-à-vis American eating habits. This he would get from Charles Mortimer, the executive who had called Clausi and the others from Battle Creek to the meeting in New York to discuss the bruising they had taken in the cereal wars. Mortimer had never clashed with the marketing side at General Foods. He *was* the marketing side, and he ran the division until he was named CEO of the company. As a child, Mortimer had been called "fatty." He was a stocky kid, like Clausi born in Brooklyn, who grew up on meat and potatoes and was something of a bookworm. But as chief executive, he placed such relentlessly high demands on his employees for results that they gave him another nickname: "How-Soon Charlie"—as in, "How soon will you have that for me?" His eleven years at the helm of General Foods, from 1954 to 1965, were viewed as the company's golden years: Sales doubled, earnings tripled, and General Foods led America to a different way of thinking about food.

"Today, consumer expectations are so high and the pace at which new products are introduced is so fast that Mrs. Homemaker usually can't say what it is she really wants—until after some enterprising company creates it and she finds it in a retail store," Mortimer said in a speech to business executives the year he retired. "I cannot think of a single General Foods product which we were selling when I became chief executive eleven years ago which is still on the grocery shelves and has not been changed importantly and, of course, for the better."

Mortimer hadn't called the Post cereal executives in from Battle Creek to chew them out. That wasn't his style. He wanted to tell them to have courage in the face of combat with other cereal makers, and more than that, he wanted to put them back on the offensive. They could turn their position of weakness to one of strength, he told them, with only a little reframing. If they were getting beaten by companies who were better at selling cereal, then they needed to figure out how to sell other things for breakfast. They might have to invent these things, because the homemaker couldn't be counted upon to think them up. But the sky was their limit, he said, and there were only a few constraints that he would place on them. These foods had to be easy to buy, store, open, prepare, and eat.

This drive for convenience had become his mantra at General Foods. His goal was to lead not only his own company into this brave new world: He felt so passionately about convenience, he wanted to engage the entire industry. In the coming years, he would share his ideas with executives from other food manufacturers and beyond, to all consumer goods. For now, however, in addressing his executives, Mortimer focused only on the company's dwindling share of the breakfast market. "Who says the only food should be cereal?" Mortimer said. "You are not just a breakfast cereal company, you are a breakfast foods company."

To drive his point home, to get his employees thinking freely, he told them about the joyful scene in his own home when his own kids came trundling into the kitchen to start their day. They didn't limit themselves to bowls of Sugar Crisps or Cocoa Puffs.

"My daughter," he said, "likes to eat cake for breakfast."

More than fifty years later, the words that Mortimer spoke that day still resonated with Al Clausi. As we sat in his office, he said that the cake story, along with the rest of Mortimer's speech, was not simply inspiring. Mortimer's exhortations gave him the means to pursue, and help, Mrs. Homemaker in a way that he had never imagined before. If she didn't know how much she needed convenience, it was up to inventors like Clausi to show her the way. "That was a mind spreader," he said.

In his forty-year career at General Foods, Clausi dabbled in numerous aisles of the supermarket—even the pet food section, which, by Clausi's estimation, was the easiest to transform. Until he and his colleagues put their minds to it, dog food had come in boxes and bags and was uniformly dry as a bone, utterly boring to the pooches. The problem was bacteria, which thrived in moisture. To keep the chow safe, it had to be dry. Having studied the chemical properties of sugar, however, Clausi saw another way.

He figured out that adding sugar to the chow would keep the bacteria away even in moist conditions, as sugar acted like a binder to make the water inaccessible to the bacteria. The result was a dog patty dubbed Gaines-Burgers, which could sit on the shelf until they were sold, just as long as the dry stuff could. The idea of using sugar to ward off bacteria is now embedded in the production of many processed foods, especially when the fat content is reduced.

The crowning jewel in Clausi's career, however, had nothing to do with dog food. It showed up one day in another aisle in the supermarket, and breakfasts in America would never again be the same. Starting in 1956, he used his chemistry and people skills to transform a natural breakfast food, orange juice, into Tang, a laboratory product that was 100 percent, nothing-natural-about-it, synthetic chemical and sugar.

The Tang project had started immediately after Mortimer's pep talk in White Plains. Before returning to Battle Creek, Clausi visited his old laboratory in Hoboken, where he took Mortimer's advice and tried thinking big. "Are you working on anything that people could eat or drink for breakfast?" he asked the technicians.

"We're developing synthetic juices, like orange," the laboratory director, Domenic DeFelice, told him. "But we've got a long way to go."

"Can you let me see them?" Clausi asked.

The Hoboken scientists had come up with some amazing concoctions, especially the orange one. It didn't taste watery like other powdered drinks that Clausi had tasted. It had a fullness, a good mouthfeel, and the flavoring brought to mind real Valencia oranges. It easily beat out the taste of what most people were drinking for breakfast at the time, Clausi told me. "People didn't have fresh orange juice back then like they do now," he said. "They either had concentrate, frozen like a hockey puck that took you half a day to defrost in the kitchen sink, and full of pulp, which children do not like. Or they had canned orange juice, which had a tinny, cooked characteristic."

But DeFelice and his lab crew had been in despair when Clausi came along. When they added in all the vitamins and minerals that were needed to replicate the nutritional profile of real orange juice, their drink tasted horribly bitter and metallic. Clausi listened to them, and then, with his diplomatic skills, he took the problem to the marketing side, where the director, Howard Bloomquist, said the technologists were being too picky—or rather, they were misreading the potential consumer concern. Bloomquist said that people mostly associated orange juice with vitamin C, not all the other nutrients the lab technicians were trying to add to their synthetic drink, and vitamin C, as luck would have it, was the one nutrient the technicians could add without hurting the taste. Clausi went back to the lab and urged them to forget all about the other nutrients they were trying to add. Thus was born Tang, the technician's gift to harried breakfasters everywhere. Released in 1958, Tang blew away yet another of the chores that moms faced at breakfast time, and the General Foods copywriters had a field day. "New! Instant! Just mix with cold water," the company ads read. "No squeezing. No unfreezing. Real wake-up taste. Always the same sunny goodness, glass after glass."

"Happiest thing that ever happened to breakfast," said another.

Tang was never intended to blow out the sugar levels of real juice, Clausi said. If people followed the instructions on the label and used only level teaspoons when scooping the crystals into their glass, Tang had only a bit more sugar than orange juice. But that was one of the beauties of Tang—its bliss point was readily adjustable. Just start rounding the spoonfuls, or throw in an extra, and Tang quickly gets as sweet as soda. The marketing power of this movable bliss point became starkly evident when General Foods began selling Tang in other countries. Clausi was on a marketing trip in China in the 1970s that included taste tests for Tang. "We started in Beijing, and the further south we went, the sweeter the people wanted the Tang," he said. Today, with annual sales having pushed past $500 million, more Tang is being sold in China and Latin America— another part of the world where people have a high fondness for sugar— than in the United States.

Tang had one other little-known attribute that contributed to its blockbuster status in the United States, albeit in a peculiar way. NASA, the space program, needed a drink that would add little bulk to the digestion, given the toilet constraints in space. Real orange juice had too much bulky fiber in its pulp. Tang, however, was perfect—what technologists call a "low-residue" food. When NASA heard about Tang, Clausi instructed a colleague: "Tell NASA we're honored to be of service, and we'll supply whatever they need—free of charge." On February 20, 1962, John Glenn returned from his triple orbit around the earth and told reporters that the only good thing about the food aboard his spacecraft was the Tang. With that endorsement, sales exploded.

In the days after Charles Mortimer's exhortation to be more imaginative, the company's cereal executives out in Battle Creek, Michigan, showed their own flair for thinking grandly. In 1961, they came up with an invention that could take the place of an entire real breakfast. It was another powdered drink, initially called Brim, and it was promoted as "breakfast in a glass." The popularity of this new "instant breakfast" was guaranteed by its sweetness. Then, two years later, the Post inventors came closest of all to replicating the cake that Mortimer's daughter ate for breakfast. They tooled their production plant to turn out two ribbons of pastry dough. A sweet fruity mash was smeared on the top of one, which was then covered by the other to make a sandwich that was cut into squares with edges crimped and then baked. These were called Pop-ups, and they met all of Mortimer's criteria for convenience: They came in a box, could stay on the shelf for months, could be eaten on the go, and could be served hot without even needing to light the stove. The toaster would do. As with most food inventions, the sure sign of success was the speed with which it was copied. A few months after the squares were introduced, Post's rival, Kellogg, executed an even more successful version of this breakfast pastry, which had scant amounts of actual fruit but loads of sugar, as much as 19 grams—more than four teaspoons—each. Called Pop-Tarts, some of the twenty-nine varieties make no pretense of being anything other than cake for breakfast, or cookies at least. Among the flavors: Chocolate Chip, Chocolate Chip Cookie Dough, Chocolate Fudge, Cookies and Creme, and S'mores.

The real beauty of this convenience was its elasticity. When sales flattened out forty years later, Pop-Tarts would be promoted not as a warm breakfast food, but as a "cold afternoon treat." Sales shot up 25 percent, according to Kellogg's account of its 2003 marketing campaign, when it found a rich snacking target: "The 30 million tweens aged 9–14 who possess an estimated $38 billion in spending power."

Every year in New York City, the top executives of companies that sold a wide range of goods gathered together under the auspices of the Conference Board, an august association best known today for conducting the "consumer confidence" survey. In 1955, the dinner speaker was Charles Mortimer, and he got right to the point. Food, clothing, and shelter were still important, he told the crowd. But now there was a fourth essential element of life that could be "expressed in a single word—convenience—spelled out with a capital 'C.' "

"Convenience is the great additive which must be designed, built in, combined, blended, interwoven, injected, inserted, or otherwise added to or incorporated in products or services if they are to satisfy today's demanding public. It is the new and controlling denominator of consumer acceptance or demand."

There is convenience of form, he said, citing the Gaines-Burger dog food patties that Clausi had invented to be as soft as hamburger but so durable that they could sit on the pantry shelf until needed. There is convenience of time, like the grocery stores throughout America that were starting to stay open in the evenings to accommodate increasing numbers of women who worked outside the home. And there is convenience of packaging, like beer in bottles that used to have to be hauled back to the store but were now disposable, and the aluminum foil pie pans that were showing up on the grocery shelves.

"Modern Americans are willing to pay well for this additive to the products they purchase," Mortimer told the executives. "Not because of any native laziness but because we are willing to use our greater wealth to buy fuller lives and we have, therefore, better things to do with our time than mixing, blending, sorting, trimming, measuring, cooking, serving, and all the other actions that have gone into the routine of living."

As if on cue, time-saving gadgets and gizmos started arriving in the grocery store that year that helped the modern homemaker trade a little more of her new wealth for some extra time away from the kitchen. Ready-to-bake biscuits appeared in tubes that could be opened by merely tugging a string. Special detergents came out for electric dishwashers that had special compounds to get off the water spots. One entrepreneurial firm even made plastic lids with spouts that snapped on cans of milk or syrup for easier pouring.

As more food companies followed his lead and conveniences arrived in every last aisle in the supermarket, there was only one real obstacle to the social transmutation that Mortimer had envisioned: the army of school teachers and federal outreach workers who insisted on promoting home-cooked meals, prepared the old-fashioned way. These educators numbered in the tens of thousands, and they were spread throughout the country, teaching kids and young homemakers not only how to cook from scratch but also how to shop to avoid processed food. Those preaching this ideal included a few thousand government employees known as extension agents, who worked for the federal and state departments of agriculture and who made house calls to teach young homemakers the ins and outs of gardening, canning, and meal planning with nutrition in mind. The main force of this army, however, was the twenty-five thousand teachers who taught the high school classes known as home economics. Home Ec was the field of formal study that taught how to manage a home and community.

If there was anyone who epitomized the Home Ec teacher, it was a thirty-year-old former farmgirl named Betty Dickson. She had been raised in York County, South Carolina, a heavily wooded and historic part of the Piedmont region just to the south and west of Charlotte, which had been developed by Scotch-Irish settlers in 1750. The main crop on her parent's farm was cotton, but they also grew their own vegetables. Dickson learned to cook from her mother, without even the convenience of a freezer. She made it to college and earned her teaching credentials, but it was these practical, low-tech skills from the farm that she passed on to her high school students. "It was teaching the basics," Dickson recalled. "They knew how to boil water, or maybe not all of them. But we did the basic skills in preparing and making biscuits, or meat, vegetables, and desserts." Part of the class work was simply learning how to shop. The town had a small grocery, where she could immerse the students in dos and don'ts. She had them prepare shopping lists to avoid buying those things they didn't need and "to compare prices, because money was not as free as it would be."

Dickson belonged to the American Home Economics Association, whose founder, Ellen Henrietta Swallow Richards, had parlayed her training in chemistry at MIT into a career as a consumer activist. Richards tested commercial foods for toxic contaminants; lobbied for nutritious, inexpensive cooked food in the home and at school; and pushed back on the notion that "convenience" should be owned and controlled by the processed food companies. Homemakers could do convenience, too, and even better, the association argued. To help make its case, the association conducted a two-layer cake experiment in 1957 that pitted a commercial mix against a homemade batter. As reported in the association's journal, the homemade cake not only cost less and tasted better, it took only five minutes more than the commercial mix to prepare, cook, and serve. Moreover, for extra convenience, the homemade mix could be made and stored in big batches, for quick parceling out when a cake was needed.

But the world that Dickson and the other home economics teachers were fighting for, a society that valued home cooking, was already showing substantial signs of stress in 1955. Even then, nearly 38 percent of American women were leaving the home to work. When they returned in the evening, it was to cope with a second, even more demanding job: caring for their husbands and kids.

As food manufacturers saw it, these women needed help. They

couldn't cook meals from scratch, even if they felt that would be more nutritious for their family. Evenings became rushed. More households were getting TVs, too, which added another distraction. Who wanted to be still eating dinner or doing the dishes when *Lassie* and *Gunsmoke* were on? If the teachers of home economics couldn't see that society was changing, and quickly, then the processed food companies saw it as their mission to change the nature of home economics.

In the mid-1950s, the food industry undertook two cunning maneuvers to draw these working women into its fold. The first was to create its own army of home economics teachers. Bright and fashionable, these women worked for the companies, held their own cooking contests, set up popular demonstration kitchens, and conducted cooking classes for moms and their daughters in direct competition with the home economics teachers who taught in the schools. By 1957, General Foods had sixty of these home economists on its payroll, promoting its products and working with the company's technologists to create more convenience foods. They had glamour, and they had style, as Al Clausi, the General Foods inventor, well knew. He married one of them.

The second move by the industry was perhaps the most influential of all. To compete with the home-cooking skills being taught by Betty Dickson and the other home economics teachers, the industry wielded its very own Betty to preach the creed of convenience. Her name was Betty Crocker, and she quickly became one of the most famous women in America, notwithstanding the fact that she was entirely fake. Betty Crocker had been invented by the manager of the advertising department at Washburn Crosby, which later became General Mills, and this Betty never slept. She started out as the friendly signature on the advertising department's letters to customers, and soon she was responding to as many as five thousand adoring fans a day, like the Mrs. Springer who wrote to her in 1950 to say how much she enjoyed the company's Party Cake mix. "You will find that the PARTYCAKE Mix, DEVILS FOOD CAKE Mix and the GINGER-CAKE and Cooky Mix are all grand time savers," Betty Crocker replied.

Her catchy slogans, like "I guarantee a perfect cake, every time you bake—cake after cake after cake," rang out in radio, magazine, and television advertisements. She opened a set of show rooms, known as Betty's Kitchens, where women were taught quick 'n easy, heat-and-serve cooking with Bisquick and other General Mills products. These kitchens became so famous that Vice President Richard Nixon and Soviet Premier Nikita Khrushchev in 1959 held their famous "Kitchen Debate" in a copy of the Betty Crocker kitchen that General Mills had set up at the U.S. Trade and Cultural Fair in Moscow to epitomize the modern American kitchen. Betty Crocker also unleashed the Big Red, a string of bestselling cookbooks that went far beyond hawking desserts. As Susan Marks writes in her book *Finding Betty Crocker: The Secret Life of America's First Lady of Food*, the recipes and advice in these cookbooks helped to drive "the fundamental shift in American diets toward the factory-processed convenience foods that were becoming fixtures in the grocery aisles."

But even Betty Crocker wasn't enough to totally undermine the teachings of Betty Dickson. To do that, the processed food industry had to come up with another, more insidious strategy. Like the Hoover-era FBI pursuing its enemies list, the industry infiltrated the association of home economics teachers. This operation started with money and advertising, an archive of the association's journal reveals. In 1957 alone, General Foods funneled $288,250 into the grants and fellowship program of the home economics association, winning the gratitude of a generation of teachers. The association then devoted a special section of its journal to publicizing all the convenient products, from Stove Top Stuffing to nine-serving cake mixes. And General Foods and other manufacturers took out big ads for the hospitality booths they set up at the association fairs.

Then the food industry began sending people to further reshape the association to its own designs. It sponsored candidates for the organization's top leadership posts, candidates who would bring a decidedly pro-industrial view to home economics. Marcia Copeland, a General Mills executive who became the home economics association's president in 1987, told me that the decline of scratch cooking wasn't a corporate plot as much as it was a foregone conclusion when women acquired greater roles in American society. "When I joined General Mills in 1963, it was evident that people weren't having the time or interest in preparing meals from scratch," she said. "They would do one meal from scratch, like a pot roast, and they developed a specialty if they were entertaining, like they would do the bread or the dessert, one spectacular thing. We tried to make people at General Mills look at food to be more fun."

In the meantime, teachers like Betty Dickson were forced to alter their curriculum to deal with all of the pressing problems that came to bear on the modern housewife. It would be foolish to call her the last home economics teacher in America. They do still exist. But the focus of home economics changed dramatically through the 1970s and 1980s. Each year, the association chose a home economics teacher of the year, and when Dickson won in 1980, she was praised for having a curriculum that still included cooking and shopping. In the years that followed, however, the winning teachers were cited for teaching their students not how to produce their own things like meals but how to get jobs and be consumers.

Dickson was still only in her sixth year of teaching in 1959 when it might be said her fight was lost. *Time* did a long article on convenience foods, and after casting about for a person who would illustrate all that was new and great about cooking, the magazine chose someone else to put on the cover about convenience foods: Charles Mortimer, CEO of General Foods and the man who coined the phrase. "Modern Living," read the headline of the article. "Just Heat and Serve." Inside was a profile of a Hollywood secretary who'd thrown together a dinner party for fourteen guests, on a weeknight, after coming home from her job. She served hors d'oeuvres, shrimp cocktail, lobster Newberg, fresh salad, asparagus tips in Hollandaise sauce, rice, rolls, white cake, and ice cream. "Almost every bite of the appetizing meal she placed before her guests had been washed, cut, peeled, shelled, precooked, mixed and apportioned by 'factory maids' long before it reached her hands," the writer gushed. "Such jiffy cooking would have made Grandma shudder, but today it brings smiles of delight to millions of U.S. housewives. The remarkable rise of 'convenience' or processed foods—heralded by slogans 'instant,' 'ready to cook' and 'heat and serve'—has set off a revolution in U.S. eating habits, brought a bit of magic into the U.S. kitchen.

"No company has done more to revolutionize U.S. cooking than General Foods Corp., the world's biggest food processor," the piece continued. "It sparked the revolution with its line of Birds Eye frozen foods, still the biggest-selling brand. Last year it put its 250 products (including different flavors and varieties) into 4.5 billion packages that the housewife took home for $1.1 billion. On pantry shelves and in refrigerators from Maine to Florida, its products are household words—Jell-O, Maxwell House coffee, Post cereals, Swans Down cake mix, Sanka, Minute Rice, Gaines dog food, etc."

In one final blow to the traditional teachings of home economics, Mortimer was quoted reading the long, arduous instructions in *Fannie Farmer's Cookbook* for preparing a fresh fish, which trudged along from cleaning to scaling to boning. "And so on," Mortimer said, "through all the other gruesome procedures before the housewife could start to burn her fingers in the hot grease or fill her kitchen with clouds of fish-laden smoke."

"What does it say on a package of frozen fish sticks?" he said, triumphantly. " 'Heat and serve.' "

Betty Dickson is diplomatic about the turn that home economics took in the 1960s and 1970s, when cooking from scratch increasingly gave way to the kind of quick fare celebrated by *Time*. "We taught skills, but over the years that changed. It became more consumer education," she said. "I'm so thankful that jobs became more available, and people had more resources. But that wasn't always for the best. The change came in how they used their resources. The boys in high school had to have a car, and they had to get a job to get the car."

Charles Mortimer died in 1978, and he is buried on the horse farm he owned in New Jersey, which one of his grandsons has turned into a winery. His legacy is left for Al Clausi to defend, and he had a bit of a struggle with it when we spoke. Today, he told me, the most remarkable aspect of Mortimer's convenience doctrine is not the speed with which pudding can be made, or how a few spoonfuls of sugar powder can avoid the hassle of squeezing oranges, or even how multi-course dinners can be pulled out of the freezer and refrigerator, already prepped by "factory maids." The most remarkable aspect of the doctrine, he said, is how it is now being challenged by newer generations of consumers—the sons and daughters and grandchildren of the people he and other food technicians had wooed with the quick-to-cook packaged foods.

"Convenience is still very high in the consumer's mind," Clausi said. "But it is not what it used to be. Now there are more questions being asked. How is it convenient? What are the ingredients? What am I trading for the convenience?"

Clausi still works as a consultant to the food industry, and he had to chuckle to himself recently when one of General Foods' old rivals called on him for some advice. It was Kellogg, the cereal maker, looking for ways to boost sales. Keeping in mind the doubts that consumers were starting to have about convenience, Clausi told Kellogg to think about something other than sugar to draw their interest. "Why can't you make breakfast cereal from a protein source like nuts?" he told them. "They have a good nutrition profile."

This was the same company, however, that had relied heavily on sugar in trouncing General Foods back in the early 1950s and in maintaining its lead over other cereal makers ever since. Kellogg had gone so far down the road with sugar, in fact, that there was no easy way to turn back. If consumers were getting antsy about the health implications of sugar, getting rid of it was not a viable way out for Kellogg. The biggest cereal maker in the world would have to find another way to keep drawing its customers in, and it would find that that way was in the hands of a section of the processed food industry that was gaining in stature every day: marketing.

chapter four

"Is It Cereal or Candy?"

John Harvey Kellogg had one thing in mind when he created his sprawl-ing health complex on the prairie of Michigan in the late 1800s. He wanted to cure people of what one observer had called "Americanitis"—or the bloated, gaseous stomachache caused by the ailment otherwise known as dyspepsia. The whole country seemed to be suffering from it, thanks in large part to what they were eating for breakfast. Nineteenth-century Americans typically started their mornings with sausages, beefsteaks, bacon, and fried ham, to which, as the day progressed, they added salt pork and whiskey. Grease, in effect, had become the national condiment.

As a medical student at New York City's Bellevue Hospital Medical College, John Harvey Kellogg had seen, up close, what this diet was doing to America's health. Concerned by the profusion of indigestion he saw, he ended up beating a hasty retreat to his home state of Michigan, where he decided that what America needed—as much as another doctor—was someone to promote better nutrition.

Kellogg took over a tiny health facility in Battle Creek, a town on the prairie 120 miles west of Detroit, and renamed it the Battle Creek Sanitarium. He added a solarium, a gymnasium, and a glassed-in palm garden with rubber trees. As word of the facility's salutary treatments got around, the rooms began filling up. In high season, four hundred guests were tended to by a staff of one thousand, and they happily underwent a relentless regime of baths, enemas, and exercise that included a high-stepping workout to a song that was dubbed "The Battle Creek Sanitarium March." Mostly, though, Kellogg sought to remake their eating habits with a strict dietary regimen. He served wheat gluten mush, oatmeal crackers, graham rolls, and a tea made from a South African grass. He disdained salt and abhorred sugar, citing the overconsumption of both as primary contributors to the nation's health woes, so there was none of either to be found in the sanitarium food. Nor was there much fat; his reform diet was built around whole grains and a dearth of meat.

On a trip to Denver in 1894, Kellogg met a dyspeptic entrepreneur who had invented a cereal made from shredded wheat. Enamored by the idea, Kellogg set out to make his own breakfast version of it. He returned to Battle Creek and, with help from his wife, took some leftover boiled wheat, ran it through a machine that turned the mush into thin sheets of dough, and popped them into the oven. Out came a flaked cereal, which Kellogg served to his guests and which his guests liked. Kind of. The texture was certainly novel.

That might have been the extent of his cereal's market—the captive sanitarium guests—except for a bit of treachery in the Kellogg household. John Harvey Kellogg had a younger brother named Will who worked as the sanitarium's bookkeeper. Will was far more interested in making money than his older brother, who was forever going off on some scientific lark just when the sanitarium most needed sound management. So Will took over the cereal operation, commandeering a barn out back to make the dough and bake the flakes. The Kellogg brothers called their cereal venture the Sanitas Nut Food Company, and with Will's attention to detail it did reasonably well, considering its unsweetened taste: They sold 113,400 pounds of the stuff in 1896, mostly to their own patients and Battle Creek locals. With his brother's encouragement, Will also began experimenting with flakes of corn, called cerealine, which were used by the brewing industry. They named these the Sanitas Toasted Corn Flakes.

Then came the betrayal.

In 1906, John Harvey was in Europe on a medical-science trip when Will went out and bought some sugar, which he added to the corn flake mix. These, the sanitarium patients *really* liked. When John Harvey returned, he was furious. So Will struck out on his own. Within months of leaving, he was churning out 2,900 cases a day of the cereal he called "Kellogg's Toasted Corn Flakes." The brothers ended up in court twice, fighting for the commercial rights to the family name. Will prevailed. On December 11, 1922, Will registered his company under a new name: Kellogg.

Thus, the sweetened breakfast was born, as was a core industry strategy that food processors would deploy forevermore. Whenever health concerns arose over one of their pillar ingredients—salt, sugar, or fat—the solution of choice for the food manufacturers was the simplest: Just swap out the problem component for another that wasn't, at the moment, as high on the list of concerns. In this case, the fat-laden breakfast plate of the nineteenth century, vilified for upsetting the national stomach, was largely replaced by the sugary cereal bowl of the twentieth century, and with it came a new set of health issues that would be slow to arouse widespread public concern.

Will Kellogg should not get *all* the credit, or blame, for sweetening cereal, however. One of the sanitarium's earliest guests was a marketing whiz named C. W. Post, who took the baths, ate the meals, and, inspired by what he experienced there, eventually went into business for himself. In 1892, he started a rival health spa on the east side of Battle Creek and began turning out a stream of health-conscious items: a coffee substitute called Postum; a cereal he called Grape-Nuts—"grape" for the maltose sugar he used, which he called "grape-sugar," and "nuts" for the flavor—and a sweetened corn flake cereal he called Post Toasties.

Post's cereals, however, weren't his most lasting contribution to the industry. Rather, it was his knack for marketing. In some of the first-ever advertising campaigns in America, Post sold his Postum by disparaging coffee as a "drug drink" that contained "poisonous" caffeine. He sold his first cereal with the slogan "Brains are built by Grape-Nuts." And he sold Toasties by putting an image of the prophet Elijah on the green-and-white box, an unapologetic attempt to tap into the spiritual movement sweeping America at the turn of the century. By 1897, Post was spending a million dollars a year on advertising and clearing a million dollars a year in profits.*

Will Kellogg took to marketing, too, and as he and Post began racking up their fortunes, Battle Creek turned into a cereal boom town. Entrepreneurs swarmed in from around the country to set up factories, some of which amounted to little more than an oven shoved into a tent. Soon, there were Grape Sugar Flakes, Malt-Too, and Malted Oats; Korn-Kinks, None-Such, and Luck Boy Corn Flakes. By 1911, Battle Creek was home to 108 brands of cereal, but Kellogg and Post would emerge as the dominant players. They were eventually joined by a third manufacturer, General Mills, which began making cereal at the colossal flour mills it had on the great falls of the Mississippi River in Minneapolis.

The Big Three, as they came to be known, further solidified their hold on the cereal market in the late 1940s when Post, now owned by General Foods, became the first brand to make its cereal even sweeter by adding a candy coating. In 1949, they introduced a wheat-based product called Sugar Crisp, which caused an immediate sensation. Kellogg and General Mills, of course, then answered with their own concoctions: Sugar Corn Pops, Sugar Frosted Flakes, Sugar Smacks, Sugar Smiles, and Sugar Jets. The companies had in-house dieticians who raised concerns about the health implications of all this added sugar, but as the authors Scott Bruce

---

* In 1911, in an article entitled "The Great American Frauds," *Collier's* magazine accused Post of using fictional doctors for endorsements and implying that Grape-Nuts could cure appendicitis. Post, in response, spent $150,000 on ads accusing the editors of *Collier's* of being jealous because Post wasn't advertising with them. With testimony from the magazine's ad manager, Conde Nast, *Collier's* sued Post for libel and won.

and Bill Crawford recount in their cereal industry chronicle, *Cerealizing America*, this voice of caution was quickly silenced. Jim Fish, a General Mills vice president for advertising at the time, told them, "It was overcome by marketing people who said, 'We've got to be able to move into this area to survive!' "

By 1970, the Big Three controlled 85 percent of the cereal market. This put them in an enviable position as the decade got under way and the world's appetite changed: The public's enthusiasm for cereal was growing by leaps and bounds, thanks to a dramatic rip in America's social fabric. Within a decade, 51 percent of women would be working outside the home, and when food manufacturers drilled into this data more deeply, they found even more promising news: The figure rose to 66 percent for women from twenty-five to forty-four. These women—many of whom had young children—had more money than time. Dinner was a struggle, of course, but breakfast was also a source of stress, a mad dash in which mothers tried to get everyone fed before the whole family flung itself out the front door. Convenience was key to starting the day. For the Big Three, this meant an opportunity to control the breakfast table like never before, but their power—in matters of sugar as well as money—had to be finessed.

With cereal sales surging—from $660 million in 1970 to $4.4 billion by the mid-1980s—the first trouble the Big Three faced came from the fair trade watchdogs in Washington. Kellogg, Post, and General Mills had crammed the grocery shelves with so many of their own brands that there was no room for any significant competition. In fact, they so completely controlled the cereal aisle that the Federal Trade Commission brought a complaint against the Big Three in 1976, accusing them of creating a shared monopoly in order to jack up cereal prices. Without even having a written agreement, the commission said, they were charging twenty to thirty cents more for each box of cereal than they would have been able to command had other companies been given space on the shelf to compete.

This had netted the companies $1.2 billion in consumer overcharges since 1958, and they stood to gain another $128 million each year unless the cartel was broken up. The case would not improve the FTC's reputation as a bumbling champion of the consumer. Denying the accusation, the cereal companies mounted a vigorous defense and the antitrust action lumbered along for years, with the cereal companies outmaneuvering the FTC's attorneys at every turn, until the commission voted in 1982 to drop its case.

On the more critical matter of what the cereal makers put *into* their boxes, there seemed to be no one in Washington willing to stand up to the Big Three. Indeed, Kellogg and its fellow manufacturers had a stalwart ally in the federal government—and, in particular, the Food and Drug Administration. The FDA was charged with overseeing the manufacture of cereal, along with all other processed foods except meat and poultry, which were controlled by the Department of Agriculture. It steadfastly refused, however, to see sugar as a threat to the public's health. Moreover, it repeatedly declined to require food manufacturers to disclose, on their packaging, exactly how much sugar they were adding to their products. With cereals like Kaboom and Count Chocula, two General Mills brands, and Kellogg's Sugar Frosted Flakes, the biggest seller of them all, parents could generally guess why their kids were lunging for the boxes at the breakfast table. But without specifics, sugar remained only a vague concern.

This all changed in 1975, when sugar—the keystone of the cereal makers' fortunes—suddenly became a matter of vivid distress to consumers. Where Washington had failed to act, two men working on behalf of the public took the Big Three on themselves. One was an enterprising dentist, Ira Shannon, with the Veterans Administration Hospital in Houston, who, alarmed by the exploding rates of tooth decay he'd seen in his young patients, decided that he'd had enough. (By one estimate, there were at any given moment one billion unfilled cavities in American mouths.) So the dentist took a trip to his local supermarkets, brought seventy-eight brands of cereal back to his lab, and proceeded to measure the sugar content of each with damning precision. A third of the brands had sugar levels between 10 percent and 25 percent. Another third ranged up to an alarming 50 percent, and eleven climbed even higher still—with one cereal, Super Orange Crisps, packing a sugar load of 70.8 *percent*. When each cereal brand was cross-referenced with TV advertising records, the sweetest brands were found to be the ones most heavily marketed to kids during Saturday morning cartoons.

With the dentist's report in hand, a second critic—who posed a much bigger threat to the cereal industry—took up the cause. His name was Jean Mayer, a Harvard professor of nutrition who later became the president and chancellor of Tufts University, and he was hugely influential in matters of diet, starting with poverty and hunger. As an advisor to President Richard M. Nixon in 1969, he'd organized the White House Conference on Food, Nutrition, and Health, which led to the introduction of food stamps and expanded school lunch programs for needy children. That endeared him to the food industry, since those programs expanded its market for sales.

But what made Mayer an industry threat was his pioneering research on obesity, which he called a "disease of civilization." He is credited with discovering how the desire to eat is controlled by the amount of glucose in the blood and by the brain's hypothalamus, both of which in turn are greatly influenced by sugar. He became an early critic of sugar, which he saw as one of the most dangerous additives in food, citing its link to diabetes, and he hotly disputed the industry's claim that sugar played a valuable role in food by delivering inexpensive calories. In 1975, taking his growing concern about sugar to the cereal industry, he penned a piece of advocacy journalism that newspapers around the country ran under the headline, "Is It Cereal or Candy?" In it, Mayer made his view perfectly clear. Citing the dentist's report and the FDA's abdication of its responsibility to protect the health of consumers, Mayer conceded one point to the industry. Many of their brands *were*, in fact, fortified with added vitamins and minerals. But the fortification was merely a ruse. Some candy bars had more protein than many cereals. Mayer dubbed them "sugar-coated vitamin pills" and wrote, "I contend that these cereals containing over 50% sugar should be labeled imitation cereal or cereal confections, and they should be sold in the candy section rather than in the cereal section."

With Mayer continuing his crusade and parents looking at cereal with growing qualms, the Big Three, remarkably, didn't push back. Sugar took center stage at the 1977 conference of newspaper food writers and editors, where several food manufacturers scrambled to address the public's concerns. The chairman of Gerber, for one, said that his company, under pressure from nutrition activists, had recently dropped two highly sweetened items from its lineup of baby foods, Blueberry Buckle and Raspberry Cobbler. "We never said they were particularly nutritious," he said. "We just said they tasted good." Kellogg, in turn, was asked how its sugary cereals could even be called cereal—as in, food made from grain. The answer was provided by Kellogg's vice president for public affairs, Gary Costley, who would go on to run the company's North America division. "The candid answer is—to meet a lifestyle," Costley replied. "Maybe we should quit calling them breakfast cereals and call them breakfast foods. These are mini–meal replacements. We don't care whether it's grain or not."

But Kellogg was hardly throwing in the towel on sugar. Rather, Costley's comments were revealing of another, more strategic shift that would define the company's positioning for decades to come—decades that would be marked not by Kellogg's supremacy but by its efforts to beat back a relentless assault on its dominance of the cereal market. Faced with growing consumer concern about sugar and with competition from manufacturers other than Post and General Mills, Kellogg would seek to bolster its sales by downplaying sugar. Some of these efforts were not so subtle. It de-sweetened the name of its leading brand, Sugar Frosted Flakes, by changing it to, simply, Frosted Flakes. The other manufacturers quietly dropped the word *sugar* from their brand names, too.

The deemphasizing of sugar would go deeper than the name on the box, however. The cereal industry would come to realize that the public's anxiety about sugar required a reboot of its marketing schemes. Companies couldn't keep touting the sweetness of their cereals without hurting their revenue. Their advertising, so crucial to the success of their sales, needed more powerful, more hopeful themes.

At Kellogg, the strategy developed to draw the consumer's attention to something other than sugar would evoke some of the creativity that its rival, C. W. Post, had used in his advertising copy a century earlier. The shift would also transform the essence of the company, empowering a breed of executive whose faith and expertise lay not in the product being sold but in the selling itself. And at Kellogg, the changes would come in the nick of time, just as the federal watchdogs, who had let sugar slide for so long, geared up for their own assault.

The battle in Washington over sugar began, oddly enough, with a pile of rotten teeth. In 1977, twelve thousand health professionals had signed petitions asking the Federal Trade Commission to ban the advertising of sugary foods on children's television shows, and the consumer groups who had joined them decided to add a little theater of their own. They collected two hundred decayed teeth from pediatric dentists, bagged them, and sent them to the FTC along with the petitions for the advertising restrictions.

The FTC's response caught the industry by surprise.

For much of its sixty-three-year history, it had been considered a dumping ground for political patronage, with a staff so inert and poorly qualified that it could manage only the most trivial of projects. But a housecleaning by the Nixon administration had attracted a cadre of young, idealistic attorneys, and they were finally starting to pick some serious fights with various industries over price gouging and deceptive advertising. In early 1977, President Jimmy Carter gave the FTC a new activist chairman, Michael Pertschuk, who had proven himself a staunch consumer advocate in his previous role as chief counsel for the Senate Commerce Committee. Pertschuk saw the children's advertising issue as more than a worthy crusade; he saw it as an opportunity to galvanize the FTC. Here, at last, was an issue that could connect with the public emotionally and become "the principal vehicle to demonstrate that we are serious."

"As with cigarette advertising, we are not dealing with a single commercial or set of commercials that are allegedly deceptive or misleading, but rather with children's advertising as a whole," Pertschuk said. "The effect of which has been to shape the environment of the child in a manner which may well be unintended but which nevertheless raises certain clear and disturbing danger signals."

Consumer advocates were asking only that the commission go after the marketing of sugary foods to children. The commission staff, however, laid out a set of recommendations that included a total ban on *all* advertising to children—for any product, food or otherwise. The Carter administration was not known for its political acumen, and indeed, this broad, far-reaching attack on advertising had a $600 million problem: Next to the salt, sugar, and fat in their formulas, advertising was far and away the most powerful tool the industry had to create allure. At times, it was the only thing that companies could use to distinguish themselves from their competitors.

Advertising's power is particularly evident in the cereal aisle today, where high profit margins have led to severe overcrowding. In any given cereal aisle, two hundred cereal brands—and their spinoffs—compete for the shopper's attention, so food manufacturers now spend nearly twice as much money on advertising their cereals as they do on the ingredients that go into them. But cereal makers were already large advertisers in the 1970s; taken altogether, advertising aimed at children for all types of goods generated $600 million in yearly revenue for media companies.

One man, arguably the most famous consumer activist of all, warned the FTC that any assault on this mountain of riches would be folly. This man, Ralph Nader, already legendary for his work in exposing the poor safety record of the Chevrolet Corvair, told FTC Chairman Pertschuk that the public's concern about children's advertising was simply not strong enough to win the fight to the death that industry would wage to preserve this kind of revenue. "If you take on the advertisers," Nader told Pertschuk, "you will end up with so many regulators—with their bones bleached—in the desert."

Pertschuk and the FTC, however, pressed ahead and ran smack into the industry's most formidable team of lobbyists. Tommy Boggs, of the Washington powerhouse firm Patton Boggs, assembled a group of thirty-two advertisers, food companies, and television networks to fight the commission's proposals. In their battle with the FTC, they would be able to draw from a reported war chest of $16 million, which was one-quarter the size of the commission's annual budget. Boggs's group got Pertschuk disqualified from overseeing the commission's hearings, claiming he had prejudged the matter, and actively worked to win the all-important media over to its side.

Until then, the editorial board of *The Washington Post* had supported the commission's work in general, portraying it as necessary to balance the power of private industry. But in this matter of children's advertising, the paper turned fiercely against the FTC with an editorial whose headline labeled it "The National Nanny." Getting children to eat less sugar may be a laudable goal, the *Post* said, practically regurgitating the industry line that regulatory intervention was uncalled for, "but what are the children to be protected from? The candy and sugar-coated cereals that lead to tooth decay? Or the inability or refusal of their parents to say no? The food products will still be there, sitting on the shelves of the local supermarkets after all, no matter what happens to the commercials. So the proposal, in reality, is designed to protect children from the weaknesses of their parents—and the parents from the wailing insistence of their children. That, traditionally, is one of the roles of a governess—if you can afford one. It is not a proper role of government."*

---

* Thirty-five years later, the "nanny" label would get resurrected by a soda-industry group that sought to defeat a proposal brought in 2012 by the New York City mayor, Michael Bloomberg, to bar the sale of mega-sized sodas in certain venues. The group's full-page ad depicted him in a long dress and scarf under the headline, "The Nanny. You only *thought* you lived in the land of the free." This time around, it was the editorial board of *The New York Times*—where the soda group's ad ran—that mirrored the food industry's position. "Promoting healthy lifestyles is important," the paper's editorial said. "In the case of sugary drinks, a regular reminder that a 64-ounce cola has 780 calories should help. But too much nannying with a ban might well cause

Not only did the proposed curbs on advertising to children founder, the FTC itself nearly capsized as, one by one, it lost key friends on Capitol Hill, who objected to the curbs as intrusive. On May 1, 1980, the commission's officers were actually shuttered for a day when its funding ran out—the first such closure in the agency's history. At that point, Bruce Silverglade, one of the commission's young activist attorneys, quit and joined the consumer group that had brought the petition, the Center for Science in the Public Interest. He now works for a lobbying firm that represents food companies, and he believes that the FTC's one-day closure in 1980 foreshadowed the shutdown of the entire federal government years later, when President Bill Clinton fought with House Speaker Newt Gingrich, and was a terrible omen for consumer advocacy. "It became a pivotal moment inside the Beltway," Silverglade told me. "That's when the whole concept of 'overregulation' started."

Pertschuk was ousted as chairman, and though he remained a commissioner for several years, his agenda was abandoned by the new, less-aggressive FTC leadership. "They have suppressed its energy, neglected its tasks, wasted its resources, while wallowing in intellectual self-indulgence," he said when his term ended in 1984. "While they have fiddled, consumers have been burned."

The incoming chairman, James Miller, a longtime critic of government regulation, brushed Pertschuk's criticisms off, saying that he had had his chance to effect change. "I don't make any bones about it," Miller said at the time. "There's been a change of emphasis and philosophy at the Federal Trade Commission. We're not going to engage in social engineering."

Pertschuk's efforts had not gone completely for naught, however. In waging its fight, Pertschuk's staff had prepared an investigative report that did a great deal to expose the dominant role that sugar played in the industry's advertising and the influence this had on America's children.

---

people to tune out." What the editorial failed to address, however, was the changed world since *The Washington Post* used the nanny line that made overconsumption a problem for everyone. With the soda industry spending $700 million a year on advertising to push soda drinking higher, New York City and the country at large were having to shell out more than $90 billion a year on medical treatment related to the devastating health effects of obesity.

The report ran 340 pages long, and it threw down the gauntlet in its first paragraph: Small children were so gullible, it said, that they couldn't help but view commercials as informational programming. Not only that, they were unable to comprehend "the influence which television advertising exerts over them"—especially when it came to sugar. The typical American child in 1979 would watch more than twenty thousand commercials between the ages of two and eleven—and more than half of those ads were pitching sweetened cereals, candies, snacks, and soft drinks. "Sugar was promoted as many as four times per half hour on each network," the report said, "and as many as seven times per half hour if fast-food advertising is taken into account." The report made another point, equally alarming to nutritionists. Food companies were not simply trying to get us to eat more sugary fare; they were diverting attention from other, healthier foods that had the potential to reduce children's consumption of sweets.

In urging the voting members of the commission to act, the FTC staff added, "The largest single part of the television advertising addressed specifically to children is for sugared foods, consumption of which poses a threat to the children's dental health, and possibly to other aspects of their health as well," the report said.

The commission staff didn't throw these accusations around lightly. To compile their report, they went out and gathered hard data, conducting a nine-month survey of weekend daytime TV to show how stacked the decks were in favor of sugary fare. There were 3,832 ads for mostly sugary cereals, 1,627 for candy and gum, 841 for cookies and crackers, 582 for fruit drinks, and 184 for cakes, pies, and other desserts. The total number of ads for unsweetened foods, like meat, or fish, or vegetable juice, on the other hand? Four.

The FTC report didn't stop there. The report named names and quoted from the industry's own documents, including a Kellogg memo that summed up the bottom line on children's advertising quite succinctly: "Television advertising of ready-to-eat cereals to children," the memo said, "increases children's consumption of these products." The commission also went after the broadcasters, citing an exuberant house ad in *Broadcast* magazine that offered some blunt advice to advertisers. "If you're selling, Charlie's Mom is buying," it said. "But you've got to sell Charlie first. His allowance is only fifty cents a week, but his buying power is an American phenomenon. When Charlie sees something he likes, he usually gets it. Just ask General Mills or McDonald's. Of course, if you want to sell Charlie, you have to catch him when he's sitting down. Or at least standing still. And that's not easy. Lucky for you, Charlie's into TV.

"And, of course, Charlie won't be watching alone!" the magazine added. "You'll also be reaching Jeff and Timmy, Chris and Susie, Mark and his little brother John.

"That's what we mean by Kid Power."

The outraged staff continued: "The examples we have collected include a commercial in which children are taught that breakfast is 'no fun' without a particularly heavily sugared brand of cereal, and another in which the message is that a certain brand of heavily sugared fruit-flavored cookies is actually preferable to fresh fruit—as is shown by a fruit peddler's abandoning of his entire stock of fruit after being introduced to the cookies. We have also collected a great number of commercials in which the message is that eating sugar is desirable and fun, that this is the normal, accepted way to satisfy hunger, either at breakfast or between meals, and that boys and girls who do this are healthy and happy."

Dubbed "kidvid" by the media, the FTC's proposal to curb TV advertising aimed at kids caught fire with reporters, who broadcasted the findings. Even when the FTC's crusade ended in 1980, the sugar in processed foods continued to garner public attention. In 1985, the group that had started the proceeding, the Center for Science in the Public Interest, released a handy wall chart for consumers that served as a guide to the sugar levels in the most popular brands of food. In writing about the chart, Jane Brody, the influential *Times* health specialist, expressed what every American who saw the chart likely thought: "The amount of sugar commonly consumed at one time is astonishing."

The persistent attacks on sugar had an effect. That same year, Post changed the name of its Super Sugar Crisp Cereal to Super Golden Crisp, though its sugar levels remained at more than 50 percent. A spokeswoman said at the time that the change was made in "recognition that there's a sensitivity to the word sugar."

"It's a marketing tool to give a modern image to an old product," she added.

This followed Kellogg's earlier move to drop the word *sugar* from two of its own 50-percent-plus mega-sellers: Sugar Frosted Flakes became Frosted Flakes, and Sugar Smacks turned into Honey Smacks. But if touting the sugar in cereal was no longer a smart marketing move, Kellogg would soon find itself under intense pressure to find another way to sell cereal that was better than smart.

The 1990s opened with nothing but trouble for Kellogg. For starters, the cereal aisle, once the exclusive domain of the Big Three, was invaded by retailing giants like Safeway and Kroger. They began selling their own generic knockoffs of the name brands. They also avoided the Big Three's costly advertising, which brought their prices down by a third and sent their annual sales surging to nearly $500 million by 1994, or nearly 10 percent of the cereal market.

Even more disconcerting to Kellogg: An old rival, General Mills, was gaining ground in the cereal aisle by wielding a brash new pricing strategy. For years, Post, Kellogg, and General Mills had all maintained a steady gain in profits simply by raising their prices in unofficial lockstep. Then, in the spring of 1994, General Mills broke from the group and dropped its prices. At the same time, it stepped up its marketing efforts so that it could make up for the lower prices by selling more cereal. Stephen Sanger, the president of the General Mills cereals division, had a watchword for attracting consumers to his brand: flux. The company's products had to stay in constant motion. Every time shoppers hit the cereal aisle, they should find something different about their favorite cereals, something that would compel them to buy as much as, if not more than, they did on their last trip through the store. He called this "product news," and he excelled at it. Product news could be a cereal that had more crunch, from more sugar in the formula. Or it could be a prize, known within the industry as an "incentive," like the three-part collectable poster of Michael Jordan folded into boxes of Wheaties. Product news was anything that said to the consumer: This cereal is new and exciting. Executives from consumer research, product development, sales, and legal all pulled together to give the cereal continuous buzz, said Jeremy Fingerman, who held the position of marketing manager for children's cereal at General Mills from 1990 to 1992. "Sanger pushed for product news," Fingerman told me. "In this business, you have to stay fresh and nimble all the time."

Sugar drove much of the product development at General Mills. Even Cheerios—its more wholesome brand, at just 3.5 percent sugar by weight, got a sweeter version in 1988: Apple Cinnamon Cheerios, which clocked in at 43 percent sugar. General Mills also chased hard after America's growing appetite for snacks that could be eaten on the run—pizza, bagels, soda, and toaster pastries were the fastest-growing foods in the American diet, along with presweetened cereals. One key to their success was the product design and packaging that made them easy to wolf down on the go. General Mills jumped out early on this front in 1992 with a superconvenience food called Fingos, a cereal shaped to be eaten by the handful, rather than poured into a bowl. They even widened the mouth of the box to better accommodate a plunging hand.

Outmaneuvered, Kellogg's share of the cereal market slipped a full 1 percent in 1990 to 37.5 percent, down significantly from its peak, in the 1970s, of 45 percent. The erosion seemed especially ominous given how fierce the competition had become with General Mills. "Getting a 0.5 percent share in this market is a real battle," the Kellogg CEO, William LaMothe, said at the time. Kellogg had its own "product news" operation under way, but as LaMothe conceded in a 1991 interview, its development arm was running blind, introducing strings of cereal products—as many as four a year—but without doing the necessary market testing or, even worse, ignoring the results when testing showed low consumer enthusiasm. "You can get swept up in this," LaMothe said, "and so you launch, and the product doesn't do well and you've spent the money and don't get the return."

On the verge of panic, Kellogg went back to the drawing board, and this time, a total reset on its marketing strategy would be required. Nothing would be held sacred. Not the company's famously strict—and, at times, bizarre—corporate etiquette, which rewarded rank over achievement and put a damper on creativity. (These rules, at one time, extended to the company parking lot, where only the president was allowed to drive up in a Cadillac. Vice presidents were allowed to drive Oldsmobiles, managers could have Buicks, and everyone else settled for Chevrolets.) Not the dress code, which was strictly suits and ties. Not even the rules on where its employees could socialize after work, which was something of a problem in tiny Battle Creek; they could hit the Tac Room at the Hart Hotel but not the Wee Nippy a few blocks away, where the competition gathered. Most pointedly, Kellogg, in rethinking how to make better products, lifted its longstanding rule that outsiders be kept from seeing the company's most sensitive operation—its research and development laboratories—for fear of corporate espionage. This shroud of secrecy had even applied to executives from the company's ad agency, Leo Burnett, who had always been banned from the company's labs, where the food inventions they were selling were born.

With Kellogg's share of the cereal market in a free fall, all of these rules fell by the wayside. Rather than rely on food technicians, who traditionally held the reins when it came to inventing more cereals, Kellogg now put its marketing department in charge. The marketing folks, in turn, set up a special team whose members were exempt from the company norms. They left their suits in the closet and wore jeans instead. They went out on the town to brainstorm over booze and barbecue. They set up in the most sensitive corner of Kellogg's operation, a building where the cereal puffers and other top-secret machinery were developed. The room they inhabited resembled a war room and was kept under lock and key. Boxes of cereal from all of the competing brands were brought in and stacked against the walls, forming what looked like a giant map detailing the enemy's positions. They pored over these cereals like generals, but of course, the other food companies were not the target.

The target was the civilians who were buying the rival cereals.

In the most telling break from tradition, the Kellogg war room was opened to the same people who had been barred from the company's sensitive operations: the advertising executives from Leo Burnett. With the company under pressure to come up with better-selling products, these ad men were not only put on the team, they were also given the most prominent seats at the table, relegating some of Kellogg's own executives to the margins of the room. "You know how at meetings the junior people will be sitting away from the table, against the wall?" recalled Edward Martin, a marketing analyst at Kellogg who was assigned to the team. "Well, we'd have the Leo Burnett guy right at the table, with the assistant brand managers sitting against the wall. It set a tenor. The top guy at Leo obviously had access to the CEO of our company, and that filtered all the way down to our working team."

This team would turn the traditional Kellogg way of creating products on its head. Instead of having the food technicians toil away in their labs experimenting with tastes and textures, the marketing folks hunted for ideas that suited the advertising needs at Kellogg first and worried about pleasing the palates of consumers second. The driver for this reversal was the recognition that branding was overwhelmingly important, explained Martin. The Kellogg icons—whether Rice Krispies or Frosted Flakes or Special K—all had distinct identities, carefully honed by hundreds of millions of dollars of advertising. Increasingly, image was all that stood between these icons and the less expensive private label knockoffs. Each brand had its own image to convey. Corn Flakes suggested tradition. Frosted Flakes, fun. Special K, nutrition and strength.

Kellogg had labored to burn these brands into the minds of American consumers over the years, and with this as their guide, the team would reject whole slews of great-tasting candidates that did not fit the image they needed to convey for each of the brands. "They'd come in with seven or eight different varieties, in little bowls, and we'd chow down and say, 'Well, these taste good but they don't really live up to the brand concept,'" Martin said. The war room at Kellogg began generating its own wild ideas for cereals that seemed to have blockbuster potential, but no one knew if they could actually be made. A case in point was the team's takeoff on its legendary sweet snack Rice Krispies treats.

The concept drew on the psychology of perceptions. If a cereal could evoke the joy of an afternoon snack, it could generate sales not only as a breakfast food but also as a snack, in and of itself. Kellogg had made Rice Krispies since 1927 and had been promoting the homemade dessert— a combination of cereal, butter, and marshmallow—on the side of its box for nearly as long. What the team saw when they looked at these two parts—the cereal and the dessert—was a dessert-like cereal called Rice Krispies Treat Cereal that would have a huge, built-in, and powerful driver: Its homey image would evoke happy childhood memories for the moms and dads who would buy cereal for their kids. But when the team dispatched the technicians to turn this vision into reality, they came back weeks later and said they could not make it work. In trying to mimic the dessert, they had ended up with gooey clumps that turned to mush as soon as they were combined with milk. "Mush in the bowl was death," said Martin. "Kids, especially, like crunch."

Even when they upped the sugar content to get more crunch, they could not make it work. The technicians could not get both the crunch and the gooey marshmallow to coexist once milk was added. That's when the marketing folks applied some of their magic. They set up focus groups to ask consumers about the idea of Rice Krispies Treat Cereal, and the consumers said the cereal didn't actually have to be gooey like the dessert. It just had to have the *flavor* of gooey. In food marketing lingo, this is known as "permission." It's what people allow manufacturers to take away from their food in exchange for convenience or price. Yes, the consumers would have preferred a bowl of the real Rice Krispies treats they grew up on, but they were willing to settle for less. "The lightbulb moment finally came when consumers gave us that permission," Martin said. "We didn't have to be literal. We only needed the flavor to be spot on."

Launched in 1993, Rice Krispies Treat Cereal helped catalyze Kellogg's new marketing-driven development scheme. Strong sales that first year rocketed the cereal to eleventh place in the company's vast lineup, handily beating out Smacks, Cocoa Krispies, and most of the company's "better-for-you" brands like NutriGrain and All-Bran. The TV commercial that heralded the launch, crafted by Leo Burnett, captured the concept perfectly. It depicted a plate of Rice Krispies treats cut into squares and stacked in layers five high, spinning magically into a large bowl of the cereal. The bowl looked like it easily held four or five servings—a sugar load of eight teaspoons, as much as in a can of Coke. And as the kid in the ad dug in with gusto, the narrator exclaimed, "What a thought! The taste of Rice Krispies treats, in a big way!"

There was only so much the product development team could do for Kellogg, however. New products are exceedingly difficult to bring to market, and they fail far more often than they succeed. By 2005, Kellogg's share of the cereal market had slipped again, even further this time, falling below one-third as the private label grocery brands grew to nearly half its size. If Kellogg was to regain its supremacy, it needed to invent ways to reinvigorate its existing brands. For this, the company turned once again to the marketing side of the business, including the advertising specialists from Leo Burnett. Based in Chicago, the agency had always distinguished itself—and proudly—from the New York firms by being homey and a little corny. Its creations included the Jolly Green Giant, Charley the Tuna, and Tony the Tiger. The growing consensus among the advertising trade, however, was that homey no longer worked as well as edgy.

So Leo Burnett got edgy.

In 2004, it rolled out a new campaign for one of Kellogg's marquee cereals, Apple Jacks, which embraced this change. In the commercial, three girls sit around a table eating the cereal as two cartoon characters appear. One is a cinnamon stick named CinnaMon, who is agile and amiable, tall and thin, with a West Indian accent. The other is an apple named, astonishingly, Bad Apple. He is short, round, grouchy, and scheming. "When you pour a bowl of Apple Jacks cereal," the voice-over said, "sweet CinnaMon races to you. But there's a Bad Apple who's trying to get there first." And with that, the race is on. CinnaMon is jumpy with energy as he surfs subway cars, hops through open windows, and leaps park benches. Bad Apple, the dumpy grouch, gets his due at every turn. He trips, stumbles, is smashed into pieces. The voice-over delivers the punch line: "Once again the sweet taste of CinnaMon with new CinnaMon-shaped marshmallows . . . is the WinnaMon."

Why Kellogg felt compelled to go after the apple is not entirely clear. Forty years earlier, when Apple Jacks was invented, fruit in the cereal aisle was novel and exciting. One of the cereal's creators, William Thilly, was a sophomore at MIT interning at Kellogg for the summer, and he told me he had been inspired by the apple farm where he grew up. "I was used to cooking with apples and knew it would fit in with lots of foods," he said. The early advertising even stressed the nutritional power of apples, depicting a kid who was scrawny and bullied until he ate the cereal. The talking apple that appeared in these ads was big, strong, and friendly. Somewhere along the line, Kellogg appears to have started to worry that kids, in fact, didn't like the taste of apples all that much, though it's also not clear how much apple taste the cereal has. The largest ingredient in Apple Jacks is sugar, with three teaspoons per cup, or 43 percent of the cereal.

Kellogg responded to a complaint from the Better Business Bureau by agreeing to give the apple a softer demeanor, but insisted that children who saw the ads came away with the view that apple flavor was not an appealing taste in cereal, rather than apples themselves being bad. Consumer advocates, however, were aghast and worried about the potential damage to one of the central tenets of better childhood nutrition. The federal government had been redoubling its efforts to encourage children to eat fresh fruit, and here was Kellogg giving it an evil face. "Though Apple Jacks contains very little apples—less apple or apple juice concentrate than salt—it is inappropriate for Kellogg to disparage the taste of apples," the Center for Science in the Public Interest wrote to chief executive and chairman of the board of Kellogg, James Jenness. "Also, it is more likely that Apple Jacks tastes sweet because it has more sugar than any other ingredient, not because of the added cinnamon."

Jenness was no ordinary Kellogg CEO. Traditionally, and to a degree that exceeded most other food companies, Kellogg had been run by men who worked their way up through the ranks, selling cereal and even driving a truck like Jenness's predecessor, Carlos Gutierrez, had done. When Gutierrez stepped down in 2004 to become the Bush administration's commerce secretary, however, Kellogg felt pressed to break with tradition. Jenness had never worked at Kellogg but had spent much of his career in advertising, at Leo Burnett. He had what Kellogg felt it needed to compete. "With the game we're in and the quality of the competitors, it's dog eat dog," Jenness told a group of Rotarians after he'd been on the job for two years. "The moment you let up . . . you're gonna get nailed."

At its peak, Apple Jacks held no more than 1 percent of the cereal market, tenth place in Kellogg's own lineup. Yet, as the company pushed to regain its dominance, even the smallest brands had their marketing campaigns honed to maximize sales. For the largest brands, Kellogg would pull out all the stops the moment they showed even the slightest sign of weakness.

In 2006, Frosted Mini-Wheats—the largest brand in the Kellogg stable, next to Frosted Flakes—wasn't just starting to flag. It was in the midst of a full-blown identity crisis. The problem was bran, with its halo of health. Flour that is made from the entire grain, including the bran, had become the rage in the cereal aisle. Nutritionists were linking bran to lower cholesterol, less heart disease, better intestinal health, and a reduced risk of obesity, and federal officials warned that Americans were not eating enough of it. Kellogg's rivals at Post had just pulled off a striking feat:

Spending a mere $12 million, a pittance in cereal advertising, on an ad campaign that touted their whole grains, Post had reversed a seven-year slump in its Grape-Nuts and Shredded Wheat brands and sent their sales soaring by 9 percent. Kellogg had whole grains in its Frosted Minis, too, but with more than two teaspoons of sugar in a single cup, they were a harder sell to people who were looking to be healthy. In an analysis of the situation, Kellogg concluded that the Frosted Mini-Wheats brand had "lost its connection" and "needed an insight that ran deeper than basic nutrition and into the hearts of consumers." The company went on an offensive to reverse its fortunes.

Kellogg didn't cut back on sugar to emulate Grape-Nuts. Fundamentally, the allure of the Frosted Mini line was all about sweet. Even the names of its product extensions—Cinnamon Streusel, Little Bites Chocolate, Vanilla Crème—evoked dessert. The company couldn't suddenly undermine that foundation. This was the cereal's *branding.* It was still trying to appeal to kids, and kids still wanted dessert for breakfast. But it couldn't afford to lose the people it needed to make the sale: parents. To convince them, Kellogg devised an ad campaign that sold Frosted Minis as brain food.

The ads evolved, culminating in a commercial of early 2008 that centered on the premise that Frosted Mini-Wheats would help children get better grades. "Help your kids earn an A for attentiveness," the company said in a media release that touted the ad campaign.

The scene was a classroom. A teacher standing at the whiteboard loses her train of thought. "Okay," she asked the class. "Where were we?" Her young students looked weary, slumped at their desks. They used their arms only to prop up their heads. One boy shot his hand into the air, bright-eyed and eager, fingers waving. "We were on the third paragraph of page 57, and you were explaining that the stone structures made by ancient Romans were called aqueducts," he said. "And as you were writing that up on the board, your chalk broke. Into three pieces."

"Right," said the teacher, amazed.

Then a voice-over brought the message home: "A clinical study showed kids who had a filling breakfast of Frosted Mini-Wheats cereal improved their attentiveness by nearly 20 percent. Keeps 'em full. Keeps 'em focused."

The ad ran widely on TV, the Internet, and various modes of print, including the sides of milk cartons. One could almost imagine stressed-out parents doing the math on what, exactly, a 20 percent boost would mean for their own kids. *Let's see. Billy got a 70 on his last test. Add 20 percent, that's an 84. A solid B!* There was just one hitch: The claim wasn't true. The clinical study cited in the classroom campaign had, in fact, been commissioned and paid for by Kellogg. That should have made it suspect right off the bat, since, as every good scientist knows, the results of a study can be preordained by its design. But the truly remarkable aspect of the campaign is that the company study, even if taken at face value, did not come close to supporting the claim in its advertising. Half of the children who ate bowls of Frosted Minis showed no improvement at all on the tests they were given to measure their ability to remember, think, and reason, as compared with their ability before eating the cereal. Only one in seven kids got a boost of 18 percent or more.

These were the findings of the cereal industry's old nemesis, the Federal Trade Commission, which had been trying to claw its way back to relevancy after the blows it suffered following the children's advertising debacle of 1980. To its credit, the commission, quick to get wind of the suspect research behind the Frosted Mini ads, opened a legal proceeding. It called the ads false or misleading. Kellogg's campaign, to be sure, was not in the same league as the ads run by its old rival, C. W. Post, a century earlier, in which he was accused of insinuating that his cereal, Grape-Nuts, would cure appendicitis. But with Kellogg spending $1 billion a year on advertising that can deeply influence America's shopping habits, the commission was incensed.

"It's especially important that America's leading companies are more 'attentive' to the truthfulness of their ads and don't exaggerate the results of tests or research," the FTC chairman quipped in a statement. "In the future, the commission will certainly be more attentive to national advertisers."*

But behind the scenes, the case stretched on for so long that the resolution may have done little to diminish the ad's effectiveness in shaping consumer perceptions. The FTC declined to release detailed records of the case to me, citing its standard policy of not divulging information that might hinder the competitiveness of a company whose practices the commission scrutinizes. Kellogg declined to provide the scientific study on which the brainpower claims were based. (In 2011, Kellogg agreed to settle a separate class action lawsuit brought by consumers by paying up to $2.8 million in refunds on purchased Frosted Minis and donating $5 million worth of its products to charities.) "Kellogg has a long history of responsible marketing and takes any concerns about our advertisements seriously," the company said to me in an email. "When we received feedback from the FTC, we adjusted our communications to incorporate the guidance."

Through the Freedom of Information Act, however, I was able to obtain emails and other records showing that the FTC first contacted Kellogg about the commercial in March 2008—questioning the veracity of the ad and seeking proof from Kellogg that the near–20 percent attentiveness claim was true. But the agency then plodded for more than a year before issuing a decision that barred Kellogg from using the claim. The FTC told me its powers in such cases are limited.

By then, Kellogg had already stopped running the ad on its own accord, but it didn't do so until late September 2008—*six months* after the

---

* The chairman had more harsh criticism for Kellogg a year later, in 2010, when the company settled a second deceptive advertising case brought by the FTC. In this case, Kellogg agreed to stop claiming that its Rice Krispies, with their added vitamins and antioxidants, would bolster children's "immunity" from disease. In noting how closely this advertising had followed on the heels of the Frosted Mini-Wheats case, the chairman said, in announcing the settlement, "We expect more from a great American company than making dubious claims—not once, but twice—that its cereals improve children's health. Next time, Kellogg needs to stop and think twice about the claims it's making before rolling out a new ad campaign, so parents can make the best choices for their children." In an accompanying statement, the chairman wrote, "Kellogg must not shirk its responsibility to do the right thing when it advertises the food we feed our children."

FTC first contacted the company raising concerns. (Kellogg, in its defense, said that even that late date in September was "about a month before we had our first substantive discussion with the FTC of their concerns.") Six months is a long time in commercial campaigns, especially for one as effective as the classroom ad. Like other companies, Kellogg pays close attention to how well its ad dollars are spent, and in this case, the influence these dollars had on consumers was impressive indeed. A resounding 51 percent of the adults surveyed were not just certain that the claim about attentiveness was true; they believed it was true *only* for Frosted Mini-Wheats. That is, only by dropping that cereal into their shopping carts would their kids get ahead in class. Despite their high sugar content and a public growing more wary of sweetened cereals, Frosted Mini-Wheats in 2008 achieved a 3.5 percent share of the market, even as Frosted Flakes slipped a notch in popularity.

Within months of the FTC's order on Frosted Mini-Wheats, Kellogg was back with another brainpower campaign, though this one had a new twist. Rather than compare its cereal with those of its rivals, this new ad stacked the Frosted Mini-Wheats against having *no breakfast at all*— a claim that would presumably survive the FTC's scrutiny, if not the moral compass of consumerists: "A clinical study showed kids who ate Frosted Minis had 23 percent better memory than kids who missed out on breakfast."* The campaign's main focus was still on the fears of women with school-age children, and it seemed to play on these fears. The new campaign featured a Kellogg-funded website called "Mom's Homeroom" where mothers could discuss how best to help their kids succeed in school. "My son still struggles so much with his reading," one mother wrote in. "I don't know what else to do. Please HELP!"

Mom's Homeroom won an industry advertising award in 2010, and in accepting the award Kellogg explained the reasoning behind this line of attack: "After years of Frosted Mini-Wheats 'Full and Focused' campaign

---

* If Kellogg compared its cereal with a breakfast recommended by nutritionists, like oatmeal and whole-grain toast, it wasn't saying in this Frost-Minis-or-nothing claim.

positioned around success in school for kids, moms still weren't buying it. The times had changed and we needed a different strategy. So we stopped talking at her and joined in on the dialogue she was already having. Pulling together all of her trusted resources, creating a one-stop shop online for all of Mom's school-related needs, Frosted Mini-Wheats proved that we were not only talking the talk, we were Mom's true partner in helping her kids succeed in school."

chapter five

"I Want to See a Lot of Body Bags"

Jeffrey Dunn's first job at Coca-Cola confirmed everything he'd heard about the company growing up. His father had worked there since Jeffrey was five, first as a sales director and then as a pioneer of Coke's renowned marketing, which had singlehandedly put the soda into the biggest sports-entertainment venues around the world. Every evening, his father would regale him with some fresh and rousing story about his valiant efforts to block his archnemesis, PepsiCo, and prevent them from getting a single account. One day, he would be keeping McDonald's from falling into his rival's hands; the next, he would be fighting for his monopoly at Yankee Stadium. "We were always keeping track of how my father was doing relative to fighting off the 'no-good bastards' of Pepsi and maintaining the integrity of the Coke brand," Dunn said.

Now it was Jeffrey's turn. In 1984, at age twenty-seven, he joined the division that was Coca-Cola's equivalent of the Marines: fountain sales. His job was to go out on the road and get Coke into the carbonated drink dispensing machines at fast food chains and convenience stores, from Hardee's to 7-Eleven, and Dunn, a brawny former athlete who hated to lose more than he loved to win, was an ideal recruit. In fountain, there could be no complacency. These were the front lines of Coca-Cola's campaign to dominate the soda business and reshape America's eating habits. Fountain was all about taking beachheads and holding ground, and Coke ruled over Pepsi in these outlets two to one. This was where the supersize phenomenon was born, dreamed up by the marketing corps as a way to sell yet more Coke with hamburgers and fries. The skirmishes with Pepsi were endless and intense. Around the offices, they had a name for losing one of these fights—they called it "being positioned." And with Jeffrey Dunn, the company could count on one thing: He was not about to be positioned.

"There was no status quo, because everyone in the marketplace is constantly positioning," he told me. "You were either going forward or you were going backwards. They called it positioning because of where you stood in relation to the rest of the universe. The other companies were constantly pushing on you, trying to capture customers. And you gotta push back, because if you're not defining and delivering on your position, then you are by definition *being* positioned. So you really learn this in the soft drink business. It's hyper-competitive, and you're constantly working on not just, What do I want my brand to stand for? but also, How do I want to position it versus every other brand in the market?"

Kellogg and General Mills and other food manufacturers might think they are pretty good at this positioning stuff, but their efforts pale in comparison to those of Coca-Cola, which isn't so much a company as a $35 billion institutional force. Coke didn't just set up a war room, like Kellogg did with its special team dedicated to identifying and targeting the fears and desires of consumers. At Coca-Cola, the whole organization was a war room. The desks and tables in Coke's headquarters complex in Atlanta were papered with charts that mapped out the company's strategy, and every employee was expected to devote long hours to the cause. Coke prided itself on being progressive, but at one company meeting in the 1990s, a female executive asked whether Coke might consider creating a day-care facility to ease the scramble at 6 P.M., when children needed picking up long before the day at Coke was done. The company president, Douglas Ivester, who had no kids and often worked seven days a week, stared at her for a moment and then said, "There will never be a day care on this campus."

The man who instilled this ethos, Robert Woodruff, was a classic corporate warrior. He was working for an automobile maker, the White Motor Company, in 1923 when his father asked him to move to Atlanta. He needed help running his newly acquired company, Coke, which was foundering. The elder Woodruff, Ernest, had led a group of bankers in buying Coca-Cola for $25 million four years earlier when Coke's profits had gone flat, but the company's prospects had only grown worse. Sales were falling, despite Coke's attempts to boost consumption through the introduction of a cardboard carton that could hold six bottles. Coke was also distracted by fights with its bottlers—the franchises, numbering 1,200 at the time, who had the plants where the Coke concentrate was combined with sugar, water, and carbonization.

Robert Woodruff—who would oversee Coca-Cola for six decades—is widely credited, among many other things, with two brilliant innovations. In 1927, he created a division called the Foreign Department, which introduced Coke to the rest of the world. Then, at the onset of World War II, he publicly declared that every soldier in uniform would get Coke for five cents a bottle, no matter where they were stationed or what it cost the company to put those bottles into their hands. As a result, a generation of men and women came home hooked on Coke.

Woodruff, however, had another insight—this one not as frequently discussed in the business school case studies—that would help take the company from solid to spectacular. He figured out how to tap into people's emotions better than anyone else in the industry of consumer goods, whether food or beer or cigarettes. His method didn't require slogans or celebrity endorsements or the kind of money the company would spend every year on advertising, though all those things helped. It went deeper than that. It focused on getting Coke into the hands of people, especially kids, when they were most vulnerable to persuasion—those moments when they were happy. That is how Coke came to be partners with America's favorite pastime. "The story they always tell at Coke," Dunn said, "is Mr. Woodruff saying, 'When I was a kid, my father took me to my first baseball game, and there was nothing more sacred to me than that moment with my father. And what did I have to drink? I had an ice-cold Coke, which became part of that sacred moment.'

"The idea was to be in all those places where these special moments of your life took place," Dunn continued. "Coke wanted to be part of those moments. That was, if not the most brilliant marketing strategy of all time, probably one of the best two or three. You not only had the imagery, it's like somebody was in their own television commercial. You're in the moment, you're drinking the product, you have that emotional context that sets it. And Coke really came to have a very high share of those experiences. It was about having a ubiquitous presence. Inside Coke, it is called the 'ubiquity strategy.' In simple terms, Mr. Woodruff's words for that were: 'Put the product within an arm's reach of desire.' " This helped turn the soda into much more than a product. To the envy of every food company on earth, Coke became the most powerful *brand* in the world—a brand that was deeply rooted in people's psyches, able to generate staggering heights of consumer loyalty.

As Coke's sales doubled and tripled and kept going up—along with those of Pepsi and other soft drinks—so too did America's inclination to overindulge. In nutrition circles, where the causes of obesity are discussed, there is no single product—among the sixty thousand items sold in the grocery store—that is considered more evil, more directly responsible for the crisis than soda. The problem, as growing numbers of nutritionists see it, is not the calories in soda, though calories are ultimately what causes us to gain weight. Rather, it's their form: Research suggests that our bodies are less aware of excessive intake when the calories are liquid. Health advocates don't blame the single can of Coke with its roughly nine teaspoons of sugar. What made Coke evil—or, depending on who you are talking to, wildly successful—was the supersizing. As the obesity crisis was building in the 1980s, those cans gave way to 20-ounce bottles, with 15 teaspoons of sugar; liter bottles, with 26 teaspoons; and the 64-ounce Double Gulp sold by the 7-Eleven stores, with 44 teaspoons of sugar. Beyond the size of each serving, Coke's success came from the numbers of these cans and bottles and cups that people, especially kids, were drinking every day. By 1995, two in three kids were drinking a 20-ounce bottle daily, but this was merely the national average. At Coca-Cola, executives didn't speak of "customers" or even "consumers." They talked about "heavy users," people with a habit of two or more cans per day. As Dunn's career stretched into its second decade, the numbers of these heavy users was only going up.

In pursuing this massive consumption, Dunn rose nearly to the top of the company. He became president for North and South America, a job that entailed winning the brand loyalty of nine hundred million people. He lived Coke and loved his work and the company, a devotion shared by many at Coke, and for all those years he had no qualms about what he sold. He achieved this peace of mind, he said, by simply not thinking about what he sold. Rather, he thought only about the selling, and the selling was great, until it wasn't anymore. This moment came one day in 2001 when his lieutenants took him to a part of the world that excited them like no other: Brazil. The economy there was booming, and the population there had the potential to match the soda consumption levels in the United States; Coke only had to show them the way. As Dunn toured some of the targeted neighborhoods, he felt his stomach sink. Suddenly, the kids there, along with the kids in the United States, seemed so unfairly lured, so help-less in the face of the company's tactics, so utterly vulnerable to the addic-tive powers of Coke, that Dunn decided his company had gone too far. After trying over the next four years to steer the company back to saner nutritional policies, he resigned. For the first time since then, he agreed to discuss some of the company's deepest secrets that ultimately led to his own deepest regrets.

Jeffrey Dunn is no ordinary whistleblower. He doesn't look back on his time at Coke with bitterness, nor does he view his former colleagues as evil. Rather, he said, they are blinded by the desire to win. "At Coke, I do think they believe they are doing the right things," he said. "If you really think you are doing the wrong thing and covering it up, it's hard to deal with that emotionally. I've still got friends there, and I suggest to them, 'It's just very hard to see yourself from the inside.' "

"But the obesity trend is an epidemic," Dunn continued. "And there is no question its roots are directly tied to the expansion of fast food, junk food, and soft drink consumption. Whether you can identify any one of those things is probably a fair question. Soft drink guys prospect on that all the time. But you can look at the obesity rates, and you can look at per capita consumption of sugary soft drinks and overlay those on a map, and I promise you: They correlate about .99999 percent. As they say, you can run but you can't hide."

Jeffrey Dunn can't quite pinpoint the moment when he first knew he would work for Coca-Cola. He guesses he was seven or eight. And he probably wasn't the only kid in his family who felt that way. He grew up in the San Fernando Valley with four older brothers. The Dunn boys played baseball. They surfed. They tangled with one another, and—this being the 1960s—they grew their hair long. Their mother had been a cartoonist at the Disney studios, but she traded that career to wrangle her boys full-time or, as Dunn likes to say, "to keep us out of jail." In the evenings, when Jeffrey and his brothers would tumble through the door, the day's real entertainment would begin: Their father would come home and transfix them with stories of his job.

Walter Dunn worked for Coca-Cola, but he could have passed for a U.S. senator. Tall and handsome with a big head of white hair, the elder Dunn also had the gift of speech. The five boys would sit, rapt, as he spun his latest war stories, which invariably involved the competition, Pepsi. "When other kids were coming home and talking about how school was, Walter would come home and tell stories about Pepsi making a challenge, here and there," Dunn said. "He worked in the fountain department of

Coke's offices in Los Angeles, and one time when 7-Eleven decided to put Pepsi into their stores alongside Coke, Walter was called in over the Christmas holiday to help stop it."

In 1970, Walter Dunn moved his family to Atlanta, where Coke is headquartered, to take a much bigger job. He was put in charge of the prestige accounts, the company's most valued relationships—and, at this point, the stories around the dinner table got even more colorful. It was during these years that Walter Dunn developed—invented, really—the enterprise known as sports and entertainment marketing. Under chairman Woodruff's direction, Walter Dunn's job was to put Coke's logo into stadiums, movie theaters, amusement parks, fair grounds, and every other venue in the country where people had fun. He cut endorsement deals with athletes and teams and stadiums, which for Jeffrey, now a teenager, was a dream come true. "He took his job very seriously," Dunn said. "Coke had about an 80 percent share of what you would define as prestige accounts, so every one of these that came up, Pepsi would try to take them away. Walter took this personally. He was maintaining the integrity of the Coke brand. I was always hearing about the Buffalo Bills or the Dodgers or the Yankees, and if you're a kid growing up, all those names *meant* something to you."

Listening to his father, Jeffrey Dunn knew that he had the work ethic needed to succeed at Coke. But it wasn't until one day in high school that he knew he could do more than work hard—that he, too, could lead and inspire others to give themselves over to something larger. He was the captain of the basketball team, and early in one heated game his coach pulled him off the court after he committed a foul. Dunn, feeling that the coach was being too timid, picked up a chair and threw it eight rows into the stands—at which point, the coach promptly sent him to the locker room. His teammates, however, who thrived with Dunn as their captain, had other ideas. They confronted the coach at halftime and insisted he put Dunn back in the game. Which is just what the coach did.

In deciding he wanted to work for Coke, Dunn faced one small hurdle. The company had a strict rule against nepotism, and his father had not been just any Coke employee. The riches Walter had brought to the company had made him a star, making it all the more difficult to overlook when Jeffrey came knocking on the door, résumé in hand. The twenty-seven-year-old Jeffrey had already earned his stripes through a stint with E. & J. Gallo Winery, selling door to door to liquor stores in Mississippi, where he picked up some tricks in handling store owners, merchandising, and working the competition. He also worked for Seagram, where, in the course of less than two years, he rose to the company's director of sales for seventeen western states. Still, getting into Coke, where he had always wanted to work, was an ordeal.

In early 1985, he tried in vain for weeks to land an interview with a Coke executive, Charlie Frenette, who wouldn't return his calls. Undeterred, he got a sympathetic secretary to tell him when Frenette was traveling next, and Dunn flew to Atlanta and boarded the same flight. "He was up in first class," Dunn said. "I was in coach. When they turned the seat belt lights off, I walked up and said, 'Hi Charlie, how are you doing? I've been having a hard time getting in to see you, so I thought the best thing would be for us to spend a few minutes on the plane.' And he looked at with me this kind of look—oh, really—and said, 'I'm kind of busy. I have a big call. I'll see if I have any time at the end of the flight.' " Dunn still didn't get an interview, but he did get a test. Just before landing, Frenette had him come up to first class, where he asked him to critique a presentation he'd prepared for the Denny's restaurant chain. "Next thing I know, he had hired me," Dunn said. "And what's funny about that, we got to be good friends, and he would tell that story to sales people all the time. 'Let me tell you about somebody who figured out how you get to see somebody. You just don't accept no for an answer.' "

Dunn started off in the fountain business at a regional office in Irvine, California, where his first big account was the Carl's Jr. hamburger restaurant chain. This was also his first experience with the supersize craze that would sweep through the fast food industry and move into the grocery stores with ever larger cups and bottles of soda. "It was bigger, better,"

Dunn said. "We had a whole marketing division within fountain that looked for opportunities. Coke went to its customers, starting with McDonald's, with the idea of bundled meals that included a Coke. At the time, the restaurant chains didn't do combos—like hamburgers with fries—but we figured out that if they did this, we'd get a lot more people to buy Coke. From 1980 through 2000 at least, that was the predominant marketing strategy of Coke to build consumption within fast food outlets. At Carl's Jr., when I was running that account, we not only put Coke into their equivalent of combo meals. We actually had all-you-could-drink beverage bars added, too—you know, buy a drink and get as many refills as you want. All of that was about instilling more value into the fast food experience and ensuring that people bought a soft drink along the way."

By the early 1990s, Dunn was in charge of his own battalion in Coke's army—a force of eight hundred people who handled fountain sales to convenience stores, restaurants, and cafeterias, with annual sales of $3 billion. And like any beloved leader, Dunn was given a nickname by the people who worked for him. It happened one day when he had assembled his staff for a pep talk. "Sales people, by definition, like to keep score," he told me. "You generally don't make it in sales unless you are good with people and you like to keep score. It's just the nature of the beast. So here was this big army of sales people and I was giving a speech about Pepsi. Coke has about a 70 to 80 percent market share of the fountain side of the business, and every five years, Pepsi would make a run and decide they were going to take fountain. So I gave this speech about winning and I said, 'It's like we're at war. And the way you keep score in war is how many body bags get carried off the field. The key is to have more of their body bags carried off the field than our body bags. I want you all to go out and ramp up our scorecard. I want to see a lot of body bags.'

"I said it a little more intensely than that," he told me. "The body bags were the Pepsi sales people who were going to get fired as a result of not getting our accounts. So my nickname for the next ten years was Body Bag."

. . .

It would be difficult to overstate the animosity between Coke and Pepsi or the extent to which they looked upon one another with suspicion. But things reached a low point in 1984, after PepsiCo pulled off a stunning coup by signing the world's biggest star, Michael Jackson, to film a commercial for them, a move that appeared to seize them the high ground. Relations deteriorated even further the following year when Coke, perhaps feeling some pressure from the Jackson endorsement, prepared to introduce New Coke—and watched helplessly as PepsiCo pulled off yet another publicity coup. A day before Coke's announcement, PepsiCo ran ads in newspapers around the country, presenting Coca-Coca's move as a triumph for Pepsi. For years, PepsiCo had been claiming that its sweeter soda was better liked than Coke, and here was Coke, practically admitting to the world that it agreed. New Coke, by PepsiCo's analysis, was 4 percent sweeter than regular Coke. And to celebrate the reformulation, PepsiCo gave its employees a day off.

From Wall Street to the mass media, this rivalry between the two soda titans became known as the Great Cola War. The companies, however, weren't fighting each other as much as they were pulling together to drive up consumption overall. Coke crushed Pepsi in the 1960s, and Pepsi won the 1980s, and Coke came back strong in the 1990s. But what few outside the companies realized was that winning or losing was immaterial: In each of those decades, the sales of Coke and Pepsi *both* went up. Roger Enrico, the CEO of PepsiCo, was the first to let slip that, in reality, the Great Soda War caused neither company to shed much blood.

"If the Coca-Cola Company didn't exist, we'd pray for someone to invent it," he wrote in his 1986 autobiography, *The Other Guy Blinked.* "You see, when the public gets interested in the Pepsi-Coke competition, often Pepsi doesn't win at Coke's expense and Coke doesn't win at Pepsi's. Everybody in the business wins. Consumer interest swells the market. The more fun we provide, the more people buy our products—*all* our products."

To be sure, much of the "fun" they provided came from the product itself, and in this matter, sugar was key. It is the largest ingredient, after water, with caffeine not far behind. From time to time, other elements of the company's well-guarded recipe would leak into the media, and these reportedly include extracts of coca, lime, and vanilla.

As Dunn would learn, however, what makes Coke's formula so addictive goes beyond sugar or any secret flavorings. The precise nature of this allure was not even known to Coke until the late 1990s, when Charlie Frenette, the man who had hired Dunn and was now the chief marketing officer, decided to dig deeper into Coke's formula. With the utter secrecy that shields all matters relating to Coke's recipe, he hired a famous Swiss manufacturer of flavors and fragrances, Givaudan, to divine the fundamental aspects of Coke's appeal. Reporting back to Frenette, Givaudan pointed out that the bubbles in the soda themselves are quite enticing, which a sip of flat Coke will demonstrate. But Givaudan found something else as well, and it stems from a quirk of our biology—one that the entire processed food industry has, of course, learned to exploit. Its premise is this: We like foods that have an identifiable strong flavor, but we tire of them very quickly.

So, for instance, meat eaters will give out on a plate of highly seasoned turkey tetrazzini much faster than they will on a serving of plain hamburger of the same size, even though the first bites of the turkey will be more exciting. Even more problematic for food manufacturers, those same meat eaters are likely to remember this the next time they go shopping and buy the plain hamburger more often. Food scientists speculate that this behavior stems from our instinctual need for varied nutrients, which are more easily attained by eating a variety of foods. Get too much of one thing, and the brain starts sending out signals of satiety, or fullness, to compel us to move on to different foods.

This was the phenomenon known as "sensory-specific satiety," or the power of one overwhelming flavor to trigger the feeling of fullness, which would complicate the efforts of food scientists like Howard Moskowitz to hit the perfect bliss point for sugary foods and drinks. In creating products that will sell consistently, they learned to walk a line between the extremes of an exciting first bite or sip and the utterly familiar. More than any other product, Coke had mastered this balancing act, Givaudan told the company's marketing officer. "They said what's fascinating about Coke versus the other soft drinks is that it really, truly is the most balanced," said Dunn, who was looped into the project. "When you drink it, there is no edge to it. Their analogy was a fine wine that's balanced so you drink it and you're not left with any kind of lingering edginess. I think, intuitively, the technical guys at Coke knew that all along. But from a marketing standpoint, this was the moment of 'A-ha.' "

Givaudan's findings remained locked up at Coke, since they weren't exactly the makings for a flashy ad campaign. The flavor experts from Switzerland were basically saying that Coke was so dominant because of a recipe that made it *forgettable*—at least in the way the balance of flavors caused the brain to flash a continuous green light for more. To parse this out a bit, I reached out to John Hayes, a food scientist who directs the Sensory Evaluation Center at Penn State University. In evaluating the seductive powers of Coke, he drew on more than scientific expertise. In his younger days, he had been a true soda junkie, drinking *six* 12-ounce cans a day until, realizing that "that was not good for me in a whole host of ways," he cut back. Reformed as he was, I could still hear excitement in Hayes's voice as he spoke about Coke. "From an anatomical sense, we always mention smell and taste," he said. "But in terms of flavor, there is that third leg of the stool that everyone forgets about, and that is the somatosensory, or the touch component, and this includes things like the tingle from carbon dioxide bubbles, or the bite from chili peppers, or the creaminess. In the case of Coca-Cola, what's so interesting about it is you're really activating *all* those modalities. You have those nice aromas from the vanilla and the citrus and the whole family of brown spices, like cinnamon and nutmeg. Then you have that sweetness. And there's the bite of phosphoric acid, the tingle of the carbon dioxide. You really end up stimulating all the different parts of the flavor construct that we experience."

Still, as good as Coke is—with a world-class formula of incredible power—it became clear to Dunn in his years at Coca-Cola that there was more than sensory power behind the soaring sales. Coke's allure, he realized, is derived as much from what goes onto the can or bottle as from what goes into it. This is the logo, the brand known as Coke. "Everybody asks, why couldn't you just match Coke by finding out what's in it," Dunn said, holding up an imaginary can as he spoke. "But once you take the trademark off, it's a different brand." Studies have found that people like Coke much better when they know what they are drinking is in fact Coke and not one of the knockoff colas sold by grocery chains.

Coke's efforts in marketing its brand were restrained through much of the 1970s, when Dunn was watching his father establish the sports endorsement business at Coke. But 1980 was a watershed for Coke, just as it was for America's obesity rate, which had started to surge. That year, Coke switched from using table sugar to high-fructose corn syrup, which was less expensive and blended more readily with the flavoring concentrate. The revered but aging chairman, Robert Woodruff, chose an unsmiling taskmaster, the Cuba-born Roberto Goizueta, to be the new CEO. This was also the year that Coke intensified its marketing, more than doubling the money it spent on advertising, reaching $181 million by 1984.

The executive who commanded the company's marketing at the time, Sergio Zyman, was known as a merciless pursuer of the consumer. With Zyman leading the charge, Coke hired Bill Cosby to tout Coke as "the real thing," which implied Pepsi was not. It designed 12-packs to look like cheerfully wrapped gifts during the Christmas season, and then, being an equal-opportunity marketer, targeted Muslims by shifting its advertising to run at night during the Ramadan holiday, when they abstain from food and drink until sundown. "The job of marketing is to sell lots of stuff and make lots of money," Zyman wrote in *The End of Marketing as We Know It*, his account of the battles with Pepsi. "It is to get people to buy more of your products, more often, at higher prices. In fact, though some marketers will tell you it's impossible, the real job of a marketer is to sell everything that a company could profitably make, to be the ultimate stewards of return on investment and assets employed."

To illustrate the global scope of Coke's take-no-prisoners approach to marketing, Zyman tells the story of the crisis Mexico found itself in when the government devalued the peso in 1994. He was skiing, he writes, when he heard the grim news, and he got to a phone as fast as he could to call Douglas Ivester, Coke's president. He urged Ivester to make sure that Coke's operators in Mexico did not cut their marketing campaigns. Overnight, the rich became poorer and the poor got hungry, struggling with the soaring prices. But Zyman saw that as more reason to work harder at getting them both—rich and poor—to drink Coke. "We were no longer in a battle for share of market or share of mind," Zyman explained. "We were in a battle for disposable income. We were going to have to compete with every other product and service in the Mexican marketplace; the idea was to get in and make sure that consumers remembered to buy Coke." The strategy worked perfectly. Coke sales didn't slump with Mexico's economy; in fact, they grew—three times as fast as the competition, as Mexicans from all walks of life responded to Coke's advertising.*

The targeting that Coke performed in the United States was no less ruthless or importunate. "Why does Coke market?" Dunn asked me. "Why does McDonald's market? The answer is because you're either going forward or you're going backwards. You do big conceptual maps, and you look at the different attributes of what you are selling, and the communication strategies. The communication is very much about, 'How do I want to be seen as relevant to my target consumer, relative to my primary competitors.' Relevance, salience, and competitive position all go into what Coke is today."

The intensified targeting by Coca-Cola focused on two metrics. The first was per capita consumption, or how much Coke people drank, on average, each year. This told Coke how it was doing relative to the growing population. It wasn't enough just to be selling more Coke. The "per caps,"

---

* Similarly, hard economic times in the United States, including the recession that started in 2008, have proven to be boons for large parts of the processed food industry, as shoppers pinching their pennies find it easier to buy soda, snacks, and frozen entrees than more costly groceries, like fresh fruits and vegetables.

as the average person's consumption was known, had to be going up. The second metric was market share, or how much of the world's total soda consumption Coke owned. "Everything else flowed out of those two things," said Dunn. "If you were growing per caps, and you were capturing market share, you'd make money." For Coca-Cola stockholders, the years from 1980 to 1997 were especially sweet. Sales more than quadrupled from $4 billion to $18 billion. The per caps were equally impressive. By 1997, Americans were drinking 54 gallons of soda a year, on average, and Coke controlled almost half of the soda sales, with a 45 percent share. The rising consumption, which had more than doubled from 1970, also had staggering implications for the nation's health. With diet sodas accounting for only 25 percent of the sales, the sugary soda that people drank each year—more than 40 gallons—delivered 60,000 calories and 3,700 teaspoons of sugar, per person.

By 1994, Coke's marketing efforts became even more intense, driven by competition from new sources: sweetened teas and sports drinks. Even bottled water was making it hard to push the per caps for soda any higher. More and more, Dunn found himself participating in efforts that directed Coke's marketing muscle toward particularly poor and vulnerable parts of the country where consumption seemed to know no bounds. Places like New Orleans, where people were drinking twice as much Coke as the national average. Or Rome, Georgia, where the per cap hit 1,000—nearly three Cokes a day. Coca-Cola executives never used the word *addiction* to describe this behavior, of course. The food industry prefers not to speak of addiction. Instead, when describing their most valued customers, they chose a term that evokes an image of junkies pursuing their fix.

In the war room atmosphere of Coke's headquarters in Atlanta, these consumers were not called "loyal customers." They were called "heavy users," and their importance to Coca-Cola was rooted in a principle named for an Italian economist, Vilfredo Pareto. He created a mathematical formula to describe the unequal distribution of wealth in his country, having observed that 80 percent of the land in Italy was owned by 20 percent of the people, and like many other things, the consumption of Coke worked the same way. Eighty percent of the world's soda was consumed by 20 percent of the people. "Your heavy-user base is, by definition, very important to the business," Dunn said.

"The other model we use was called 'drinks and drinkers.' How many drinkers do I have, and how many drinks do they drink. If you lost one of those heavy users, if somebody just decided to stop drinking Coke, how many drinkers would you have to get, at low velocity, to make up for that heavy user. The answer is a lot. It's more efficient to get my existing users to drink more."

One of Dunn's lieutenants, Todd Putman, who worked at Coca-Cola from 1997 to 2000, said he was astonished by the ferociousness with which the company pursued consumers. The goal became much larger than merely beating the rival brands; Coca-Cola strove to outsell every other thing people drank, including milk and water. "It was a mind-bending paradigm shift for me," Putman said. "We weren't trying to get share of market. We weren't trying to beat Pepsi or Mountain Dew. We were about trying to beat everything."

And when it came to per caps for Coke, Putman said, the marketing division's efforts boiled down to one question: "How can we drive more ounces into more bodies more often?"

One aspect of this pursuit involved playing with the price to jack up demand. The country, as Dunn put it, became a "battlefield grid." On the same Memorial Day weekend, for instance, a liter of Coke might sell for $1.59 in San Francisco but only ninety-nine cents in Los Angeles, based on the company's reading of consumer demand and habits during that holiday. In pursuing heavy users, however, Coke went beyond mere pricing. It began going after the group of people who had not yet decided if they were Coke or Pepsi lovers. These were the future heavy users, whose habits and brand loyalty were still unformed and pliable, and Coke pursued them like it had pursued nothing before.

"Teenagers became the battleground for early brand adoption," Dunn said.

• • •

There was one caveat in Coca-Cola's pursuit of kids in which Dunn, at first, could find a measure of comfort. The company was an early adopter of self-imposed curbs on its advertising, and it drew a bright line at marketing to kids under twelve. Coke abstained from placing its advertising on any programs—television, radio, mobile phones, or the Internet—where more than half of the viewers were eleven years old or younger. In 2010, they made this policy even stricter by lowering the threshold: Coke will now walk away from programs where only a third of the viewers are under twelve.

The company touts this policy as part of a sweeping agenda in social responsibility that includes everything from the efficient use of energy to preserving water supplies in regions of water scarcity to a program it calls "active healthy living," which ranges from offering kids low-calorie drinks including bottled water to running an ad campaign called Move to the Beat that promotes dancing as a means of exercise. "There are more than 680 million teens on the planet," Coca-Cola says on its website. "An investment in their future is one of the most critical investments we can make."

The advertising policy was a point of pride to Coca-Cola employees, Dunn said, and he credits the company for taking this stance. But the self-imposed restraint on children, he pointed out, had its limits. In reality, it applied only to media advertising, not the invaluable marketing that Robert Woodruff had first identified: kids in their special moments. "If you think in terms of Coke's presence in ballparks and every place kids go, there was certainly marketing to kids going on," Dunn said. Moreover, once those kids turned twelve, even before they could be officially called teenagers, they were lumped with the 680 million teenagers on the planet who were fair game for every last ounce of marketing firepower Coke could muster.

"Magically, when they would turn twelve, we'd suddenly attack them like a bunch of wolves," said Putman.

In many ways, teenagers are even fatter targets than younger kids. Starting at twelve, kids have more allowance to spend, travel to and from school on their own, and often leave the school grounds for lunch. Most critically, they begin to form the likes and dislikes that will define them for the rest of their lives. Coke studied these metrics, of course, and planned its campaigns accordingly. "Say kids started drinking 250 soft drinks a year," Dunn told me. "They tend to carry that consumption behavior all the way through their life. Then it was a brand battle from that point on, because the core brand decision—i.e., I'm a Coke drinker, I'm a Pepsi drinker, I'm a Mountain Dew drinker—tends to be made by the time people are in their mid to late teens."

As important as teenagers were to Coke in establishing loyalty to the brand, much of the company's marketing effort was directed at young adults, where the goal was to sustain and grow consumption rates. In this matter, Coke left nothing to chance. It created an entity whose task is to guide the marketers toward their targets with laser precision. Called the Coca-Cola Retailing Research Council, it plumbs the social science of shopping to identify the ways in which both teens and adults can be made more vulnerable to persuasion. Soda already rivals bread in grocery sales and easily tops other staples like milk, cheese, and frozen foods. In 2005, however, the council produced one of the largest studies ever undertaken about America's shopping habits, and it was loaded with tips and advice for grocers to increase their soda sales further still. The study included a "shopper density map," done up in bright yellows and reds to mark the "hot spots" where most shoppers go. Whisked through the front doors, they typically start on the right side of the supermarket—moving counterclockwise and, in a surprise, from back to front. Thus, the main racks of soda should be placed toward the rear of the store, on the right side. By contrast, much of the center of store has light traffic, the report warns, calling this area the "Dead Zone."

Coca-Cola, in this study, also urges grocers to find ways to catch shoppers off guard. Federal health officials who are fighting the obesity epidemic advise consumers never to enter a grocery store without a shopping list, which helps to ward off the impulse to load up on sugary, salty, and fatty snacks. But Coke's study offers the grocer numerous strategies for snagging even the wariest consumer. "Engage the shopper early," the study says, with giant, eye-catching displays of soda, up front on the right for maximum traffic. These should be parked outside the aisle where sodas are usually found. Nor should gum, candy, and magazines get exclusive use of the most valuable part of the store, the checkout zones, where impulse buying is at its highest. Tall coolers loaded with Coke should be placed right next to the cash registers. "Sixty percent of supermarket purchase decisions are *completely unplanned*," the Coke study says. "Anything that enables the shopper to make a faster, easier, better decision" will help spur these unplanned purchases.

Over the years, Coca-Cola has also paid careful attention to how sales are affected by the gender, race, and age of consumers. Dunn told me that Coke deepened its demographic knowledge by mining the customer loyalty cards of grocery chain shoppers. It learned, for instance, that African Americans tend to like drinks that are not only sweeter but fruit-flavored too. "We could tell you by shopping basket, by market, by demographic, what people bought," Dunn said. "And then we made targeted offers to those people based on what they'd be most likely to consume. Buy two liters of Coke and get a free bag of potato chips, or whatever it was."

The company's shopper study cites the sweet tooth of minorities, along with the benefits of marketing soda in combination with other grocery items. It also lumps American shoppers into five basic groups—from rural to suburban upscale to urban ethnic—and provides details on each group's drink preferences so that grocers can calibrate their displays. The new energy drinks have the best chance with the "urban upscale" shopper, while the "urban ethnic" and "rural" shoppers remain slightly more loyal to soda. Depending on its clientele, "each store has a unique DNA," the report says.

Perhaps the greatest influence that Coca-Cola has had on American shopping habits is in the arena of the convenience store, or "C-stores," as they are known in the trade. These range from mom-and-pop groceries in the inner city to the national chains of drive-up food-and-gas stores in the suburbs. Besides convenience, they sell foods that have the heaviest loads of salt, sugar, and fat. To nutritionists, these stores are to obesity what drug dens were to the crack epidemic. The C-stores attract young kids and teenagers because they are closer to home and sell single drinks. Inside is a layout calculated to grab these kids at every turn. The staples—the bags of rice, canned soup, and bread—are all in the rear of the store. Up front, typically right by the door, are the stacks of soda bottles, joined by the racks of chips and pastries, with the soda cooler on one wall and inexpensive candies next to the cash register to snatch up any leftover change. In big cities like New York and Philadelphia and Los Angeles, there are thousands of corner stores strategically located near the schools, to catch kids coming and going.

As powerful a force as the C-stores might be in the nation's health, they didn't get that way without considerable help. Indeed, the number of C-stores surged in the 1980s as a direct result of the marketing strategies developed by Coke and Pepsi, along with the snack food manufacturers, like Frito-Lay and Hostess. These companies have divisions of employees or contractors who visit and service the convenience stores every week to deliver their products. Paid by how much they sell, these workers stock and clean their displays, maximizing their visibility by making sure no other items encroach on their space. In fact, such companies actually *own* the racks and the coolers. I met one C-store owner in Philadelphia who tried to improve the nutritional profile of his offerings by positioning bananas up front, only to be scolded by a soda delivery crew, who claimed this space as their own. But it's the rare C-store owner who would look upon the deliverers with anything but the utmost affection. The soda and snacks are not just the most profitable items in the C-store; they make the C-stores the cash cows that they are. Grocery industry officials told me that C-stores are now bought and sold by syndicates who make loans at exorbitant rates, which only deepens the owner's need for profits.

The industry marketing strategy that begat this boom in C-stores has a name: "up and down the street," as in driving the delivery truck up and down the streets of a neighborhood, from one C-store to the next. For the soda and snack companies, the goal in this wasn't just selling more goods; they wanted to win the loyalty of the kids who frequent these stores. "Up and down the street" became a rally cry among marketers, something they returned to time and again to boost sales and expand their customer base. "Coke was doing it and Pepsi was doing it, and the candy guys were figuring out the same thing," Dunn said. "All the food companies started to engineer a strategy around immediate consumption, and as they put more effort into it, the sales in those stores went up, and there was a huge build out of convenience stores. So now you go to a city like Atlanta, and on every corner there's a convenience store."

"You start to get into the question of what drives what," Dunn said. "Does the preference for soda and snacks drive the availability of soda and snacks, or does availability drive the preference? None of the players stop to think about whether people should really be eating a bag of chicken wings and a bag of potato chips and a 2-liter Coke. They're thinking, 'Is this going to get me an increase in sales?'"

In 2005, the research arm of Coca-Cola sought to answer that question with another shopping report, this one aimed at the owners of convenience stores. Focused on "building loyalty with the next generation," it revealed that the most profitable person who walks through the door is not who the owner may think it is.

"Who's worth more to your store?" the study said. "The 32-year-old who just spent more than $10.00, or the teen who rang up a Coke, a sandwich and a candy bar? Surprisingly, the teen is worth nearly as much as the 30+ shopper today. Teens spend less, but they visit more often. If C-stores can hold on to teens' business as they move into their 20s, these customers have the potential to be worth substantially more." Even in the suburbs, where older teens visit convenience stores most often to buy gasoline, their second most-cited reason is to "satisfy a craving," and these urges present a huge opportunity for growth. "Teens buy a little gas, a lot of times a month," the study said. "Retailers need to recognize and take advantage of this frequency by making it easy for them to enter the store."

Suburban or inner city, kids offered an opportunity to create lifelong brand loyalty. Or, as the study put it, "Teens are at a crucial stage on the learning curve of 'how to be me.'"

Jeffrey Dunn wasn't around when that study's findings confirmed what he already knew.

One day in 2000, a book arrived at Dunn's corner office in the Coca-Cola headquarters complex, unsolicited, and set in motion a chain of events that would convert him from the loyal soldier to the disbeliever he is today. The book was called *Sugar Busters!*, and the team of authors included two physicians from New Orleans. In it, they argued that the rapid increase in sugar consumption had caused a massive disruption to America's health, and they placed much of the blame on soda. "During the meteoric rise in adult and childhood obesity in the last thirty-five years, the consumption of soda has roughly tripled," they wrote. "To put 10 teaspoons of added sugar per regular soft drink into perspective, how many of you would scoop 10 teaspoons of sugar into a glass of tea and then sit and drink it?" Even when mixed with healthy snacks, the physicians argued, the sugar in soda encouraged the body to store the calories as fat.

Dunn took the book home to read, and as he turned the pages, two thoughts began running through his head: This makes sense, and this isn't good.

That same year, he became engaged to a woman who unsettled his view of Coke even more. She was a free spirit, rail-thin, who consumed no sugar and was very anti–junk food. She traveled repeatedly to the Amazon rain forest, and after every trip she returned home with new arguments for why Dunn should apply his talents to something other than selling Coke. "I'm marrying her, I'm reading this book, and I'm simultaneously in the running to be the next president of the company," he said.

In early 2001, at age forty-four, Jeffrey Dunn was already directing more than half of the company's $20 billion in annual sales as president and chief operating officer for Coca-Cola in both North and South America. He made frequent trips through Mexico and on to Brazil, where the company had recently begun a push to increase consumption of Coke. Brazil was a huge potential market with a surging economy and a booming young generation that was poised to become the country's new middle class. But many of these Brazilians still lived in barrios, had limited savings, and had little familiarity with processed foods. The company's strategy was to take over the barrios by repackaging Coke into smaller, more affordable 6.7-ounce bottles, just twenty cents each. Coke was not alone in seeing Brazil as a boon or in embracing the strategy of miniaturization. The food giants, Nestlé and Kraft, were starting to shrink much of their grocery lineup, too, from Tang to Maggi instant noodles, putting them into smaller containers so that they could be sold for less. Nestlé began deploying battalions of ladies to travel the barrios hawking these American-style processed foods door to door, enticing people who, although they still cooked from scratch, aspired to the trappings of middle class. But Coke was Dunn's concern, and as he walked through one of the prime target areas, an impoverished barrio of Rio de Janeiro, he had an epiphany. "A voice in my head says, 'These people need a lot of things, but they don't need a Coke.' I almost threw up. From that moment forward, the fun came out of it for me."

He returned to Atlanta, determined to make some changes. He didn't want to abandon the soda business, but he did want to try to steer the company into a healthier mode. First, he developed Dasani, Coke's bottled water company. Then he pushed to stop marketing Coke in public schools, where the financial incentives to sell soda soon became all too apparent. The independent companies that bottled Coke viewed his plans as reactionary. The largest bottler's chairman, Summerfield Johnston, wrote a letter to the Coke chief executive and board asking for Dunn's head. "He said what I had done was the worst thing he had seen in fifty years in the business, just to placate these crazy leftist school districts who were trying to keep people from having their Coke," said Dunn. "He said I was an embarrassment to the company, and I should be fired."

In February 2004, the company underwent a restructuring, and Jeffrey Dunn was indeed fired by one of his rivals for the presidency, Steven Heyer. Before leaving, Dunn gave one last speech to his colleagues, who gathered in the auditorium to say goodbye. "I had asked Peter Ueberroth, who was on the board and was kind of my mentor. I said, 'They're not going to want me to do this, but I really would like to say goodbye. The company has been in my family since I was born.' And so Steve introduced me and I walked by and I hugged him and whispered in his ear, 'Thank you.' He looked at me and said, 'For what?' And I said, 'You did for me what I would never have done for myself. I would have never left Coke.'"

Dunn told me that talking about Coke's business today was by no means easy, and, given that he continues to work in the food business, not without risk. "You really don't want them mad at you," he said. "And I don't mean that like I'm going to end up at the bottom of the bay. But they don't have a sense of humor when it comes to this stuff. They're a very, very aggressive company."

Dunn does not see himself as a whistleblower, not like the tobacco industry insiders, anyway, who accused their companies of manipulating nicotine to increase its potency. "I may know more about it than other people," he says, "but it's not like there's a smoking gun. The gun is right there. It's not hidden. That's the genius of Coke."

On April 27, 2010, Jeffrey Dunn walked into the Fairmont Hotel in Santa Monica with the blueprints for selling America on a novel snack. He was meeting with three executives from Madison Dearborn Partners, a private equity firm based in Chicago with a wide-ranging portfolio of investments. They had recently hired Dunn to run one of their newest acquisitions—a food producer in the nearby San Joaquin Valley—and had flown out to California to hear his plans for marketing the company's product.

As they sat in the hotel's meeting room, however, with the stunning views of the Pacific Ocean just outside, the men from Madison listened to a pitch like none they'd ever heard before. Dunn was certainly formidable enough for them. His résumé was superb. His twenty years with Coca-Cola had clearly left him with an elite set of marketing skills, and in his presentation he deployed them all.

He talked about giving the product a personality that was bold, irreverent, confident, clever, and playfully confrontational, with the goal of conveying a promise to consumers: that this was the ultimate snack food. He went into detail on how he would target a special segment of the 146 million Americans who are regular snackers—people, he said, who "keep their snacking ritual fresh by trying a new food product when it catches their attention."

He helped the investors visualize these people by flashing mock bios up on a screen. The targets were people like Aubree, thirty-four, the on-the-go mom who wants to give her kids "all the fun in the world" and feeds them Oreos, Go-Gurts, and Delmonte fruit packed in syrup; Kristine, twenty-seven, the busy professional who is drawn to Starbucks, trail mix, and the new, dip-ready chip; and college student Josh, twenty-three, on his own for the first time, seeking adventure fueled by Doritos and Mountain Dew Code Red.

He explained how he would deploy strategic storytelling in the ad campaign for this snack, using a key phrase that had been developed with much calculation: "Snack on That." He had considered other wording, including "Snack That," and "Snack This," but adding the word *on* made it more thought-provoking. "It's language we use in culture for evaluation and reappraisal," he said. Snack on That, as a marketing tool, would "work harder" for them.

He then went through the details of the proposed product launch, including a media buy with commercials on *House, CSI,* and *Survivor;* a grassroots guerilla PR campaign with the product's own video game; and digital media with blogger outreach and *seeding* message boards to accelerate the pickup.

Forty-five minutes later, he was done. He clicked off the last slide. "Thank you," he said.

This was a fairly typical meeting for the executives from Madison, except that Dunn was a cut above the brand managers they were used to having on their side. The rub in the presentation, however, came in the snack that Dunn was now preparing to promote. This wasn't a new concoction of salt, sugar, and fat whose appeal was well known to these investors. Madison's $18 billion portfolio had contained the largest Burger King franchise in the world, the Ruth's Chris Steak House chain, and a processed food maker called Pierre whose lineup includes a champion of handheld convenience, the Jamwich, a peanut butter and jelly contrivance that comes frozen, crustless, and embedded with four kinds of sugars, from dextrose to corn syrup.

The snack that Dunn was proposing to sell: carrots. Plain, fresh carrots. No added sugar. No creamy sauce or dips. No salt. Just baby carrots that are peeled, washed, bagged, and then sold into the deadly dull produce aisle. Carrots were the flip side of Coke. They weren't selling because of the way they were being sold. To fix this, Dunn said, would require unleashing the proven techniques of processed food marketing.

"We act like a snack, not a vegetable," he told the investors. "We exploit the rules of junk food to fuel the baby carrot conversation. We are pro–junk food behavior but anti–junk food establishment."

In describing this new line of work, Dunn would tell me he was doing penance for his years at Coca-Cola—or, as he put it, "I'm paying my karma debt." That day in Santa Monica, however, the men from Madison were thinking about sales. They had come all the way from Chicago to hear this pitch, and they loved it. They had already agreed to buy one of the two biggest farm producers of baby carrots in the country, and they'd hired Dunn to run the whole operation. Now, after his pitch, they were relieved. Dunn had figured out that using the industry's own marketing ploys would work better than anything else. He drew from the bag of tricks that he mastered in his twenty years at Coca-Cola, where he learned one of the most critical rules in processed food: The selling of food matters as much as the food itself. If not more.

chapter six

"A Burst of Fruity Aroma"

At 2 P.M. on a Monday afternoon in late February of 1990, twelve of the most senior Philip Morris executives gathered in a conference room at company headquarters in midtown Manhattan. The austere, gray-granite building stood on Park Avenue, twenty-six stories tall and situated directly across from the main entrance to Grand Central Station, with features that bespoke the company's affluence. It had underground parking for the executives, a high-ceilinged lobby with art curated by the Whitney Museum, and sweeping views of the New York harbor far to the south. As the operations center for the largest tobacco company in the world, it also had a special accommodation for employees who smoked: Most of the office floors had ceiling fans. The executives met on the top floor, in a space called the Management Room, where six tables had been pushed together to form a large block, with a pad, pen, and water glass placed at each seat. These dozen men formed the brain trust at Philip Morris, and they assembled like this once a month, in what they called the Corporate Products Committee, to hear from the managers of the company's most valuable brands.

As usual, the chief executive, Hamish Maxwell, took a seat at the table. He was joined by two of his predecessors—Joseph Cullman III and George Weissman—who, though now in their seventies, continued to serve as high-level advisers. Cullman, the great-grandson of a German cigar maker, had set the stage for the company's first diversification beyond tobacco when he bought the Miller Brewing Company back in the late 1960s. Weissman, a two-pack-a-day smoker and one-time reporter for the *Star Ledger* in Newark, New Jersey, had helped develop the masculine image for Marlboro cigarettes and famously said in 1978, when he became the company's chief executive, "I'm no cowboy and I don't ride horseback, but I like to think I have the freedom the Marlboro Man exemplifies. He's the man who doesn't punch a clock. He's not computerized. He's a free spirit."

This month's meeting was chaired by one of Maxwell's direct reports, a fifty-two-year-old Australian-born financial manager named Geoffrey Bible. He wouldn't take over the chief executive spot himself for another four years, but the job of chairing the meeting rotated among the executives. It was fitting that Bible should take the lead at this particular session, where much of the agenda would be devoted to company products other than cigarettes. Just one month earlier, Maxwell had asked him to immerse himself in—and gain some control over—the newest addition to the company's roster of consumer goods: the vast and unwieldy division of processed food.

Thanks to its acquisitions of General Foods and Kraft, ten cents of every dollar that Americans spent on groceries now belonged to Philip Morris, which dramatically altered the balance sheets at the tobacco giant. Philip Morris was amassing mountains of cash from its cigarette sales and saw the food business as a way to diversify and put those profits to work. When it finished merging the two food giants in 1989, their combined annual sales of $23 billion accounted for 51 percent of the total revenue at

Philip Morris. Food had not only become its largest division, the tobacco executives were suddenly also running the largest food company in the country, in charge of icons like Cool Whip, Entenmann's, Oscar Mayer, Lunchables, Shake 'n Bake, Macaroni & Cheese, Velveeta, Jell-O, Maxwell House, Tang, and the Post cereal lineup of Raisin Bran, Grape-Nuts, and Cocoa Pebbles.

Once tidy and contained, the agendas of these monthly product meetings were now careening wildly through the aisles of the grocery store, and everywhere the Philip Morris executives looked, they saw battles under way with rivals intent on stealing their turf. In getting ready for this particular meeting, the food brand managers had spent days preparing strategy memos, sales charts, and testing reports, but the tone in the room remained low-key and cordial, as always. The Philip Morris executives were seasoned corporate brawlers, supremely confident in their ability to win the loyalty of consumers. The Marlboro brand had been a loser back in the 1940s, pulled from the market and taken for dead, before the Marlboro Man ads started running in the 1960s and turned the cigarette into the country's—and eventually the world's—top seller. Geoffrey Bible, moreover, had developed an empathy for the managers in the Kraft General Foods division (whose name was later shortened to Kraft Foods), who were in an endless struggle to fend off their many competitors. He had spent time in the field with their salesmen, and he came away awed by the challenges they faced, from the arduous task of convincing the grocers to give them space on the shelf to creating the emotional lures in their advertising and packaging that, along with the actual formulas, would compel shoppers to pick their products up.

I met Bible in late 2011 in the office he used in Greenwich, Connecticut, after retiring from Philip Morris in 2002. At seventy-three, he was twenty years older than Jeffrey Dunn, the former Coca-Cola executive, but both men had strong handshakes and deep tans and were careful eaters, avoiding too much of the kind of foods and drinks their companies sold. Where Dunn could exude laid-back California and Bible still had traces of his Australian upbringing, they were also each known to their peers as fierce corporate gut-fighters with an instinct for the jugular and no tolerance for fools.

When Bible took a seat at his desk, the place where he monitors the stock market and engages in varied business activities, one artifact seemed conspicuous in its absence: There was no ashtray. He had smoked as much as a pack a day until 2000, when he stopped on his doctor's advice. "We were very blessed in tobacco, because we had the biggest brand in the world," he told me. "The trade was desperate to get our brand. Not the case in food. You were desperate to get *their* business. I was shattered to find the attitude of the buyers in these various grocery chains towards even large companies like Kraft and General Foods. It's brutal stuff. 'What are you doing in here? I told you to get out of my office the last time you came. That promotion was a disaster. Get out.' You'd move from the meat buyer to the mayo buyer, and he'd say the same thing."

The effort required in marketing food to consumers was, if anything, even more demanding and also very different from tobacco, which was promoted through idealistic imagery like the rugged cowboy in the Marlboro Man commercials. "Cigarettes are much the same to look at, and their advertising and marketing is much more aspirational than it is for food," Bible said. "In food you have to really find a way to convey the product better, and its worth. It's much more, 'This product is good for you because it has the following ingredients, or it has whatever pizzazz.' And it's got to have that product differentiation, that reason to buy it and consume it."

With these challenges in mind, the Corporate Products Committee on that winter day in 1990 took mere minutes to work through the company's plans for marketing Marlboros in Hong Kong and the L&M brand in Germany and spent only slightly more time with the new nonreturnable 7-ounce bottles that Miller was introducing to the eastern and southern states; they wanted to make sure these regions were considered "strong 7 oz. markets." The committee then turned its attention to food—specifically, a discussion of one of the most profitable parts of its lineup:

the beverages known as fruit drinks. Consumers were spending nearly $1 billion each year on powdered drinks, and the company's own Kool-Aid, Country Time, and Tang brands were pulling in an 82 percent share. But as Bible and the other committee members opened their folders to examine the memos and charts that had been prepared on these beverages, the Kool-Aid brand seemed especially vulnerable. Kool-Aid was a throwback to the 1950s, when the flavored drink's mascot, the smiling pitcher known as Kool-Aid Man, was created by ad execs to battle Coke and Pepsi with his warm and cuddly antics. Now, Kool-Aid looked to be fading fast into that storied history, as determined challengers were vying to shrink its take. It was the committee's job to keep that from happening, and the Philip Morris executives listened quietly as the managers who ran the Kool-Aid brand presented the first in a series of plans that were breathtaking in both scope and strategy.

The schemes would all share one theme. Where some of these drinks were every bit as sweet as Coke, they wouldn't be pitched like that, given the public's increasing concern about its sugar load. In marketing these drinks to kids and their parents, the brand managers now working for Philip Morris would use something else to create allure. They would use fruit, or rather the intimation of fruit, to create an even more powerful image for their drinks: a chimera of health.

There was a touch of irony in tobacco executives coming to the rescue of Kool-Aid. The drink had been invented in 1927 by a Nebraskan man named Edwin Perkins whose other creations included Nix-O-Tine, a horrible-tasting mixture of herbs and silver nitrate that became a popular cure for tobacco addiction. But there was a certain marketing genius in the development of Kool-Aid that Philip Morris would have appreciated, one that set the tone for the current efforts to revitalize the drink.

Perkins was a mercantile wholesaler, selling various products to grocers that included bottled flavorings for drinks. These were mediocre sellers and cumbersome to distribute. So Perkins, who liked to tinker with mixes and powders, converted the flavorings into powders that could be easily shipped in packets. He called them Kool-Ade, later changing the spelling to Kool-Aid, and they were an immediate sensation. America readily took to the packets of artificial flavors, bright colorings, and sugar— until the Great Depression hit, after which sales skidded. By then, Perkins had ditched all his other products to focus on Kool-Aid, and with his company on the verge of bankruptcy, he came up with another inspired move: He slashed the price of his Kool-Aid packets from ten cents to five. And that did the trick. People no longer saw Kool-Aid as a frivolous luxury. At a nickel each, they saw the packets as an affordable way to enjoy soft drinks during the tough economic times. By 1953, when Perkins sold his company to General Foods, he was producing more than a million packets each day.

General Foods pushed Kool-Aid to far greater heights. Eventually, Americans would stir up and drink 569 million gallons of the stuff a year, and Kool-Aid would come to dominate the company's lineup of powdered soft drinks—a lineup that topped $800 million in sales. But the brand began to flag again in the 1980s. This time, it wasn't the economy. Soda was killing it, as the juggernauts of Coca-Cola and PepsiCo lured more and more kids to their bottled drinks. On top of that, General Foods was outmaneuvered by its rival. In 1987, General Mills introduced a product called Squeezit, which was really just a novel form of packaging. With 23 grams of sugar per serving, this brightly colored drink was sweeter than Coke, and kids went wild. Sales hit $75 million in the first year, which prompted the managers of supermarkets to make room for every one of the dozen flavors that General Mills quickly turned out. Suddenly, Kool-Aid was getting pushed off the shelf. Sensing the urgency, Bible and the Philip Morris Corporate Products Committee made fixing it a priority.

To regain this lost turf, the Kool-Aid team invented their own squeezable bottle, with an added touch: It had a bendable neck, which made drinking all the more fun. They named it Kool-Aid Kool Bursts, and in a detailed memo presented to the committee members, the brand managers laid out precisely how they would overtake General Mills. Much of the strategy involved promotion, including ways to target kids that Philip Morris executives themselves could no longer deploy in marketing cigarettes. Since 1965, the tobacco industry had sought to defuse the growing political pressure against smoking by not using promotional materials that were aimed directly at kids, including, for example, comic books. That didn't preclude General Foods from using these magazines to sell sweet drinks, however. Indeed, it had completed a hugely popular six-issue run of *The Adventures of Kool-Aid Man*, published by Marvel comics and distributed, for free, by General Foods. But the campaign for Kool Bursts would go a step further. General Foods had mass-mailing lists composed entirely of the names and addresses of children, in order to better target them with promotions. In their memo to the products committee, the Kool-Aid managers said they would put these lists to work on behalf of the Kool Bursts: "Gain kid demand through targeted events using General Foods kid mailing list."

But the real genius of their marketing plan was found in a contrivance that would appeal both to kids and moms. The drinks were made mostly with sugar, artificial flavors, and preservatives. In each plastic bottle, however, the company would add a splash of real fruit juice. It was barely half a tablespoon of juice, a mere 5 percent of the total formula, company records reveal, but the Kool-Aid managers already knew that even a hint of fruit was worth a zillion times its weight in marketing gold.

Fruit's value had been established three years earlier in repositioning another of the company's stalwart sugar-based drinks: Tang. In 1987, soon after Philip Morris acquired General Foods, the beverage managers put Tang into little boxes, added two tablespoons of real fruit juice, decorated the cartons with pictures of fresh oranges and cherries, and rebranded them the Tang Fruit Box. The results were gratifying, and not only in terms of sales. In 1992, the Tang Fruit Box won a coveted award from the advertising industry for an ingenious campaign that marketed the boxes as healthy and fun. The slogan was "Nutrition in Disguise," which the company had trademarked for use in "soft drinks and powders, syrups and concentrates used in the preparation of soft drinks." Besides the splash of real fruit juice, the "nutrition" part of this slogan was the added vitamin C, which had been a selling point for the original Tang. Moms who bought Tang Fruit Boxes were applauded for sneaking this good stuff into the hands of their kids via a drink that, to them, looked liked nothing but fun. This was compared to the other tricks parents use to disguise things like carrots, peas, and string beans in the food their kids ate or, as the ad called it, "four clever ways a mom can disguise nutrition."

Building on this fun-but-healthy theme, the Kool-Aid brand managers didn't stop with adding a dash of juice. The Kool Bursts were engineered to evoke the image of fresh fruit in as many ways as possible: They were made in a variety of imitation fruit flavors, including cherry, grape, orange, and tropical punch, and they were given the most enticing imitation aromas that lab technicians could devise so that when the bottles were opened, they emitted powerful fruity smells. Even the bottles promulgated the mythology of health: Their plastic sides were embossed with the shapes of fruit. The managers promised the committee that these fruit-evoking attributes would appeal to kids and, most crucially, to their mothers. "To kids 6–12, Kool-Aid Kool Bursts is the brand of beverage that is the most fun," the managers said. "Fun means: the great taste of Kool-Aid, a burst of fruity aroma, and the most enjoyable package from which to drink. To moms, Kool Bursts is the brand of 'Fun Bottle' that they know their kids will love. Moms can feel better about Kool-Aid Kool Bursts because it's from a brand they trust."

The Philip Morris executives on the products committee had a few thoughts of their own, asking about the test marketing, and wondered if each fruity flavor should have its own matching-colored bottle. Then they authorized the beverage team to spend $25 million on an initial advertising campaign, which sent the Kool Bursts on their way to eclipsing the Squeezit with $110 million in first-year sales. By 1992, Philip Morris was touting its success to its stockholders, noting that the beverage division was showing "excellent" results "fueled by the national introduction of Kool-Aid Kool Bursts."

Kool Bursts only whetted the company's appetite for the marketing power of fruit, and fortunately for Philip Morris, the acquisition of General Foods had given it the means to fulfill that desire. It now had possession of the largest and most advanced research center in the processed food industry, and at the very moment the products committee was green-lighting Bursts, the scientists at this facility were putting the finishing touches on a remarkable bit of chemistry that sweetened the taste of sugar.

The facility was known as the Technical Center. It had been built by General Foods in 1957 to replace the old and crowded labs in Hoboken, where Al Clausi had invented instant Jell-O pudding a decade earlier. The new center consisted of four three-story buildings and was situated on a beautiful, sprawling campus near Tarrytown, New York, twenty-five miles north of Manhattan. Nine hundred people worked at the center, including 530 scientists and their staff, all devoted to pioneering research in food. Each of the major brands had its own crew and spacious laboratory. The Jell-O group lived on the second floor of Building Two. Maxwell House was on the top floor in Building Three, where it was joined by Kool-Aid in a suite of adjacent rooms.

On rare occasions, the technical center was opened to visitors who were treated to demonstrations of what science was doing for modern processed food: the creation of artificial flavorings, the process of ridding fats of their natural odors, and the engineering that allowed for high-speed production in factories. During one such open house in 1977, guests at Kool-Aid's lab in Bay D-365 were told, "You can 'taste for yourself' why a balanced flavor system is important in powdered soft drinks, and you'll find out why there is a close relationship between color and flavor recognition in beverages." The center was a fun house of illusion and discovery for the technicians, overlaid by the excitement of seeing their experiments turned into blockbuster commercial products.

One such achievement came in 1990, when a small group of researchers set out to improve on a keystone of processed foods: sugar. At the time, manufacturers had many ways to sweeten their products: corn syrup, dextrose, inverted syrup, malt, molasses, honey, and table sugar in granulated, powdered, and liquid form. They typically mixed and matched these various forms to achieve maximum allure at minimum cost. The chemical formulations of most of these sugars, however, have a key component in common: fructose. Fructose is a white crystalline compound of twelve hydrogen molecules sandwiched by six carbon and six oxygen, and it has one overarching quality that generated considerable excitement in the Kool-Aid labs. By itself, fructose is much sweeter than the sugar in sugar bowls.

The precise role of pure fructose in commercial sweeteners is still widely misunderstood. Table sugar, whose formal name is sucrose, is half fructose and half glucose. Likewise, the sweetener known as high-fructose corn syrup, in its most common formulation, is also roughly half fructose and half glucose. (In its earliest incarnations, back in the mid-1960s, the syrup had higher levels of fructose, thus the name.)

Fructose in its pure form was discovered by a French chemist in 1847, and 140 years later this white, odorless crystalline solid would prove to be a boon for the food industry. In the late 1980s, a commercial version called crystalline fructose first appeared on the market, and salesmen pitched it to food manufacturers as an additive with a variety of wondrous technological powers. Pure fructose is highly soluble but does not decompose as readily as other sugars, so it can remain effective for the long shelf life that processed foods demand. It resists forming crystals, which helps keep food like soft cookies from hardening. When baked, it delivers an alluring aroma and a crisp, brown surface that mimics the finish achieved in cooking at home, and when frozen, it blocks the formation of ice. As a result, fructose started turning up in a whole range of foods, from yogurt to ice cream, cookies to breads. The annual production reached 240,000 tons.

The true power of fructose, however, lay in its sweetening powers. It is far sweeter than glucose, the other component of table sugar. On a relative scale, with the sweetness of table sugar marked as 100, glucose clocks in at 74, while fructose hits 173.

When the fructose salesmen called on General Foods, the beverage division was intrigued, but there was a problem. Fructose is very sensitive to water. This poses no trouble in syrup, but when fructose is left in its dry form, the slightest exposure to the moisture in air will cause it to cake. A packet or jar of Kool-Aid, in other words, would quickly become a brick. At the Technical Center in Tarrytown, the small group of researchers—who called themselves the "Fructose Team"—was tasked with developing a noncaking fructose.

One of its members was Fouad Saleeb, an Egyptian-born chemist who amassed so many inventions in his three decades at General Foods that he became known as the "Patent King." Making fructose waterproof was one of his more exhilarating challenges. He kept it from getting moist by adding starch, and then used agents like calcium citrate, tricalcium phosphate, and silicon dioxide to prevent the caking. "It took us maybe two or three months to develop the anti-caking materials," he told me. "With the rigid quality controls, we had to keep it for twelve more weeks at the highest temperatures to be 100 percent sure it was stable."

Saleeb had to come up with one more invention before the company could put this noncaking process to work with Kool-Aid. General Foods needed to buy vast sums of raw fructose to keep pace with its production of powdered drinks, and the dilemma was how to store all that fructose before the anti-caking agents could be added. So Saleeb designed a gigantic diaper-like device to slip over the silos where it was stored to keep the moisture out. General Foods was now ready to reap the benefits of waterproof fructose, their new supersugar.

First, it allowed the company to cut back on the sugar in its powdered drinks by 10 percent or more, which would mean lower production costs and higher profits. In 1990, a General Foods manager named Toni Nasrallah estimated that this move alone would increase profits by $3.7 million each year. And second, the lower sugar content gave the company a way to tout its formulas as drinks that are good for you. As Nasrallah wrote in a presentation to Philip Morris executives, Tang could now be advertised as having "10 percent less sugar with more orange flavor." And Kool-Aid could be made more attractive to moms with a similar claim: "25 percent less sugar than Coke or Pepsi."

The lower-sugar claim would hold up only if consumers—often little kids—carefully measured their scoops of powdered Kool-Aid according to the label's instructions. Still, reducing the sugar in products would seem like a solid step toward better nutrition and higher sales, given the bad rap that sugar was getting. The FDA was still unwilling to ascribe anything worse to sugar than tooth decay. But in 1990, the same year that General Foods developed its noncaking waterproof fructose, sugar was coming under attack from a variety of quarters. A Yale study made headlines for finding that children who were given two cupcakes suffered a tenfold increase in adrenaline and exhibited abnormal behavior. Separately, the World Health Organization proposed changing its nutritional guidelines to lower the recommended daily levels of sugar to 10 percent of a person's caloric intake, citing various research that suggested links between sugar and diabetes, cardiovascular disease, and obesity.

The WHO eventually withdrew that proposal after taking withering fire from the food industry, but sugar's reputation sunk lower still as researchers launched an even more worrisome line of inquiry, linking sugar to addictive substances. In 1993, at the University of Michigan, a scientist named Adam Drewnowski took a fresh approach in examining the problem of bingeing, or compulsive overeating. Drewnowski knew there were links between sugar and addiction to opiates; studies showed, for instance, that sweets sometimes eased the pain of withdrawal. So he treated his subjects as if they were drug addicts. He gave them a drug that counters the effect of opiates; called naloxone, this drug is given to people who overdose. Drewnowski then offered his subjects a variety of snacks—ranging from popcorn, which was low in sugar, to chocolate chip cookies, which were loaded with sugar, as well as fat. His findings: The drug worked best in curbing the appeal of the snacks that were highest in both.

If anything, high-fructose corn syrup has a worse reputation among consumers, though the issue should not be whether eating too much of the syrup is worse for one's health than table sugar—experts now agree they are equally bad. Rather, at a time consumers were trying to cut their sugar consumption, food companies doubled down on the syrup—it's cheap and convenient for manufacturing—which drove the production of soda and snacks to record heights.

Despite all the scrutiny, however, pure fructose has largely gotten a free pass—until now. New research on fructose is raising concern. (Nutrition science, it needs to be stressed, is generally far less authoritative than studies that involve rigorous, months-long trials, such as those for pharmaceuticals, so these studies on fructose, like those on sugar, should be viewed with caution.) In 2011 an independent group of researchers at the University of California at Davis reported on their examinations of pure fructose and they made what could be a significant find: In a two-week trial, they sequestered young adults in a lab to track their eating more accurately and gave them a drink at each meal alternately sweetened by glucose, fructose, or corn syrup. The glucose group emerged largely unscathed, but those who got the fructose or corn syrup beverages experienced a 25 percent jump in their triglycerides, LDL cholesterol, and a fat-binding protein, all markers for heart disease.

Kraft, when I asked about this new research, said fructose is considered safe by regulatory officials, but that it would "continue to monitor the research and respond to any regulatory recommendations that result." John White, a veteran sugar industry researcher who helped develop sweeteners including high-fructose corn syrup, said he, too, is waiting for more studies to be done before rendering a verdict on how fructose might be affecting the American diet. "The testing has involved high concentrations of fructose, so I think it's premature to point at fructose," he told me. Still, where fructose was once hailed as the innocent nectar of fruits, it is now looming large as a health concern at least as great as table sugar.

When it comes to flying under the public's radar, however, even fructose can't match the spectacular PR that food companies have garnered for a sweetener known as "fruit juice concentrate." Typically made from grapes and pears, with a huge global market, this concentrate is now being added to a staggering array of products, from fruit leather to pastries to cereal to almost any sweet product that the manufacturer wants to link to the healthy image of fruit.

Juice concentrate is made through an industrial process that is highly variable, including any or all of the following steps: peeling the fruit, thereby removing much of the beneficial fiber and vitamins; extracting the juice from the pulp, which loses even more of the fiber; removing the bitter compounds; adjusting the sweetness through varietal blending; and evaporating the water out of the juice. At its extreme, the process results in what is known within the industry as "stripped juice," which is basically pure sugar, almost entirely devoid of the fiber, flavors, aromas, and or any of the other attributes we associate with real fruit. In other words, the concentrate is reduced to just another form of sugar, with no nutritional benefit over table sugar or high-fructose corn syrup. Rather, its value lies in the healthy image of fruit that it retains. "The advantage that the fruit juice concentrate people have from a marketing standpoint is this product appears on labels in a very healthy context," White, the industry scientist, told me. A company like General Foods can use this stuff and still put the comforting words *contains real fruit* on the box.

General Foods was not the first to recognize the marketing potential of fruit concentrate in processed foods, but it used this supersugar to great effect in one of its biggest moneymakers: a "fruit drink" called Capri Sun, which Philip Morris acquired in 1991 for $155 million. Five years later, in what Geoffrey Bible praised as a "staggering" achievement, the drink reached $230 million in annual sales, with a volume that was rising a spectacular 26 percent each year. A portion of this success was due to some technical heroics in the factory, where engineers figured out how to retool the manufacturing process to cycle more quickly through the drink's twenty-one flavors, which greatly enhanced productivity and the bottom line. But there was more to it than that. Like Kool-Aid and Tang, Capri Sun was sweetened mainly by high-fructose corn syrup, but it also now contained juice concentrate, which allowed the drink's label to boast, for the first time, "Natural fruit drink. No artificial ingredients." This was a huge selling point for moms who, as a result, felt more comfortable adding the drink to their kids' school lunches and snacks.

I asked Capri Sun's former brand manager, Paul Halladay, whether the drink's formula could have been altered to avoid using the fruit concentrate without changing the taste. "Yes, you could do that," he told me. "It was not a major part of the sweetener. But Capri Sun has always had some fruit concentrate. It helps with the validity of the 'natural' in the advertising to have the natural in there."

"Kraft has always taken pride in labeling its products clearly and accurately and in a manner that is not misleading to consumers," a company spokeswoman told me. "The nutritional information resulting from the addition of real fruit juice and use of the natural claim was in keeping with the labeling regulations." But Capri Sun's use of "natural" in its marketing would come under fire in 2007, when a Florida grandmother named Linda Rex picked up a case for a young relative visiting from Ireland. "When I saw 'All Natural' on the label, that sounded healthier than soda," she said. "But when I got home and got out my glasses, I threw it in the garbage, when I realized it contained high-fructose corn syrup and was nearly identical to soda." Some of Capri Sun's flavors, in fact, were higher in sugar than soda. Wild Cherry, for instance, had 28 grams of sugar—more than six teaspoons—in each 6.76-ounce pouch. Coke, in its larger 12-ounce can, has 39 grams—28 percent less per ounce. Working with an attorney for the Center for Science in the Public Interest, Rex sued Kraft for deceptive marketing. Eighteen days later, Kraft announced it would replace the words *all natural* with the phrase *no artificial colors, flavors, or preservatives*, and thanked the group for its work in resolving the matter. Kraft later set out to reduce the drink's sugar load to 16 grams, the company said.

Whether Kraft lost any sales from these concessions, however, is not clear. It was projecting a 5 percent drop in 2008 due to a variety of factors, but a new advertising campaign —"Respect the Pouch"—aimed at making the drink cooler with six- to twelve-year-olds, sent consumption soaring again by more than 17 percent. But Capri Sun has been helped by another scheme, which was first deployed back in the 1990s, and this was an idea that the Philip Morris executives could claim as their own.

When Philip Morris acquired General Foods and Kraft, its executives were faced with one overriding challenge: They knew almost nothing about processed foods. Moreover, the people who ran these two food giants disliked and distrusted one another. Their operating styles could not have been more different. General Foods, with its throngs of food scientists, was cerebral and painstaking in the way it rolled out products or adjusted its marketing to exploit consumer-driven trends like fiber or low-fat. One former Kraft executive who started out with General Foods described the latter as Ancient Greece, studied and cultured and not especially keen on warfare. By contrast, he viewed Kraft as the imperial Roman army on a brutal march to conquer the world. It boasted a powerful lineup of mega-brands and ever-changing fast food sensibilities. Its president, Michael Miles, was a former executive at Leo Burnett, the advertising agency, and chairman of Kentucky Fried Chicken. Shortly after arriving at Kraft, he recruited a number of Ivy League MBAs and Procter & Gamble executives to add to Kraft's skills. They did things like increase prices and advertising simultaneously to take the lead over competitors. Following the merger, Miles was made CEO of the combined food divisions, and he brought the top executives from both companies to Key West for three days of team building. By the end of 1990, however, the merger looked more like an acquisition by Kraft: Only two of the thirty-five executives who remained had come from General Foods.

The Philip Morris executives, led by CEO Hamish Maxwell, had an easygoing management style that might have made them more partial to the reserved manners at General Foods, but they valued even more the revenue gains from Kraft. Their answer to merging these two "nation-companies" as smoothly as possible was to send Geoffrey Bible to the Kraft headquarters near Chicago and have him show the way. His rallying cry was "synergy," and Philip Morris had some strategies of its own to offer on this front. In the coming months, the vast sums that Philip Morris spent advertising tobacco won discounted ad rates for the company's Miller beer; products were jointly promoted, such as cigarettes and Post cereals in the Virginia Slims tennis tour; and the pacts that Marlboro had with 7-Eleven stores leveraged the sale of an extra $20 million a year in Oscar Mayer hot dogs. Philip Morris also made sure that the technicians and brand managers throughout its empire talked to one another to share the secrets of their marketing triumphs.

"The concept of 'synergy' derives from the powerful idea that two or more entities have greater strengths combined than they could ever claim apart," Bible told Kraft managers at a strategy meeting in late 1990. "That's certainly true of the family of companies represented here today. If the tremendous creative resources of KGF*, Miller and the Philip Morris companies can be brought together to interact on behalf of understanding the consumer—power can be released on the market unlike any of us could do on our own. That's our mission for this conference, in a nutshell. To start a chain reaction of synergy throughout this corporation. A chain reaction whose ultimate goal is to better understand the men and women who buy our products."

Nowhere did this message resonate more loudly than in the beverage division. By 1996, the company's fruity drinks—created by General Foods but now marketed by Kraft—were dominating a large stretch of the beverage aisle. Not only had their annual sales moved to the cusp of the hallowed mark of $1 billion, Kool-Aid and the company's other brands were now in solid third place behind the titans of soda, Coke and Pepsi.

The beverage managers at Kraft fully embraced the concept of synergy in responding to Bible's call to better understand and target the consumer. In the summer of 1996, they were back in front of the Corporate

* The combined food entities were known as Kraft General Foods before becoming just Kraft Foods in 1995.

Products Committee at Philip Morris, presenting a detailed account of their victories. The meeting minutes, in turn, reflect the celebratory air, with the tobacco executives doling out nothing but praise.

"The Beverage division, consisting of seven core trademarks, is approaching the one billion mark in both pound volume and revenue," one of the Philip Morris executives who attended the meeting, Nancy Lund, wrote in the minutes. "1995 was a turning point, 1996 is on track for a record year."

The details of this accomplishment were presented to the committee by James Craigie, a Harvard-trained MBA who had joined Kraft thirteen years earlier and risen to executive vice president and head of beverages, and they offer a window on more than just Kraft's efforts to accelerate its sales. The beverage division's work reflected the culmination of the food industry's decades-long love affair with sugar and the cunning developed by processed food managers, whether gleaned from laboratory experiments or the war rooms of marketing experts. All of this skill and resourcefulness was channeled into a colossal, sustained push to remake and exploit one of the America's biggest dietary habits: the nonalcoholic drink.

To achieve their gains, the Kraft beverage managers went into the suburbs, where the principal target was moms who had grown worried about the health implications of sugar. They rolled out products whose formulations were still guaranteed to generate bliss, but with fruit motifs that disguised the sugar as something more nourishing. One such new line for Kool-Aid, called Island Twists, "received extremely high scores from Moms who found the real fruit flavors to be very wholesome," the presentation to the products committee said. They handily beat, by more than two to one, the sales of Snapple, then owned by rival Quaker Oats.

Having reached the moms, the beverage division went after African Americans next, targeting their preferences. It used pinpoint-accurate studies of black consumers to nail down their likes and dislikes and then adjusted the company's advertising accordingly. "Consumer research has revealed that African Americans like to customize their Kool-Aid by adding fruit or mixing flavors," so the marketing division used this "consumer insight" to produce a more effective marketing theme: "How do you like your Kool-Aid?"

Kraft then went into supermarkets with new clever strategies to increase the power of their displays. Each April, in grocery stores throughout the country, the company's sales force installed thirty-thousand stand-alone racks with five shelves each and a banner on top to display their drinks, towering over the aisle to draw the shopper's attention. These usually stayed up only for the summer, when sales for sugary drinks peaked. But Kraft convinced the stores to keep these racks up—and extend America's sugary drink habit—until winter by agreeing to share the shelf space on the racks with puddings and other desserts from their sister divisions.

The urban centers of America don't have many supermarkets, so there the drink managers focused their efforts on corner stores, which are laid out like traps for the unwary. Kraft had to work hard to get its drinks on the shelves, since it didn't deliver directly to the stores like Coke and Pepsi did through their "up and down the street" campaigns. On this front, however, Kraft had its own secret weapon, borrowed straight from Philip Morris. The beverage division hit the phones to call these stores and sell the owners on the virtues of carrying Kraft's drinks, first and foremost among which was their low pricing to suit the low incomes of their customers. But they didn't leaf through the phone book; they used targeted lists prepared by the tobacco company in selling cigarettes—yet another example of the synergy Philip Morris had been advocating.

"Consumers in these stores represent prime prospects for our value-oriented brands, but have been inaccessible," the beverage division explained. "As such, we have leveraged Philip Morris' scale by utilizing their tobacco data base to develop a list of carefully selected stores to target via telemarketing. Our initial test of this program in the first quarter generated over $1 million" in added sales.

They even targeted people who may have overindulged on the company's drinks in the first place: diabetics, whose growing ranks were, ironically, opening up a hot market. Or, as the beverage division put it, this "targeted marketing effort involves new programs on our sugar-free brands that are focused against diabetics."

"Diabetics already represent 12 percent of the U.S. population and this figure is unfortunately expected to steadily grow as the large Baby Boomer segment ages," the committee was told. Unfortunate for those afflicted, perhaps, but not for sales of the company's artificially sweetened Crystal Light. "We believe there is significant untapped opportunity through advertising and promotion programs aimed at gaining trial with diabetics," which Kraft would leverage by combing the Crystal Light diabetic campaign with another developed for sugar free Jell-O.

Finally, they dusted off one of the early stars of processed foods, turning back to the first product General Foods created in the wake of the 1956 speech by its CEO, Charles Mortimer, who implored his food developers to get creative: Tang. With sales now flagging, Kraft drink managers aimed to rejuvenate the brand. They looked at the age of the people who drank Tang, and decided to go further than even Coke dared to go. Where Coca-Cola had drawn the line at age twelve in its pursuit of kids, Kraft went after a younger set. "We restaged the brand by changing our target consumer from Moms to Kids age 9–14, otherwise known as 'tweens,' " the report disclosed.

Lund, the Philip Morris executive who prepared the meeting minutes, summed up the Tang presentation in this way: "For Tang, it's a three-part restage—new target, new positioning and a fully loaded marketing plan."

Tang and Kool-Aid were among the highlights of this Corporate Products Committee meeting, which took place on June 24, 1996, but they were really just two among many. It turned into one of the committee's longest sessions ever, an all-day affair in midtown Manhattan. The morning started with Marlboro and the introduction of a new cigarette box in the brand's most recently captured territory: the kingdom of Nepal. Lunch was served as the beverage division delved into all its feats, and if that conversation was all about sugar—from its power to attract to the power of alternative sweeteners when sugar becomes overwhelming—what came next on the agenda was something else. This discussion moved on to frozen pizza, whose allure was now being enhanced by the addition of ever greater amounts of cheese, on top and in the crust, so as better to compete with the fast food pizza chains.

The fat in this cheese and a range of other foods in the Philip Morris portfolio would bump up against its own consumer backlash, for which the company managers would need all of their cunning and skill. Through the 1990s and beyond, fat would in some ways grow to be even more powerful than sugar, delivering untold riches to Philip Morris and other food manufacturers. It would also bring them some of their biggest troubles.

part two fat

chapter seven

"That Gooey, Sticky Mouthfeel"

There is a piece of lore, cherished among food scientists, that Aristotle was the first to explore our ability to detect flavors in food. This ability, called taste, is one of the five basic senses that include sight and smell, and the study he made of all of these senses was part of the remarkable observations on life that established him as a founding figure in Western philosophy. A student of Plato, who in turn had studied under Socrates, Aristotle had been tutoring Alexander the Great and other future kings of ancient Greece in 335 B.C. when he established his own school in Athens known as the Lyceum. It was there, over the course of twelve years, that he is believed to have written his series of elegant treatises that ranged from physics to music, ethics to zoology, politics to poetry. Among these writings was *De Anima*, which examined the life force in plants and animals, and it was in this book that Aristotle attempted to parse the nature of taste. He was fond of creating lists, and first and foremost on his list of tastes was sweet, which he described as pure nourishment. The others that followed, which included bitter, salty, harsh, pungent, astringent, and acid, were mere "relish" that served as a counterbalance, "because the sweet is over-nutritive and swims on the stomach." The final entry in his lineup of basic tastes, however, was one whose power to generate pleasure was on par with sweet. Aristotle called this the "fat or oily."

Twenty-four centuries later, fat is seen as one of the most potent components of processed food, a pillar ingredient even more powerful than sugar. As Aristotle pointed out, fat is indeed oily, in some of its forms. Canola, soy, olive, corn, and the other oils are all liquid fats, viscous and flowing, easily spotted and identifiable as fat. In other cases, fat in our food is a solid at room temperatures, and not readily recognized. A hunk of cheddar cheese is one-third fat, along with protein, salt, and a little sugar, and even that statistic understates the force that fat brings to food. Two-thirds of the calories in that cheese are delivered by the fat, which packs more than twice the energy of sugar.

When it comes to divining the allure that it brings to food, however, the taste of fat is a bit harder to pin down. It is not part of our official roster of primary tastes, which currently consists of just five members: sweet, salty, sour, bitter, and a more recent addition known as umami, which is a meaty, savory taste derived from an amino acid called glutamate. Some food researchers have argued for adding fat to the list of five primary tastes, but they face one substantial hurdle: The entry rules for this group requires that scientists know how each taste interacts with our taste buds, and no one has yet figured this out when it comes to fat. All the other tastes have receptors in the taste buds that have been identified and labeled as their hosts. It is through these receptors that the sweet taste and other flavors get delivered to the brain.

No such receptor for fat has been found.

And yet, because of fat's remarkable powers, the processed food industry relies on it like no other component. Fat turns listless chips into crunchy marvels, parched breads into silky loaves, drab lunchmeat into savory delicatessen. Like sugar, some types of fat furnish processed foods with one of their most fundamental requirements: the capacity to sit on the grocery store shelf for days or months at a time. Fat also gives cookies more bulk and a firmer texture. It substitutes for water in lending tenderness and mouthfeel to crackers. It lessens the rubbery texture in hot dogs, deepens their color, keeps them from sticking to the grill, and, as an added bonus, saves the manufacturers money, since the fattier trimmings of meat they use in making hot dogs cost less to buy than the leaner cuts. Indeed, the entire hamburger industry—which turns out seven billion pounds or more of ground beef each year—revolves around fat. Hamburger is a mixture of beef carcass trimmings that are purchased from slaughterhouses through-out the world, based on their fat content. The fattiest scraps are called "fifty-fifties," as in half fat and half protein, and these are mixed and matched with less fatty cuts, like "ninety-tens," to achieve the desired fat level in the final ground beef. When retailers like Walmart place their or-ders for ground beef from the meat companies that make the hamburger, they do so by specifying the fat content, which ranges between 5 and 30 percent. Surprisingly, fat is even the key determinant of the nutritional value of ground beef. The Department of Agriculture has a handy online calculator, and depending on the percentage of fat that is entered, the levels of calcium, niacin, iron, and other elements in the meat go up or down—as do, of course, the loads of saturated fat, which is the type of fat associated with heart disease.

Fat also performs a range of culinary tricks for food manufacturers, thanks to another of its extraordinary powers. It can mask and convey other flavors in foods, all at the same time. This can be seen in a dollop of sour cream, which has acidic components that, by themselves, don't taste so great. Fat coats the tongue to keep the taste buds from getting too large a hit of these acids. Then, this same oily coating reverses direction, and in-stead of acting as a shield, it stimulates and prolongs the tongue's absorp-tion of the sour cream's more subtle and aromatic flavors, which, of course, is what the food makers want the taste buds to convey to the brain. This act of delivering other flavors is one of fat's most valued functions.

Fat has a final trait, however, that makes it even more essential than sugar in processed foods. Fat doesn't blast away at our mouths like sugar does; by and large, its allure is more surreptitious. As I spoke with scientists about the way fat behaves, I couldn't resist drawing an analogy to the realm of narcotics. If sugar is the methamphetamine of processed food ingredients, with its high-speed, blunt assault on our brains, then fat is the opiate, a smooth operator whose effects are less obvious but no less powerful.

Aristotle's observations in taste were all the more remarkable given how poorly he actually understood the mechanics of the human body. He rejected the concept of the brain as the mind's organ, which his teacher Plato had embraced, and chose instead to view the brain as a regulator of the heart's temperature. The heart, by his estimation, played the starring role in matters both physical and psychological; some scholars believe he even saw the heart as the primary organ of taste, with the tongue a mere facilitator. Today, of course, scientists are turning to the brain to understand the allure in food and our ability, or lack thereof, to control our consumption. Some of the more intriguing studies on this subject have emerged from Oxford University in England, where a neuroscientist named Edmund Rolls has been investigating, to put it broadly, how the brain processes information. Rolls is not a food scientist, though some of his work on the brain's role in thirst and appetite has been funded by Unilever, the global food giant based in England. Rather, he roams widely through the field of brain research, using medical imaging machinery to monitor the brain's responses to various stimuli. In 2003, he published on the results from an experiment in which he charted the brain's response to two substances: sugar and fat.

It was already well established that the ingestion of sugar will light up the nucleus accumbens and other areas of the brain that are collectively known as the reward centers, generating intense feelings of pleasure when we engage in acts of self-preservation like eating. Sugar's effect on the brain is so strongly and consistently exhibited in these studies that some scientists have come to see certain foods as potentially addictive. At a federal research facility in Long Island called the Brookhaven National Laboratory, scientists have studied the brain's reaction to processed foods and drugs like cocaine, and have concluded that some drugs achieve their allure, and addictive qualities, by following the same neurological channels that our bodies first developed for food. Where the Brookhaven scientists used foods that were sweet, or both sweet and fatty, in their studies, Rolls wanted to know whether fat *alone* had the same narcotic-like affect on the brain. He recruited a dozen adults, healthy and mildly hungry, having not eaten for three hours. One by one, they entered the tunnel of a functional magnetic resonance imaging machine, or fMRI. Once inside, they couldn't move their arms, so plastic tubes were placed in their mouths, through which they were fed a solution of sugar and another solution of vegetable oil. Purchased at a local supermarket, the oil was made from rapeseed, also known as canola, and came fully loaded with fat in all three of its basic modes: saturated, monounsaturated, and polyunsaturated. In addition to the sugar and fat solutions, a third served as the control by mimicking plain saliva.

As they tasted and swallowed, Rolls watched the machinery register their brain's response. As expected, the saliva generated no evident stimulus. No surprises with the sugar solution, either: It provoked a vivid response, with the images generated by the machine depicting the brain's electrical activity as patches of bright yellow. But the shock came when his subjects got hold of the fat: Their brain circuitry lit up just as brightly for the fat as it did for the sugar. Moreover, the images showed that this brain activity occurred precisely where neuroscientists would expect to see this activity. The sugar and fat stimulated areas of the brain associated with hunger and thirst, but they also lit up the reward center, which generates the feelings of pleasure. "Fat and sugar both produce strong reward effects in the brain," Rolls said when I asked him which was more potent, sugar or fat. It's a toss-up.

In recent years, some of the world's largest food manufacturers have been conducting brain research of their own to assess the depths of fat's allure. Unilever alone invested $30 million on a twenty-person team that used brain imaging and other advanced neurological tools to study the sensory powers of food, including fat. The scientist who led the Unilever team until recently, Francis McGlone, described its operations as a free-wheeling exploration of a rapidly expanding corner of science, where $3 million brain scanning devices and other neurological testing can reveal more about consumer likes and dislikes than companies could ever glean from focus groups. Unilever has a massive lineup of health and beauty aids, from Dove to Alberto VO5, as well as packaged food, from Ben & Jerry's to Knorr, and McGlone roamed across the whole range of products hunting for ways to improve upon them. For the most part, he sought to discover precisely what made certain groups so alluring. Like many specialists in basic science who go to work for food manufacturers, he brought with him the dispassionate language of researchers who see consumers as experimental subjects. "I went there to build a research focus that looked at the reward-based systems that underpin their business," he told me. "Their business was basically all feeding and grooming, involving 6.7 billion people or, in my view, 6.7 billion primates. And I saw feeding and grooming as very stereotypical human behaviors. There is not a lot to be gained from asking people *why* they like something, because they don't bloody know. These are very low-level processes that drive these fundamental behaviors, and I'd gotten into imaging because it's a good way to sort of bypass the mouth, if you like, so you can see just what the neural processes are underpinning a behavior."

McGlone didn't have to bother talking to his subjects; he could peer into their brains. And the discoveries made by his team underscored the complex and varied ways in which processed food can be made ultra-alluring. They explored all five of the basic senses. To examine the role that odor plays in foods, for example, they let their subjects smell a glass of Hershey's Chocolate Cookies 'n' Cream Milkshake, and found this excited the brain's pleasure zones just as if they were tasting the drink. To study the power of hearing, one of the team's scientists, Charles Spence, amplified the sound made by potato chips when they were eaten. This study—which won an Ig Nobel, the prize awarded to research that is brilliant but quirky—showed that the louder the noise, the deeper the allure; the noisiest chips were rated by test subjects as the freshest and crispiest. McGlone has studied how the mere sight of food can excite the brain.

Being the world's largest ice cream maker, with brands like Breyer's and Ben & Jerry's, Unilever itself got quite excited by his work on how the brain responds to the silky smooth fat and sugar in ice cream. This project started in 2005 when McGlone had a conversation with the company's research director for consumer insight. They determined there might be a substantial commercial payoff if he could establish that ice cream made people happy—through scientific methods, that is. So McGlone put eight graduate students in an MRI and then scanned their brains as an assistant tipped a spoon of vanilla ice cream onto their lips, letting it melt into their mouths. McGlone is a bit sheepish about the scientific weight of this experiment: He told me that he would never seek to publish the results, since there were too few subjects and too many variables to qualify as solid, peer-reviewed science. But the resulting images—which show the brain's pleasure centers lighting up as the subjects tasted the Unilever ice cream—thrilled the marketing arm of the company. "This is the first time that we've been able to show that ice cream makes you happy," a Unilever vice president, Don Darling, told a food industry publication. "Just one spoonful of Carte D'Or lights up the happy zones of the brain in clinical trials." Unilever released the results, generating a flurry of publicity for the company and its ice cream in news reports throughout the world including the U.S. media with the slogan: "Ice Cream Makes You Happy— It's Official!"

Even without these brain studies, however, food manufacturers have long understood the power of fat to make their products more attractive. The industry's reliance on the stuff runs so deep that suppliers of fat, like Cargill, hold training seminars. Based near Minneapolis, Cargill is one of the world's largest privately owned companies and a dominant provider of ingredients to food manufacturers. It sells seventeen types of sweeteners, forty types of salt, and twenty-one oils and shortenings, from coconut for spraying on snacks to palm for candies to peanut for deep-fat frying. In a recent presentation to food manufacturers who purchase its fats, a Cargill manager empathized when a customer asked for advice in reducing the amount of fat that snacks absorb in being fried.

Lessening the amount of fat in processed food—like reducing the sugar or salt—is no simple matter to the manufacturers. They can't allow this to diminish the taste or texture, or they will lose sales. Nor can they let a reduction in fat cause their production costs to rise too high, or they will lose profits. The X factor is often how much more money consumers are willing to spend for a healthier product. In this case, the Cargill manager pointed out, fiddling with the fat used for frying had serious implications for the bottom line of its customers. Sure, they could cut down on the fat in their foods. All they had to do was turn up the temperature of the oil. But the higher the temperature, the less often the oil can be reused before going bad, which would send the food manufacturers running back to Cargill more often for fresh oil. "It doesn't work all of the time, but the hotter the oil, the less absorption of the snack, in principle," the manager, Dan Lampert, said. "We like it because the hotter the oil, the more oil we sell. Just kidding."

In one respect, fat is considerably less powerful than the other two keystones of processed foods, sugar and salt. Fat's public image has always been horrid.

Sugar—at least until the surge in obesity in the 1980s—has been something that manufacturers have eagerly touted in their foods with a long list of charming euphemisms. The words *honeyed, sugarcoated, sweet, syrupy,* and *candied* were effective marketing tools in attracting consumers. More broadly, the word *sweet* was used to connote anything good, innocent, or attractive. Likewise, until blood pressure rates in America went up in the 1980s, salt had a favorable image, too, helped along by colloquialisms like, "the salt of the earth." Picture in your mind a hot pretzel with big white crystals of salt on top; your brain is probably, at this very moment, sending you signals of pleasure.

Now picture that same pretzel dipped in oil. That is not such a positive image, is it? There are some exceptions to this, to be sure. (What's a lobster without a dish of hot melted butter?) By and large, however, and for as long as anyone in the food industry can remember, fat has been saddled with more than its share of negativity. (No kid's grandmother will say to them with a pucker: "Give me some fat.") For starters, its lingo is deeply unappealing. If a food isn't "fatty," it's "greasy" or "oily" or "heavy." Even worse, fat in food is equated with fat on the body, and there is ample justification for this. Fat is an energy colossus. It packs 9 calories into each gram, more than twice the caloric load of either sugar or protein. Surveys have shown that grocery shoppers who stop to read nutrition labels look first and foremost at the fat content of foods. This has led to the proliferation of products that claim to have less fat or lower fat, and it has spurred a host of marketing tricks the industry uses to make it seem like they have cut back. Take milk, for instance. Through the 1960s, sales of milk plunged as it bore the brunt of public concerns about fat, both in terms of its calories and its links to heart disease. At the same time, however, the dairy industry figured out a way to soften this blow to their business by putting the phrases "low-fat" and "2 percent" on milk in which a little of the fat had been removed. The popularity of this defatted milk grew so fast that it now outsells all other types of milk, including skim, which has no fat at all. But there is a marketing scheme at work in this: The "2 percent" labeling may lead to you to believe that 98 percent of the fat is removed, but in truth the fat content of whole milk is only a tad higher, at 3 percent. Consumer groups who urge people to drink 1 percent or nonfat milk have fought unsuccessfully over the years to have the 2 percent claim barred as deceptive.

While fat's PR has suffered greatly, the food industry has privately treated fat as a cherished friend, one whose quirks and mysterious ways it has labored hard to understand and cultivate. At the General Foods research center in Tarrytown, New York, fat became the lifelong obsession of a Polish-born scientist named Alina Szczesniak, who retired in 1986. One of her more lasting contributions stemmed from her realization that fat, in one respect, is not about taste at all. Nor did people have to like the sight of oil pooling atop their pizza to be enthralled by what happens inside their mouths. Szczesniak was the first to grasp that fat is about feel, or texture, and that it is an enormously powerful force in processed food that often flies under our radar, drawing us in without the blaring horns that a dose of sugar or salt will set off in the mouth.

Part of Szczesniak's job involved evaluating new versions of products like Jell-O and imitation whipped cream toppings. She used ordinary citizens as guinea pigs, sitting them down in a room with some samples to taste and a rating chart to describe the textures. As she developed these tests, Szczesniak accumulated a long list of terms to describe the feel of fatty foods, including *smooth, firm, bouncy, wiggly, disappears, slippery, gummy, melts, moist, wet,* and *warm.* Her tasting system is still used today by manufacturers, and these textural attributes became known as the "mouthfeel" of fat. There is strong neurological science backing her up on this notion that fat is as much a feeling as it is a taste. We now know that we feel fat through a nerve called the trigeminal. This critical part of our anatomy hovers above and behind the mouth near the brain with tentacles that extract tactile information from the lips, gums, teeth, and jaw, which it then conveys to the brain. The trigeminal nerve is how we distinguish between sandy and smooth, and why grit in a salad causes us to cringe. When it comes to fat, it detects the enthralling crunch in fried chicken, the velvet in melting chocolate and premium ice cream, the creaminess in cheese. And it delivers these sensations with plenty of muscle, a recent brain study by Nestlé shows.

Nestlé, which has picked up on fat research where General Foods left off, has good reason to want to deepen its understanding of fat. Back when it was founded in the mid-1800s, the company had one product to worry about: milk chocolate. But today, Nestlé is a $100 billion global giant with a portfolio of processed foods and drinks that rely on fat, from Häagen-Dazs ice cream to Kit Kat bars to DiGiorno frozen pizzas, which have up to

8 grams of saturated fat in a single serving—half of the recommended daily maximum for adults.*

The indispensability of fat to Nestlé's balance sheets becomes all the more evident to the company whenever it tries to cut back. In the early 1980s, one of its food scientists, Steve Witherly, was trying to save the company money by lessening the amount of cheese in a sauce. He used substituting chemicals designed to impart a cheese-like tang, but the fat in cheese, he realized, provided more than just flavor. It gave the sauce its silky, rich texture, the mouthfeel that people wanted—and that was something no chemical could replicate. "We were always trying to make it cheaper," he told me, "but people could always detect if we started messing around with the cheese. It's the texture of cheese sauce people go crazy for. That gooey, sticky mouthfeel, kind of like a peanut buttery mouthfeel that really made people want to be on my taste panels. Something about the cheese made people go nuts."

At Nestlé's research and development center near Geneva, Switzerland, the scientists include a German-trained biophysicist named Johannes Le Coutre who is currently using some of the same brain-mapping science that academic centers like Oxford employ. His tools include electroencephalography, or EEG, in which a net of electrodes is affixed to the head to explore how the brain responds to various stimuli. In 2008, he wired up fifteen adults to an EEG machine and showed them pictures of foods that were either low or high in fat. At first, he wanted to see if their brains would recognize the difference, and they did. But then he made another noteworthy discovery. He timed the signals given off by the food pictures, and found that they raced to the brain in a mere 200 milliseconds. The brain was identifying fat with incredible speed. In his quest to learn more, Le Coutre rounded up fifty of his colleagues in industry and academia and asked them to help produce an "all known facts" compendium on fat. Published in 2010 with 609 pages, the resulting book, *Fat Detection: Taste,*

---

* In 2010, the USDA's panel of experts who set dietary guidelines issued a new standard calling for saturated fat not to exceed 7 percent of total calories, about 15.6 grams in a 2,000-calorie-a-day diet. The average intake is about 11 percent to 12 percent.

Texture, and Post Ingestive Effects, serves as a roadmap for companies looking to harness the power of fat in their food and drink. "Why is fat so tasty?" Le Coutre asks in the introduction. "Why do we crave it, and what is the impact of dietary fat on health and disease?"

To answer the part about craving, the book turned to an American scientist who had made an intriguing discovery about sugary chocolate chip cookies—that the compulsion to overindulge these and other sweets could be suppressed by the same drug that doctors use to block and counter the effects of heroin. This was one of the earliest pieces of evidence that obesity had parallels to drug addiction, but this scientist, Adam Drewnowski, has been making equally important discoveries about the role that fat alone plays in driving people to eat.

Drewnowski's work has been pioneering in several areas of nutrition science, including the links between the epidemic of obesity and processed foods. A professor of epidemiology at the University of Washington at Seattle, he directs the school's Center for Obesity Research. In recent years, he has focused on the economics of eating, studying the factors that make processed foods more attractive than fresh fruits and vegetables, and the decisions people make in choosing what to put on the table. "I want to know where people compromise," he said. "You have to take into account the cost, but there are other constraints. When you have kids, the question becomes, *What can I buy that won't cost much, that the kids will eat, and that won't take long to prepare?* Beans and eggs have good nutritional value at low cost, but you have to cook them. Most veggies are going to be more expensive, though not potatoes and carrots. For them, the question becomes, How many dishes can you cook with potatoes and carrots before you say, 'Kentucky Fried is not so bad after all'? My other question is, At what point is not wanting to feel hungry going to outweigh the nutritional value of the product? Such as tomatoes, at two dollars a pound. They are nutritious but won't keep me satisfied. And here is a pizza. It's not nutritious, but I know I will be full at the end. This all gets much starker in looking at a big bag of potato chips versus veggies."

Drewnowski started asking questions about fat in 1982. He had a degree in biochemistry from Oxford, and he was hunting for something to focus on as a doctoral student in mathematical psychology at the prestigious Rockefeller University in New York City. The field of nutrition, in which he was interested, was a close-knit world where everyone kept tabs on each other's work. He knew that his peers had already trammeled the ground on sugar: He followed the progress that Howard Moskowitz had made in pinpointing the bliss point for sweet taste, and he had read the scientific papers that Szczesniak at General Foods had written on the texture of fat, and he had seen the rating system she devised that many food scientists used. In fat, however, he saw an area of research that remained largely uncharted. No one had yet tried to measure with any precision just how alluring it really was. To the contrary, he noticed that scientists who were studying food cravings were making a mistake that could be obscuring the power of fat. They wrongly identified things like candy bars as sugary foods, when in fact they were also loaded with fat. "I came to the realization that most of the 'sugary foods' in our diets were not just pure sugar," he told me. "They were really linked up with fat."

Drewnowski devised an experiment. Sixteen undergraduates, eleven women and five men, were given twenty different mixtures of milk, cream, and sugar. He then asked them how much they liked each combination; to sort out their answers, he used his math skills and an early-model computer. (His partner on the 1983 study, M. R. C. Greenwood, went on to have her own illustrious career that included a stint in the White House as associate director for science.) Two significant findings emerged from the data. Drewnowski knew about the bliss point for sugar, how our liking for sugary concentrations goes only so far; after a point—known as the break point—adding more sugar only lessens the appeal.

"But there was no bliss point, or break point, for fat," Drewnowski told me. The sixteen people in his experiment never once cried uncle in working their way through the increasingly fatty mixtures. The fat, no matter how rich the food, was so pleasing to their brains that they never gave the signal to stop eating. Their bodies wanted more and more fat. "The more fat there was, the better," he said. "If there was a break point, it was somewhere beyond heavy cream."

The second finding concerned the relationship the fat had with sugar. He found that the heaviest cream tasted even better to his subjects when he added a little sugar. There was something about this combination that created a powerful interplay. They boosted one another to levels of allure that neither could reach alone.

Given the vast numbers of products on grocery shelves that are loaded with sugar and fat, Drewnowski assumes that the processed food industry was already aware of this synergy, if only in broad, practical terms. Still, being an inquisitive type, he had yet more questions to ask and answer. Was the brain just being the body's servant in extreme gluttony, seeing fat as the best way to store energy for emergencies down the road? Or was there something else going on between the sugar and fat? A few years later, Drewnowski had fifty college students taste and rate fifteen different formulations of cake frosting in which the sugar and fat content was varied. The tasters were able to taste and quantify the sugar content of each sample quite accurately, but not the fat content; the participants in his study found it difficult to detect its presence with any precision at all. On top of that, when sugar was added to the fattier formulations, the students mistakenly thought the fat had been *reduced*. In effect, the fat had gone into hiding. This meant the food manufacturers could use fat as an allure in their products without ever having to worry about a backlash from people's brains, which they do with abandon. Many soups, cookies, potato chips, cakes, pies, and frozen meals deliver half or more of their calories through fat, and yet consumers won't identify these as fatty foods, which is great for sales. For some extra insurance on this, all the manufacturers have to do is add a little sugar.

Drewnowski published his study, "Invisible Fats," in 1990, and it showed that fat was a double-edged sword when wielded by the processed food industry. In certain circumstances and with certain foods, manufacturers might be able to reduce the fat content without causing a significant drop in the product's allure. (Depending on the product, adding more sugar might be needed to maintain the allure.) On the other hand, these same manufacturers could crank up the fat content as high as they wanted, and unless people studied the nutrition label carefully, the fat would get eaten in bliss without setting off any alarms in the body's system that help regulate our weight by telling us we are eating too much.

"A dish or a drink could be very high in fat and people wouldn't be aware of it," Drewnowski said. "So it can cut both ways. Good if you're reducing fat, and not so good if the diet is already heavy in fat and people aren't aware of it. Fat is trickier than sugar. My point, back when I did my studies, was that in these mixtures of sugar and fat you find in so many products, most of the calories come from fat. I had this disagreement years ago with researchers who were working on the hypothesis that obesity is caused by carbohydrates, which is what sugar is. They were using things like Snickers bars and chocolate M&Ms and thinking, 'A-ha, sweet foods, carbohydrates.' And my point was, yes, they *are* sweet, and there *is* sugar in them. But they are not carbohydrate foods—60 to 70 to 80 percent of their calories was coming from fat. The fat was invisible, even to the investigators themselves."

chapter eight

"Liquid Gold"

Dean Southworth was enjoying a quiet retirement in Florida after thirty-eight years as a food scientist for Kraft. He and his wife, Betty, were living in a modest house in the palm-lined island town of Fort Myers Beach, smack between the inlet that runs to Estero Bay, with its luscious sunrises, and the Gulf of Mexico, with its magnificent sunsets. Southworth, finally, had the time to take in both. During his years at Kraft, he had spent long days trying to develop new products, trying to stay ahead of the competition. Now, he did things like take long walks and help run the local Kiwanis Club. He hadn't abandoned his previous life completely, though. Whenever he got the urge, which was quite often, he would enjoy the fruits of one of his finest inventions: the spread known as Cheez Whiz.

Southworth had been part of the team that created Cheez Whiz in the early 1950s. The mission had been to come up with a speedy alternative to the cheese sauce used in making Welsh rarebit, a popular but laborious dish that required a half-hour or more of cooking before it could be poured over toast. It took them a year and a half of sustained effort to get the flavor right, but when they did, they succeeded in creating one of the first mega-hits in convenience foods. Southworth and his wife, Betty, became life-long fans and made it part of their daily routine. "We used it on toast, muffins, baked potatoes," he told me. "It was a nice spreadable, with a nice flavor. And it went well at night with crackers and a little martini. It went down very, very nicely, if you wanted to be civilized."

So it was with considerable alarm that he turned to his wife one eve-ning in 2001, having just sampled a jar of Cheez Whiz he'd picked up at the local Winn-Dixie supermarket. "I said, 'Holy God, it tastes like axle grease.' I looked at the label and I said, 'What the hell did they do?' I called up Kraft, using the 800 number for consumer complaints, and I told them, 'You are putting out a goddamn axle grease!' "

Cheez Whiz was already something of a horror to nutritionists. A sin-gle serving, which Kraft defined as just two level tablespoons, delivered nearly a third of a day's recommended maximum of saturated fat as well as a third of the *maximum* sodium recommended for a majority of American adults. Sit down with a drink in front of the TV and start heaping it onto salty, buttery crackers, and both daily limits would quickly be blown.

As for its taste, Southworth conceded that the spread had never been in the same league as a fine English Stilton. But it hadn't pretended, even *wanted* to be. In the laboratories at Kraft, in fact, Cheez Whiz had been designed to have the mildest flavor possible for the broadest public appeal. Upon its release on July 1, 1953, the advertising emphasized its expedi-ency, not its taste: "Cheese treats QUICK. Spoon it, heat it, spread it."

Nonetheless, in his kitchen that day, Southworth knew that something had changed. Staring at the label, parsing the list of ingredients, he even-tually found the culprit, though not without some effort. There were twenty-seven items listed in all, starting with the watery by-product of milk called whey, taking him through canola oil, corn syrup, and an additive called milk protein concentrate, which manufacturers had begun import-ing from other countries as a cost-cutting alternative to the higher-priced powdered milk produced by American dairies. One crucial ingredient was missing, however. From its earliest days, Cheez Whiz always contained real cheese. Real cheese gave it class and legitimacy, Southworth said, not to mention flavor. Now, he discovered, not only was cheese no longer prominently listed as an ingredient, it wasn't listed at all.

Not surprisingly, Kraft kept this change to itself. I couldn't find any public discussion of it even nine years later, when Southworth related his story to me. So during a visit to Kraft's headquarters in 2011, I asked if he was right, if Kraft in fact had taken the cheese out of Cheez Whiz. Actually, a spokeswoman told me, there was still some cheese left in the formula, just not as much as there used to be. When I asked how much, she declined to say. It no longer appeared on the label, she added, because Kraft—in attempting to simplify its long lists of ingredients—had switched from citing components, like cheese, to listing their parts, like milk. "We made adjustments in dairy sourcing that resulted in less cheese being used," she told me. "However, with any reformulation, we work hard to ensure that the product continues to deliver the taste that our consumers expect."

Southworth was more blunt in his assessment of what happened to his creation. "I imagine it's a marketing and profit thing," he said. "If you don't have to use cheese, which has to be kept in storage for a certain length of time in order to become usable, flavor-wise and texture-wise, then you've eliminated the cost of storage, and there is more to the profit center."

Southworth's grievance was surely heartfelt; he even phoned his food-scientist friends who still worked at Kraft to complain. But Cheez Whiz had other, deeper troubles beyond its sixty-year-old formula being fiddled with, beyond it being cheese or not cheese. The spreadable dip that transformed American snacking and cocktail parties when it first came out had already become something of a dinosaur, overrun by Kraft's own indefatigable efforts to unleash a slew of newer, snazzier cheese-related products. Granted, many of these items—Easy Cheese, Velveeta, American Singles, Philadelphia Cooking Creme, and a group of blends called Philadelphia Shredded Cheese, which combine real cheese with cream cheese—defy definition. Federal regulators have resorted to terms like *cheese food, cheese product,* and *pasteurized processed American* to describe what the industry itself loosely calls cheese. Taken together, however, the effort by Kraft and its smaller competitors to recast and expand the traditional provision known as cheese has achieved stunning results.

Americans now eat as much as 33 pounds or more of cheese and pseudo-cheese products a year, triple the amount we consumed in the early 1970s. During that same time, beverage makers managed only to double the per capita consumption of carbonated soft drinks to 50 gallons a year; in fact, in recent years they have seen a dropoff, as consumers switched to other sugary drinks. America's intake of cheese, by contrast, continues to swell, increasing 3 pounds per person per year since 2001.*

The nutritional math, when it comes to cheese, is staggering too. Depending on the specific product, 33 pounds of cheese delivers as many as 60,000 calories, which is enough energy, on its own, to sustain an adult for a month. Those 33 pounds also have has many as 3,100 grams of saturated fat, or more than half a year's recommended maximum intake. Cheese has become the single largest source of saturated fat in the American diet, though it is hardly the only culprit. Day in and day out, Americans on average are exceeding the recommended maximum of fat by more than 50 percent.

The soaring amounts of cheese we eat is no accident. It is the direct result of concerted efforts by the processed food industry, which has labored long and hard to transform the very essence of cheese and its role in our diet. Some of this effort is focused on changing its physical nature, converting cheese into a form that is durable as well as quick and cheap to produce. The key to this makeover is the product called processed cheese, which Kraft pioneered nearly a century ago and which fueled its rise to the position of America's largest manufacturer of cheese, with annual global sales of $7 billion.

---

* The source of this figure is the U.S. Department of Agriculture, which monitors the production of cheese along with most other foodstuffs, and it likely overstates consumption by ignoring spoilage or waste. The more accurate sum for how much cheese people eat could go as low as 27 pounds a year, but the trend remains the same: consumption has tripled since 1970.

By itself, however, the industrialization of cheese does not explain the surge in consumption. To triple America's intake in forty years, the food industry has also worked vigorously to change the way cheese is eaten. It is no longer a rare treat to be savored with guests, before a meal. In the hands of food manufacturers, cheese has become an *ingredient*, something we add to other food. And not just any ingredient, either. Cheese is now being slipped into packaged foods that are found in almost every aisle of the grocery store, from the frozen pizzas that now boast "triple cheese," to peanut-butter-and-cheese crackers, to packaged dinner entrees that tout their contents with names like "extreme cheese explosion," to the breakfast sandwiches stocked in the meat cooler. Moreover, to boost the usage at home, the dairy aisle has been loaded with cheese made more and more convenient for use in recipes. Where there used to be a few blocks of cheddar and Swiss and some packs of sliced cheese on the shelf, there are now vast hanging displays of cheese—shredded cheese, cubed cheese, blended cheese, string cheese, crumbled cheese, spreadable cheese, bagged cheese, cheese mixed with cream cheese.

This deployment of cheese as a food additive has proven to be a windfall for food companies, driving up sales of cheese as well as the products that now use it to increase their allure. As a result, Kraft has become not only the largest cheese maker, it has climbed to the top of all food manufacturing. For consumers, however, the results may be far less thrilling. Cheese as an additive, with all of its undeniable bliss, has equally big implications for overeating.

The first step in the industrialization of cheese came in 1912 when a thirty-eight-year-old Chicago street peddler named James Lewis Kraft found his calling. He had been selling traditional cheddar to grocers from a horse-drawn cart, rising before dawn each day to get his cheese from the South Water Street market downtown, the pricey, high-quality stuff his customers valued. Sales were strong, but there was one problem: constant spoilage, which ate into his profits. "Made up loss-and-gain account for December," he wrote in his diary. "Found loss of seventeen cents. Worse than I expected."

Some grocers wouldn't buy his cheese at all in the summer, because it wilted in the heat. Others grumbled about how much was getting wasted each time they sliced off a wedge for a customer and a hard crust formed on the exposed surface. Kraft lost no time in trying to salvage his livelihood. He had no formal training in food chemistry. His first job, after leaving the family's farm in Ontario, had been clerking in a grocery store. Undeterred, he started tinkering at night in the boarding house where he lived. He ground up several kinds of cheddar, and cooked them in a copper kettle, ending up with a glop of stringy, greasy goo. The heat separated the oil and protein molecules, leaving Kraft with an unsightly mess.

The experimentation went on more or less for three years until, one day in 1915, Kraft stumbled upon a solution. He was stirring a pot of cheese continuously as it melted, for fifteen minutes. When he looked down at the pot, he saw that the fat hadn't bled out. The agitation from the continual stirring had kept the fats and proteins together. Now smooth and homogenized, the mixture poured easily into containers, where it solidified again. He rounded up some 3½- and 7½-ounce cans, sterilized them, filled them with the cheese, and embossed the label with his name, "Kraft Cheese," and a promise that would soon get the whole country excited: This was a "cheese of creamy richness" that "will keep in any climate." Before long, he ditched the horse and cart. He needed trucks to fill all the grocery store orders for his cheese-in-a-can.

Traditional cheese makers were appalled. They tried to get lawmakers to force Kraft to label his canned cheese with any number of caustic descriptors, including *embalmed, imitation, made-over,* and *renovated.* The U.S. Department of Agriculture, which oversees the manufacture of cheese and other dairy products, finally settled on a variety of more palatable terms like "American cheese food" and "American cheese product." But the name that stuck came from Kraft's own patent, in which he described his invention as a "process of sterilizing cheese and an improved product produced by such process." Henceforth, the broad category of cheese that is industrially improved became known as "processed cheese."

Notwithstanding the critics, Kraft's cheese turned out to be a perfect field ration for soldiers. He sold six million pounds to the federal government in World War I, and the idea of cheese that could sit around for months on end without needing refrigeration gradually caught on with grocers, too. Given the demands of the job, Kraft was soon joined in business by his four brothers, and by 1923 they had turned their company into the largest cheese manufacturer in the world, adding factories and an endless stream of new technology that sped up the fabrication while lowering production costs.

One of its most popular brands was Velveeta, which Kraft didn't invent but acquired from another entrepreneur in 1928. Velveeta was made directly from milk, milk fat, and the whey that dairies previously discarded. The stirring that Kraft had done in his copper kettle was replaced by sodium phosphate, a chemical additive, which acts as an emulsifier and prevents the fat from separating from the protein in milk. It also more than doubled the sodium content of processed cheese, and it siphoned away—via the chemicals—much of the cheese flavor, which is why processed cheese tastes so mild.

Over the ensuing decades, the technicians at Kraft pulled off one miracle after another in making the fabrication of processed cheese faster and cheaper. In the 1940s, James Kraft's brother Norman invented a contraption called the chill roller on which hot, melted processed cheese was rapidly cooled so that it could be cut into thin slices. By the 1960s, those slices were getting individually wrapped in plastic for minimum mess and maximum convenience. In the 1970s, enzymes were being used in larger amounts to shorten the aging and flavoring process, which spurred a 70 percent jump in production that decade.

But the crowning achievement came in 1985, when Kraft opened two factories in Minnesota and Arkansas that used cutting-edge technology to speed up the process like never before. Kraft still produced huge amounts of natural cheese (cheddar, Swiss, mozzarella), which required as many as eighteen months or more, start to finish, to reach ripeness. But for years, company officials had been dreaming of a better, less costly way, even creating a "SWAT team" of technologists and presenting them with a challenge: "Forget about the way cheese is made today. Look at the problem with fresh eyes."

Nearly a decade had passed, but with the two new factories up and running, the revolution could begin. In one single continuous process, fresh milk would enter one side of the plants and come out the other end as cheese. In between, the milk was put through a rigorous straining called ultrafiltration, enzymes were added at various stages and agitators worked with the chemical emulsifiers to keep the fat molecules blended in. Where traditional cheese took a year and a half or more to prepare and age, the new process whittled that time down to mere days. This final innovation got a name to match its grandeur: "Milk in, cheese out," as they said at Kraft.

With the making of cheese taken to warp speed, all that was left was getting people to eat more of it, and this was no easy feat. It would require the combined efforts of the dairy industry, the federal government, and Kraft all pulling together to overcome a major hurdle: The people were not so inclined.

By 1985, in fact, much of the country was trying to *avoid* high-fat dairy products, especially milk. Women and girls had led the way. In a long, slow—and, for the dairy industry, painful—shift that started in the 1950s, they had come to see milk as an easy and obvious sacrifice in watching their weight. A 12-ounce glass has 225 calories. Starting in the 1960s, the fat in milk was linked to heart disease as well. The same glass has 7.5 grams of saturated fat, or about half of a day's recommended maximum. (Milk is also surprisingly flush with sugar; 12 ounces has four teaspoons of sugar from the lactose in the milk.) By 1988, for the first time ever, grocery stores were selling more lower-fat milk than whole milk.

This effort by Americans to cut back on fat thrust the dairy industry into crisis. It was suddenly drowning in surplus whole milk, as well as the fat that was being taken out of whole milk to make the skim. This extracted fat is called milkfat, and it was piling up due to a simple fact of nature: Cows can't make skim milk. They can make only full-fat milk, so milkfat became something that had to be removed and then stored somewhere. The dairy industry's problem, however, was not just the cow's mammary system. The cows that the industry increasingly came to own were no longer ordinary cows turning out modest sums of milk. They were milk machines. In the old days, dairy cows idled in pastures, just a few to a farm and tended by milkmaids, and they were mainly located in Wisconsin, where the cows had to expend a good deal of their energy just to stay warm. By the 1980s, however, the center for dairy was shifting to California, where balmy weather was only the start of big things to come for the milk cow. The typical dairy operation came to have herds of 500 to 2,000 cows, genetically bred through artificial insemination. They were moved into gigantic sheds where artificial lighting extended their workday. This industrialization, along with a heartier diet of corn and added fats, transformed the American dairy cow into a prodigious producer. Where each animal used to give barely a gallon and a half of milk a day, the modern cow puts out more than six gallons each. Six gallons of full-fat milk.

If people were cutting back on milk, one might ask, why didn't the dairies cut back on their production, rather than send it soaring to new heights? The answer is that they didn't have to cut back. Milk is one of the most stunning examples of overproduction in the American food supply system, with huge consequences on obesity, but a bit of explanation is required to appreciate the industry's full illogical splendor.

Dairies are no ordinary companies. They are not beholden to the constraints of a free market economy. Since the 1930s, the federal government has viewed milk as vital to the nation's health, and thus, it has labored to ensure that dairies never go under. It subsidized the industry by setting price supports and used taxpayer money to buy any and all surplus dairy products. As a result, the dairies didn't have to bother with the normal commercial concerns in selling food. They didn't have to mess with super-sizing or target heavy users or concern themselves with any of the other marketing tactics deployed by food manufacturers to boost consumption. The government simply bought as much as the dairies could make.

It wasn't just milk that the government subsidized, either. It protected the milkfat as well, since the dairy industry couldn't be expected to just toss the fat away and remain financially healthy. This had a consequence. With the cows making more milk than anyone wanted to drink and the milk that people did want to drink being stripped of its fat, the industry devised an ingenious solution: It started turning all that unwanted milk and extracted milkfat into something else. It started turning it into cheese, which soaks up milk and milkfat like a sponge. (One pound of cheese takes a gallon of milk off the dairy industry's hands.) Production began to surge, and just like the excess milk, the dairies didn't have to worry too much about selling the cheese. Whatever the grocers didn't buy, the government did, citing its responsibility to subsidize the dairy industry.

These government purchases hummed along rather quietly until 1981, when the dairies got greedy. By that point, there were so many opera-tors sending so much excess milk and milkfat to cheese makers that the government was buying more cheese than it could ever give away. This cheese, along with surplus butter and dried milk, accumulated into a stack that weighed 1.9 billion pounds, and it cost taxpayers $4 billion a year. With more truckloads arriving daily, this milkfat mountain was growing faster than the national debt. The storage fees alone were running upwards of $1 million a day. It grew so large, in fact, that the government began secreting it away in caverns and a vast, abandoned limestone mine near Kansas City, where *The Washington Post*'s agriculture reporter described an astonishing scene: "Deep beneath the ground here, in more bags, bar-rels and boxes than the mind can imagine, the awesome triumphs of the prodigious American milk cow rest enshrined in dark, cool and costly comfort. What they're keeping here is government-owned milk, butter and cheese. It keeps piling up, costing the treasury millions upon millions of dollars, and nobody knows what to do with it."

Enter the Reagan administration and its commitment to slash the federal budget. In looking around for programs to cut, the new secretary of agriculture, John Block, discovered the cheese vaults and set out to put a stop to the government's buying of surplus, not to mention its storage fees. This required some astute wrangling on his part, since the mega-dairies wielded considerable political clout. At one point, Block felt compelled to perform a little show and tell. He requisitioned hunks of stored cheese that had grown moldy, and showed these to members of Congress who needed some extra convincing. Block's stunt rankled some people, since so much of the stored cheese was, in fact, of the processed variety, which was designed to withstand being locked away. "Some of us were aggravated that this guy would hold up moldy cheese," the executive vice president of the Kansas City storage facility said at the time. "Processed cheese will keep for five years under proper conditions."

Ultimately, Block won. Processed or not, the government stopped buying the excess dairy. Washington tried to help out by discouraging, in the form of incentives, excess production. It paid operators $955 million to make less milk, and the country's dairies pledged to do their part by sending 339,000 milk cows to an early slaughter. This effort, however, was riddled with loopholes and ended with negligible results when the dairy operators simply rebuilt their herds by adding fresh cows.

In 1983, a sympathetic Congress devised another solution. Cows weren't the problem, the elected officials decided, not even the modern supercharged cow. The problem was the consumer, who had caused this whole surplus problem to start with. The people simply weren't drinking enough milk, so Congress created a system to boost the consumption of dairy products. (The law was actually called the Dairy and Tobacco Adjustment Act, since it also offered some aid and comfort to the cigarette industry.) Under this plan, the federal government allowed a special assessment to be levied on every milk producer in the country, with the money to be spent on marketing schemes that were aimed at making milk and cheese more alluring.

This left only one question: Why would people who shun fatty milk eat more fatty cheese?

The answer, in part, is because they had no choice. There is no nonfat cheese worth eating, at least nothing that comes close to the real thing. The dairy industry has put some effort into finding a way to make low-fat cheese as attractive as low-fat milk, but by and large the taste and texture of these fat-stripped cheeses is appalling. As a result, more than 90 percent of the cheese sold today remains full fat.

There is another reason, however, why people who shun whole milk will devour a full-fat cheese. Cheese has something going for it that whole milk does not: It is not as readily identified as a fatty food. True, cheese is loaded with fat, especially with saturated fat, the kind that is linked to heart disease. It has much less of the other kind of fat, unsaturated, that nutritionists have increasingly come to view as a good fat. Better sources of this good fat are oils like canola, olive, and safflower. But in one of the great perversions of nutritional science, the bad fat, saturated, doesn't look or feel like fat. It remains solid at room temperature, where it locks up with the protein molecules and hides from view.

Not everyone in the country is worried about fat, of course. There are many people who drink whole milk and eat cheese and eat it in huge quantities, enjoying it for its unique flavors and velvety mouthfeel. I met one such person in the winter of 2010, and his affection for cheese was a marvel to see. His name is Ulfert Broockmann, and he's a German-born cheese expert who spent forty-seven years as a technician in the dairy industry. He did two five-year stints with Kraft, ending in 1984, though there is no love lost between him and the company. He said he won a substantial legal settlement from Kraft after being fired, which he attributed to his disgruntlement with the company's turn toward speedier cheese production. He disliked especially the increased use of enzymes to replace the aging process. "They made everything cheaper," he said during my visit to his home in Libertyville, Illinois, just twenty miles from the company's headquarters. "It's a shame."

As we talked cheese at his dining room table, I asked to see his larder. One entire shelf of his refrigerator was devoted to cheese. He had cheddar and jack, blue and Gorgonzola, Brie, Camembert, and Swiss, neatly arranged on ceramic plates. I started salivating, but eating cheese in the Broockmann household requires time and discipline. It can't be rushed. Before he eats any cheese, he told me, he takes it out of the fridge and sets it on the counter to warm up to room temperature, which brings out the flavors and tang. For a man in his early seventies, Broockmann was impressively fit, tall, and slim, still capable of 100-mile rides on his bike, and he is unconcerned about the fat in his food. In fact, he credits his good health to a diet that is heavy on cheese.

"I eat it in the morning, with bread," he told me. "It's a European-type breakfast. We set out four or five types, with butter. And I eat it at night, with a glass of wine." None of the cheese he buys, not an ounce, is made by Kraft. He said that he can taste high amounts of enzymes, and he prefers artisanal brands that still rely on eighteen months or more of aging.

For all his love of cheese, however, Broockmann's ways with the stuff were not going to fix the dairy industry's problem of having too much milk and milkfat. He is way too particular about what he considers cheese and far too methodical in how he eats it. To triple the per capita consumption to 33 pounds, cheese would have to be eaten much faster, in newer, more convenient ways, and in much looser formulations. It wasn't long after Broockmann left Kraft that officials there got to work on a more realistic solution to the milkfat mountain.

In the early stages of its quest to make cheese more convenient to eat, Kraft stumbled badly. The company's cheese division managers started with one of their biggest brands, Philadelphia Cream Cheese. The idea was that busy people would use cream cheese more readily if it was sold not in its famous foil-wrapped blocks but pre-sliced and -wrapped in 1.2-ounce portions. In May 1989, the company made three hundred thousand pounds of sliced cream cheese and shipped it to test markets in up-state New York and Kansas City. Kraft's cheese division had predicted a jump in annual sales of $61 million and 27 million pounds of additional cheese being eaten, explaining its reasoning in an internal memo that was distributed that summer to other company officials. Cream cheese in brick form was being used mainly on bagels and toast, and only for breakfast. The new sliced version would extend that reach into lunch and dinner, with lots of new recipes made easier by the handiness of the slices. "The introduction of new forms of cream cheese drives cream cheese consumption," the memo said. "Usage of cream cheese during lunch and dinner occasions represents a significant opportunity for greater cream cheese consumption."

The slices, however, flopped. Consumers were put off by the whole concept; in this case, Kraft determined that the added convenience didn't compensate for the pleasure people took in taking a knife to the brick themselves.

Fortunately for Kraft, the company had recently been purchased by Philip Morris, and its top lieutenant, Geoffrey Bible, had just arrived at Kraft headquarters in 2000 when the disappointing data came in, marking the cream cheese venture as a failure. He did not hold back in dispensing guidance to the cheese managers. To come up with winners, he reminded them, one has to think long and hard about just what it is people like. "Now, I don't mean to pick on Philadelphia Cream Cheese, because it's a shining star in our product crown," Bible said in one meeting. "But here's an example of what happens when you take your eye off the customer and pursue an interesting technology too far without validating it first, with consumer input. We figured out how to create a cream cheese slice and put it on the shelf. It was a very impressive technological accomplishment. The question was did it really address a need? Sure, we were the only people in the world who could do it. Unfortunately, we were also apparently the only people in the world who cared. No one bought it. You know what we found out too late about consumers and their cream cheese? They'd rather spread it themselves! It's fun! The great thing about cream cheese is the wretched excess of how much you can glom onto your bagel in the morning. It turns out involvement is part of consumer need when it comes to cream cheese."

The cheese managers took Bible's words to heart. Cream cheese was no Oreo cookie, but it could be fun, too. They also saw no reason that they couldn't adopt the marketing strategy deployed by that other great sugary product, Coke. If Coca-Cola could get people to drink more Coke by targeting those who already drank a lot, why couldn't Kraft do the same with cheese? The managers even adopted Coke's language, referring to cheese lovers as "heavy users." To target them, they produced a new line of flavored cheese spreads called Kraft Crockery that hit on both these themes. "The fun is spreading," promised the advertising.

In an internal memo on tactics, the cheese managers pulled back the curtain on their strategy. "These products will be targeted to people who snack on cheese, primarily heavy cheese users," it said. "Media selection will be skewed to female principal shoppers who are heavy processed cheese users, representing 67 percent of total processed cheese volume. The copy strategy positions Crockery as a whole new way to add fun, exciting new cheese tastes to any food."

As sales of the Crockery line boomed, Kraft realized something else about cheese that made it every bit as attractive as sugary food, if not more so. People have their limits on sweetness. They can take only so much sugar in their food, and thereafter their liking—and sales—will drop. This is the famous bliss point that food scientists study and parse. But cheese is different. Cheese has fat, and as Adam Drewnowski in Seattle and other food scientists had discovered, the more fat in our food, the better we like it. This meant that cheese could be added to other food products without any worries that people would walk away. To the contrary, the added fat could be counted upon to make them more attractive.

Much of Kraft's early efforts in this arena focused on the company's famous Macaroni & Cheese. Known internally as "the Blue Box," it sold for a mere $1.19 and was a stalwart seller. But it was the eighteen new versions—most of them featuring added cheese—that would push the Blue

Box into the club of elite mega-brands, with sales of $300 million a year. The lineup included Potatoes & Cheese, Pasta & Cheese, and Rice & Cheese, with each of the broad categories sliced into several subtypes, like Cheddar Broccoli, Cheddar Chicken, Cheddar Pilaf, and Three Cheese. In their strategy memos on this move, the cheese managers referred to the Blue Box "leveraging its cheesiest point of difference."

Kraft used this same strategy to increase consumption of its packaged, just-add-meat dinners like Velveeta Cheesy Skillets, which featured added cheese and were spun off into varieties like Ultimate Cheeseburger Mac, Nacho Supreme, and Zesty BBQ Chicken. They sold for a mere $2.39, but contained up to fifteen grams of saturated fat per package—a fat load that soared even higher when the recipe was completed by adding the mixture to ground beef. In the television ad campaign for these meal supplements, a strapping and handsome blacksmith dips a ladle into a pot of melted yellow cheese and brings the thick velvety goo up slowly while singing, in baritone, "Liquid Go-o-o-o-o-o-ld."

Kraft's use of added cheese as a lure in its packaged foods, of course, sent other food manufacturers scrambling to keep up. As an analytical firm called Packaged Facts noted in tracking this gold rush, "There exists an opportunity for cheese ingredients in every aisle of the supermarket." Walmart, for one, started selling its own brand of soup called Loaded Baked Potato that included processed cheddar cheese, and contained 9 grams of saturated fat—more than half of a day's recommended maximum. Its affiliate, Sam's Club, came up with a four-cheese artichoke dip. Nestlé, through its Stouffer's brand of ready-to-eat packaged foods, brought out a frozen Three Cheese & Ham Panini and added cheddar to its Grilled Mesquite-Style Chicken.

One of the biggest free-for-alls took place in the freezer aisle. Frozen pizza used to be made with the bare minimum amount of cheese, as manufacturers were always looking for ways to save on ingredient costs. But the new math on cheese turned that upside down. The more cheese that was added, the better the pizzas sold, and the better they sold, the more Kraft could charge. Kraft and other companies started turning out frozen pizza that boasted two, three, and four different cheeses, including even a tangy blue, and then they tucked more cheese into the crust. By 2009, frozen pizza had reached $4 billion in annual sales, with Kraft alone pulling in $1.6 billion from DiGiorno and its other brands, and there appeared to be no end in sight.

For years, Kraft had been keeping an eye on the public's concern about the health implications of eating too many fatty foods. In a confidential strategic plan the company drew up in 1993, Kraft cited this nutritional worry first among the topmost "weaknesses" in the company's cheese-filled lineup of products. It possessed, Kraft lamented, "a portfolio weighted towards businesses in categories that lack vitality because they are out of consumer favor due to ingredient and/or fat orientation."

And yet, the food industry's rush to embrace cheese—the fattest of all fat-based products—as a way to increase sales put Kraft's cheese division on a tear. In this same strategic plan, Kraft said, "Competition is intensifying across all categories. Spending is up. Healthy Choice (Con Agra) has entered Cheese. Competitive strategies are converging, with all Peers trying to establish category leadership positions. Peer leaders are reportedly targeting 3+ percent annual growth volume. The implications for Kraft USDA is that we need to leverage our scale and do 'faster, better, and more completely' versus the competition." By 1995, Kraft was reporting to Philip Morris officials that it had achieved a string of "strong years," hitting $5 billion in revenue and two billion pounds in cheese.

With the industry working so hard to turn cheese into an ingredient to tuck away in other foods, the consumption rates climbed precipitously, with hardly anyone noticing. Even consumer advocates, in their efforts to steer Americans toward healthier diets, overlooked cheese. The Department of Agriculture, however, tracks all of the basic staples that Americans eat, and it has kept a close watch on cheese. And nearly every year, the numbers in its tally set a record. Where Americans, on average, were eating 11 pounds of cheese a year in 1970, they were up to 18 pounds in 1980, 25 pounds by 1990, 30 pounds in 2000, and 33 pounds by 2007, when the rates dipped in the recession before resuming their surge.

Remarkably, the growth in cheese has mirrored the plunge in whole milk, which American consumers identified—mistakenly, it turned out—as the primary source of the saturated fat they wanted to avoid. Milk drinking went from 25 gallons per person in 1970 to the current average of six. For the country as a whole, trading cheese for milk has been a poor bargain indeed. The net gain per person at the current rates is roughly 200 grams of saturated fat a year. Few people, of course, realized how much more cheese they were eating. But by 2010, the floodgates for cheese—as an ingredient—were opened wide.

It had been twenty years since the sliced cream cheese debacle had subjected the cheese managers at Kraft to a scolding from the executives at Philip Morris. As the cigarette makers pointed out to the food technologists, playing with the shape of products was pointless without an equal amount of energy spent on divining the minds of consumers—that the "selling" of food counted as much as the food itself.

By 2010, however, the cheese managers at Kraft had fully internalized this message, and it was with no small amount of satisfaction that they built one of their most spectacular "divination" campaigns around the same product that had defeated them before: Philadelphia Cream Cheese.

The operation they launched was called the Real Women of Philadelphia, and its stated goal was to capture some of the estimated $7.3 billion that shoppers were spending each year on fat-laden additives for cooking at home. This field was cluttered with sour creams, shredded cheeses, sauces, and canned soups as ingredients for recipes, and if Kraft wanted in, it knew it would have to do something special to stand apart. "We couldn't win in this category with a traditional approach," Kraft said in an analysis of the campaign. "We needed to listen more closely and respond more generously to our customers.

"Philadelphia Cream Cheese was happy to be America's favorite schmear for bagels and main ingredient for cheesecakes. But growth had flattened out, and our challenge was to find new reasons for people to buy our product. Our goal was to sell more product and shift brand perception toward cooking. We needed to encourage consumers' use of cream cheese in their recipes and increase the frequency with which they purchased the product, a measurement that had been flat for five years."

The idea was to identify women who cook and show them new ways to use cream cheese. Kraft, however, did not want to rely solely on traditional advertising. For all its power to influence shopping habits, large numbers of American consumers saw paid commercials for what they were: pure hype. Kraft believed it could increase the credibility of its marketing by having real people do the promoting on its behalf. Thus the slogan "Real Women," and the concept was brilliant. This was like having a neighbor tell you over the fence about the new recipe she had tried that included cream cheese as a novel, luscious ingredient.

But Kraft didn't want to rely on everyday women alone. It wanted someone of stature to lead them. Some companies trot out their CEO to stand up in TV commercials and lend some homespun credibility to the product, but many more realize what Kraft concluded, that it "didn't have sufficient credibility to inspire broader use of Philly cream cheese. But a celebrity partner who oozed credibility, loved Philly, and used it a lot, *would*, especially when engaging daily with a community of 'real' women."

Kraft needed Paula Deen.

Deen, whose appearances on the Food Network had turned her into a star, was perfect for the role. Her show, Paula's Home Cooking, featured Southern-style fare that is heavy in butter, mayonnaise, and anything else with saturated fat as a main component. One of her demonstrations was fried macaroni and cheese. For this, she scooped baked macaroni and cheese from a casserole, wrapped the balls in bacon, and deep-fried them in oil. As one online reviewer who awarded the recipe five stars wrote, "It's like eating pure cholesterol! Delicious and fun to make and eat!"

On Kraft's behalf, Deen appeared on the daytime talk show *The View* and other television programs, joined contest winners in writing a cream cheese–based cookbook, and opened her vast social media network to the company's new campaign for cream cheese. The centerpiece was a contest in which Kraft offered a $25,000 prize to each of four winners who came up with the best recipe that used cream cheese as an ingredient. And the contest was run by Deen.

Every week for four months, Deen starred in videos that aired on YouTube in which she would demonstrate the entered recipes, praise the winners, and show video snippets that contestants themselves had submitted. These videos, along with the other promotional work by Deen and a website that Kraft devoted to the campaign, produced precisely the reaction that Kraft had wanted. Home cooks deluged the company with an avalanche of recipes for using cream cheese in their cooking. It had taken Kraft's own test kitchens a decade to devise five hundred recipes that deployed cream cheese, but the Real Women campaign put that to shame. It generated five thousand recipes in three months, which Kraft began promoting through the social networks of Facebook, Twitter, and Google advertising.

Sales of Philadelphia Cream Cheese surged 5 percent almost overnight, the first increase the cheese had had in five years. More telling, shopper tracking data showed that while the traditional usage of the cream cheese as a spread had declined, its use as an ingredient had gone up.

The only glitch came in January 2012, when Deen revealed that she had been diagnosed with diabetes three years earlier. She made this disclosure in announcing a new deal to publicly represent Novo Nordisk, the world's largest maker of insulin and other diabetes drugs. Much of the food world went nuts. The problem for Deen was the nature of the fat-laden cooking she'd been selling, which was viewed by critics as the surest path to diabetes.

Deen went on *The Today Show* to air her side, where she was interviewed by Al Roker, who had dealt with his own weight issues by undergoing a stomach-banding operation in 2002. When he asked if she planned to change her eating habits, Deen said she had never intended for anyone to use her recipes day in and day out. "I've always encouraged moderation," she said. "I share with you all these yummy, fattening recipes, but I tell people, 'In moderation, in moderation.'"

In examining Kraft's cream cheese campaign, along with other efforts by industry to promote the increased consumption of cheese, I phoned the chair of Harvard's Department of Nutrition, Walter Willett. He was deeply familiar with saturated fats, having spent years studying America's consumption patterns. Still, he was taken aback by how big a player cheese had become in the American diet. "We don't have to eliminate cheese, that's for sure," he told me. "A small amount of good cheese can be compatible with a healthy diet. But consumption in the U.S. is enormous and way too high." He worried especially about cheese being used as an additive in foods where its main function, increasing the allure, runs counter to an important nutritional strategy. It's better, he said, to eat things that are high in fat and calories, like cheese, directly, when they can be savored, rather than tucked away in other foods where their downsides—the saturated fat and the calories—are not so readily noticed.

In 2008, a team of Dutch researchers conducted an experiment to see whether people will eat any more or less, depending on whether they can easily see the fat in their food. "The products we used were foods that are commonly consumed in the Netherlands, but we manipulated them in order to create a visible- or hidden-fat version," the team leader, Mirre Viskaal-van Dongen, told me. Tomato soup was served with a vegetable-oil slick floating on top and then, in the hidden-fat condition, with the oil emulsified into the soup. Bread was served with butter spread on top of the slices, so it was visible, and, alternatively, baked into the loaves, so it was not. "We also used a small bun with a sausage inside," he said. "I am not sure whether these are available in the U.S., but in the Netherlands they are quite common. In the visible-fat condition, the bun was made of puff pastry, which has a very fatty appearance. It is shiny, and when you hold it in your hands, you get greasy fingers. In the hidden-fat condition, the bun was made of dough that does not have the fatty appearance."

In order to measure the effect of the visible fats more accurately, the study used more butter and oil than the fifty-seven participants were perhaps accustomed to, so that the effect would likely be less obvious in real life. Nonetheless, the results were striking. The participants were first asked to estimate the amount of fat—and calories—in the food, and in the versions where the fat had been tucked away, they sharply underestimated the levels of both. Next, they dined on the foods, having been told to eat as much as they wanted. The visible fat group got fuller faster, while the other group, downing the hidden-fat recipes, remained hungry and kept eating. In a key—but commonly overlooked—aspect of obesity, weight gain can be caused by the slightest increases in consumption, if it continues day in and day out. A mere extra one hundred calories a day will, over time, put on the pounds. The participants in the Dutch study hit that mark exactly. When they couldn't see the fat in their food, they ate nearly 10 percent more or about 100 extra calories.

This may be bad news for the heaviest users of fatty ingredients like cheese, when the cheese is tucked in or out of sight, when the oil shimmering atop a triple-cheese pizza hardens and disappears from view as the pie cools. The fat might well show up when they next step onto a scale. But the gains in consumption to be had from hidden fats was certainly not bad news for the food industry. More food eaten equals more food sold. And hiding the fat in processed foods would become an industry theme, one that would involve far more than just cheese.

"Lunchtime Is All Yours"

In the summer of 1988, an assembly line clattered to life at Oscar Mayer in Madison, Wisconsin, just off Packers Avenue as it skirts the eastern shore of Lake Mendota. It wasn't much of an assembly line, more cobbled together than engineered, and set up not in the vast processing plant where 1,800 workers turned out cold cuts, ham, and hot dogs but in the company's headquarters building, up on the seventh floor.

There, in a large open space the company's research and development staff used to test food ideas, a crew of twenty men and women took up positions alongside the makeshift conveyor belt. At first blush, what came down the line was unremarkable: little white subdivided plastic trays, so small and light they flitted rather than bumped along. Behind the workers were tables piled high with the product waiting to go into the trays: sliced bologna.

Bologna was a signature item for Oscar Mayer, but over the years it had been steadily losing appeal with the American public, in part because of its hefty loads of saturated fat and salt. The company had always sold it by itself, in the deli meat section, sliced in half-pound packs. On these trays, however, the meat would play a less prominent role. It became a component, one among many, slipped into a package that didn't suggest meat as much as it signaled fun. The trays had compartments, and the workers started off by tucking eight pieces of bologna into one of the slots. Down the line, each tray also received eight pieces of yellow cheese, eight butter crackers, and a yellow paper napkin. The trays were then sealed with plastic, wrapped in a school bus–yellow cardboard sleeve, and packed into cartons for a journey that, if all went well, would take them from warehouse to distribution center to grocery stores across America, where they would get stacked in the meat-section coolers.

Standing off to the side, the man responsible for this product, called Lunchables, watched the crew with a measure of trepidation. For two and a half years, Bob Drane had led a team of food technicians and designers on a long, difficult quest to invent these little trays. At one point, Drane's team hid out in a hotel meeting room they dubbed the "Food Playground," where they gathered for days on end with bags of groceries and art supplies, snipping and taping and tasting their way to the perfect marriage of package and food. Now, as the first trays rolled off the line, Drane worried that they'd gotten it all wrong.

Drane had been Oscar Mayer's vice president for new business strategy and development since 1985. He had been through enough launches to know that the odds of success were long. In the great churn of processed food merchandising, 14,000 newly hatched products show up every year in the grocery store, each of which typically carries between 15,000 and 60,000 items; two of every three products will fail to last a few months. One in ten of those that do survive will achieve what the industry views as a modest success: $25 million in annual sales. All in all, inventing processed foods is a bit like drilling for oil: The big money is made through the endless pumping of mediocre wells, knowing that occasionally, a gusher will come along.

As it turned out, Drane was right to worry about the rollout of Lunchables, but not for the reason he thought. The trays did not get yanked immediately from the stores: They flew off the shelves. The sales of Lunchables were phenomenal from the start, hitting $217 million in the first twelve months. Grocers scrambled to make more room for them in their coolers, and Oscar Mayer's salesmen, who at first had refused to pitch the puny 4.5-ounce trays, rushed back to Madison clamoring for more and more trays, as fast as the line workers in the factory could get them out.

Drane's problem lay in trying to balance the books. While sales were spectacular, so were production costs, as Oscar Mayer struggled to expand its modest factory line to keep up with the deluge in orders. The trays were priced as low as $1.29, and the more they sold, the more money the company lost. The first year's tally for Oscar Mayer? A net loss of $20 million.

"There's a huge, huge scramble going on," Drane told me one afternoon in his home office in Madison. "How can we produce millions of these units at a reasonable cost? Because while we *thought* we knew how to do that, the truth is, we didn't. Oscar is making hot dogs and bologna and stuff like that, but it has no experience with assembly operations, where you've got a tray and you fill up the tray and do all that kind of stuff. As we start to roll out with this thing, there is an awful cost structure, with huge amounts of waste. The red ink at the bottom line is piling up, and my bankers are sitting across from me every single day, saying, 'What's going on here? You're having a lot of fun selling lots and lots of volume to consumers but we're not making any money, and what are you going to do about it?' "

Those bankers, as Drane referred to the company's accountants, would soon grow even more worried. A few months after the launch, Oscar Mayer merged with Kraft, where a cadre of Ivy League bean counters seemed to have one overriding thought: Blow this project up and shut it down before they all lose their jobs. Drane was asking for ten new production lines at $3 million each to meet demand, and the money men were terrified that the trays would turn out to be a short-term fad. If the sales crashed, they would be left holding more than a product that never turned a profit; they would own multiple factories with now-useless manufacturing lines.

At this point, Drane packed up his data and flew to New York City, where he appealed to a far different breed of executive: men who had seen some difficult product launches in their day and had laughed in the face of catastrophe. These were the leaders of Philip Morris, whose recent purchase of Kraft and General Foods had put hundreds of grocery items into their hands, more than fifty mega-brands in all. Bob Drane's little trays were now their little trays.

The head of Philip Morris was Hamish Maxwell, a pack-a-day smoker who was viewed as a master tactician in marketing cigarettes. As the chief executive of the newly merged company, he needed to know that Lunchables had serious long-term prospects. A stickler for details, Drane walked Maxwell through the early sales data showing that more than half of the buyers were returning for more, which, for new grocery products, was about as good as it ever gets. At the end of the meeting, Maxwell turned to Drane and told him to worry no more.

"The hard thing is to figure out something that will sell," Maxwell said. "If you've got something that's selling, you'll figure out how to get the cost right."

So Drane walked out of the Philip Morris headquarters building on Park Avenue with the money he needed to expand and streamline the production and boarded the Philip Morris helicopter, which would take him back to the airport. The aircraft was parked at a heliport on the edge of Manhattan, for easy access by the tobacco executives, and it rose up over the East River with the city unfolding below him. "On the way out to New York, there had been a daily pounding from the Oscar Mayer sales force. 'Hey, you finally got something right and everybody wants this and all you are telling us is you can't achieve the production. We are really getting ticked off, and you are about to lose this thing,' " Drane said. "And now, instead of coming back with my tail between my legs, I'm up in the helicopter looking down on the Big Apple, feeling pretty good."

Whether they fully realized its potential or not, the tobacco men in the coming years would do more than merely hand over the cash to exploit this gusher called the Lunchables. They would help turn the trays into a processed food colossus, one that would break industry records by soaring to nearly $1 billion in annual sales. The little trays, by transforming bologna into a product kids were suddenly clamoring for, would also accomplish one of Drane's own goals, which was to save the jobs of the Oscar Mayer workers who made the fat-laden meats that were running afoul of the public's concern for its health.

Lunchables, however, would play a part in exacerbating those same health concerns. The trays created an entirely new category of food, one that exposed Americans, especially young kids, to the thrills of fast food that heretofore were the purview of restaurant chains like McDonald's and Burger King. Back in the late 1980s, when Lunchables were first introduced, food manufacturers—despite their push for more convenient foods and their heavy reliance on salt, sugar, and fat—had not yet realized that they could mimic the fast food chains by making whole meals that were ready to eat at school, on the go. Even more remarkably, these fast food wonders could be sold through the grocery store and without the need for a microwave oven. "Chilled prepared foods," this category was called, and it took the Lunchables to turn this light on. But the grocery makers embraced this conceptual breakthrough at the very moment when the power of these foods was becoming all the more problematic for consumers. Obesity began surging, and Bob Drane, who fathered the Lunchables with the best of intentions, would eventually have to face what he had wrought.

Best known, perhaps, for the Wienermobiles that tour the country promoting its hot dogs, Oscar Mayer cherished its status as America's favorite meat company. It cultivated a warm, friendly image (perfectly embodied in the iconic TV jingle "Oh, I wish I were an Oscar Mayer wiener," which first aired in the 1960s) and a stout reputation for caring about the consumer. The company got its start in Chicago in 1883 as a champion of quality meats. The founders were two Bavarian brothers, Oscar and Gottfried, who sought to distinguish themselves from the sordid practices that tainted the industry, like letting rat poison fall into the sausage-making machines and bleaching weeks-old meat so it could be sold as new—horrors that were later exposed by the muckraking journalist Upton Sinclair in his book *The Jungle*.

The Mayer brothers were among the first to put their names on packages of bacon, linked sausage, and lard as a means of avowing their product's excellence; in the days before labeling requirements, many meat producers ducked scrutiny by remaining anonymous. They were also early participants in the principal reform that Sinclair's exposé generated, a system whereby federal workers monitored and inspected meat plant operations, which started out as a program companies could join at their discretion.

Oscar Mayer's strong commitment to sanitation helped establish its reputation through much of the twentieth century until one hundred years after its founding, when the company was faced with a public concern that went beyond the safety of its food. Red meat was increasingly being seen as unhealthy. A single slice of beef bologna, for instance, has 3.5 grams of saturated fat, along with 330 milligrams of sodium, nearly a quarter of a day's recommended maximum for most American adults.

Fat was becoming synonymous with cholesterol, clogged arteries, heart attacks, and strokes. And as a result, between 1980 and 1990, red meat consumption fell more than 10 percent. During that same time, the consumption of poultry, which has less saturated fat, rose 50 percent. This signaled a potentially huge swing in eating habits, and no one worried more about it than Oscar Mayer.

"From 1986 to 1988, fat and sodium grew to be big issues in the hot dog and bologna category," Tom Coffey, an Oscar Mayer manager for new product development, told Philip Morris officials in a confidential 1990 presentation. More and more people who worried about fat and salt were changing their diets to reduce consumption of red meat—or avoid it altogether.

The company's first response to this crisis was to reformulate some of its meats to offer customers a version that was healthier than the mainline product. Within a few years, it introduced a lower-fat bologna blended with turkey and hot dogs made with chicken instead of beef. But these were slow to catch on, and overall sales continued to slip.

The company also retooled its advertising to appeal to a broader audience. Bologna did not wear well with its fans; kids lost interest as they grew older. Oscar Mayer's marketing department set up test panels to poll adults and found that men turned to ham, turkey, and roast beef. On a scale of 1 to 10, men gave the bologna sandwich a meager 4 or 5—but there was a glimmer of hope. Bologna's image seemed to be worse than the meat itself. When the marketing people handed out actual sandwiches to taste, the rating men gave to bologna rose to 8 or 9. Encouraged, Oscar Mayer sought to expand its market for bologna from kids to men by developing new ads that featured men loving bologna. At the same time, the company tried to reach more children. In 1995, they launched a promotion called "Talent Search," in which ten Wienermobiles were dispatched to fifty cities, where they looked for a child star to sing the company's famous jingle.

"The early results of Talent Search are outstanding," the Oscar Mayer unit president, Robert Eckert, told Philip Morris executives in the fall of 1995. "We completed over 700 events and had nearly 45,000 kids audition. And, during the promotion, retail sales volume for participating products like Oscar Mayer hot dogs and bologna was up over 10 percent vs. last year."

Oscar Mayer also worked on the cost of bologna to bolster sales. On one end, it zeroed in on the production side of things, looking for savings through various changes in the factories as well as in the formulations of its products. Like other food companies, Oscar Mayer was continuously seeking less expensive ingredients that could be substituted without diminishing the quality, and Eckert, in his presentation to the tobacco executives, assured his bosses that the company had been especially aggressive on this front: "90 percent of our products have been reformulated in one way or another over the past four years," he said.

The other side to the cost equation was pricing, and the bologna managers at Oscar Mayer worked hard to outmaneuver their competitors.

They had to get the price of bologna low enough so people would buy more, but the price had to stay high enough to make a profit. By slashing the price of a pack of sliced bologna to $1.99, Oscar Mayer seemed to do fairly well: It held on to a 29 percent share of the bologna market. But this was a Pyrrhic victory. The company had a solid one-third share of a sinking ship. Through the 1990s, bologna sales in general—no matter what manufacturer—fell 1 percent each year; by 1995 the annual drop had accelerated to 2.6 percent.

Oscar Mayer had to face facts: People were falling out of love with bologna. What it needed was a new vehicle, something other than bread and mustard to draw people's interest—something with enough pizzazz to overcome the growing hesitancy about the fat in red meat. This was the business of product developers, the people who toil away in laboratories and test kitchens looking for ways to repackage and present foods that fall out of favor. And fortunately for Oscar Mayer, its product developers had a head start. Just as the sales were growing stagnant in the mid-1980s, the product developers had cleared off their stations and gone to work looking for ways to sell the company's luncheon meat, beyond the stacks of plastic-wrapped slices.

In late 1985, Oscar Mayer asked Drane to take the lead in finding a better way to repackage bologna and any of the company's other meats that needed an overhaul. I met Drane at his home office and went through the records he had kept on the birth and development of what would become his solution to the company's red meat problem: the Lunchables. Among the records he saved was a presentation, 206 slides in all, he had prepared to convey the project's details to other food developers. With bologna sales only starting to slip, Drane told me, "Oscar Mayer was not in dire straights. It was literally like, 'You guys go out and try to figure out how to contemporize what we've got. We are a famous lunch company and we have famous brands of lunch and so why don't you concentrate on lunch and see what you get.' "

But Drane understood the changing dynamics—and the stakes for a company whose legacy was red meat. "Alarm bells ringing!" says the twenty-sixth slide in his presentation. A brown bag lunch with bologna on Wonder Bread was depicted under the caption, "Lunch of the 50s," next to another, "Lunch of the 90s," which had a large question mark, which was followed by a photo of Drane with three of his team members in their white smocks with the red Oscar Mayer logo, arms folded and looking determined.

Drane's first move was to try to zero in on how, exactly, Americans were feeling about lunch. He organized focus group sessions with the people who had been buying bologna: moms. As they talked, he realized the most pressing issue was not fat, it was time. Working moms and busy moms strove to provide healthy food, of course, and thus sales of lower-fat turkey were rising. But day in and day out, finding time to prepare any sort of food for their kids was increasingly difficult. The mothers spoke at length about the morning crush, that nightmarish dash to get breakfast on the table and lunch packed and shoes tied and kids out the door. He summed up their remarks for me like this: "It's awful. I am scrambling around. My kids are asking me for stuff. I'm trying to get myself ready to go to the office. I go to pack these lunches, and I don't know what I've got. They want them to be special, and I want to take care of them and, by the way, I like to take care of myself, but I might not have stuff in inventory."

With his large, black-frame glasses and professorial demeanor, Drane did not rank as the company's most ruthless executive. But this revelation from the moms brought out the shark in him. Drane smelled blood in the water—or, as he put it to me, "a goldmine of disappointments and problems."

He assembled a team of about fifteen people with varied skills, from design to food science to advertising, and he enrolled this crew in what he called "Montessori School." To bail out bologna, they couldn't just copy some trick another food manufacturer had used. They needed to come up with something new and fresh, and this kind of challenge was right up Drane's alley. For Montessori School, Drane developed a curriculum designed to help his team tap their imaginative powers.

Having set themselves up in Oscar Mayer's headquarters building, they got started by studying other vulnerable designs in consumer goods that underwent successful transformations, such as the boom box (which morphed into the Walkman), kids' shoelaces (which became Velcro), and exploratory surgery (which gave way to the MRI). They took field trips to Krispy Kreme, the doughnut maker that, at that moment, was driving the country wild with its enthralling feature: It was served warm, the sugary glaze and fatty dough perfectly poised to deliver a double whammy of bliss. They pulled out their markers and brainstormed a wish list of attributes that would give their bologna sandwich replacement, whatever it may turn out to be, that level of power over consumers. To keep their discussions lively, they used alliteration: "Faster, fresher, foolproof, fortified, flavorful, flexible, funner, and for me."

The creative juices now flowing, Drane and his team made a key decision: They settled on creating a convenient prepackaged lunch. The questions then became, What kind of container? And what would go in it?

Of course, they would have to use the company's red meat. That was the whole point of this project, after all, to kick-start stagnant sales. So sliced bologna and ham became the first building blocks. They wanted to add bread, naturally, because who ate bologna without it? But this presented a problem: There was no way bread could stay fresh for the two months their product needed to sit in warehouses or in grocery coolers. Crackers, however, could do that, so they added some Ritz rounds.

In choosing the lunch's basic components, the toughest decisions involved the cheese. Using cheese was an obvious move, given its increasing presence in processed foods. (When word of the Lunchables project first leaked out in 1987, the addition of cheese had sent ripples of excitement through the dairy industry—offering, as it did, another outlet for their product. The company's merger with Kraft in 1988, however, nipped that joy in the bud. Oscar Mayer didn't have to shop for cheese anymore; it got all it wanted from its new sister company, and at cost.) But what kind of cheese? Natural cheddar, which they started off with, crumbled and didn't slice very well, so they moved on to processed varieties, which could bend and slice and last forever. Then the question became, What shape should the cheese be? Through tests on consumers, they discovered that cheese sliced into little rounds was a bit more exciting than squares. In their likability matrix, the rounds came in at 80 on a scale of 100, while the squares mustered only a 70. But they also needed to keep their production costs as low as possible, or the retail price would have to be set beyond what people would be willing to pay. Square cheese was easier to cut than round, so they went with that. They looked at everything through the matrix of shrinking the production costs any way they could without hurting the flavor or texture too much. They could use the processed cheese made by Kraft, which was already cheaper than regular cheese, or they could knock another two cents off the per unit price by using a lesser product called "cheese food," which had scored poorly in the taste tests. Likewise, they compared things like real pepperoni to pepperoni flavoring, a cardboard tray cover to a printed, clear film.

Now that they had the components, the meat, cheese and crackers, and the right shapes, Drane's team moved their venture into a nearby hotel, where they set out—with no distractions—to find the right mix of components and container. "What principles drive success?" Drane reminded them. "Self-contained, individualized, compact, portable, ready to use, fun, and cool." They gathered around tables where bagfuls of meat, cheese, crackers and all sorts of wrapping material had been dumped, and they let their imaginations run. In the end, they came up with twenty designs that ranged from the ridiculous (a jumble of meat and cheese in a box with a tiny cellophane window) to the mundane (a single piece of meat wrapped around some cheese on tiny foam tray). A myth later arose, repeated by the company's top executives, about how the team finally settled on a white plastic tray with several components—that this had been inspired by the Japanese bento box. The reality, Drane told me, was far less exotic: After snipping and taping their way through a host of failures, the model they relied on was the American TV dinner.

Drane's Montessori School had one task left: bestowing a catchy, approachable name on the trays. The team hung butcher paper up on the wall and picked *Lunchables* from a long list of puns and catchwords for fast, fun, and flexible food, including *On-Trays, Crackerwiches, Mini Meals, Lunch Kits, Snackables, Square Meals, Walk Meals, Go-Packs*, and *Fun Mealz*. At the end, when they'd finally chosen a name, the right components, and a prototype tray, the team asked itself: Just how likely was it, really, that America would go for a lunch of plain meat, crackers, and cheese?

Their bosses at Oscar Mayer were asking the same question, so they ran one final test. An outside research firm was hired to perform a process called BehaviorScan, which would help determine if the Lunchables was attractive to schoolchildren, or parents, for their own lunches, and what kind of advertising would compel the most consumption.

A few dozen families were recruited in Grand Junction, Colorado, and Eau Claire, Wisconsin. They were given shopping cards that would record their purchases, that is, how often they bought the Lunchables. Then their TV sets were wired into an electronic device that hijacked their normal programming to display commercials that their neighbors did not see. They were shown commercials for the Lunchables, and the frequency, timing, and tone of these ads were adjusted to test various strategies on how and when to pitch the trays.

The testing, which went on for months, surpassed Oscar Mayer's highest hopes. Not only did the people in the experiment go for the trays after being exposed to the advertising, the familiarity of the contents, however plain they were, proved to a foundational theorem in processed foods, which Drane calls "the weirdness factor": If a new product is too unusual, shoppers get scared. "I use the term, '80 percent familiar,' " Drane told me. "If you've got a new thing, it better be 80 percent familiar, or you'll have people scratching their heads wondering what the hell it is."

While the Lunchables tray itself was an alien sight in the supermarket aisles, the stuff inside was deeply familiar. The testing also told the company where to start marketing the trays. "The sales we saw in Grand Junction were twice as strong as the sales we saw in Eau Claire," Drane told me. "And we scratched our heads on that. We had thought meat and cheese and crackers would be right on for good old Eau Claire in the Midwest, and that Grand Junction in the West would be more kind of leading edge. But no. So we went to the West to roll out the Lunchables, and they started to sell. Then everybody else started to demand it across the country, and we were racing along on the manufacturing side, adding machines and capacity like crazy."

In the coming months, Drane and his team would uncover even richer insights into who liked the Lunchables and why. But first, they would get some invaluable help from the executives who oversaw not only Oscar Mayer but all of General Foods and Kraft. These were the men who ran Philip Morris, and they were taking a keen interest.

By 1990, Philip Morris had all but cornered the market for cigarettes. Its share of sales had grown to 42 percent, while the nearest rival, R. J. Reynolds, had slipped below 29 percent. With the purchase of General Foods and Kraft, it had also become a consumer goods goliath, posting $3.5 billion in annual profits on $51.2 billion in sales, with 157,000 employees worldwide. Half of its revenue now came from food, but tobacco, led by the Marlboro brand, was still the more lucrative enterprise, pulling in 70 percent of the profits. It was, as Hamish Maxwell said when he retired as the company's CEO, "a lovely business, because it's so relatively easy. Cigarettes have tremendous brand loyalty, you don't have to bring out new products every five minutes."

When they did make any changes at Philip Morris, the decisions were quick, almost instinctual. One Kraft executive recalled being in awe of the way the tobacco executives ran their Corporate Products Committee. At one of the monthly meetings, Marlboro's manager for Australia had traveled to New York to ask for permission to change the iconic pack design. "Here is the old one," he said, sliding it down the table. "And here is the new one." Go for it, the committee said.

The new food division, however, injected some strain into their handling of the company's affairs. Philip Morris had acquired the two food giants as a way to take the vast sums of cash the company was earning from cigarettes and put it to work making more money. General Foods (with its Jell-O and Post cereals), and Kraft (with its Velveeta cheese and Miracle Whip) were seen as ways to broaden the company's portfolio to include brands that were less controversial but still powerful. But it had paid dearly for General Foods, shelling out some $5.7 billion to buy the food giant in November 1985, and three years later it paid even more handsomely for Kraft in a deal valued at $12.9 billion. The Kraft purchase especially drew complaints from Wall Street that they had overpaid. Though not overly anxious about this criticism, the Philip Morris executives were resolute: They would get their money's worth.

This is how Geoffrey Bible ended up spending more than a year at Kraft's headquarters north of Chicago, abandoning his family to sleep in a company apartment three-quarters of a mile down the road, and devoting his days to learning the food trade. "Hamish Maxwell was a brilliant guy, in my opinion the best CEO we ever had," Bible told me. "He was the architect of all this buying of food companies and his attitude was, 'If you gotta do it, do it big, don't fiddle around.' We had sort of screwed around with the smaller companies we acquired and hadn't done well with any of them. He asked me if I'd go out there for a period of eighteen months or so to learn about the food business and, I suppose, maybe as a backup. A little bit of a safety valve."

I asked Bible about his first impressions of Kraft, whose executives were decidedly more formal and yet less steadfast in their devotion to the company. They tended to build their careers by moving from company to company within the consumer goods and fast food industries, whereas the Philip Morris executives stayed put.

"I never really worried much about the culture there," he said. "Cultures are cultures and you can't change them. Believe me, I've been through too many acquisitions to think they're going to change. They were different from us, and I sensed there was a certain . . . resentment isn't the right word, but we were a tobacco company, and tobacco wasn't highly thought of. We had had General Foods for a few years, and to some degree that was helpful, but there was a clash. The General Foods and the Kraft people didn't really hit it off. They had different styles. But they both had terrific brands, and I'd say that's what attracted Hamish, the great brands."

One of Bible's goals was to help smooth the merger by fostering a synergy between the food giants that could tie all of their expertise together, from the laboratories in Tarrytown, where people like Al Clausi, the chemist, labored to keep the brands fresh and attractive, to the sales force that roamed the country making sure that those products got the most prominent placement in the grocery store, to the advertising executives at the Leo Burnett agency who dreamed up the campaigns that convinced people to pick up those products and take them home. (The Burnett agency not only worked on food, such as Velveeta cheese for Kraft; in 1955 it created the cowboy known as the Marlboro Man.) To push this concept of synergy along, Philip Morris brought its far-flung staff to a Marriott hotel on the North Shore of Chicago, where they held a two-day retreat in December 1990 that was billed as the "Philip Morris Product Development Symposium."

Bible helped kick things off with a speech that was part war stories, part pep talk. He focused on the one thing that every one of the food managers needed to do if their products were to continue to dominate the processed food world. They had to understand, deeply, the mind of the consumer. "The simple beauty of the Kraft General Foods challenge is that everybody eats," Bible told them. "This is part of the new job I'm especially enjoying: The potential is at once limitless and incredibly daunting. The fascinating challenge is to discover unmet needs surrounding this behavior that has been with mankind since day one. The needs are there, waiting in the detritus of modern life to be excavated and defined as likely today to center around time or convenience as they are around taste, value or nutrition, and as likely to involve the subtleties of how, when, why, or where people eat as much as what they eat. So that's point number one. We don't create demand. We excavate it. We prospect for it. We dig until we find it."

For added inspiration, the food managers were treated to the inside story of how Philip Morris turned its own famous brand, Marlboro, from a loser nobody wanted into a cigarette that hooked more people than any other brand in the world, and how it added new brands and line extensions. Philip Morris didn't accomplish this by being the smartest cigarette maker; it did it by being the fastest and most aggressive in spotting the consumer's ever-changing vulnerabilities, as Philip Morris research and development official John Tindall explained. The company had gone from a 9 percent share of the cigarette market in 1954 to a 42 percent share in 1989 not by being the trendsetter but by quickly following its rivals when they came up with blockbuster innovations, like the slimmer cigarette called the 120s, which lent some needed glamour to smoking. It spun potentially devastating developments into gold by always keeping the mind of the consumer at the forefront of everything it did. Lesser companies might have panicked in 1964 when the Royal College of Physicians and Surgeons released its first report on smoking and health, but the Philip Morris managers seized upon it with a brilliant response. They began selling filtered cigarettes as a "healthier" alternative, which in turn broke open an entire new market for sales: women. "Suddenly, because of the smoking and health publicity, filter cigarettes became not only acceptable but necessary," Tindall said. "Filter cigarettes offered what smokers perceived as a health benefit, and the rapidly growing demographic segment, smoking women, could smoke filter cigarettes without getting tobacco in their mouths, and with only one end of the cigarette leaking tobacco into their purses."

One of the best examples of Philip Morris responding quickly to marketplace shifts was happening right at that moment, Tindall said. With the addictive properties of nicotine becoming more widely known, the company was working to create a low-nicotine cigarette, and in this endeavor it had the food scientists to thank. Philip Morris was borrowing the technology General Foods used to extract caffeine from coffee to pull the nicotine out of tobacco. "Obviously, there was concern that a low-nicotine cigarette might put the cigarette industry out of business," Tindall said. "The long-term management philosophy prevailed, though; we would compete in any category that had a chance for success."*

In the audience that day were 86 research and development officials from General Foods and another 125 from Kraft, who represented all the major brands, from boxed cereals to frozen desserts. But none of them would benefit more from all the talk about divining the consumer's mind and chasing trends than the people from Oscar Mayer, who at that moment were poised to take their own product, the Lunchables, to new heights.

For a brief moment, when production costs were outstripping revenue, it looked like Philip Morris had made a bad bet on the Lunchables. Right after Hamish Maxwell signed off on giving the trays more development money, which kept the Kraft bankers from shutting the whole venture down, sales dropped, and Bob Drane's team scrambled to slash production costs. Drane even gave up his most treasured part of the tray, the yellow napkin, "which I fought like crazy to hang on to. It was like one and a half cents, but every element was examined in detail to figure out how to reduce the costs without screwing up the quality." Oscar Mayer also gradually learned how to accomplish high-tech assembly, in which workers were replaced by machinery that accelerated and automated the factory lines, further reducing costs. Projected to lose $6 million in 1991, the trays instead broke even; and the next year, they earned $8 million.

Having extinguished this fire, the Lunchables team could focus its attention, once again, on boosting sales. And it did this by turning to one of the cardinal rules in processed food: When in doubt, add sugar. "Lunchables with Dessert is a logical extension," an Oscar Mayer official reported

---

* The low-nicotine cigarette, dubbed the De-Nic, turned out to be short-lived. Within a year of its release in 1992, Philip Morris pulled it from the market, citing slow sales.

to Philip Morris executives in early 1991. To accomplish this, they would have to spend $1.2 million to retool the production lines yet again. But the "target" remained the same as it was for regular Lunchables—"busy mothers" and "working women" aged twenty-five to forty-nine, he said—and adding cookies and puddings would bring several advantages. The "enhanced taste" would attract shoppers who had grown bored with the current trays; the added sweets would let the company charge thirty cents more per unit; and the dessert line would keep Oscar Mayer a step ahead of competitors who were reacting to the Lunchables success by putting out their own versions of cold, ready-to-eat lunch.

A year later, with the trays increasingly being eaten by kids, the dessert Lunchable morphed into the Fun Pack, which came with a Snickers bar, a package of M&Ms, or a Reese's Peanut Butter Cup as well as a sugary drink. The Lunchables team started by using Kool-Aid and Cola but switched to Capri Sun in 2000 when Philip Morris added that drink to its stable of brands.

By 1995, six years after their launch, the Lunchables were giving the tobacco executives some of the only good cheer in the financial reports from Oscar Mayer. In appearing before the Corporate Products Committee that fall, Bob Eckert, president of the Oscar Mayer unit, went through all the bad news in red meat: Bologna sales were down; bacon was down; even hot dogs had sunk 4 percent. "Our processed meat categories get more than their fair share of negative stories about fat, leukemia, nitrates and the like," Eckert lamented. In response, Oscar Mayer had begun making a new line of fat-free meats—hot dogs, bologna, sliced ham—that were projected to reach $100 million in sales.

The Lunchables, however, used the regular products and were already a superstar in the Oscar Mayer lineup. It had gone from being a money loser—or, as Eckert put it, "a bleeder"—to being "a growth engine," a foundation of the company's profits. "We're leading the hottest segment of the supermarket's refrigerated case," he said. That year, the Lunchables hit a string of milestones: 100 million pounds in trays sold, half a billion dollars in revenue earned, and $36 million in profits. Lunchables had come so far, so fast that Oscar Mayer was scrambling to find more places to make the trays. "We must expand manufacturing capacity," Eckert told the tobacco executives.

Sugar wasn't the only catalyst being used to advance the Lunchables sales. All three components—salt, sugar, and fat—would get hefty boosts. A line of the trays, appropriately called Maxed Out, was released that scoffed at the federal government's guidance on nutrition. These and other permutations had as many as 9 grams of saturated fat, or nearly an entire day's recommended maximum for kids, with two-thirds of the max for sodium salt, and 13 teaspoons of sugar.

When I asked Geoffrey Bible, former CEO of Philip Morris, about this shift toward more salt, sugar, and fat in meals for kids, he did not dismiss the nutritional concerns that this raised. Indeed, he said, even in their earliest incarnation, Lunchables were held up for criticism. "One article said something like, 'If you take Lunchables apart, the most healthy item in it is the napkin.' "

Well, they did have a good bit of fat, I offered.

"You bet," he said. "Plus cookies."

But speaking in general about the nutritional aspects of the products that Philip Morris sold through its food division, Bible said the company was in a tough spot. The prevailing attitude among the company's food managers—through the 1990s, at least, before obesity became a more pressing concern—was one of supply and demand. "People could point to these things and say, 'They've got too much sugar, they've got too much salt,' " he said. "Well, that's what the consumer wants, and we're not putting a gun to their head to eat it. That's what they *want*. If we give them less, they'll buy less, and the competitor will get our market. So you're sort of trapped."

Bible said the nutritional aspects of the company's products were typically left in the hands of brand managers, who faced an uphill battle whenever they sought to introduce a new product. But given the consumer's fickleness, the risks of failure were even greater if they tried to pull back on the keystones of their formulations, the salt, sugar, and fat. Bible said the most vivid example of this that he could recall involved Robert McVicker, a Kraft vice president for technology who died in 2001, and Michael Miles, the company's former CEO. "Bob was very keen to get a low-fat peanut butter," Bible said. "Peanut butter wasn't a big business for us, but it was big in the country, so if you find one it could pay. But it was going to cost a lot of money. So Mike had a rule, which I thought was a pretty sensible rule. He said to Bob, 'If you can find a brand manager who's prepared to absorb the R&D cost, go for it.' Now, if I'm the brand manager, and they say, 'Geoff, this is probably going to cost you $5 million and if you want to put it in a test market, another $10 million, and then if we roll it out to a bigger test market, this thing will cost you $30, $40 million.' And I say, well, 'No thanks.' You see your bonus disappearing. So it doesn't work, unless you can find somebody who's prepared to say, 'Okay, I'll take the punt. If it doesn't work, I'll eat the money, and I may lose my job, because that's what I'm paid to do, pick winners not losers.' A lot of these initiatives didn't really get out of the box because it's hard to find the funding, the champion who will get behind them. I think everybody did their best, but again, it's what the consumer wants that we tend to make."

When it came to Lunchables, they did try to add healthier ingredients. Back at the start, Drane had experimented with fresh carrots and sliced apples but quickly gave up on that; these fresh components didn't work within the constraints of the processed food system, which typically required weeks or months of transport and storage before the food arrived at the grocery store. The carrots and apple slices wilted or turned brown within days. Later, a low-fat version of the trays was developed, using meats and cheese and crackers that were formulated with less fat, but, like the low-nicotine cigarette, it tasted inferior, sold poorly, and was quickly scrapped.

When I met with Kraft officials in 2011 to discuss their products and policies on nutrition, they said that they were trying to improve the nutritional profile of Lunchables through smaller, incremental changes that were less noticeable to consumers. Across the Lunchables line, they said they had reduced the salt, sugar, and fat by about 10 percent, and new versions, featuring mandarin orange and pineapple slices, were in development. These would be promoted as healthier versions, with "fresh fruit," but their list of ingredients—containing upwards of seventy items, with sucrose, corn syrup, high-fructose corn syrup, fructose, and fruit concentrate all in the same tray—have compelled some reviewers to attack. "Snack Girl makes frequent visits to her local supermarket to check up on the latest," Lisa Cain, a biologist and mother of two, wrote in November 2011, on the website she calls Snack Girl. "Guess what I found in the shampoo aisle? Peanut Butter and Jelly Sandwich Lunchables! Right there next to shaving cream, toothpaste, and assorted hair products was Oscar Mayer's kid friendly MRE (meal ready to eat) for our children. Now, if we were in a hurricane situation—I would say, 'Stock up on those bad boys. They will last forever!' "

She added five "reasons to avoid" the new Lunchable: The sugar, at 37 grams, nearly matched that in a 12-ounce can of Coke; the $3 price tag far exceeded the cost of her homemade PB&J and fresh fruit; the packaging was not reusable; the bread was not 100 percent whole-grain; and the ingredients included "artificial colors, flavors and something called 'carnauba wax'—I use wax on my floors and car—not for food for my children."

Kraft has been deftly defusing criticism like this since the earliest days of the Lunchables, of course. One of the company's counterarguments was that kids don't eat the Lunchables every day, so even the versions with the heaviest loads of salt, sugar, and fat were just part of their overall diet that parents could supplement with healthier foods. They also pointed out that there was nothing automatically healthy about the brown-bag lunch, if parents loaded them up with their own brownies and cookies and soft drinks. As for the kids, the company pointed out that they were unreliable—even when their parents packed fresh carrots, apples, and water, they couldn't be trusted to *eat* it. Once in school, they often trashed the healthy stuff in their brown bags to get right to the sweets.

Kraft's use of this notion that kids are in control of their eating dates back to the earliest days of the Lunchables. In 1994, when a pediatric cardiologist called the trays a "nutritional disaster," a Kraft spokeswoman,

Jean Cowden, shot back, "This is not some big corporate plot to fatten up kids. This is what kids want. There are very few kids out there who will eat rice cakes and tofu."

This idea would become a key concept in the evolving marketing campaigns for the trays. In what would prove to be their greatest achievement of all, the Lunchables team would delve into adolescent psychology to discover that it wasn't the food in the trays that excited the kids; it was the fun, the cool, and most of all, the feeling of power it brought to their lives.

"If you had lunch with Michael Jordan tomorrow, what would you eat?"

That was the question Bob Drane put to kids in the mid-1990s, as his team began searching for tricks to keep the Lunchables sales growing. "And guess what came back?" Drane told me. "Pizza."

It made sense. Pizza, back then, was booming. Throughout the country, sixty thousand pizza restaurants were turning out $26 billion worth of the stuff each year. Pizza had become the hottest convenience food in the country, which, in turn, only helped fuel the entire fast food market. The big chains—from Pizza Hut to Domino's to Jack-in-the-Box—which had generated $6 billion in sales in 1970, were pulling in nearly $93 billion by 1995, or roughly a third of all restaurant sales nationwide.

But what did this pizza insight possibly have to offer them, the Lunchables team wondered. All those pizzas and burgers sold by restaurants and craved by kids had something the Lunchables could never replicate: They came out of an oven. They were hot. Lunchables came off the shelf of the cooler section of the grocery store and then went into kids' lunches from the fridge at home. Pizza would never be a possibility for them, right?

Wrong.

"We went through the Montessori School process again, asking, 'What could a pizza be like that would fit into the Lunchables world?' " Drane said. "We started to make them, and they had this characteristic of being cold. They could have been heated but not as a carried lunch. It was impractical, so we created little crusts and little sauces and toppings and stuff and stuck them in a package and showed them to moms." Not surprisingly, he said, "the moms told us, 'This is an awful idea, a really awful idea.' It was a disaster in the making, who would ever eat cold raw pizza, on and on. I think, in our testing, the concept got the worst score in our history."

And yet, Drane wouldn't let go of the idea. The potential windfall was just too huge. Not only were Americans buying $26 billion worth of pizzas from restaurants, they were spending another $1.7 billion on frozen pizzas they heated up at home. It was these frozen pizzas that gave Drane hope. Even when cooked, the crust on many of these was pale and soggy and tasted like cardboard. Surely, they could do better. So Drane and his team persevered, and a few months later, they encountered some good news. Moms may have been revolted by the idea of serving their kids a cold, raw pizza, but kids were a different story. The team whipped up a prototype; according to Drane, when "we showed it to kids, they said, 'Wow, that's really cool. I love it!' "

This disconnect between moms hating the idea of cold raw pizza and the kids loving it had to do with their distinct approaches to eating in general. Adults use their mouths when they eat, tasting whatever it is they are eating. By contrast, kids tend to use their eyes, judging the food—initially, at least—by how it looks. In a Lunchables with cold raw pizza, they saw nothing but fun. And to amp up the fun quotient, Drane's team didn't lay out the pizza in slices, as if it had been cut from a pie. They put it into the trays unassembled, in order to maximize the fun. The crust went into one compartment, the cheese, pepperoni, and sauce into others. That way, the kids got to make their own pizza right at school, while their schoolmates looked on with envy.

Kids weren't the only ones being targeted, however. Lunchables, in all of its incarnations, were powered by some potent psychology aimed at moms as well. In the beginning, the trays were wrapped in a cheerful, yellow cardboard sleeve that evoked the image of a gift, giving working moms who felt guilty for leaving their kids something special to give them in the morning as they headed out the door. "The box was there as a gift, something precious to elevate its specialness," Drane said. A few years after the launch, the cardboard sleeve was dropped in response to environmental criticism that the Lunchable was overpackaged. "It was one of those hold your breath moments," Drane said. But the impression of gifting was already so well established, it seemed to work just as well with a sleeveless box. "People tend to buy out of the right side of their brain, using emotions, and so we learned over time that for moms, this was a gift for their kids, and for kids it was a badge for their classmates."

Ultimately, it was the kids themselves who would make or break the Lunchables, so Kraft honed in on this concept of self-empowerment with all the marketing power it could muster. A few years later, the CEO of Kraft, Bob Eckert, put his finger on the psychology of this phenomenon of self-empowerment. "Lunchables aren't about lunch," he said in 1999. "It's about kids being able to put together what they want to eat, anytime, anywhere." Drane added, "Kids like to build things and play with food."

In response to this targeting of kids, Kraft shifted its advertising strategy. (The first campaign had targeted mothers with a theme called "The Bad Week." These ads proffered the trays as the solution to their mad dash to get out the door in the mornings.) As the focus swung toward kids, however, Saturday morning cartoons started carrying an ad that offered a different message, one of independence and empowerment.

"All day, you gotta do what they say," the ads said. "But lunchtime is all yours."

With this powerful marketing strategy in place and pizza Lunchables proving to be a runaway success, the entire world of fast food suddenly opened up for Kraft to pursue. Chains like Taco Bell were hooking America on the speedy, cheesy nature of "Mexican" food, so Lunchables came out with a Mexican Lunchables called Beef Taco Wraps. (Like the pizza, the taco filling was packed separately so that kids could be their own chefs at school.) Hamburgers, of course, were still the most popular fast food of all, and McDonald's reigned supreme for kids with its Happy Meal, so Lunchables went after that too. It created the Mini Burgers Lunchables, packing the tray with two meat patties, Kraft processed cheese, two buns, and a choice between ketchup or mustard, soft drink, and a candy bar. The Mini Hot Dog Lunchable was not far behind, which also happened to provide a synergistic way for Oscar Mayer to sell its wieners. This was followed by a line of Lunchables that extended the product's reach beyond lunch to other times of the day, including breakfast. By 1999, pancakes—which included syrup, icing, Lifesavers candy, and Tang, for a whopping 76 grams of sugar—and waffles were part of the Lunchables franchise as well.

This entire array was meant to be eaten cold, and the kids weren't bothered by cold pancakes any more than they were by raw pizza. Annual sales kept climbing, past $500 million, past $800 million; at last count, it was close to $1 billion. In food industry parlance, the Lunchables became more than a hit: It became a category. And it sustained Oscar Mayer at a time when its red meats were flagging.

Eventually, more than sixty varieties of Lunchables and other brands of trays—including Armour's Lunchmakers, which included a processed ham and cheese item called Cracker Crunchers and a Nestlé Crunch bar—were showing up in the grocery stores, mostly aimed at kids. In 2007, Kraft even came out with Lunchables Jr. for three- to five-year-olds.

Not surprisingly, much of this chilled processed food has been found lacking nutritionally. Convenience, of course, does have a price. Loads of salt, sugar, and fat are used not only to boost the allure of the foods; they are needed to make them safe for eating weeks or months after they were manufactured. And by 2009, when an advocacy group took a look at the explosion of fast foods in the grocery store, the price of this convenience was no longer being measured only in surging rates of childhood obesity. Children were succumbing to diabetes in greater numbers, a trend that was marked by some shocking studies. Nearly one in four American adolescents may be on the verge of developing type 2 diabetes or already have it, compared with one in ten in the 1990s. Type 2 is the most common form of diabetes, with obesity cited as the primary cause. In 2008, doctors who used ultrasound to peer inside the bodies of seventy children, many of them obese, found that kids as young as ten had the stiffened, thicker-walled arteries of forty-five-year-olds and other abnormalities that greatly increased their risk of heart disease.

The group, called the Cancer Project, that examined the prepackaged Lunchables-type meals, sized up nearly sixty ready-to-eat meals sold by grocery stores and found a nightmarish mix of salt, sugar, and fat in nearly all of them. Among the five rated worst by the group was a bologna and crackers kit sold by the Armour company, which delivered 9 grams of saturated fat, 39 grams of sugar, and 830 milligrams of sodium. Three of the worst-rated meals were from the Lunchables line, including, in the number one spot, a ham and cheese tray from the Maxed Out line. It had all the fat of the bologna tray, but with 57 grams of sugar—nearly 13 teaspoons—and 1,600 milligrams of sodium, which is two-thirds of the daily recommended maximum for kids. Under pressure from attacks like this, Kraft has dropped the Maxed Out line and is lowering the salt, sugar, and fat in other Lunchables to improve their nutritional profiles.

Bob Drane had moved on to other projects before many of these Lunchables lines were developed. But looking back to the earliest days, when he secured the funding he needed from Philip Morris to ramp up production, he said that he was not surprised by their success. "All things started to become clear," he said. "The volume goes up. The revenue goes up. The costs come down. The margins go up. The returns turn from red ink to black ink. You get what we call a platform, which becomes what we call a growth engine, and it goes on from there for a long, long time."

In the trove of records that document the rise of the Lunchables and the sweeping change it brought to lunchtime habits, one item drew my attention perhaps even more than the memos detailing the tactical pursuit of moms and kids or the nudging and gushing praise from Philip Morris executives. It was a photograph of Bob Drane's daughter, which he had slipped into the Lunchables presentation he showed other food developers. The picture was taken on Monica Drane's wedding day in 1989, and she was standing outside the family's home in Madison, a beautiful bride in a white wedding dress, holding one of the brand-new yellow trays.

I kept coming back to that photograph over the months that I spent researching the Lunchables. Something about it kept nagging at me. Was she really that much of a fan? I finally decided I had to ask her about it. "There must have been some in the fridge," she told me. "I probably just took one out before we went to the church. My mom had joked that it was really like their fourth child, my dad invested so much time and energy on it."

As we started to talk about the Lunchables, however, she said a far different moment in her life came to mind. It was the day a few years later, when she had moved to Boston to work in a district office of Congressman Barney Frank, and she was having lunch with a few other staffers and volunteers. "I came in with a Lunchable, feeling some measure of pride that my dad had created this cool, nifty package. And one woman there, a volunteer, was horrified. 'Do you realize all that plastic is going into the landfill? And all those nitrates in that ham?' "

"I had gone to a liberal arts college in Minnesota, and I had maybe the beginnings of an interest in healthier food, but not really. I shrank to about the size of a Lilliputian, thinking, 'Oh my gosh, she's right. Look at this awful yellow plastic. Look at the ingredients.' And I don't even know if there were ingredient lists then, but I had enough awareness to think, 'Oh wow, this really *is* pretty awful.' "

Monica Drane had three of her own children by the time we spoke, aged ten, fourteen, and seventeen. "I don't think my kids have ever eaten a Lunchable," she told me. "They know they exist and that Grandpa Bob invented them. But we eat very healthfully."

After the Boston incident, Monica said she used to get after her dad, berating him for "how junky Lunchables are, and now that I'm older I realize how thoughtless that was. For him, it was an effort to create jobs in the Madison community. He was deeply committed to finding ways to employ people. That drove a lot of his pursuit. He also saw it from a cultural stand-point, that there was a need for something like a Lunchable for people who didn't have the resources that I have. And maybe the outcome wasn't the most desirable product, but the impulse was right."

Bob Drane didn't strike out entirely with his kids—one of his two sons became an enthusiast, Monica said, sending his own kids off to school with the trays, but Drane said it was not unusual for product developers like him to find little in the way of inspiration in their own households. There is a class issue at work in processed foods, in which the inventors and company executives don't generally partake in their own creations. Thus the heavy reliance on focus groups with the targeted consumer.

"People who work in these companies have very little in common, frequently, with their audience," he said. "They're super-educated, and their incomes are much higher, and their lifestyles are frequently very different. They're the folks that invent things for the middle of the market, and they frequently are clueless, so the voice of the consumer is the voice you have to pay attention to, and that's one of the principles of success. Don't listen to the senior vice president. Let the people that you're going to sell something to tell you what they want."

Having done just that—delivered what people wanted, saved a few hundred jobs, and eased the morning crush of harried families—Bob Drane paused only briefly when I asked him if, looking back today, he was proud of creating the trays. "Lots of things are trade-offs, of course," he said. "And I do believe it's easy to rationalize anything. In the end, I wish that the nutritional profile of the thing could have been better, but I don't view the entire project as anything but a positive contribution to people's lives. On balance, it did a lot of things within the convenience world that served people, and the benefits outweighed, I think, the negatives. It established the model of a preprepared, prepacked lunch. And one of the things I love about innovation is for subsequent generations to go back, having a model, and continuously improve it. I'm still believing that model will long endure and will serve society, kids, and moms, in various ways, and that over time, people will adjust in the direction it needs to be adjusted."

Today, Bob Drane is still talking to kids about what they like to eat, but his approach has changed. He volunteers with a nonprofit organization based in Madison that seeks to build better communications between school kids and their parents who are less well off financially, and right in the mix of their problems, alongside the academic struggles, is childhood obesity. Drane has also prepared a précis on the food industry in discussing obesity with students at the University of Wisconsin. And while he does not name his Lunchables in this document, he holds the entire industry accountable for the epidemic, citing the "rise in corporate cooking, processed and preserved foods, often high in sugar/fat/salt/etc. More calories in, less calories burned, obesity up.

"What do University of Wisconsin MBA's learn about how to succeed in marketing? Discover what consumers want to buy, and give it to them with both barrels. Sell more, keep your job! How do marketers often translate these 'rules' into action on food? Our limbic brains love sugar, fat, salt (scarce and high energy). So, formulate products to deliver these. Perhaps add low cost ingredients to boost profit margins. Then 'supersize' to sell more (# users x amount/user). And advertise/promote to lock in 'heavy users.' Plenty of guilt to go around here!"

There is no magic pill to resolve the nation's weight problem, Drane writes. Rather, he proposes a long list of partial solutions and pokes the manufacturers of processed food as hard as his daughter used to poke him. The industry, he writes, must recognize that " 'corporate cooking' now plays a dominant role in our diets and 'whatever sells' can no longer be a stand-alone yardstick." It must start reducing or removing ingredients that cause obesity, and "invent more products with less sugar, fat, salt, etc." It needs to fund research "to discover how 'corporate cooked foods' might come closer to delivering the nutritional benefits of old fashioned scratch cooking. We need some across-the-board breakthroughs here, in ingredients, and processing/preservation systems, and shorter/faster distribution."

In holding the industry accountable, Drane's list of ways to fix the obesity problem had one notable gap: the federal government's own role in tempering the processed food industry's zeal. But there was a reason for this. As food manufacturers know very well and as I would find out by moving the reporting for this book from Madison to Washington, when it comes to nutrition, the role the government plays is less a matter of regulation than it is promotion of some of the industry practices deemed most threatening to the health of consumers.

chapter ten

"The Message the Government Conveys"

The Department of Agriculture is headquartered on the National Mall, a mere stroll from the Washington Monument. It is the only cabinet-level agency with this distinction, and in keeping with the open-door policies of its neighbors—the museums of the Smithsonian—it maintains a modest visitors center for tourists. With 117,000 employees, the agency prides itself on being of service to the country at large, a populist arm of the government. After all, when President Abraham Lincoln created it in 1862 for a country that was still heavily agrarian, he called it "The People's Department."

There are actually two buildings that form the headquarters of the Department of Agriculture, and both are massive. The main one, which houses the top brass, was built in sections starting in 1904. Its two wings, detailed with white marble, stretch for one-sixth of a mile along the Mall and are braced by the gigantic white Corinthian columns typical of the Beaux Arts style. Behind this stands the South Building, which went up in

1936 to house the agency's expanding operations. Its 4,500 rooms and seven miles of corridors gave it the distinction of being the largest office building in the world until the Pentagon was built a few years later.

Inside the Department of Agriculture, where the public is less welcome, the agency pursues an agenda that is every bit as massive as the buildings themselves: Overseeing the food that Americans eat. Its principal mission is to ensure the integrity of the country's most fundamental life-giving force, from farm to fork. But in this matter, the People's Department of Lincoln's imaginings has long been enmeshed in a conflict of interest that undermines its populist roots. On one side are the 312 million or so people of the United States and their health, which the USDA is charged with safeguarding. On the other side are the three hundred or so companies that form the $1 trillion industry of food manufacturing, companies that the USDA feels obligated to placate and nurture. Nowhere is the tension between what is good for the companies and what is good for the people more evident than in one of the pillars of processed foods: fat.

Fat, of course, is the lubricant that sustains the $90 billion trade in snack foods, providing that crucial element known as mouthfeel to corn chips and crackers, ice cream and cookies. But in a little-known fact of nutrition, neither chips nor desserts are pumping anywhere near the levels of fat into our bodies as two other mainstays of processed foods. In fact, the biggest deliverers of saturated fat—the type of fat doctors worry about—are cheese and red meat, and it is in producing and selling these two products that the food industry has shown its greatest ability to influence public policy. With the American people facing an epidemic of obesity and hardened arteries, the "People's Department" doesn't regulate fat as much as it grants the industry's every wish. Indeed, when it comes to the greatest sources of fat—meat and cheese—the Department of Agriculture has joined industry as a full partner in the most urgent mission of all: cajoling the people to eat more.

• • •

To meet the employees of the Department of Agriculture who work on the people's side of things, protecting their nutritional health, you have to hop on the Washington Metro, ride under the Potomac River, and then transfer to a bus, which takes you to an intersection in the far western edge of Alexandria, Virginia. From there, you still have to walk a third of a mile to a stone-and-glass building and ride an elevator up to the tenth floor. Here, finally, is a division called the Center for Nutrition Policy and Promotion. Its lowly rank in the pecking order is not only reflected in its satellite office status, it is reflected in the amount of money it's allowed to spend in pursuit of healthier food. The center's annual budget is a paltry $6.5 million, which amounts to 0.0045 percent of the agency's overall outlays of $146 billion. Given this constraint, the center channels much of its energy into a single modest endeavor: creating and promoting an official guide to better eating.

This guide, which sets the framework for the government's policies on nutrition, was first published in 1980, when obesity was starting to surge. It gets updated every five years with help from a panel of experts that works with the center to assess the state of America's eating habits. This group includes dieticians, educators, research scientists, and epidemiologists, and over the years they have zeroed in on the biggest culprits in overeating. Their lengthy, heavily detailed reports have documented the country's addiction to sugar and charted our dependence on salt as well. Some of the panel's most compelling work came in preparing its latest report, published by the USDA in 2010.

Saturated fat, the panel concluded, has been on a tear.

This type of fat—so named by chemists for the way it is fully saturated with hydrogen atoms, without the double-bonded carbons that characterize unsaturated fats—has long been associated with heart disease, the panel noted. It is a primary cause of high cholesterol in the bloodstream, a waxy substance that leads to heart attacks and strokes, and a significant profit center for the pharmaceutical industry. An estimated thirty-two million Americans are taking drugs to reduce their cholesterol levels. But for the first time, the panel also stressed that saturated fat was partly responsible for another health epidemic: type 2 diabetes, the kind caused by poor diet. The latest estimates were that 24 million Americans had type 2 diabetes, with another 79 million people having pre-diabetes. Even more disturbing, a small but growing number of kids—many of them obese—were getting type 2 diabetes, with 3,600 new cases diagnosed each year.

The USDA panel had access to federal data on how much salt, sugar, and fat Americans were eating, and it found the levels for saturated fat to be chronically high, especially among children. To account for the differences in how much we eat overall, nutritionists measure the fat in our diets as a percentage of all the calories we consume. The consumption data showed that kids between one to three years were ingesting the most saturated fat of anyone—more than 12 percent of their total caloric intake. They were followed closely by older kids, at 11.5 percent, and adults, who clocked in at roughly 11 percent. These, of course, were averages, which did not take into account the people the food industry targets as "heavy users," whose intake of fat knows no bounds.

"Deliberate public health efforts are warranted to reduce intakes of saturated fats," the panel said in its 2010 report. So it took the bold step of lowering its recommended maximum allowance of saturated fat for everyone, kids and adults. The old limit was 10 percent. Now, said the panel, everyone should strive to reduce their intake to 7 percent, or barely more than half what kids are consuming today on average.*

Finally, the panel was granted access to the federal government's research on where Americans were getting all this fat, and the findings were stunning. Topping the list of culprits was cheese, followed by pizza, which is basically a vehicle for conveying cheese. Together, cheese and pizza contributed more than 14 percent of the saturated fat being consumed. Second on the list was red meat in its various forms, which accounted for more than 13 percent of the fat in our diet. In third place—at a bit less than 6

---

* Using the standard of 2,000 calories a day, an average on which the nutritional labeling on packaged foods is based, a person would need to consume no more than fifteen-and-a-half grams of saturated fat—about three scoops of ice cream or two glasses of whole milk—to reach the 7 percent level.

percent—were all those grain-based desserts like chocolate cake and cookies, which are laden with oils. The list stretched on, meandering through the grocery aisles, from boxed frozen dinners to candy. Chips, from potato to corn, contributed only 2.4 percent of the saturated fat in our diet.

Taken together, the agency's report on saturated fat—the health trouble, the overconsumption, the dominance of cheese and meat as the biggest sources—would seem to lead to a logical conclusion: We should stop eating so much cheese and meat. Which was precisely the conclusion reached by some of country's smartest independent thinkers on nutritional health, including a man named Walter Willett, who leads the nutrition program at Harvard's School of Public Health. Willett is blunt in urging people to cut back on cheese and red meat. Red meat, he says, should be slashed from the current average of one serving a day to no more than two servings a week. Moreover, red meat that has been processed into bacon, bologna, hot dogs, sandwich meats, and other products with added salt is best avoided altogether. Numerous other foods can supply the protein that people require, including chicken and fish, while their calcium needs can be met through vegetables and, if need be, a supplement.

But here is where consumer advocates and the consumer advocacy at the USDA diverge, and strikingly so. For starters, the 2010 guide buried the information about where we are getting all our saturated fat, slipping it into a single chart that appears on page 26 of the 95-page report. More significantly, nowhere in the document was there any explicit talk about reducing consumption of meat and cheese. Mum on this matter, too, was the reader-friendly graphic, shaped like a dinner plate, that was released in 2011 to help convey the message of better eating to the greatest number of Americans, including children.

Following the release of the guide, Willett and Margo Wootan, the director of nutrition at the Center for Science in the Public Interest, publicly confronted a spokesman for the USDA's nutrition center. Appearing on a popular radio talk show based in Washington, D.C., in February 2011, Willett and Wootan accused the agency of being reluctant to point a finger not only at cheese and red meat, but at any specific food or product known to be a contributor to poor health. "If you really want people to reduce solid fat intake, you've got to talk about reducing consumption of red meat, consumption of cheese, ice cream, and other products like that," Willett said. "That needs to be said *clearly*. . . . Unfortunately, I think the finger-prints of big beef, big dairy are still all over these guidelines."

In reply, the deputy director of the nutrition center, Robert Post, launched into several familiar points that did little to assuage his critics. The agency was acting with full transparency, he said, opening the panel's meetings to the public and not just industry representatives, with every-one's input posted online. In his view, the science of nutrition revolved around nutrients, not particular foods, and the best strategies for achieving optimum health required the consideration of a person's entire diet. "The idea isn't to eliminate any specific food," he said.

If that was all the People's Department did in its guidelines—*not* name names when it came to helping people improve their diets—nutritionists might not have been so angry with the agency; people might still have been able to figure out for themselves that cheese and meat were the most obvious things to cut back on. But the USDA went further toward helping the food industry. The 2010 guide did, in fact, mention cheese. In a sec-tion titled, "Foods and Nutrients to Increase," cheese was included among the foods that people should eat *more* of, not less. As for meat, the guide suggests eating more seafood for its omega-3 fatty acids, a "good" fat that appears to lower the risk of heart disease, but meat is touted throughout the report with the added assurance that neither it, nor milk products, have been specifically linked to obesity: "These foods are important sources of nutrients in healthy eating patterns."

The agency offers one caveat with these recommendations: The cheese and meat we eat should be of the non- and lower-fat varieties. But there was a problem with this nuance, out in the real world. Since nonfat cheese tastes awful and the low-fat varieties aren't much better, grocery stores mostly offer the full-fat varieties. Meat is even more problematic. There are no whole cuts of red meat in the grocery store that fall within the USDA's definition of "low-fat," which is 3 percent fat or less.

The closest they come to this standard is 5 percent fat, known as extra-lean, and 10 percent fat, known as lean. A piece of lean meat just over three ounces has four-and-a-half grams of saturated fat, nearly a third of the recommended maximum for a day's intake. Nonetheless, this was precisely the kind of meat that the USDA was urging people to eat.

These lean-type meats—even with their third of a day's saturated fat in each serving—aren't what people envision when they think of meat. They often lack the deep flavor and silky mouthfeel that comes from a highly marbled steak, where the heated fat swims over the tongue to send signals of joy to the brain. But even if more people *wanted* to follow the USDA's advice and eat lean meat, finding it in the grocery store would be no piece of cake. In fact, it can require considerable skill in the game of hide and seek. (Shopping for meat is not like shopping for cereal, where sugar content is required, by law, to be listed on the box.) A little explanation in the ways of Washington is needed to understand why.

Another federal agency, the Food and Drug Administration, quite apart from the Department of Agriculture, oversees all of the food in the grocery store except for the meat and dairy. The FDA has its own issues in balancing the needs of consumers and the needs of industry, but starting in the 1990s it took a major leap forward on behalf of consumers: It required food manufacturers to spell out on the packaging exactly how much salt, sugar, and fat their products contained so that shoppers could make better assessments of what they are eating.* By contrast, the Department of Agriculture is only now starting to move in this direction with meat—and an awkward start it has been. In selling most meats, grocery stores are merely required to post a guide—listing the fat content of generic cuts—somewhere in the vicinity of the cooler. This chart can be placed high, it can be placed low, it can even be placed on the other side of the aisle; in short, it can be made very easy to miss. To help out, the beef in-

---

* The Nutrition Labeling and Education Act of 1990, passed by Congress, required the FDA to set food labeling rules.

dustry has created an online guide that discloses the fat content of generic cuts of meat, and suggests that consumers who want less fat look for clues on the label, including the words *round* or *loin*.

In 2012, the USDA required this information to be placed directly on packages of ground beef, but even this came with a gift to the meat producers. At the industry's urging, the Department of Agriculture allowed them to put the word *lean* on their packages even when the meat is not lean by the agency's own definition. For example, the fattiest hamburger sold in stores has six or more grams of saturated fat in three ounces. And yet the label approved by the USDA will read: "70 percent lean, 30 percent fat." Of course, there is a good reason the industry wants to use the word *lean*. According to surveys done by consumer advocates, the lean-fat labeling causes shoppers to think the meat has less fat than it really does—if they are looking at the label at all. For many, if not most, people, the decision-making stops at the price, and here, too, there is a perverse real-world issue that cancels out the federal advice to eat lean meats: The more fat that meat has, the less it costs. In 2012, stores were charging $1 more a pound for the leaner grades.

In one respect, it's hard to blame the USDA for pulling its punches on meat and cheese. Long ago, the manufacturers of processed foods, having identified the agency's nutritional guide as a key battleground, devoted considerable resources to influencing the 2010 panel before their work even started. USDA records show that seven of the panel's thirteen members were nominated by the Grocery Manufacturer's Association. The members I interviewed all vouched for their independence, but the association—in its nomination letters to the USDA—made its position clear: If the panel was going to be talking about healthier diets, it needed "to include expertise and perspective related to food product development," and thus, it needed members who *understood* the industry's needs and challenges. For instance, one of its nominees, Roger A. Clemens, was the associate director of regulatory science in the School of Pharmacy at the University of Southern California, but earlier in his career he had spent twenty-one years developing products for Nestlé, which gave him, he told me, a deep appreciation for matters like the essential role that salt plays in shielding processed food from harmful bacteria.*

At the same time, the Grocery Manufacturers Association, whose members include Kraft, Kellogg, Nestlé, PepsiCo, and almost every other major manufacturer of processed foods—more than three hundred companies in all—joined other food industry groups and individual companies in pressing the panel to tread lightly in considering their big concerns, especially salt, sugar, and fat. This lobbying took the form of letters and supporting documentation submitted to the panel, through which the companies sought to challenge the panel's assessment of the health risks posed by these additives. The food manufacturers also recited the hurdles they face in reducing their own dependence, such as the diminished texture and taste in cereal with decreased sugar or fat loads.

This intense lobbying effort went on for months, with hundreds of submissions to the USDA, but a single day's mail, July 15, 2010, provides a representative view of the war over fat that was waged by consumer and manufacturer alike. The typical consumer's view was voiced by Bonnie Matlow, a librarian from Shepherdsville, Kentucky, who also happened to be diabetic. "It is a shame entire generations have lost the ability to cook a good meal from local ingredients," she wrote to the panel, "because money was shifted to corporate farms to underwrite the growing of energy dense, nutritionally deficient grains that require supplementation to justify its inclusion in the guidelines, unpronounceable preservatives to last on the shelf, and sugar/HFCS [high-fructose corn syrup] to be palatable."

That same day, a 17-page letter arrived from the USDA's other, more monied constituency. The sender said he represented an industry with $2.1 trillion in annual sales, 14 million jobs, and $1 trillion in "added value

---

* Other special interests like egg producers, cereal manufacturers, and a second food industry funded group, the International Food Information Council, won their own panel members, while four others were nominated by academic institutions. But none of the thirteen members was nominated by a consumer advocacy organization. The nominating letters were released to me through a Freedom of Information Act request.

to the nation's economy." It was from the Grocery Manufacturers Association, and it started off with a gripe: "We find that the Dietary Guideline Advisory Committee report repeatedly suggests that Americans would benefit from consuming less processed foods. This supposition is not science-based, discounts the value of the U.S. food supply, and perpetuates a misguided belief that processed foods are inherently nutrient poor." To the contrary, the association said, food processing allowed for a huge variety of fortified, convenient foods to be eaten year-round. The association then did its best to persuade the panel from being any more specific if it did persist in urging Americans to eat fewer processed foods. (In a separate letter written three months earlier, the association had said, "There are no inherent 'good foods' or 'bad foods,' " and it reiterated this notion that better nutrition was instead a matter of total diet.)

The GMA also spent more than a page of its letter arguing against the panel's move to lower the recommended daily maximum for saturated fat, saying, among other things, that the previous, higher limit was easier to achieve and thus "more consumer friendly." But while the manufacturers ultimately lost on this matter when the panel held firm and lowered the rate, they pointed out that the change posed little real threat to them. Merely lowering the maximum limit *without* offering specific advice on how to accomplish this would do nothing to alter America's eating habits. "Reducing saturated fat intake from 10 percent to 7 percent is an abstract concept to consumers," the association told the panel.

Trekking out to Virginia to lobby the Department of Agriculture officials who speak for the health of consumers, of course, is only one small part of the job description for those who represent the food industry. Much of their time is spent prowling the corridors of agency headquarters on the National Mall, where their influence is free from any significant challenge. There, the food manufacturers don't spend much time pressing the USDA to go easy on its regulations, though that is certainly part of their mission. Instead, they have used their power to turn the agency into a partner in promoting their products. And when it comes to meat and cheese, this relationship has gotten the food companies out of some of their toughest jams—like how to get even more meat and cheese into the shopping carts of Americans, even as they are growing more leery of fat.

The Department of Agriculture's role in promoting cheese and meat began in earnest in 1985, when the Reagan administration sought to curb the federal government's subsidies for milk. As John Block, the incoming secretary of agriculture, saw it, the problem was too much production, so he set out to shrink the nation's milk cow herds. But the proposed fix for Big Dairy—the government would pay for slaughtering 339,000 of their cows—caused some grief for Big Beef. All that meat would flood the market and send beef prices plunging.

Enter a sympathetic Congress.

"I am concerned about the American cattlemen," Senator Steve Symms, a Republican from Idaho, told his colleagues in 1985. They were hashing out the latest incarnation of the Farm Bill—which sets government policy on agriculture and food—and Symms came from cattle country. "The cowboys are one group of farmers who do not come into Washington and have their hand in the federal trough. I do not know the answer, but I do have a great deal of concern for the American cattlemen, and I think they deserve our heartiest congratulations. I guess one thing we could all do is encourage everyone to go buy some beefsteak—that might help them as much as anything. We could also drink a couple extra glasses of milk and do our part to help get rid of the dairy surplus."

As it turned out, the dairy cow buyout failed to make much of a dent in the overproduction of milk, since the dairies simply stocked up on new cows, and the ongoing overproduction of milk went toward making more and more cheese. But the ranchers would still get some relief by way of the 1985 Farm Bill. In the short run, the legislation required the Department of Agriculture to purchase 200 million pounds of beef over the next two years for distribution to the needy. Over the long term, however, the Farm

Bill had another, more ingenious solution to the surplus problem. It created a system through which meat and cheese producers could aggressively market their products directly to the entire American public and thus encourage the consumption of beef like never before.

Marketing had never been one of the beef and dairy industry's strong points. To the extent that they understood the power of marketing, they quarreled among themselves too much to develop any kind of organized effort. The ranchers and dairy operators needed help, and Congress had just the solution in mind. It created two marketing programs, one for beef and one for milk, and it put the Secretary of Agriculture in charge of them both.

The programs became known as "checkoffs," so named for the scheme put in place to raise the money needed to pay for the marketing. Here is how it worked: the nintey-thousand-plus milk cow owners were required to pay fifteen cents to the checkoff for every 100 pounds—about 12 gallons—of milk they produced. For beef, the levy was based on transactions: Every time a cow was sold, such as from ranch to feedlot or from feedlot to slaughterhouse, the seller was required to pay one dollar into the marketing program for beef. Not everyone liked this idea of marketing beef as an undifferentiated mass. Some ranchers view their beef as superior, which they understandably want to promote through their own, specifically tailored advertising. When ranchers were asked to approve the creation of the checkoff program, one in five voted against it, but it wasn't enough: The majority cast its lot with the Department of Agriculture, so everyone was required to pay the levy.

The dollars for marketing beef added up to more than $80 million a year, and over the years, the total money raised has topped $2 billion. That is, essentially, $2 billion for selling America on more beef, compared with the $6.5 million the USDA's nutrition center gets each year to nudge Americans in the other direction—of cutting back, not only on fat but on sugar and salt as well. It hasn't been a fair fight.

The money arrived in the nick of time. Public consumption of beef had been trending downward since 1976: The average person's yearly consumption of red meat slipped from 94 pounds to 65 pounds, with hamburger accounting for about half of all beef consumed. At the same time, Americans were eating more and more chicken and, to a lesser extent, fish—both of which have far less saturated fat.

This was a real source of concern for beef, but with its new war chest it began mapping out a strategy to maneuver around the public's concerns. It spent some of the money on market research and found that beef faced the same problem that cheese used to have. People had been stuck eating cheese by itself, or with crackers, until Kraft—supported by the dairy industry's marketing program—got the idea of transforming the public's concept of cheese, which sent sales and consumption through the roof. Why couldn't beef do the same thing?

Mark Thomas, a biochemist, was working for a research and development arm of the beef industry when this lightbulb went on. His unit didn't have a fancy research laboratory, so it set up a contest to solicit beef-as-an-ingredient ideas from all manner of potential inventors, from cattle growers to grocery manufacturers large and small. The mission: put beef into a prepared and packaged meal that needed only to be heated before being served.

"I thought it was a dumb idea," Thomas told me. "We'd have these products sent to our test kitchen in Chicago and then presented to a group of judges who would pick five, with a top prize of $50,000. But we put all our advertising weight behind this new category. Fast forward to today, and you will find five to eight brands of ready-to-cook entrees that use beef, from Tyson and others. Hormel has a huge selection, Tips & Gravy, Pot Roast, that you microwave for fifteen minutes. I serve a pot roast to guests, and they think my wife made it."

With the rise of chicken and its huge success in McNugget-type convenience foods, the industry then put its money to work creating finger foods using beef. A team of food technicians fiddled with beef every which way they could, wrapping it in pancakes with eggs and cheese, adding cheese to it and wrapping it around a stick, and stuffing it into a hollowed-out roll that had the added feature of standing upright on the plate, for a little dining pizzazz. These technicians worked for a Denver-based group known as the Cattlemen's Beef Board, which was funded by checkoff monies and had 106 members, all of whom were appointed by the Secretary of Agriculture. On its website, the board said that the impetus for all these finger-beef foods was the demise of the American family dinner, which, while lamentable, should be viewed as an opportunity. "We've done a lot of research over the last couple of years regarding today's youth and today's adult consumer, and especially with the adult consumer," a beef board official said in one promotional video. "They are on the go, and the same with kids, they are rushed as well. They are going to school, to various practices, to after-school events, and then spend a lot of time doing homework, and we ate at the dinner table every night, and we understand that today's consumers don't do that necessarily. So we try to make new convenient products that fit into their lifestyles. Based on the research, with people on the go, we tried to make these products as easy and convenient as possible and as portable as possible."

If Americans were intent on snacking their way through the day, beef would be there for them. In this effort, the beef industry discovered it had a natural ally in dairy. They combined forces to develop recipes that used both beef and cheese, and worked together to promote more fast food sales as well through campaigns like "Double Cheeseburger Days," which launched in 2006, targeting college students. The beef industry's own analysis has found that the checkoff program has been boosting the consumption of beef between 3 and 5 percent each year since its founding in 1986.

As it was promoting new convenience foods that used beef, the beef marketing program also went in the other direction. It developed new cuts of beef that had less fat, including one called the Flat Iron, which was taken from the animal's shoulder. Today, the beef industry says it has at least twenty-nine cuts of beef that meet the government guidelines for being lean: 4.5 grams of saturated fat in a serving, which, remember, is still nearly a third of the daily recommended maximum. It also rolled out an intense lobbying campaign that sought to dispel the notion that beef was inherently fatty and, at the same time, emphasize its nutrients, such as zinc and vitamin B12. "Beyond beef's leanness and favorable fatty acid profile, beef's bundle of nutrients is beneficial for growing, developing and maintaining overall health through all life's stages, from gestation to the senior years," the National Cattlemen's Beef Association, an affiliate of the beef board, wrote to the USDA's nutrition panel during the deliberations for the 2010 nutrition guide.

Behind the scenes, however, the industry has struggled with these leaner cuts. Some suffer greatly from having less fat, with an inferior mouthfeel and tough chewing. One of the industry's solutions to this has been to soften up the muscular tissue in the processing plant by running the leanest meat through a device that deploys rows of steel needles or blades to pierce the meat, in what is known as "mechanical tenderization"; some 50 million pounds of meat is currently being softened in this fashion each month. Another method is to treat the meat with a briny solution that softens the tissue.*

One of the most successful approaches to marketing lean beef turned out to be the most controversial. It didn't involve needles or brine or merely trimming fat off with a knife. It involved ammonia. This created the leanest, least expensive, most-commonly eaten burger America had yet seen—that is, until the public caught on and the lean, ammonia-processed beef came to be known as "pink slime."

This material—which the USDA preferred to call "lean finely textured beef"—is produced by taking pieces of beef from the fattiest parts of the cow—ranging up to 70 percent fat—that has previously been diverted to pet food or tallow. The material is then put through a high-speed centrifuge that spins much of the fat off, leaving a mash that has the virtue of being quite lean, with all but ten percent of the fat removed. It is then

* Worries have arisen about both of these methods, despite the industry's conviction that they are safe. The needles used in mechanical tenderization could push E. coli and other harmful pathogens into the center of steaks where, normally, the cooking temperature is not high enough to kill the bugs. As for the brining, some of the solutions in use have added hefty loads of salt to the meat.

formed into 30-pound blocks, frozen, and shipped to meat plants, where the blocks are combined with other beef trimmings to make hamburger.

The defatted beef became popular with the companies that make hamburger for another reason: It was 15 percent cheaper than the naturally lean meat from South America, where ranchers raise their cattle on grass, forgoing the fat-inducing process of corn feeding that is typical in the American beef industry. The money to be saved was significant, and not only to grocers and restaurant chains like McDonald's, who bought hamburger made with the defatted beef. The USDA itself realized that it could shave up to three cents off the price of every pound of hamburger it was buying for school lunch programs.*

In the early 1990s, the USDA gave the green light to its burger suppliers to start using the defatted processed beef as a component in ground beef. The largest producer was a company called Beef Products Inc., based in South Dakota, but it had an additional step in its production that would prove to be its undoing. Beef Products Inc. began treating its processed meat with ammonia gas to kill any pathogens that might be present. This threat of contamination was more of an issue with the defatted material because it came from parts of the cow carcass most exposed to the feces that harbor E. coli. Meat gets tainted by E. coli in the slaughterhouse when these feces accidently get smeared on the meat during butchering. Adding the ammonia—which also gave the material a pink hue that was brighter than normal beef—was tricky. The company's experiments in methodology led to cases where the ammonia either failed to kill pathogens or tainted the meat with its powerful smell. In 2003, officials in Georgia returned nearly 7,000 pounds to the company after cooks who were making meatloaf for state prisoners detected a "very strong odor of ammonia" in 60-pound blocks of the trimmings. "It was frozen, but you could still smell

---

* The actual savings varied year to year, depending on how much burger was served and the percentage of defatted material used. In 2012, before the pink slime controversy forced the USDA to backpedal, agency officials said that they had planned to purchase 111 million pounds of ground beef using the defatted material at less than half the typical rate of 15 percent, which would have saved them 1.5 cents a pound, or $1.4 million.

ammonia," Charles Tant, a Georgia agriculture department official, told me. "I've never seen anything like it." Nevertheless, ammonia was soon being used as an additive in an estimated 70 percent of the hamburger sold by grocery stores and restaurants.*

Disturbed by the ammonia, officials in the USDA's school lunch program fought to have its presence disclosed on the labeling but were overruled by others at the agency who were persuaded that ammonia should be viewed as just one of the many chemicals the industry uses in processing meat that are not subject to public disclosure. But the issue didn't go away. In 2002, a USDA microbiologist, Gerald Zirnstein, sent an email message to colleagues in which he wrote, "I do not consider the stuff to be ground beef, and I consider allowing it in ground beef to be a form of fraudulent labeling." In this same email, he called the processed beef "pink slime."

Zirnstein's "pink slime" moniker became public when I first published it in 2009, having obtained his email in the course of reporting on Beef Products Inc.'s struggles with the ammonia treatment. The article I wrote set in motion a cascade of events. The company vowed to improve its methodology, the USDA pledged to step up its scrutiny, and some parents—in Manhattan and Boston—contacted me to say that they had begun pressing their school districts to stop serving burger that used the defatted material. Far more significantly, one of the biggest users, McDonald's, would initiate a slow-burn change in corporate policy that led, in 2011, to the chain discontinuing use of the defatted beef in the hamburger it served. Beef Products Inc. staunchly defended its product as safe and nutritious, but when word of the move by McDonald's got out, a surge of public scrutiny led to a plunge in Beef Products' sales.†

---

* Despite the ammonia's intended purpose of killing pathogens, testing the processed meat turned up instances of contamination, in which the tainted product was diverted before it could reach consumers.

† Among the de-fatted beef's critics was Bettina Siegel, a Harvard Law School graduate who had previously worked for the food giant Unilever scrutinizing the legal aspects of its marketing and advertising. In early 2012, however, as a mother of two, she was writing a blog about food called the Lunch Tray from her home deep in meat country (Houston, Texas), and she organized an online petition drive to bar the processed beef from schools. Her petition quickly drew 200,000 signatures and caused the USDA to cave: In March 2012, the agency announced

And still, the USDA tried to vouch for pink slime, using an argument that the meat industry had been wielding for years in its effort to get Americans to eat more beef. Sure, the stuff was cheap, and yes, the ammonia was making it safe to eat. But what made it vital to the U.S. food supply system was something else: its low level of fat. This made it a crucial ally in the war against childhood obesity, as the secretary of agriculture, Tom Vilsack, said in a press conference on March 28, 2012. "That's one of the reasons we have made it a staple of the school lunch program," he said. "We are concerned about obesity levels, and this is an opportunity for us to ensure that youngsters are receiving a product that is lean and contains less fat."

By then, however, the meat industry was starting to worry that pink slime had opened up a Pandora's box of issues with the potential to erode the sale of all meat. Experts were quoted saying that a tipping point may have been reached in which people in all walks of life, without regard to their ability to pay more money for food, were becoming aware of, and anxious about, what went into manufactured foods. As Phil Lempert, a food industry consultant, told one reporter, "I think we are going to see a whole new concern and interest in what's in our food and I think that is just going to build."

In 2007, an international group of twenty-one scientists meeting in Washington was poised to open another, even more threatening Pandora's box that the meat industry would scramble to close. The scientists were nearing the end of a five-year effort to identify the most likely causes of cancer. Rather than undertake their own research, the scientists waded through seven thousand published studies to reach a consensus on the cumulative findings. They paid close attention to the quality of the research, dismiss-

that schools would be able to choose burger without the material. It also allowed meat manufacturers to identify the processed beef as something other than "beef" on their labels, if they so chose.

ing results they saw as unfounded or flawed by their methodology. Some of the most obvious suspects were let off the hook for lack of evidence. For instance, foods heavy in sugar, particularly fructose, had been linked to cancer in some studies, but the group of reviewing scientists found this evidence to be "limited" and so downplayed the significance. They didn't want to overstep or be alarmist. Indeed, this was the second report from the scientists, who were working under the auspices of two groups, the World Cancer Research Fund and the American Institute for Cancer Research, and when they released their first report in 1997, they found the evidence linking meat to cancer was equally poor.

This time, however, the scientists reached a very different conclusion about red and processed meats: They found that a decade of subsequent studies offered "convincing" evidence that these meats increased the risk for colon cancer. In this case, the culprit, if there is one, may not be saturated fat. The scientists cited a natural substance in meat called haem, which they identified as promoting the formation of potentially carcinogenic compounds. They also suggested that cooking meat at high temperatures produced a group of more than one hundred substances—known as heterocyclic amines and polycyclic aromatic hydrocarbons—that can cause cancer in people with a genetic predisposition. The risk of cancer may be especially acute in processed meats and tracks with the quantity eaten, the scientists noted. The studies they examined indicated that eating red meat was safe at amounts up to 18 ounces a week. But the scientists said that they could find no level of consumption at which processed meats were safe. Every 1.7 ounces of processed meats consumed per day increased the risk of colorectal cancer by 21 percent, they said.

All this presented a threat to the beef industry that was potentially worse than any panic about saturated fat, which it was handling quite adeptly. Cancer was far scarier to consumers, as it was impossible for the industry to fix with solutions like trimming fat or promoting the zinc in beef. Nine months before the scientists' report came out, word of their conclusions reached the ears of the beef producers. Duly alarmed, they turned to the most powerful weapon at their disposal: the beef marketing program, created by Congress and overseen by the USDA. Using the checkoff monies, the industry launched a massive preemptive strike to undermine—and, if possible, discredit—the scientists' report before it reached the American people.

Getting behind the scenes of this undertaking would normally require some investigative reporting, but because of the public nature of the beef marketing program, the effort is laid bare in hundreds of pages of records, records that are available to the public—one has only to ask. According to these records, the industry used $1.2 million in checkoff funds to activate an internal management group it called the "Cancer Team." With these same funds, it also retained the services of a consulting firm called Exponent, which provides expert witnesses to industrial clients under legal duress. In recent cases, Exponent helped win a favorable settlement for an insurance firm whose client had allegedly exposed Peruvian villagers to a mercury spill, assisted Uruguay in defending a new pulp mill from environmental concerns raised by Argentina, and helped defend an oil company the government of Yemen had accused of damaging farms. For the beef producers, Exponent conducted its own analysis of the research examined by the scientists for their cancer report. It found flaws in the studies that it said weakened the evidence; later, the firm found mistakes in the cancer report itself. The scientists and cancer organizations defended themselves by arguing that the flaws were minor and inconsequential to the overall findings, but Exponent was firm in its conclusion: The scientists had overreached, and the evidence linking beef to colon cancer was unreliable.

The Cancer Team also set to work shaping the media's coverage of beef and thus public opinion. The team's activities on that front were detailed in an audit performed for the Cattlemen's Beef Board, which oversees the collection of checkoff monies from cattle growers. Cancer, the audit noted, was "an emotional and frightening issue," and several industry officials interviewed called it much more of a threat than the mad cow disease scare that had surfaced a few years earlier. Indeed, these officials said, one would have to go back to 1977 to find a menace comparable to the cancer report. (That was the year that the U.S. Senate Select Committee on Nutrition and Human Needs, chaired by Senator George McGovern, released a report that claimed high-fat diets caused cancer, and unlike the USDA's own nutrition guide, the committee urged people to reduce their consumption of red meat.)

The Cancer Team used an analytical firm, Carma, which evaluates media coverage for a wide range of clients, from Apple to JP Morgan Chase to General Mills, to study the recent media coverage of beef. The Carma reports tracked everything from published recipes to articles about issues like food safety, animal rights, and diet and health; identified industry foes and friends; and kept a special eye out for journalists who were unfriendly toward beef.

With this guidance in hand, the Cancer Team then used focus groups to pinpoint the most current consumer concerns about diet, exercise, and nutrition. They then prepared stories to give to beef-friendly media outlets and first showed them the focus groups, choosing the ones that were likely to produce the warmest feelings for beef among consumers. Using that feedback, it developed a string of messages designed to undercut the cancer report's conclusions.

"Cancer risk is not about diet alone," one such message said. "Lifestyle factors—including tobacco and alcohol use, obesity, and lack of physical activity—can significantly increase cancer risk." Another one: "Put risk in perspective. Obesity and lack of physical activity have a 2–3 times higher risk association."

In the end, the blows from the cancer report were significantly softened by the industry's counterprogramming that called the causes of cancer "complex" and placed the "emphasis on moderation and balance," the audit found. News coverage focused on many other aspects of the scientists' work on cancer, including links to body fat and the possible preventative powers of garlic. From the beef industry's perspective, the cancer report proved to be merely a close call. "Overall, beef checkoff messages reached more than 3.1 million consumers, and media reports frequently noted that red meat is safe in moderation," the audit said. "Media coverage increased consumer awareness but there was no change in consumers' likelihood to eat less processed meat or red meat."

The USDA's responses to my questions about the beef marketing program were cautiously defensive. Like the program for cheese and other dairy products, the marketing efforts were paid for entirely with the levies placed on the producers themselves, the agency stressed, and were overseen by the Secretary of Agriculture in large part to maintain support for the program among the cattle growers. Moreover, they pointed to the agency's own work on obesity as evidence that it can handle multiple missions.

One of the most stinging barbs hurled at the marketing programs, however, has come from the other end of the National Mall, in the halls of the United States Supreme Court. It was there that one of the justices, Ruth Bader Ginsburg, came across the inherent conflict in the federal government's pursuit of better nutrition for the American people. Her scrutiny of the beef marketing program came during a legal challenge that reached the high court in 2005. The case was brought by several disgruntled people in the cattle industry who sued the secretary of agriculture to overturn the marketing program, arguing that its generic promotion of beef undermined their efforts to market their particular beef products as special. The Supreme Court ruled against them. However, the case turned not on the merits of the marketing efforts but on who was doing the marketing. If this was a private program, the dissenters would have had standing to sue. But this was no private program, the court decided. All of the effort to make beef appear leaner, more convenient, and more useful as an additive in processed foods was, for all intents and purposes, an effort by the people of the United States. That is, it was a government program. It mattered not in the least that the money used to fund the marketing program came from the cattle growers themselves, the justices said. The secretary of agriculture played such an extensive role in determining how these millions were spent that the checkoff program was a form of "government speech," which protected it from legal challenge. "The Secretary of Agriculture, a politically accountable official, oversees the program, appoints and dismisses the key personnel, and retains absolute veto power over the advertisements' content, right down to the wording," the majority opinion, written by Justice Antonin Scalia, said. "And Congress, of course, retains oversight authority, not to mention the ability to reform the program at any time."

Ginsburg joined with the majority in upholding the marketing program but had a quibble that prompted her to write a separate opinion. She said she could simply not support the notion that the marketing activities were "government speech." How could they be, she asked, when others within the USDA were trying to urge people to eat *less* meat? Even Ginsburg had to work hard to put this message together, citing the relevant pages from the panel's 2005 guide on nutrition in her opinion. The part about Americans needing to eat less saturated fats came from one section of the report, and the part about meat being a big source of these fats from another. But the panel's intent was clear, she said. "I resist ranking the promotional messages funded under the Beef Promotion and Research Act of 1985, but not attributed to the government, as government speech," she wrote in conclusion, "given the message the Government conveys in its own name."

Ginsburg, of course, could have said the same thing—and a good deal more—about the government's other big checkoff, the one for dairies, which put the beef marketing to shame. At a time when the USDA, in its own publications, was urging Americans to eat less cheese-laden pizza, the dairy marketing program was boasting of its huge success in getting Americans to eat more cheese on their pizza, in their snacks, and in products scattered all over the grocery store. The dairy marketing program has even teamed up with restaurant chains like Domino's to help foster concoctions like "The Wisconsin," a pie that has six cheeses on top and two more in the crust. "This partnership sells more cheese," the checkoff's manager explained in a 2009 column published by a trade publication. "If every pizza were made with one additional ounce of cheese, it would require an additional 2.5 billion pounds of milk annually."

Each year, the USDA reports to Congress on the marketing program's victories on behalf of the dairy industry, focusing largely on its prowess in getting Americans to eat more of the stuff. With Kraft's efforts to transform cheese from a food into an ingredient, it could claim only partial credit for the tripling of consumption since 1970. The USDA, however, has given the dairy marketing program several million dollars in taxpayer money each year to promote cheese consumption overseas, and its success on this front can be more rightfully claimed. It even caused the Department of Agriculture to gush in its 2002 report to Congress. "In Mexico, a joint promotion with Domino's Pizza featured the USDEC logo on all Domino's pizza boxes with the slogan, 'Made with 100% U.S. Cheese.' Domino's delivers more than 1.6 million pizzas a month in Mexico." The following year, the agency reported that Domino's had added "cheesy bread" to its Mexico offerings, and this alone led to 36 tons of additional cheese sales each week. There was one thing the 2002 report did not mention. At the same time that taxpayer money was being used to promote cheese in Mexico, the people of Mexico were on their way to having the highest rates of obesity in the world after U.S. citizens.

This zeal at the USDA for boosting the consumption of cheese, along with red meat, helped explain what I found in the next phase of my reporting. At one point, even Kraft grew wary of its efforts in promoting processed foods. A cabal of concerned insiders convinced Kraft's leadership to reexamine some of its policies with an eye toward easing the company's impact on the obesity crisis. It was a remarkable effort, with mixed results, but there was one thing about it I could not square: The Kraft officials didn't feel they could wait for the Department of Agriculture to pursue a new course. Kraft knew, or at least it would learn, that with the agency's conflicted role in fighting obesity, those in the industry who wanted to do the right thing by consumers would have to do it on their own.

chapter eleven

"No Sugar, No Fat, No Sales"

Ellen Wartella was never one for processed foods. She took cooking classes, and both she and her husband loved to spend time in the kitchen. Together, they plied their two sons with homemade dinners, and while she tolerated their fondness for junk food and things that came in a box, she didn't exactly encourage it. "When my kids were growing up, we bought Kraft Macaroni & Cheese because they loved it," she said. "And I remember being appalled by that."

In middle school, she recalled, one of her sons swooned for another of Kraft's mega-hits, Lunchables, especially the version with pizza. His crush, however, soon extinguished itself. By the time they reached high school in the late 1990s, both boys had been exposed to the dark side of public health and marketing. They came to loathe the cigarette companies, in particular, for deliberately hooking the country on a habit that killed people in horrible, untimely ways.

Wartella worked as the dean of the College of Communications at the

University of Texas in Austin, where she had amassed some opinions of her own regarding industrial marketing. She had spent thirty years researching the affects of media on children, including TV violence and advertising, and her twelve books and 175 reports and papers had made her one of the country's leading experts on the subject. In 2003, she got a call, out of the blue, from a senior executive from Kraft. He asked her if she would join a panel of health and marketing experts that the company was putting together for guidance on how to deal with obesity. The panel sounded to Wartella like something the august Institute of Medicine might assemble to examine a health crisis: Kraft had recruited two medical doctors versed in diabetes and public health, a psychologist who studied behavior and obesity, and a food nutrition researcher who specialized in obesity and heart disease—nine experts in all, with Wartella being asked to make it an even ten.

At the time, Kraft had two people acting as CEO, and both issued statements when the panel was formed explaining why the largest food company in the world was undertaking a mission that heretofore had fallen squarely within the domain of government, not private industry. "The council will give Kraft access to a range of important voices from outside the company," said Betsy Holden, one of the CEOs, "who can play an invaluable role in helping us develop our response to the global challenge of obesity." To which her partner, Roger Deromedi, added: "We welcome the council's knowledge, insight, and judgment, all of which will help us strengthen the alignment of our products and marketing practices with societal needs."

Wartella was heartened by the notion of a publicly traded company talking about society's needs and actually taking steps to learn how it might better serve them. Companies, after all, existed to make money for their stockholders, and Kraft was tied to one of the biggest moneymakers of them all: Philip Morris. The tobacco giant had owned Kraft for fifteen years, and this was a problem for Wartella's kids. When she told them she'd been invited to join the panel, they responded with outrage. "Both my boys were appalled at the idea of my joining an advisory board for Kraft, because both my children are very antismoking," she told me. "They said, 'How could you work for a company that is pushing cigarettes?' "

Wartella, however, had an inkling she might be able to do some good. She was no expert on obesity, but Kraft was a principal player in a recent development she had been tracking with increasing dismay: the targeting of vulnerable kids through the use of online games and various social media marketing schemes. "My early research was all on helping young children distinguish between the editorial content of TV and the persuasive intent of the advertisements, which they have difficulty separating," she told me. "Now, these new strategies were coming along that completely erased that."

And kids were responding. Obesity was setting all sorts of records in 2003. The average adult was 24 pounds heavier than in 1960. One in three Americans—and nearly one in five kids, aged six to eleven—were classified as obese. As scientists poked at and measured the obesity crisis, one fact emerged from their studies that shocked people more than any other: Obesity was a lasting, seemingly incurable affliction. Kids who were overweight tended to stay that way for life.

Despite the proclamations from Kraft's CEOs and her conversations with the Kraft executive who wanted her to join the advisory panel, Wartella had her doubts about the sincerity of Kraft's undertaking. How could she not? Expert after expert was pointing the finger at processed food, and until now, Kraft had joined the rest of the industry in ducking blame. Why should she believe all this talk about society's needs?

Wartella finally decided to join the advisory group, but only after making a vow to herself and her kids: She would quit if it turned out to be more of the same old obfuscation.

After the group's first two meetings at Kraft's headquarters near Chicago, Wartella's fears about the company's sincerity seemed to be justified. The talks roamed across the landscape of obesity, but only broadly, touching on nutrition, exercise, and portion sizes. Always, the conversation was deferential toward Kraft, the $35 billion elephant in the room. This changed, however, in the third session. Wartella had been asked to discuss marketing, and she arrived having done her homework. The session started out with Kraft officials presenting a rosy view of the company's practices, which included a policy of not advertising to children younger than six. Wartella begged to differ.

In truth, she said, Kraft's own websites were riddled with tricks that lured young kids to their sweetest and fattiest products. She cited games that entailed counting up Oreos, or going on hide-and-seek missions to find Barney Rubble, whose role in the game was to tout the company's Fruity Pebbles cereal. These were marketing tricks that clearly circumvented the self-imposed advertising ban on children, she said, as did the company's use of cartoon characters to hawk its mac and cheese and cookies. Even its packaging was decorated with Shrek and Dora the Explorer, the better to seduce young kids.

"I pointed this out, and I said, 'You are at best disingenuous, and at worst you're outright lying.' The nutrition scientists and the other people on the advisory board were kind of appalled by the strength of my statements. One or two people came up to me afterwards and said, 'They're going to get you off this thing.' "

But that did not happen. The officials at Kraft listened. Not only that, they asked Wartella to dig even deeper into the company's marketing practices and come back with more stinging critiques, which she did. Wartella came to believe that her original fears were unfounded. The panel *was* making a difference, and Kraft seemed to be, incredibly, starting to address the ways its own practices were contributing to the obesity crisis.

This was no small thing. For the processed food industry, 2003 was shaping up to be a furious, competitive race to boost America's consumption of its products. Not only were wars taking place in which the sole objective was to flood the grocery aisles with items with ever higher loads of salt, sugar, and fat, a huge new player in groceries had accelerated the competition for space on the shelf. Wal-Mart had begun selling food, and just since 2000 the retailing giant had boosted its grocery, candy, and tobacco sales by 46 percent to $39.4 billion, sending food manufacturers rushing to the company's headquarters in Arkansas to pitch their wares.

The big manufacturers were in a separate race to the bottom when it came to the economics of food, seeking out new ways to cut their ingredient costs, lower the price of their food, and thus turn processed food into the only logical choice shoppers could make.*

Kraft was no stranger to this contest. Its product managers were turning out some of the most enticing, supersized, and cheapest items of all, from the fruit drink called Capri Sun (later "up-sized" to the Big Pouch) to the fat-laden Lunchables (expanded into the Maxed Out size) to the Cheese Stuffed Crust Supreme DiGiorno frozen pizza (with three meats added to with the extra cheese, delivering more than two days' worth of the recommended maximum of saturated fat and sodium in a single pie weighing nearly two pounds). "Build and defend," was the rallying cry in Kraft's internal pep talks. "Drive consumption."

Inside this same company, however, a heretical view had emerged. Starting in the late 1990s, a small group of senior Kraft officials had been watching America's massive weight gain with growing alarm. They didn't buy the industry's view that consumers were to blame for the obesity crisis by being slothful or lacking in willpower. The small group of insiders had a different take on America's gluttony. Some were emotionally vested, believing that they had an ethical and moral imperative to help resolve the epidemic of obesity, for which their industry was in large part responsible. Others made a more practical argument: The consumer backlash on processed foods, when it came, would exact a heavy toll on the company's profits. "We were trying to convince senior management that we would be better off in the long run if we gave up a little to save a lot, in terms of our long-term business reputation and success," said Kathleen Spear, a senior vice president and member of this cabal at Kraft.

---

* In 2012, two USDA economists sought to refute the perception that healthy foods were more expensive. They acknowledged that this is certainly true when foods are measured by their energy value. Calorie for calorie, broccoli is far more expensive than cookies. But noting that too many calories is, in fact, central to the obesity crisis, the economists developed an alternative calculation. They compared foods by how much they weighed, and by this metric, broccoli had a lower cost, per pound, than cereal and other packaged foods that rely on the high-calorie/lightweight pillars of processed food: sugar and fat.

The group got Kraft to empanel the experts, and it then used their testimony as ammunition in convincing Kraft to act. At first, the steps the company took were modest in scope, starting with urging restraint in the company's marketing strategies. But that was just window dressing. In order to change the company, these Kraft officials quickly realized, they had to confront the fundamental nature—the heart and soul—of processed food.

Since its earliest days, Kraft had directed every last shred of its talent and energy toward making its products as enticing as possible. Central to this mission were the formulations of salt, sugar, and fat that made the products attractive. The bliss point was no abstraction. Kraft's legacy was built on doing this bigger and better than any other manufacturer. Yet this was precisely where the Kraft officials concerned about obesity saw they would have to go: into the actual product formulations, and their loads of salt, sugar, and fat. What if these formulations were causing people to buy and eat *too* much? they asked. Could they find a way to help people ease up without killing off their own company?

Had federal regulators dared to ask these questions, they would have been branded as traitors to free enterprise. This was, after all, the most sacrosanct part of the business, the most staunchly defended. The insiders who worried about obesity had to tread very carefully in how they parsed the issue at hand: the desire created by their products. "We're a food business," Spear recalled thinking. "We wanted people to delight in the taste of everything we made, particularly when it came to snacks and cookies. We were mindful that we were selling confectionaries and snacks and not rice cakes. It was never, 'Gee, we ought to cut back on the allure.' Rather, it was, 'We ought to make sure we're not directly or indirectly or subliminally encouraging overconsumption.' "

However the equation was approached, the idea of a food giant exploring the question of how to get people to eat less was astonishing, and in the coming months Kraft would dive more deeply into the psychology of overeating than any manufacturer had ever gone before. But as I examined this extraordinary moment at Kraft, it became apparent that there was yet another force at play influencing the company's decisions. For years, much of Kraft's motivation in getting people to eat more of its convenience foods had come from the bosses at Philip Morris. The tobacco executives encouraged them to find ever more potent ways to attract consumers and then applauded the victories when sales surged. They even supplied Kraft with their own marketing apparatus and strategies that had been so successful in selling cigarettes—precisely the relationship that Ellen Wartella's boys had disdained in trying to stop her from joining the panel on obesity.

But behind the scenes, in the private rooms where the most senior officials gathered to account for their actions and receive their guidance for going forward, a dramatic shift occurred. In this confidential setting, I discovered—from secret documents and interviews with officials who spoke publicly for the first time on these matters—the same tobacco-steeped overlords in New York who had spent their own careers promoting cigarettes and denying addiction did the unthinkable: They fell in with the cabal and began urging Kraft to make changes in response to the growing epidemic of obesity.

Salt, sugar, and fat may have been the formula that carried Kraft to the apex of the processed food industry, the tobacco men said. But just as nicotine had turned on them, becoming a yoke that sunk their profits, so too would salt, sugar, and fat become Kraft's millstones, dragging the whole company down with them.

In 1925, an advertisement began appearing in newspapers and magazines across America. It depicted a slim woman with short hair standing on a diving board, clad in a one-piece bathing suit, looking pleased with her herself. But next to her, in shadow, stood her future self: dowdy and obese. "This Is You Five Years From Now!" read the caption. "When Tempted to Over-indulge, Reach for a *Lucky* Instead."

The ad, for Lucky Strike cigarettes, was made by American Tobacco, which was the first cigarette manufacturer to realize that obesity could be used as a marketing cudgel. Until then, smoking had been an overwhelmingly male pastime. But in looking to expand sales, the cigarette manufacturers began pitching tobacco to women as an appetite suppressant. The industry eventually stopped making all health claims, deciding at a 1953 summit that some of the ads—especially those touting filtered smoke as "better for your health"—were hurting sales by implying that smoking posed risks. So when Philip Morris introduced its own brand for women, Virginia Slims, in 1968, it took the more subtle route of associating the cigarette with women of style, women who were elegant, successful, slim. Only internally did Philip Morris spell out the unspoken allures, which included the brand's weight-loss appeal. The marketing slogans it tested on focus groups included concepts like this: "A satisfying cigarette, specifically made to curb your appetite for food."

As the health risks in smoking became more apparent, there was even a brief time when cigarette makers saw fat as a potential ally. Researchers had begun connecting lung cancer to diets high in fat, and the interest this generated among tobacco executives was understandable, given how it might take some of the heat off cigarettes. One study—funded by the National Cancer Institute—examined the dietary and smoking habits of people in forty-three countries and found a correlation between fat and lung cancer that might help explain why Japan—with its high level of smoking but low-fat diets—had less lung cancer than the United States. "High fat diets may promote lung tumors by decreasing normal ability to destroy new cancer," the study said. Any comfort this might have been to the tobacco industry, however, was especially short-lived for Philip Morris. When this study came out in 1986, executives there marked their copy "very confidential" before adding it to their files. Philip Morris was no longer just a tobacco company. It was on the way to becoming the country's largest manufacturer of processed foods as well. This gave it a much different view of fat. The firestorm that would later envelop the tobacco industry was still only a string of scattered lawsuits and pesky critics that Philip Morris felt confident it could contain. In the 1980s, when it started buying the food giants, Philip Morris saw them less as a replacement for tobacco than as an opportunity to supplement its own burgeoning stable of blockbuster brands. That said, the food brands did have an issue the Philip Morris executives quickly recognized as something they would have to deal with, just as they were having to deal with nicotine: saturated fat, which was starting to rival sugar as a public health concern. Within a few years, the top Philip Morris officials began referring to fat not as an ally but as a matter of concern that, like nicotine, needed careful tending.

In 1990, the battalion of attorneys who worked for Philip Morris gathered for a retreat in La Jolla, California, where the company's general counsel, Fred Newman, issued a call to arms. The Marlboro brand, he said, "ranks as one of the great product success stories of all time," having skyrocketed from a 1 percent share of the cigarette market in 1954 to 26 percent that year; the number of smokers it had attracted equaled the population of New England plus the cities of Dallas, Detroit, and Washington, D.C. But as an expanding conglomerate, he added, Philip Morris was saddled with a slew of new consumer issues. "These concerns involve not just tobacco, but also alcohol, red meat, dairy products, saturated fat, sugar, sodium, caffeine, and other common ingredients in many of our products," he said. "You already know a great deal about the challenges we face in the tobacco business—challenges ranging from excise taxes and disputes over labeling, marketing, and advertising restrictions to product liability. In the future, we can expect these challenges to also confront us in alcoholic beverages and food. And, as these brand categories come to represent larger and larger parts of our business, our need to protect our interest in them will also rise proportionately. Clearly, many of the people in this room will have a key role to play in building and maintaining our interests in these areas. Your actions on that ultimate battleground—the courtroom—will have impact all over the country. Growth from working together is the cornerstone of the future success of all the companies and brands of Philip Morris."

That same year, in addressing the food-side managers at Philip Morris, the chief executive, Hamish Maxwell, said that they—like the company's attorneys—would also have to be sensitive and responsive to a wide range of public concerns. "As new management coming into our companies, I'm sure you also have thought about public health concerns and some of the more controversial aspects of our business," he said. "We want to respond to the whole range of consumer concerns. We've modified our food products to remove fat or lessen the calories, and we've developed lighter cigarette products."

To be sure, in these early days of handling fat, Philip Morris viewed the public's worries as entirely manageable. It merely had to deploy a strategy, used by the entire consumer goods industry, known as the line extension: When people clamor loudly enough for healthier products, enough so that they are willing to sacrifice some of the pleasure these products provided, companies produce a better-for-you formulation. Whether it's low-tar cigarettes, low-calorie beer, or lower-fat potato chips, these healthier versions are no threat to the mainline products. In fact, if done right, they can boost sales for the original full-calorie and full-fat versions by attracting new shoppers to the overall brand. The food managers working for Philip Morris put line extensions in motion throughout the grocery store.

As for the mainline versions of its brands, Philip Morris showed little inclination to do anything but market these products with all the skill and vigor that had once made Marlboro such a resounding success. Having learned with cigarettes that being first was not as important as being quick and aggressive in responding to trends, Philip Morris urged this same tactic upon its food managers. If Americans were craving foods that were fast and convenient, Philip Morris wouldn't try merely to best its competitors in the grocery store; it would aim to capture a piece of the huge market owned by the fast food chains, adopting their formulations and, in some cases, even their mega-brands. Among these achievements was an ultra-convenient meal called the Taco Bell dinner kit—a boxed set of tortillas, cheese sauces, and recipes that Kraft started selling in 1996 after acquiring the rights to the brand name. With clinical precision, Philip Morris touted these efforts to Wall Street.

"In order to continue to deliver strong financial performance, Kraft will need to respond to several major environmental trends," the chief operating officer, William Webb, told a gathering of investors and analysts in 1999. "First, consumers are becoming busier. Seventy-seven percent of women in the U.S. age 25 to 54 are now in the work force, versus 51 percent in 1970, and this is expected to increase to about 80 percent by the year 2010. As consumers have gotten busier, the number of meals prepared at home has declined. Since 1990 the average consumer is preparing one half of a meal less per week at home, preferring instead to eat out or take-out from restaurants or other food-away-from-home venues. Kraft is responding to this trend. For example, we're helping busy consumers with an extensive lineup of easy-to-prepare meal products like Taco Bell dinner kits, Easy Mac single-serve macaroni and cheese, and Lunchables lunch combinations; ready-to-eat snacks like Jell-O pudding, Handi-Snacks gels and Kraft cheese cubes; and ready-to-drink beverages like Capri Sun, Kool-Aid Bursts and Kool-Aid Splash. We also know that the number one question in America at 4 P.M. is not, 'How did the market do today?' It's, 'What's for dinner?' And most consumers don't have a clue." The Taco Bell kits, he noted, had quickly reached $125 million in annual sales.

But even as Philip Morris pushed more fatty products into the American diet, its executives were tracking the public's concern about how fat, as well as salt and sugar, related to obesity. And on this front the news was growing increasingly worrisome. Between the 1960s and 1980s, obesity rates had held fairly steady. Among children, it hovered around 5 percent. In 1980, however, the rates had begun to surge for all ages. Moreover, the media was starting to draw the public's attention to the implications of the country's weight gain. Philip Morris had long used tracking surveys to monitor issues of public concern, and when obesity was added to the list of questions in 1999, the company's polling identified it as a significant threat to the manufacture of processed food: Eight in ten people viewed obesity as a serious risk to public health. And while one in three cited "lack of exercise" as a cause, a far greater number of people, nearly half of the respondents, blamed "unbalanced diets." In other words, too much fatty and sugary food.

"Obesity is literally an epidemic in this country, and some people's ideas for addressing this public health issue could directly or indirectly affect the entire agriculture industry, from farm to consumer," a Philip Morris vice president, Jay Poole, warned an agricultural economics group that year. "They're talking about punitive taxes on certain foodstuffs, limits on marketing of certain foods, regulation of others."

Just as Philip Morris was gearing up to defend its food from attacks like these, however, the nature of its battle over cigarettes took a sudden turn, an event that altered the company's view on how Kraft should deal with obesity. Through much of the 1990s, the tobacco giant had remained steadfast in its determination to fight the antismoking lawsuits being brought by individuals and the government alike. It might not win every case, the company would tell investors, but the damage would be contained. Then a lawsuit emerged to end all tobacco lawsuits. It was brought by more than forty states, whose health-care systems were buckling from having to cover the growing numbers of people made sick by smoking-induced illnesses. The states accused the tobacco industry of a wide range of deceptive and fraudulent practices, and they rallied behind Mississippi's formidable attorney general, Mike Moore, who said that the lawsuit was "premised on a simple notion: You caused the health crisis, you pay for it." In 1998, the states won. Philip Morris joined the other big tobacco manufacturers in settling the litigation by agreeing to pay the states a stunning $365 billion to revive their moribund health care systems. They also agreed to endure possible regulation of cigarettes by the FDA and to add stronger warnings on their cigarette packs.

What worried Philip Morris even more than this states' case, however, was the sea change in public opinion that seemed to arise from the accusations of fraud and deception. Where people used to see smoking as a willful decision by individuals, they were now starting to hold the industry responsible, given their marketing tactics and the foreknowledge they had about smoking's risks. In the months after the settlement, tacticians at Philip Morris conducted a sweeping review of the company's operations, producing a 1999 strategy paper that they dubbed "Lessons from the Tobacco Wars."

This manifesto called for a new accommodation to consumers on the part of Philip Morris: "Pay close attention to public concerns and, most important, address them. Denial is not enough, think about solutions. It's like good marketing. Don't argue with the customer. Respond to the customer's need and belief. Our business interest lies with public acceptance." While nicotine had become a yoke around the tobacco industry's neck, the strategy paper warned, the food divisions were saddled with more than just one big potential disaster. They had three, or more. "The media are ready and eager to write alarming stories about fat, salt, sugar, or biotech products in people's diets," it said. "And just because your critics are shrill or even slightly nuts—and just because some reporters are irresponsible—does not mean you can afford to ignore them. They won't go away by themselves. If your opponents do enough shoveling—while you just stand there shaking your head—some of the stuff they throw at you will stick. And before long, the public may not be able to see you through the muck."

The person in charge of Philip Morris during this tumultuous period was Geoffrey Bible, who was also the one tobacco executive who knew the most about the company's food business, having spent eighteen months at Kraft's operations center near Chicago. Now, in 2001, as the chief executive of Philip Morris, he drew on this experience in handling the food managers as they faced the growing public concern about the health effects of their foods. "We'd been through a pretty hard time," Bible told me. "You need to have been there to understand it. Eyes were being focused upon food, and so we were asking, 'If we are working hard to align our tobacco business with what we call society's needs, how does the food industry look?' Because we don't need to go through the ringer again."

One of the main lessons from the tobacco wars had to do with Philip Morris's relations with other tobacco companies—or, rather, the lack thereof. Instead of relations, there was growing suspicion and alarm. When Philip Morris took the step of publicly accepting some responsibility for the public health crisis caused by smoking, its rivals looked darkly upon its motives. They saw it at best as a public relations gambit, and at worst, a ploy to buy time so that Philip Morris could shift more of its focus to selling tobacco overseas, where there was less public concern about lung cancer. For this reason, Philip Morris also assumed that it would be on its own—nay-sayed and nit-picked by its rivals—when it came to handling the food division's problem.

So Bible did not try to engage the whole food industry on obesity. Nor did he simply come out and order his food managers to act, having learned from his time in Chicago that they did not have the same depth of loyalty to the company as did executives in the tobacco industry. "The food people were a different breed," he said. "There's not the same sort of allegiance that we had in our company. It's also very hard to convince them of things. They'd say, 'Well, you don't understand, it's what the consumer wants, and you've got to make it.' So it's balancing your business objectives and targets with what's the right product for the consumer."

Rather, Bible began to talk more subtly about salt, sugar, and fat—about the high levels to which Americans had become accustomed; about how "the right product for consumers would probably have *no* sugar, and *no* fat, but you'd have *no* sales"; about how Kraft could perhaps best position itself by straddling the line between junk and health foods, "finding something in the middle." He began speaking like this in private discussions with Kraft officials, including a man named John Ruff, a Kraft executive and food product developer who had joined General Foods in 1972. World-wise and savvy, Ruff listened with mixed emotions, finding it difficult at first to swallow Philip Morris's sudden about-face on food. It was hard not to think begrudgingly, Who are you to be telling us about corporate responsibility? "Most of us had lived through and watched Philip Morris for many, many years, basically saying, 'We make a legal product and we inform people of the risks, and it's not our fault, blah, blah, blah,' " Ruff told me. "That was the defense, for many years, and Geoff Bible, initially that was *his* perspective."

The more Bible talked, however, the more his message began to resonate. Ruff recalled one moment in 2001 when Bible explained in some detail the company's change of heart on tobacco. "He talked about why Philip Morris had gone through this mental mind check," Ruff told me.

"And he said, 'For many years we had had this "not our fault" point of view. But what we started to see is that more and more consumers were feeling like we were partly to blame, and we needed to do something about that.' "

That a company's own loyal customers would suddenly turn against it was a nightmarish concept that riveted the Kraft officials. Then Bible, having described the price being paid by tobacco for ignoring the public sentiment for so many years, cut to the chase. The same day of public reckoning was now likely to befall processed food, he said. The only difference was the nature of the public health concern. For cigarettes it had been cancer. "My prediction," Bible told his food executives, "is it's going to happen in the food industry around obesity.' "

In 2003, six years before he retired from Kraft as a senior vice president, John Ruff paid a visit to his orthopedist to see about the pain he'd been having while he exercised. The cartilage in his knee, the doctor told him after his MRI exam, was nearly gone. Daily workouts had long been his strategy to avoid getting fat, and even at that he was failing. He had run at least three miles a day for twenty years to "offset the excesses in diet and travel, and I was still overweight," he told me. Now, on his doctor's advice, he could only walk and bike, which would burn fewer calories. "I had to do something about my intake, and that's when I started to change all my eating habits," he said.

His new diet called for avoiding his own company's products in the grocery store.

Ruff knew about the emerging research in nutrition that found that the body's weight control systems were much less adept at handling liquid calories than solid food, so he stopped drinking anything with added sugar. He also dropped high-fat, high-calorie snacks. "I used to come home from work and get one of those giant bags of potato chips," he said. "The little bags are two servings, so god knows what the giant one is. There's probably 800 calories in there, and twice the amount of fat you need. Along with a martini, I would consume half that bag. On a good day I could eat the whole damn thing." Instead, Ruff swapped the martinis for diet ginger ale and the chips for a handful of nuts. "I lost forty pounds in forty weeks," he said. "I went from 210 to 170, and I've been 170 pounds ever since."*

By happenstance, Ruff was in the midst of reforming his personal eating habits when Kraft put him in charge of the company's own anti-obesity effort, and this couldn't have been a better fit. Ruff, as a worried consumer, was already walking around the grocery store muttering to himself, "I can't eat this, I can't eat that." Now, as a Kraft executive, he could walk around the same store saying, "We shouldn't sell this, we shouldn't sell that."

Joining Ruff on the obesity team was Kathleen Spear, the Kraft attorney and senior vice president who sought to distinguish products that were merely alluring from those that compelled overeating. Another member was the company's senior vice president for external affairs, Michael Mudd. It was Mudd who, back in 1999, had stood before the chief executives of the largest food companies in America and tried to enlist them in the war on obesity. When, instead, he got a scolding from these men, he had regrouped and was now making a new, more improbable proposition: that Kraft go it alone. Thus, it was Mudd who organized the panel of outside experts to advise Kraft on obesity in 2003, and it was Mudd who convinced Ellen Wartella, the kids marketing expert, to join the panel.

That fall, as the panel met, the three Kraft executives—Ruff, Spear, and Mudd—lost little time in advancing their agenda. No longer a mere cabal of company insiders conspiring on their own, their mission had been officially sanctioned by Kraft. They now had permission to roam through the company's entire operations, with an eye toward challenging any practice or policy that contributed to the obesity epidemic. When Wartella presented her damning evidence of Kraft's aggressive marketing to kids,

* I'm loath to embrace any dieting tools, but unsalted nuts are gaining some notable fans, including Harvard's head of nutrition, Walter Willett, and Richard Mattes, an expert on dietary fat at Purdue University. Nuts, they told me—besides having lots of protein and the "good" kind of fat, unsaturated—appear to have exceptional powers in the matter known as satiety: a mere handful can make you feel full, which helps you avoid unhealthy snacks. The trick is not reaching for more, since the fat in nuts gives them lots of calories that can quickly undo their positives.

the three executives championed that as their first reform. They urged Kraft to put the brakes on its advertising, which it did. No longer would Kraft pitch products to kids that lacked nutritional value. Now, these products had to have substantial amounts of whole-grain fiber, fruits or vegetables, and key vitamins and minerals.

The anti-obesity team turned next to Kraft's labeling, with the intention of making it honest. Their primary concern was the fine print known as the "nutrition facts," which the FDA had required starting in the 1990s. This information is usually listed on the back or side of the package, framed by a thin black line, and while it doesn't say "Warning," that is precisely how the obesity team came to view these disclosures: warnings to consumers about the ingredient loads inside. The nutrition facts tell you how many calories are inside, as well as how much salt, sugar, and fat.

As the obesity group saw it, the problem for consumers was the way the FDA let Kraft and other companies do the math. All this critical information was couched in terms of a single serving. Instead of telling consumers how much the whole package contained, the nutrition facts said only how much there was in a serving. This gave the manufacturers an obvious advantage: It shrank all the numbers and downplayed the nutritional risk. Take a bag of potato chips. Instead of saying 2,400 calories and 22.5 grams of fat, which were the true contents, the nutrition facts said 160 calories and 1.5 grams of fat, which were the contents *per serving*. Moreover, these things called serving sizes had been established by the FDA in the early 1990s, based on surveys from the 1970s, and had little to do with the way people really ate, especially when it came to junk food that compelled overeating.

This matter of serving size was made all the more deceptive by the super-sizing trend, which swept first through the fast food chains and then grocery stores, packing more and more food and soda in each container so people would buy more and consume more. Kraft's own boxes and bags of snack food were among the offenders. Many of its packages contained two or more of what the government defined as a reasonable serving, and there was nothing inherently wrong with that, the obesity team argued. But the formulas for these foods were engineered so perfectly to create bliss that almost no one stopped at just one serving. Kraft knew this from its own research. A 2003 survey of nearly 1,600 adults found that nearly a third acknowledged that they practiced John Ruff's own pre-diet mode of snacking: When opening a bag containing multiple servings, they would eat the whole thing.

The obesity team toyed with the idea of splashing the biggest warning—how many calories *the whole package* contained—right on the front of the label, to better alert consumers. But when the Nabisco managers complained that this would put them at a huge disadvantage in the cookie aisle, where no other company would be doing the same thing, Kraft settled on putting this number—along with the calculations for salt, sugar, and fat in the whole box or bag—in the nutrition facts. It added a second column of figures next to the single-serving set, to spell out the whole package's contents.

Kraft couldn't make this change without the FDA's permission, so in May 2004, company officials met with the agency to explain the idea and their reasoning for having a dual listing. The company showed the FDA photographs of its own products to illustrate what Kraft now considered to be a deceptive practice. Among these was a ninety-nine-cent bag of Mini Chips Ahoy! cookies, which weighed only 3 ounces but contained three servings, with all the critical nutrition information shrunk accordingly. One impetus to overeat was readily apparent right on the package: In big, brightly colored lettering, the marketing people at Kraft had blazoned "Indulge."

Some consumers could restrain themselves when they opened a bag like this, sharing the cookies or saving some for later, Kraft told the FDA, citing its polling. But many people could not. "These products can reasonably be consumed as a single serving," Kraft told the FDA. "What is the best approach to labeling products showing 2–4 servings? 'Do the math' for consumers."

The honest labeling move by Kraft would have a powerful ripple effect. Within months of the 2003 meeting, the FDA was urging the entire industry to consider adopting Kraft's whole-content listing for foods with multiple-serving foods that were conducive to overeating, and by 2012, the food industry was discussing even more changes. These included the reform that Kraft wanted to make but could not do without risking big losses in sales: putting a total calorie count on the *front* of food packages.

John Ruff had been forthright with me in discussing the team's work. We met twice, and we also spoke on the phone, and he walked me through Kraft's initial steps, noting the company's willingness to restrain itself in marketing to kids and to be honest about the portion size deception. So I asked him about the bigger, much thornier problem with processed foods and obesity: the huge loads of salt, sugar, and fat that so many products bear.

I asked him if anybody asked the question, " 'What if some of these products are so tasty, people can't resist eating them?' Is it possibly part of the problem that you have just made this stuff taste so good that people can't help but eat too much?"

"That was in constant discussion, and came up in many different forums," Ruff replied. It was, he said, the toughest issue of all for the team to wrestle with. No one at Kraft, in his experience, had ever talked about formulating the company's foods to be "addictive," he said. But then, they didn't have to use that particular word. It was a well-known and accepted fact that the entire company—from the food technicians to the package designers to the advertising copywriters—were pulling together to achieve one goal and one goal only. "You're looking for the product that people like best," Ruff told me. "We would talk about people 'desiring' foods, and at the end of the day, you make the best-tasting food you possibly can."

Thus, it was with considerable nerve that Kraft in 2004 broached the topic of its product formulations.

Since its beginnings more than a century ago, the processed food industry has viewed these formulations as a matter of inviolable corporate rights. The company chiefs, and the chiefs alone, could determine how much salt, sugar, and fat to put into their products, and if they deferred to anyone, it was their food scientists, who handled the specifics on bliss. But now, rethinking their culpability in the obesity crisis and wanting to do the right thing by consumers, Ruff and his colleagues pressed Kraft to act. The initiative they proposed in late 2003 was nothing short of heretical: In developing new products, Kraft's food scientists and brand managers could no longer add all the salt, sugar, and fat they wanted. Kraft, in fact, set caps on each of these ingredients, along with calories, across every category of food it produced. The idea was to start shrinking the salt, sugar, fat, and calorie loads of its entire $35 billion portfolio.

Today, Kraft insists it remains committed to these caps. To get a closer look at this, I visited the company in 2011, toured its research and development laboratories, and sat down with top officials to discuss the status of the anti-obesity campaign, eight years after the launch. Among the people I talked to was Marc Firestone, the company's general counsel, who came to Kraft from Philip Morris and returned to the tobacco company in 2012. The cabal of Kraft insiders who were pressing the company to fight obesity had considered Firestone an ally, but in our meeting he was restrained. For competitive reasons, he said he could not provide me with details on the caps Kraft placed on salt, sugar, and fat—either their actual amounts or any specifics on how the ingredient caps have held up over time.

But skeptics abound, especially among competitors who viewed Kraft's anti-obesity initiative as a cunning maneuver—or as the vice president for communications at General Mills, Tom Forsythe, put it to me, "a bit of a stealing of a march by Kraft. I will say that was a nice PR play, but it put the company in a difficult spot. Let's be honest, they're a cheese company, and there's a whole bunch of products that they were not going to make spiffy new healthy. So that was artfully written in a way that made them look good, but it had a lot of asterisks and or's in key places."

So I tried another approach with Firestone.

Back in 2004, I said, Kraft was saying it had managed to get something like 30 billion calories out of two hundred products. Do you know if there's a corresponding figure now?

"In Capri Sun alone we took out 120 billion calories," Firestone said. "But across the whole portfolio I can't say, because I don't think we've racked it up. We've looked at the amount of sodium we've taken out. Last year was six million pounds, and we're going to add nine billion servings of whole grain between now and 2013, so those are things where we've got major initiatives."

If those numbers sound impressive, consider what Michelle Obama managed to wrestle out of the entire processed food industry in 2010, after asking for their help in fighting obesity. "I am thrilled to say that they have pledged to cut a total of one trillion calories from the food they sell annually by the year 2012, and 1.5 trillion calories by 2015," she announced. "They've agreed to reformulate their foods in a number of ways, including by addressing fat and sugar content, by introducing lower-calorie options, and by reducing the portion sizes of existing single-serve products."

The math on all this, however, is less compelling. If everyone in America consumed the standard 2,000 calories a day, or 730,000 a year, the 1.5 trillion in saved calories would reduce our collective eating by not quite 1 percent. It's actually bleaker than that, according to some health policy experts. In reality, many of us consume far more than 2,000 calories, and processed foods make up a large part, but not all, of our diets. So the real drop in consumption from those 1.5 trillion calories is likely much less than that 1 percent. Still, it's a start.

One of the most enthused supporters of Kraft's anti-obesity initiative was the co-CEO, Betsy Holden, in what seemed like a striking turn in her career. Holden had risen quickly in the company after joining the desserts division of General Foods in 1982. She impressed everyone by her handling of brands like Cool Whip, and later, she was credited with innovations in the DiGiorno brand that turned the company's pizza business into a $1-billion-a-year behemoth. By late 2003, however, Kraft was slumping on numerous fronts. Some new products, like Chips Ahoy! Warm 'N

Chewy, had flopped altogether. Reliable standbys, like Philadelphia Cream Cheese, were falling below expectations. That summer, a conference call with Wall Street analysts turned hostile when Kraft delivered the news that its operating income had come in below expectations and that the company would need to spend $200 million trying to regain its competitive position.

"Do you think there's a bigger problem?" a Morgan Stanley analyst asked. "Because clearly you're underperforming your peers."

And what about all this talk about fighting obesity? asked an analyst from Prudential Securities. How was the company going to meet its projected sales growth of 3 percent if it was worrying about people's waistlines? "You've obviously made a statement on obesity," this analyst added. "But can you clarify the company's efforts in achieving a volume increase? You're going to try to grow your volume 2 to 3 percent domestically, it's almost got to make us fat."

Holden gamely replied that increasing the company's profits and fighting obesity were not necessarily mutually exclusive. She evoked the industry concept of stomach share. Kraft, she said, was trying to get a larger share of what people ate, not get them eating more food per se. But Wall Street was not assuaged. Just as the anti-obesity initiative at Kraft was gathering steam, through the summer and fall of 2003, the price of Kraft's shares started to fall, tumbling 17 percent for the year, compared with a 5 percent gain for its competitors.

Kraft's financial slump came at the worst moment for one key player: the parent company, Philip Morris. After nearly two decades of ownership, starting with General Foods, the tobacco giant had decided to start pulling out of the food business, but it did not want to sell its millions of shares at the battered price. (The slumped stock and other considerations would lead Philip Morris to delay selling the last of its shares until 2007, when Kraft, once again, became an independent company.)

Holden's career track at Kraft ended much faster than that. On December 18, 2003, Holden was removed from her job as CEO and put into the less prestigious position of president for global marketing. The Kraft officials I met held Holden in high regard and said that her removal stemmed in part from the awkwardness of having two CEOs, but eighteen months into the demotion, Holden left Kraft to spend more time with her kids.

Michael Mudd, the obesity initiative's biggest champion and spearhead, would leave the company at the end of 2004 as well. The panel of experts he organized, including Ellen Wartella, had done its job well, helping him and his colleagues put the company on the road to doing the right thing by consumer health. This was a path-breaking achievement of which he was hugely proud. But Mudd felt increasingly frustrated by the rest of the industry's refusal to follow suit, which isolated and put new pressures on Kraft—pressures that involved not thinking more about overweight kids but rather thinking more about returning to the basics of processed food. Namely, boosting the value of the company stock by selling more of the foods that people liked best.

On March 3, 2011, Kraft announced that a new era of fatty, sugary foods had come to India. The Oreo, which had never been marketed there before, was headed to the shelves of hundreds of thousands of stores throughout the subcontinent, backed by a media tour de force of TV commercials, billboard ads, and a brightly colored blue bus that roamed the country, from New Delhi to Mumbai, hailing kids to come aboard for Oreo games. The marketing had an educational theme: teaching the country's population of 1.2 billion how to eat an Oreo properly. "The 'Twist, Lick and Dunk' ritual has brought fun-filled moments of bonding to countless families across the world," the company's president for Southeast Asia and Indo-China said in a statement.

Fast on the Oreo's heels was Tang, which Kraft introduced to India the following month with a campaign slogan: "A refreshing drink that makes children happier and think more creatively." Next up, in July 2012, was Toblerone, the triangular chocolate bar that Kraft made in Switzerland

and now sold in 122 countries. To understand how these blockbuster items arrived on the shores of India, where a surging rate of obesity is now worrying health care officials as much as malnutrition, we must go back to a time when things were looking decidedly bleak for Kraft's cookies in American stores.

The year was 2002, and cookie sales were falling precipitously. Kraft hired researchers to find out what was wrong, and the word it got back was just short of cataclysmic: Shoppers confided that they were avoiding the entire cookie aisle, scared to death they would lose control, load up their carts, and rush home to, well, gorge.

"There was a broad market change, for which the Oreo had become the poster child," said Daryl Brewster, the executive who ran Kraft's Nabisco division at the time. "The consumers who loved Oreos, who loved Chips Ahoy!, who loved all our cookies, were finding themselves afraid to go down the cookie aisle because they might buy some and eat it all. So we learned all we could about it, this buy-and-binge behavior. Sometimes what happens in snacking is people get overhungry. They open up the package and it could be Oreo's, or it could be Lay's potato chips. They open it up, they start eating and they don't stop at one. They finish the bag. They have just consumed hundreds or thousands of calories, and now they're guilty. They feel awful."

This was no small matter for Kraft and Philip Morris. In its last food acquisition, in 2000, Philip Morris had paid $18.9 billion to acquire Nabisco, including the company's debts, and Wall Street had applauded the move. Nabisco had $8.3 billion in annual sales from a lineup of rock solid heavy hitters, from Chips Ahoy! to Ritz Crackers to the mother of all cookies, the Oreo. Three years later, however, there was only doom and gloom.

The shopper's fear of losing control was only part of the trouble, Brewster said. The Oreo was the subject of a lawsuit that took Kraft to task for continuing to rely on trans fats, a form of fat that was considered even more pernicious than saturated fat. (Today, trans fats have been widely reduced by the processed food industry.) Also, much of the country suddenly seemed to be on the Atkins diet, which disdained anything sweet or otherwise loaded with carbohydrates—with cookies at the top of the things to be avoided.

But *all* would be lost if Kraft couldn't get people to stop hurrying past the cookie aisle, so its Nabisco division got to work, and in late 2003 it came up with a move calculated to ease the minds of consumers who felt guilty just looking at Oreos. One of Brewster's marketing specialists had the idea: Why not create a cookie package that seemed less threatening, that promised to give the eater some self-control? This concept of empowerment became known as the 100-calorie pack.

Starting with the Oreo brand, Kraft reformulated the cookie so that a handful amounted to only 100 calories. From a technical standpoint, this took some doing. The creamy filling was so rich they couldn't make a dent in the fat. So they ditched the filling altogether, and added some creamy filling flavors to the chocolate wafers. Sales took off like a rocket. Not only that, but people returned to the cookie aisle in droves and started buying not just more Oreos but more of everything, including the full-fat versions. "People who otherwise didn't want to go down the aisle because they might buy Oreos also didn't buy Wheat Thins or Triscuits, because they were afraid to go down there," Brewster said. "All of a sudden now, they went down the aisle to get the 100-calorie pack, and were picking up some of the other products."*

But the 100-calorie packs worked a little too well for Kraft. Some of these other products from rival companies started selling so well that Kraft, to put it bluntly, started gnashing its teeth with envy and fear. The main threat came from Hershey, the chocolate company. When cookie sales

---

* The 100-calorie concept tore quickly through the grocery store, across all categories of snacks. By 2008, there were 285 items with 100-calorie packaging, racking up huge sales. But then, in 2009, sales started to slump. One theory why is that they may be ineffective at curbing the urge to overeat. One study, in fact, found that the small packs worked least of all with people who were most susceptible to bingeing. They finish one pack and simply open another. Moreover, as sales slumped, manufacturers responded by doing something that undermined the dieting powers of the small packs even further: they began putting a variety of flavors into the same larger box or bag. Inside would be small bags of chips, for instance, in five different flavors, which only increased the temptation to open one bag after another.

slumped in 2002 and beyond, Kraft may have concluded that the solution lay in easing the guilt that consumers felt when they overindulged. But Hershey wasn't worried about that. After all, it made most of its money in the candy aisle, where guilt-ridden consumers were par for the course. Consider its strategy with the Hershey's Kiss, which has reached the status of a retail colossus, with 12 billion of the teardrop-shaped chocolates sold each year. Whenever their sales started to flag, the company simply introduced a new variety that was so tempting no one could resist. Thus, the basic Kiss begat the Chocolate Truffle Kiss, which begat the Special Dark Kiss, which begat the Filled with Caramel Kiss, the Butter Creme, the Candy Cane, the Chocolate Marshmallow, the Chocolate Meltaway, and so on.

With that same no-holds-barred approach to marketing, Hershey invaded the cookie aisle in 2003 with a hybrid cookie-candy called S'mores. Based on the popular campfire treat, it pumped up the bliss by combining the fat in the company's chocolate, with sweet and salty graham cracker bits and marshmallow filling. With 6 grams of saturated fat in each cookie, it became a massive seller. "These guys came in attacking the cookie space with more indulgent products, which kind of put us in one of those interesting squeezes that big companies can find themselves in," Brewster told me.

Nabisco was left with cookies that had less fat—and less allure. Brewster said that he tried his best to compete by reformulating his cookies in ways that boosted their appeal without increasing their fat, experimenting, for instance, with higher grades of cocoa. Ultimately, however, to boost the allure, his cookie team would have to budge on fat, putting them at odds with Kraft's anti-obesity initiative, which had placed a cap on salt, sugar, and fat loads across every category of its food, from soft drinks to luncheon meats to cheese spreads. The cookies Brewster needed to create, in order to stay competitive with Hershey, would require an exemption.

Instead, Kraft simply created a brand-new category of cookie, dubbed the "Choco Bakery," and set its cap on fat high enough to compete with Hershey. "Our desire was to be no worse, but ideally better than the other guys," said Brewster, who left Kraft in 2006 to become the CEO of Krispy Kreme donuts. The cookies that emerged from Kraft's labs were not exactly diet busters, individually. But collectively they made the company look like someone who had just come off a failed diet to binge. The Oreo line went from the 100-calorie packs to the Triple Double Oreo, the Banana Split Creme Oreo, the Oreo Fudge Sundae Creme, the Dairy Queen Blizzard Creme Oreo, the Oreo Golden Double Stuf. In 2007, Kraft went all out with the Oreo Cakester, a soft Oreo filled with chocolate or vanilla cream and bulked up to deliver an additional gram of saturated fat, four more grams of sugar, and 92 added calories.

By the 100th birthday of the Oreo in 2012, the ever-expanding lineup of Oreo cookies had become a $1-billion-a-year seller in the United States. And that number accounted for only half of their success. Kraft, that year, hauled in an additional $1 billion from selling the Oreos in other countries. Even more than the fat cap waivers, this global expansion by Kraft put the company's anti-obesity campaign in a much darker context. At the first sign of losing market share, Kraft didn't just loosen its rules a bit. It set out to vanquish its rivals by dominating the entire global market on cookies and candy. Kraft's big move came in early 2010, when it paid $19.6 billion to buy Cadbury and then merged the two companies' snacks and marketing machines.

Cadbury was a familiar brand throughout much of Asia, and Kraft used the brand to introduce the Oreo. The logic in this move was explained by the company's new chief executive in a meeting with Wall Street analysts in 2012—the tone of which couldn't have been more different from the drubbing they gave her predecessor, Betsy Holden, back in 2003. No one asked about obesity in this call. There was no reason to. The CEO, Irene Rosenfeld, was focused on a strategy for higher profits that the analysts could only cheer: Kraft's snacks taking the world by storm, in what she called a "virtuous cycle of growth."

"Since combining with Cadbury, our category growth has accelerated, fueled by chocolate," she went on. "Take India, for example. Here, we've expanded our reach into remote villages by doubling the distribution of visi-coolers. These compact refrigerated displays are highly visible, and they keep our chocolate at the right temperature in the hot Indian weather. As a result, Cadbury Dairy Milk was up about 30 percent last year. Our biscuit business has also undergone an amazing transformation. Oreo, which is celebrating its 100th birthday this year, led the way with organic revenue up 50 percent. In fact, sales of Oreo in developing markets have increased 500 percent since 2006. That's an amazing record for a so-called mature product—or for any product, for that matter."

All told, Kraft's net revenues grew 10.5 percent in 2011 to $54.4 billion, a remarkable achievement indeed.

In 2012, Kraft brought its expanding synergy with Cadbury home to the United States. It started selling a spread that combined the fat in cheese with the fat and the sugar in chocolate: cream cheese blended with milk chocolate. Called Philadelphia Indulgence, two tablespoons of this chocolate cheese delivered a quarter of a day's maximum for saturated fat and, under the American Heart Association's recommendations, as much as half a day's maximum for sugar.

Behind the scenes at Kraft, the chocolate cheese put the company's system of ingredient caps under a new strain. A spokeswoman told me that Indulgence couldn't be categorized as *cheese*, which has no allowance for added sugar. So it was classified as a *spread* or *dip*, which does. Out on the market, this marrying of candy with cheese began racking up stellar reviews: "My wife saw this on a commercial this morning, got up and dressed and bought out the local grocery store," one man wrote on Kraft's website. "Chocolate and Cream Cheese! You better get out and buy some before Bloomberg makes it illegal to purchase without a prescription."

"This kind of blows my mind," said another. And a third: "When you run out of ideas, spread it on your hand and lick it off!!!!" And a fourth: "I want to put my whole face in it."

The tubs of chocolate cream cheese reminded me of the work done by Adam Drewnowski, the Seattle epidemiologist, in measuring the effects that fat has on the brain. Because fat is so energy dense—it has twice the calories of sugar—the brain sees fat in food as the body's best friend. The more fat there is in food, the more fuel the body can have for future use by converting the fat to body fat. Indeed, the body holds fat in such high esteem that it is slower to activate the mechanism that helps us avoid overeating. This mechanism is the signal the brain sends out to tell us we've had enough.

Drewnowski knew that this signal was quite operational for foods that are sweet. Even kids can take only so much sugar in their food before the taste buds cringe, but as Drewnowski discovered, the bliss point for fat, if there is one, is much higher, probably up in the stratosphere of the heaviest cream. Thus did cheese and beef become such powerhouse ingredients in processed foods. As Drewnowski also found out, however, there is something even more powerful in foods than fat alone: fat with some added sugar. Faced with this combination, the brain loses sight of the fat altogether. Fat becomes even more invisible in foods, and the brakes on overeating come right off.

This ability of food manufacturers to find synergy in the interplay of their key ingredients is not limited to fat and sugar, of course. The true magic comes when they add in the third pillar of processed foods: salt.

salt sugar fat **salt** sugar fat **salt** sugar fat **salt** sugar fat **salt** sugar fat **salt** sugar fat **salt** sugar fat **salt** sugar fat
salt sugar fat **salt** sugar fat **salt** sugar fat **salt** sugar fat **salt** sugar fat **salt** sugar fat **salt** sugar fat **salt** sugar fat
salt sugar fat **salt** sugar fat **salt** sugar fat **salt** sugar fat **salt** sugar fat **salt** sugar fat **salt** sugar fat **salt** sugar fat
salt sugar fat **salt** sugar fat **salt** sugar fat **salt** sugar fat **salt** sugar fat **salt** sugar fat **salt** sugar fat **salt** sugar fat
salt sugar fat **salt** sugar fat **salt** sugar fat **salt** sugar fat **salt** sugar fat **salt** sugar fat **salt** sugar fat **salt** sugar fat
salt sugar fat **salt** sugar fat **salt** sugar fat **salt** sugar fat **salt** sugar fat **salt** sugar fat **salt** sugar fat **salt** sugar fat
salt sugar fat **salt** sugar fat **salt** sugar fat **salt** sugar fat **salt** sugar fat **salt** sugar fat **salt** sugar fat **salt** sugar fat
salt sugar fat **salt** sugar fat **salt** sugar fat **salt** sugar fat **salt** sugar fat **salt** sugar fat **salt** sugar fat **salt** sugar fat
salt sugar fat **salt** sugar fat **salt** sugar fat **salt** sugar fat **salt** sugar fat **salt** sugar fat **salt** sugar fat **salt** sugar fat
salt sugar fat **salt** sugar fat **salt** sugar fat **salt** sugar fat **salt** sugar fat **salt** sugar fat **salt** sugar fat **salt** sugar fat
salt sugar fat **salt** sugar fat **salt** sugar fat **salt** sugar fat **salt** sugar fat **salt** sugar fat **salt** sugar fat **salt** sugar

part three **salt**

salt sugar fat **salt** sugar fat **salt** sugar fat **salt** sugar fat **salt** sugar fat **salt** sugar fat **salt** sugar fat **salt** sugar fat
salt sugar fat **salt** sugar fat **salt** sugar fat **salt** sugar fat **salt** sugar fat **salt** sugar fat **salt** sugar fat **salt** sugar fat
salt sugar fat **salt** sugar fat **salt** sugar fat **salt** sugar fat **salt** sugar fat **salt** sugar fat **salt** sugar fat **salt** sugar fat
salt sugar fat **salt** sugar fat **salt** sugar fat **salt** sugar fat **salt** sugar fat **salt** sugar fat **salt** sugar fat **salt** sugar fat
salt sugar fat **salt** sugar fat **salt** sugar fat **salt** sugar fat **salt** sugar fat **salt** sugar fat **salt** sugar fat **salt** sugar fat
salt sugar fat **salt** sugar fat **salt** sugar fat **salt** sugar fat **salt** sugar fat **salt** sugar fat **salt** sugar fat **salt** sugar fat
salt sugar fat **salt** sugar fat **salt** sugar fat **salt** sugar fat **salt** sugar fat **salt** sugar fat **salt** sugar fat **salt** sugar fat
salt sugar fat **salt** sugar fat **salt** sugar fat **salt** sugar fat **salt** sugar fat **salt** sugar fat **salt** sugar fat **salt** sugar fat
salt sugar fat **salt** sugar fat **salt** sugar fat **salt** sugar fat **salt** sugar fat **salt** sugar fat **salt** sugar fat **salt** sugar fat
salt sugar fat **salt** sugar fat **salt** sugar fat **salt** sugar fat **salt** sugar fat **salt** sugar fat **salt** sugar fat **salt** sugar fat
salt sugar fat **salt** sugar fat **salt** sugar fat **salt** sugar fat **salt** sugar fat **salt** sugar fat **salt** sugar fat **salt** sugar fat
salt sugar fat **salt** sugar fat **salt** sugar fat **salt** sugar fat **salt** sugar fat **salt** sugar fat **salt** sugar fat **salt** sugar fat
salt sugar fat **salt** sugar fat **salt** sugar fat **salt** sugar fat **salt** sugar fat **salt** sugar fat **salt** sugar fat **salt** sugar fat
salt sugar fat **salt** sugar fat **salt** sugar fat **salt** sugar fat **salt** sugar fat **salt** sugar fat **salt** sugar fat **salt** sugar fat
salt sugar fat **salt** sugar fat **salt** sugar fat **salt** sugar fat **salt** sugar fat **salt** sugar fat **salt** sugar fat **salt** sugar fat
salt sugar fat **salt** sugar fat **salt** sugar fat **salt** sugar fat **salt** sugar fat **salt** sugar fat **salt** sugar fat **salt** sugar fat
salt sugar fat **salt** sugar fat **salt** sugar fat **salt** sugar fat **salt** sugar fat **salt** sugar fat **salt** sugar fat **salt** sugar fat
salt sugar fat **salt** sugar fat **salt** sugar fat **salt** sugar fat **salt** sugar fat **salt** sugar fat **salt** sugar fat **salt** sugar fat
salt sugar fat **salt** sugar fat **salt** sugar fat **salt** sugar fat **salt** sugar fat **salt** sugar fat **salt** sugar fat **salt** sugar fat
salt sugar fat **salt** sugar fat **salt** sugar fat **salt** sugar fat **salt** sugar fat **salt** sugar fat **salt** sugar fat **salt** sugar fat
salt sugar fat **salt** sugar fat **salt** sugar fat **salt** sugar fat **salt** sugar fat **salt** sugar fat **salt** sugar fat **salt** sugar fat

chapter twelve

"People Love Salt"

In the late 1980s, a flurry of news reports and editorials focused the country's attention on a growing menace: high blood pressure. A public health survey found that one in four Americans were afflicted by this condition, also known as hypertension, and that the numbers were climbing steadily. Doctor groups held press conferences to sound the alarm that many patients didn't even know they had high blood pressure until they developed more evident complications, such as congenital heart failure, earning it the nickname "the silent killer." The precise cause was elusive, but several key factors were cited, including obesity, smoking, and diabetes. The other was salt.

The problem was not salt per se. The problem was sodium, which is one of the chemical elements in salt. Further complicating matters, public health officials explained, even sodium itself was not all bad: A little bit of sodium in the diet was essential to good health. The problem was, Americans were eating so *much* salt they were getting ten times—even twenty times—the amount of sodium the body needed. This was also far more than it could handle. In large amounts, sodium pulls fluids from the body's tissues and into the blood, which raises the blood volume and compels the heart to pump more forcefully. The result: high blood pressure.

In looking for ways to reduce the consumption of sodium, health officials identified one obvious target: the saltshakers on everyone's kitchen table. This certainly seemed like a logical notion. The saltshaker was not only a focal piece at dinner, passed around the table and then left there like a sentinel to guide the next meal. It had established itself as a form of Americana, something people collected and showed off. Even food companies got in the act: Coca-Cola branded a collectible saltshaker to look like a miniature can of Coke.

With all these shakers on all these tables, it was no wonder that health officials felt compelled to act. They urged Americans to trash their salt-shakers, or at the least relegate them to the knick-knack shelf. In 1989, the American Heart Association began marketing an alternate way for people to season their food. It created and sold its own shaker, which contained a salt-less blend of cayenne pepper, basil, thyme, and other herbs, and it even came up with a catchy slogan to brand it as the answer to high blood pressure: "Shaking the salt habit."

In this attack on sodium, however, no one bothered to examine, with any accuracy, the assumption that table salt was responsible for America's massive intake of salt. The quantities people were ingesting should have been a tipoff that something else, something bigger, was afoot. Teenage boys and men under forty, especially, were pulling in more than ten grams of salt a day, or nearly two full teaspoons. And this was merely an average. Untold numbers of people were even heavier users. Women and girls clocked in at a bit more than one teaspoon a day, but even their numbers should have made it clear that the shaker wasn't up to this kind of salting.

So where was all this salt coming from?

The answer arrived in 1991 when the *Journal of the American College of Nutrition* published the results of a clever experiment. To identify the true source of America's sodium problem, a pair of researchers rounded up sixty-two adults who liked to use salt and gave them pre-measured salt-shakers to use at home for a week. The bona fides of the scientists who conducted the study were impeccable: They worked for the Monell Chemical Senses Center in Philadelphia. This was the place where researchers perfected the calculation of the bliss point for sugar and explored the alluring properties of fat, pulling apart its molecular underpinnings to explain how the lower melting point of artery-clogging fats like butter causes them to liquefy in the mouth and produce instant joy. Monell, it was true, accepted substantial financial support from the largest food companies, including the manufacturers of iconic salty foods. The industry money, however, had not made the institute's independent-minded researchers shy about pointing fingers at the processed food industry. They were plainspoken in chastising food manufacturers for abusing their influence on America's eating habits, especially for the way the industry used sugar to increase the allure of its products. This, they knew from their own research, exploited the natural cravings that kids get for sweets. Now, in hunting for the source of sodium in the American diet, the Monell researchers were just as prepared to let the chips—or rather the grains—fall where they may.

The sixty-two participants were asked to keep careful track of everything they ate and drank for the week. To increase the reliability of their record-keeping, the Monell investigators spiked their saltshakers with a tracer that showed up in their urine, a particularly clever move that, through the regular samples they took, allowed the researchers to see precisely how much salt the shakers were contributing. At the end of the week, they gathered up all of the data and crunched the numbers.

There was hardly any sodium in the water they drank, so that was ruled out as a source. Some sodium occurs naturally in foods—such as Swiss chard and spinach—but the participants would have had to gorge themselves on these things for them to make any difference. The naturally occurring sodium in their meals contributed only a bit more than 10 percent of the total sodium they consumed in the week. And as for the much-maligned saltshaker: It delivered just 6 *percent* of their sodium intake.

Had they conducted this study a few centuries earlier, the Monell researchers would likely have gotten very different results. The salted fish that Swedes ate in the sixteenth century, for example, pushed their sodium intake way beyond even the levels consumed today, and until the advent of the refrigerator, people throughout the world relied heavily on salt to preserve their meat and fish. For the people in the Monell study, however, the natural sodium in their food and the salt they were adding themselves came to barely a fifth of the salt being consumed. Where was the rest coming from?

By 1991, when this study was done, cooking from scratch was in steep decline, steadily replaced by processed foods that were preassembled, precooked, and packaged to go. Like everyone else in the country, the study participants were getting the bulk of their meals at the supermarket, where the price of convenience was the salt that these groceries contained. The researchers discovered that more than three-quarters of the salt they consumed in the week came from processed foods. The companies making these products weren't just adding salt. They were dumping sack after sack of it into their boxed macaroni and cheese, their chicken à la king heat-and-serve meals, their canned spaghetti and meatballs, their salad dressings, tomato sauces, pizzas, and soups. Even items that manufacturers were making expressly for people who wanted to lose weight or manage afflictions like diabetes—the low-fat, low-sugar versions of their brands— were delivering huge doses of salt. From one aisle to the next, there wasn't much in the grocery store that didn't have added salt. As much as, if not more than, sugar and fat, the salting of processed food had become a way to increase sales and consumption.

The power of salt in food is smartly summed up by the industry's largest supplier of salt, Cargill, which says in its sales literature: "People love salt. Among the basic tastes—sweet, sour, bitter and salty—salt is one of the hardest ones to live without. And it's no wonder. Salt, or sodium chloride, helps give foods their taste appeal—in everything from bacon, pizza, cheese and French fries to pickles, salad dressings, snack foods and baked goods."

People don't just love salt, they crave salty foods. Depending on one's point of view, the supermarket is either a goldmine—or a minefield—of salt-heavy foods. For perspective on the salt loads delivered by groceries, consider the number 2,300. This is the maximum amount of sodium, measured in milligrams, that the federal government recommends people eat every day. In 2010, the government lowered this target for people who are especially vulnerable to the hazards of salt: people fifty-one years or older, blacks of any age, and anyone with diabetes, hypertension, or chronic kidney disease. These 143 million people—a majority of American adults—were now being urged to keep their sodium intake below 1,500 milligrams a day—less than a teaspoon a day.

With these lower limits in mind, it is easy to see why most of us are getting far more sodium than we should, with teenage boys and men averaging twice as much. The labels on foods in the grocery store tell the story. And going natural is no help when it comes to salt; even health-conscious manufacturers deliver heavy doses. Amy's Organic Minestrone Soup has 580 milligrams of sodium in a cup. Newman's Own Organic Pasta Sauce has 650 milligrams in half a cup. In perusing an expansive supermarket in New York City, my personal favorite was a frozen roast turkey dinner from Hungry Man. Salt made nine separate appearances in the list of ingredients on the side of the box, more than any other item. Helpfully, the list broke the dinner down into all of its parts. Not only did salt appear in the meat component, the gravy, the stuffing, and the potatoes, it was also the leading ingredient in something called "turkey type flavor" and ranked near the top in another mysterious component called "potato flavor." In all, the sodium in this microwavable dish came to 5,400 milligrams, which is more salt than people should eat over the course of two days. Unless, that is, the people are baby boomers or older, black, or suffering from sodium-sensitive disease. In this case, the Hungry Man dinner would deliver enough salt to meet their quota for half a week.

• • •

To understand why anyone would want to eat three and a half days' worth of salt in a single sitting, I turned once more to Monell. This time, however, instead of delving into the bliss points for sugar and fat, I met with its scientists to go over their pioneering work on salt. The lead researcher who performed the shaker study had since moved on to another subject, the mouthfeel of fat, but the center now had one of the foremost authorities on salt. His name is Paul Breslin, and he is a biologist trained in the field of experimental psychology. When he is not conducting research at Monell, he is forty-five miles north in Princeton Junction, New Jersey, where he teaches and runs his own laboratory at Rutgers University. I arranged to meet him there. Breslin's lab included a typical tasting room, which was divided into stations where test subjects are given a seat and asked to sample food or drink in order to test their likes and dislikes. In a smaller, adjoining space, he was completing the construction of something a little more unusual in food-science circles: Here, in a large metal cabinet that looked like a refrigerator (except the temperature was set to 77 degrees), Breslin was incubating fruit flies, which have proven quite useful in exploring the mysteries of salt. The genes of flies can be manipulated rapidly, allowing scientists to home in on particular traits. Moreover, their tastes are surprisingly similar to those of humans.

"Most of the things we love, they love, and most of the things we hate, they hate," Breslin said. "We both like fermentation, and they love wine, beer, cheese, vinegar, bread. That's why they are in our kitchens." Fruit flies also like modest levels of salt in their food. The manipulation of their genes has helped scientists identify the cellular mechanism by which our own mouths detect salt. More recently, Breslin has been studying the flies not for the mechanics of *how* people taste salt but for clues on *why* we love it so much.

It is, after all, just a dumb, white rock that gets dug out of the ground or drawn from the sea.

Breslin is a food scientist who loves the food he studies and thinks deeply about the food he loves. Like some of his colleagues at Monell, he is not shy about poking the giants of the food industry. His own pet peeves include the low-calorie lines of ice cream that companies make for people who want to lose weight, which Breslin believes only encourages them to overindulge. "I think the interest in making a low-fat, low-sugar ice cream, which is almost oxymoronic as far as I'm concerned, is to allow people to eat four gallons a day," Breslin said. "That's not what ice cream is designed for." He eats ice cream for what it is, a treat to be relished in small amounts. Then again, he has a lean build and seems in control of any compulsions to overeat. His latest infatuation—as a scientist and an eater—was the oil pressed from olives. In its finest, most expensive grades, olive oil will provoke a sting or itch at the back of the throat, which Breslin has been studying for its similarities to the irritation caused by ibuprofen, the anti-inflammatory drug; anti-inflammatory compounds, whether in drugs or foods, may prove to be effective in preventing disease. Friends started sending him expensive bottles—not to test, however, but to consume, because he also discovered that he loved olive oil for its taste. Sometimes he sips it straight, without even a hunk of bread, which only gets in the way of the bouquet.

What Breslin loves most, however, is salty food. We drove to a Greek delicatessen near his lab to pick up lunch, and ended up gorging on the stuff. The feta cheese was swimming in salt; the spinach pies were loaded too. "You should try one of these so you know what I'm talking about," he said, pointing to a bowl of cracked green olives. "They're my all time favorites." The grocery clerk handed me one, soaked in a garlicky, deeply salty brine that was, indeed, amazing. I could see the joy in Breslin's eyes when he got one of the olives to taste. "I used to be someone who is borderline hypertensive, and so I was told to worry about it," he said. "But my blood pressure has been perfectly normal for a long time now, and so I pay no attention to it. I love salty foods. I don't know if it's just because of the psychological reward of eating something that's truly yummy, or if it's physiological in terms of salt doing something for me. But my personal perception is that when I eat these foods I actually feel *better*. I don't mean feel better in that I feel like I've been exercising and feel, like, vigorous. I just feel better, like you would feel if you had a small dish of your favorite ice cream."

Back in his lab, where we got down to the science behind all that pleasure, it became clear that much about salt's powers of allure remains a mystery. The very idea of salt inducing feelings of joy seems crazy, given that it is just a mineral, dead and devoid of any sustenance. Sugar and fat, by contrast, come from plants and animals and are loaded with the calories people need to avoid withering away. It makes sense that when scientists slide someone into an MRI scanner and drip a sugary or fatty solution into their mouth, the electrical circuit in their brain lights up and floods them with feelings of pleasure. This stimulus, we know, comes from the part of the brain that rewards us for doing things that keep it alive or perpetuate the human race. Things like eating and sex.

Salt is not entirely worthless, of course. It does contain sodium, whose importance to our well-being should not be overlooked. In 1940, researchers reported the case of a child who had a condition that diminished his capacity to absorb sodium. He needed massive amounts of salt to survive, and he knew this instinctively. One of the first words he could say was "salt." At age one, he was licking salt off his crackers. Later, he ate it directly from the saltshaker. His parents and doctors were clueless about his condition, however, and during a prolonged hospital stay, the boy could get only foods that were low in salt, and he died. Even in not so dire a case, a diet lacking sufficient sodium will cause trouble, researchers have found. Rats develop less bone and muscle mass, have smaller brains. Still, most people need only tiny amounts of sodium, which makes it all the more difficult to understand why the vast majority of people are so prone to eating massive amounts of the stuff.

Part of the explanation for this goes back to the tongue map, the diagram that purports to show that we taste sugar only at the tip of the tongue. Likewise, this same map depicts salt as having a very limited zone—the edges of the tongue, and only toward the front, at that. The map, however, is as wrong on salt as it is for sugar. We taste salty foods like we do sweets, throughout the mouth. "Anyone can demonstrate this for themselves at home," Breslin told me. "All you have to do is take some lemon juice, honey, cream off your espresso, and a solution of table salt, and stick the tip of your tongue in each of them. You'll get sour, sweet, bitter, and salty, all on the tip on your tongue, which right there smashes the tongue map." The taste for salt doesn't end at the tip of the tongue. People are one big sponge for the salty taste. As there are for sugar, the body has receptors for detecting salt that go all the way through the mouth and down to the gut.

All this hardwiring for the salty taste would seem to imply that the body wants to make sure it gets a lot of salt. If we were not able to taste it so easily, and if salt were not so alluring, who would be bothered to rummage through the kitchen cabinet for those pretzels? People would stick with the sugary and the fatty. This desire for salt seems to have some grounding in evolutionary history. When everything lived in the ocean, animals had no problem getting the sodium they needed to survive. They wallowed in salty water. On land, however, the early climate was hot and dry. The pre-human mouths that crawled out of the sea may have developed the salty taste receptors as a means of ensuring that their owners didn't forget about salt when they foraged for food.

It's plausible, certainly. But people today aren't merely remembering salt; they're devouring it. Thus, the Hungry Man turkey dinner, with its half-week load of salt. Or the popcorn at Yankee Stadium that was so heavily salted one recent afternoon, I had to miss parts of two innings, the first waiting in line for the popcorn and the second getting drinks for my kids to un-kink their throats. The cravings we get for certain foods are a topic that none of the food companies supporting Monell are eager to raise. But Breslin not only freely discusses food cravings, he doesn't hesitate to link salty foods to an even more dicey subject: drug abuse.

The notion that some foods behave like narcotics goes back at least twenty years in scientific circles. One of Breslin's favorite papers was published in

1991, the same year as the saltshaker study. It was written by a professor of psychiatry at the University of Cincinnati named Stephen Woods, who compared eating to taking narcotics. Both, he wrote, pose a considerable challenge to the body's fundamental goal of staying on an even keel. This balancing trick is known as homeostasis, and eating, like doing drugs, throws things out of whack. "Ultimately whatever you eat ends up in your blood, and our body wants the blood levels of everything—from carbon dioxide to oxygen to salt and potassium and lipids and glucose—to be constant," Breslin said. "Probably our bodies would be happiest if we could never eat and just somehow magically be able to have some intravenous drip or something that would maintain those things constantly. When you eat, you're pushing all kinds of stuff into your blood, which goes against the concept of homeostasis, so your body basically responds to that by saying, 'Holy smokes, what are you doing to me? I have to deal with this now.' You have to get yourself back to some constant homeostatic level. Insulin is one of the things you release to push sugar out of the blood and into the cells. This is exactly what happens when you take drugs. When you inject heroin into your body, your body says, 'Holy cow, what have you done to me?' It has to try and metabolize these things, and there's all kinds of coping mechanisms for that."

The blood gets especially besieged when processed food is ingested, flooding the system with its heavy loads of salt, sugar, and fat. But where the links between eating and drugs get really interesting is in the brain. There, narcotics and food—especially food that is high in salt, sugar, and fat—act much alike. Once ingested, they race along the same pathways, using the same neurological circuitry to reach the brain's pleasure zones, those areas that reward us with enjoyable feelings for doing the right thing by our bodies. Or, as the case may be, for doing what the brain has been led to believe is the right thing.

One of the most intriguing accounts of salt's effect on the brain appeared in a 2008 paper by researchers at the University of Iowa entitled, "Salt Craving: The Psychobiology of Pathogenic Sodium Intake." In lay terms, this translates to the craving people get for salt at levels so high it causes disease. The authors reviewed all the brain scanning and other scientific investigations that had been done on salt to date, and they concluded that salt could be lumped with other things in life that become problematic when overdone. Salt, the authors concluded, was similar in this way to "sex, voluntary exercise, fats, carbohydrates and chocolate, in its possessing addictive qualities."

For obvious reasons, the word *addiction* is a particularly touchy subject among food manufacturers. They prefer saying a product is crave-able, likable, snack-able, or almost anything other than saying it is addictive. For them, the term *addiction* conjures images of strung-out junkies who hold up 7-Elevens at gunpoint for the money they need for another fix. Addiction also raises barbed legal issues that industry is loath to engage. In reality, processed food is so inexpensive and easy to procure that no one need rob a convenience store for a fix—never mind the fact that the convenience store itself, in this case, is the dealer of the fix.

In 2006 a law firm whose clients included both tobacco and food manufacturers produced a remarkable treatise on the legal fights the processed food industry might face if people tried to hold them accountable for the obesity epidemic. The authors conclude that the food industry overall is in good shape legally, that the strategy used in suing tobacco manufacturers wouldn't work nearly as well on food manufacturers. But a large section of the report is devoted to the subject of addiction, and the authors labor to identify a strategy that companies could use to persuade a jury that food isn't addictive. In the end, they don't deny there are parallels between overeating and drug abuse. They argue, instead, that the word *addiction* traditionally has had defining qualities, such as the severely painful symptoms of withdrawal, that are not readily applicable to the desire for food. "Labeling the perceived overconsumption of chocolate, for example, as 'chocolate addiction,' even if this practice is associated with high levels of comfort (emotional) eating and somewhat unstable eating patterns, risks trivializing serious addictions," they write.

Paul Breslin frames the question of addiction a little differently. When people abuse drugs long enough, he noted, the motivation to take more drugs becomes less a matter of wanting the benefit of the drug—the high—and more a matter of wanting to avoid the awful feeling generated by the craving itself. Similarly, when people start feeling hungry, they are not seeking the primary benefit of food, the calories needed to keep them alive. Rather, they are responding to the body's signal that it does not ever want to be put in the position of *needing* to eat. Most people in America never feel true hunger pain, the gut-wrenching result of being starved for nutrition. Consider how often people say they feel hungry during a single day, Breslin said. "With few exceptions, we can go a day without food or water with no problems whatsoever. The body has enough calories. But people who fast for a day feel awful. Your body comes to expect that we will feed it, and it has all these mechanisms in place so if you don't do it, then you start to feel awful. Ultimately you end up feeding yourself in order to feel okay."

This notion that we eat not so much for pleasure as we do to ward off an awful feeling, reminded me of the work done by Howard Moskowitz, the legendary food scientist who engineered the new flavor for Dr Pepper. In the study he dubbed "Crave It," he found that people are drawn to foods that are heavily salty, sweet, or fatty for reasons other than hunger. They are drawn to these foods by emotional cues and the wish to avoid the lousy feeling that the body generates as a way to defend against starvation. The fear of hunger is deeply rooted, and food manufacturers know well how to push the buttons that evoke this fear. (A particularly stark example of this comes from the Mars company in promoting its Snickers candy bar, which won applause from the advertising industry with this slogan: "Don't let hunger happen to you.")

As bad as the word *addiction* may be, however, the food industry has another problem when it comes to salt—one that could prove to be more problematic. In assessing the industry's culpability for the epidemic of overeating, scientists have come up with evidence that the *manner* in which people have come to crave salt, rather than the craving itself, is far more damning.

As it turns out, the manufacturers of processed foods have been creating a desire for salt where none existed before.

Babies love sugar the instant they are born. Simple experiments have demonstrated this, by eliciting smiles with a droplet of sugary water. But babies do *not* like salt. They don't like it at all until they are six months or more into their lives, and even then, they have to be coaxed.

This idea that salt is being pressed upon America's kids comes from the scientists at Monell, who have been pushing hard to pinpoint the genesis of our taste for salt. They wanted to know what caused kids to like salt, if it wasn't a natural thing for them to do. So they followed sixty-one children, starting at infancy. First, they surveyed their parents to learn how much salt the kids got in their diets, and the kids fell neatly into two camps: One group was eating what their parents ate, salty cereal and crackers and bread made by food manufacturers, while the other got baby foods that had little or no salt, like fresh fruits and vegetables.

Then the Monell researchers tested the kids to see if there was any difference in how much the two groups liked salt.

The results were published in 2012 in the *American Journal of Clinical Nutrition*, and they kicked up quite a stir among regulators and food industry officials. To test the kids' fondness for salt, the Monell investigators, led by Leslie Stein, gave them solutions of varying salinity to sip, starting when they were two months old. At that age, all the kids either rejected the salty solutions or were indifferent to them. At six months, however, when they were tested again, the kids split into two groups. Those who had been given fruit and vegetables to eat still preferred plain water to the salty solutions. But those who had been fed foods that were salty now liked the salty solutions.

Over time, the two groups—the salted and the unsalted—grew even more disparate. "Mothers reported that preschool-age children who had been introduced to starchy table food by six months of age were more likely to lick salt from the surface of foods," the study said. "There was also a trend for these children to be more likely to eat plain salt."

Of course, the kids didn't have to resort to the shaker. By preschool, the salted kids were getting foods from throughout the grocery store that were loaded with salt—potato chips, bacon, soup, ham, hot dogs, French fries, pizza, crackers.

When the study was released, Gary Beauchamp, the center's director and a co-author, talked about its significance. These were kids being studied, he stressed. Kids who were *not born* liking salt. They have to be taught to like the taste of salt, and when they are, salt has a deep and lasting effect on their eating habits. "Our data would suggest that if one wants to reduce salt in the population as a whole," Beauchamp said, "then it's important to start early, because infants and children are very vulnerable."

With this revelation, the industry's heavy use of salt moves from the realm of merely satisfying America's craving for salt to creating a craving where none exists.

As it happened, I wasn't the only one who needed help from the experts at Monell to understand the powers of salt. In 2005, when Washington put a scare into the industry by urging people to slash their intake of salt to less than a teaspoon each day, some of the largest food companies convened a group they called the Salt Consortium to figure out a way to deal with this threat to their industry. The group kept its existence confidential for fear of generating unwanted attention, but I learned about it from food company officials who also divulged that they had chosen none other than Monell to gather the facts to help them out of their predicament.

The group's goal was to learn precisely what made salt so alluring, so that they might find ways to reduce its presence in their products. As with sugar and fat, the industry has a strict bottom line on reducing salt: This effort can't hurt their sales in any way. Their products, with less salt, have to be just as alluring as they are in full-salt mode.

But the more the industry looked at salt, the more it realized that the consumer was only part of the problem. The manufacturers themselves were utterly, inexorably hooked on the stuff. Each year, food companies use an amount of salt that is every bit as staggering as it sounds: 5 billion pounds.

And that's because, for them, the salty taste that drives people to keep eating popcorn until the bag is empty is just the start of salt's powers.

Manufacturers view salt as perhaps the most magical of the three pillars of processed foods, for all the things it can do beyond exciting the taste buds. In the world of processed foods, salt is the great fixer. It corrects myriad problems that arise as a matter of course in the factory. Cornflakes, for example, taste metallic without it. Crackers are bitter and soggy and stick to the roof of your mouth. Ham turns so rubbery it can bounce. Some of salt's power has nothing to do with the food at all. In commercial bread making, salt keeps the huge, fast-spinning machinery from gumming up and the factory line from backing up: Salt slows down the rising process so that the ovens can keep up with the pace.

Among all the miracles that salt performs for the processed food industry, perhaps the most essential involves a plague that the industry calls "warmed-over-flavor," whose acronym, WOF, is pronounced something like the dog's bark. WOF is caused by the oxidation of the fats in meat, which gives meat the taste of cardboard or, as some in the industry describe it, damp dog hair, when the meat is reheated after being precooked and added to soups or boxed meals. "Once warmed-over-flavor gets going, you are pretty well dead in the water," said Susan Brewer, a professor of food science in the University of Illinois's College of Agricultural, Consumer and Environmental Science. "People can smell or taste it at very low levels. At my cafeteria, they will make a rib roast, and serve the leftovers the next day as roast beef sandwiches, and they taste nasty. That's the warmed-over-flavor. People get very sensitive to its taste."

This is where salt comes in. Once WOF sets in, salt becomes a convenient antidote for the processed food industry, which is heavily reliant on reheated meats. One of the most effective cures for WOF is an infusion of fresh spices, especially rosemary, which has antioxidants to counteract the meat's deterioration. But fresh herbs are costly. So manufacturers more typically make sure they have lots of salt in their formulas. The cardboard or dog-hair taste is still there, but it is overpowered by the salt.

To make matters worse for consumers, salt is not the only way that food manufacturers pump sodium into America's bloodstream. Companies are adding sodium in the form of other food additives, completely aside from the salt they pour into their foods. They do this through the dozens of sodium-based compounds that are added to processed food to delay the onset of bacterial decay, to bind ingredients, and to blend mixtures that otherwise come unglued, like the protein and fat molecules in processed cheese. With names like sodium citrate, sodium phosphate, and sodium acid pyrophosphate, these compounds have become essential components in processed foods, making them look and taste attractive and last longer on the shelf. Together, these compounds contribute less sodium than salt, but the grocery store nonetheless has become filled with products dependent on them. The same Hungry Man turkey dinner that listed salt nine times among its various components also had nine other references to various sodium compounds.

The industry's addiction to salt and sodium is evident on its product labels. But it is also evident behind the scenes, in how the industry reacts to the slightest nudging from Washington. In 2010, when the federal nutrition panel lowered its recommended daily maximum for sodium to 1,500 milligrams for the most vulnerable Americans, food manufacturers put on a full-court press urging the panel to back off. Kellogg, for one, sent the Department of Agriculture, which was overseeing the panel's work, a 20-page letter detailing all the reasons it needed salt and sodium—and in amounts that would not make the 1,500 level feasible. "Serious technical constraints limit the ability to dramatically reduce sodium concentrations while maintaining consumer acceptability that is essential to sustain such products in the marketplace," Kellogg implored. "We urgently request that the Committee consider these constraints."

Kellogg did not mention WOF by name but more generally pointed to salt's powers to override the dark sides of processed foods, in which all the additives being used can generate unpleasant tastes. Foods do not even have to taste salty for salt to be critical to their success, the company noted. "The ability of salt to enhance other flavors and/or mask objectionable ones (e.g., bitterness) in foods that do not necessarily taste salty is more important. Examples of foods in this broad category include baked goods, cereals, cheese, entrees and numerous other foods."

To be sure, Kellogg—like other food manufacturers—didn't miss their opportunity to shift some of the blame for the country's dependence on salt onto the people who buy processed foods. In its letter, Kellogg talked about salt as if it was a drug. It cited the "psychobiology of the innate craving for salt" and "the virtually intractable nature of the appetite for salt" and shifted the onus on consumers. "Taste is by far the most powerful factor that motivates consumers to purchase and consume foods," Kellogg said, citing some recent polling. In these surveys, people conceded that they were not doing enough to achieve a healthy diet, but three in four cited the same excuse for their failure: "I don't want to give up the foods I like."

Yet, for people at least, there's hope when it comes to salt. Addiction to salt, it turns out, can be readily reversed. All that is needed is to stop eating processed foods for a while.

This bit of wisdom—known instinctually to anyone who is forced to undergo a low-salt diet—was put to the scientific test by Monell. In 1982, when salt first landed on the radar of federal regulators, the institute's director, Gary Beauchamp, performed an experiment on salt. He studied six women and three men as they slashed their consumption of salt by half by avoiding certain processed foods. For the first few weeks, nothing much happened, apart from the subjects missing the foods they used to eat. But then, slowly, bit by bit, a radical change occurred. The test subjects didn't stop liking salt, nor did they lose their taste for it. Rather, the salt-sensitive taste buds in their mouths—the same ones that had grown used to bombardment by salty foods—became more sensitive to salt, so they needed less salt to experience its pleasures. A lot less. Enough to get them within the limits now being urged upon Americans by the federal government. "At the end of twelve weeks, after being on the low-sodium diets, we allowed them to use as much salt from their saltshakers as they wanted to, and all they added back to their diet was about 20 percent of the salt we had taken out," Beauchamp told me.

The subjects had, in effect, unhooked themselves from salt, or at least from the levels of salt that are considered potential killers.

That is the good fortune that awaits anyone trying to wean themselves off salt. As I would soon see, the food manufacturers are facing a much deeper and far more complex struggle in confronting their own addiction.

chapter thirteen

"The Same Great Salty Taste Your Customers Crave"

I arrived at a modern office complex in Hopkins, Minnesota, ten miles west of Minneapolis on a cool morning in April 2012. This is where Cargill, the $134 billion food industry giant, houses its central operations. I walked into the lobby, picked up my security badge, passed through the security gates, and took the elevator to the sixth floor. When the doors opened, I was greeted by seemingly endless rows of cubicles with low partitions, filled with men and women staring at their computer screens. The mood was decidedly dreary.

They had a good excuse to feel down, my guide explained. They had just spent months drumming their fingers on their desks, waiting for their phones to ring. This was the unit that sold road salt, and the past winter had been a relief for everyone in the country—except for these workers at Cargill. Meteorologists declared it the fourth-warmest winter on record, which meant it had rained, not snowed, throughout the entire Northern Plains, the Midwest, and the Northeast, which meant there was no ice on the roads. Icy roads are Cargill's best friend; the more ice the winter brings, the more money the company makes. "We have a saying at Cargill," the company's spokesman, Mark Klein, told me. "When winters are brown, we are blue. And when they are white, we are green."

As we moved deeper into Cargill's sixth floor, however, the mood changed dramatically. In this part of the salt division, the workers were all happily green. There was no global warming to worry about here. These sales people were downing cups of coffee not to keep themselves awake but to keep up with the frantic pace of orders. These workers had been busy for as long as anyone could remember. This was because the salt being sold here was not for the country's roads. This salt was for a much more reliable—and dependent—customer: the processed food industry.

As company officials explained to me, the salt that they sell to food manufacturers is no ordinary salt. In the processing plants that Cargill owns, this rock is transformed into a vast array of shapes and designs. Cargill's salt is smashed, ground, pulverized, flaked, and reshaped in hundreds of ways, all with one goal in mind: to maximize its power in food. Cargill currently sells forty different types of processed salt, from a fine powder to large granules, and every one of them is engineered to provide the biggest bang for the buck—or, perhaps more accurately, the biggest bang for the penny. Even the high-tech salts engineered by Cargill cost a mere ten cents per pound, which is so cheap in the grand scheme of things that some food manufacturers have to pay more money just to get clean water into their factories.

There is nothing cheap about Cargill's salt beyond the price, however. Its salts are finely tuned bliss machines. When the popcorn-makers come to Cargill for help, they get a flake that is specially designed to cling to every nook and cranny of this odd-shaped snack—the better to lash the taste buds, instantaneously, with a direct hit of salt. When processed meat and cheese companies come calling, Cargill has a salt that has been pulverized into a texture-less, fine powder, which makes for easier assimilation by our bodies and brains. Dry soup, cereal, flour, and snack manufacturers, when they knock on Cargill's door, are more keen on certain sea salt varieties, which contain additives that keep the salt from caking. "Our extensive portfolio of salts can help you delight your consumers," as Cargill says in its sales literature.

My own personal favorite is the kosher salt I often use at home to perk up everything from steamed broccoli to a roast leg of lamb.* Cargill makes this salt in St. Clair, Michigan, and sells it to food manufacturers and home cooks alike under the Diamond Crystal brand. When poured out of the 3-pound box, it looks like innocent flakes of snow, but in fact this salt is of cunning and intricate design. Its magnetism begins with the feel: Cooks like to pour it into their hand and then pinch the crystals between their fingers as they add it to food. In 2009, Cargill hired celebrity chef Alton Brown as its spokesman for Diamond Crystal, and in the videos he made for the company, he enthuses profusely about sprinkling this salt on all manner of foods, even chocolate cookies, fruit, and ice cream. "Salt!" he says. "It's the finest compound to ever grace our palate."

It's what happens after the sprinkling, however, that gives this kosher salt its greatest power in food. Produced through an evaporation technique called the Alberger process, the crystals are quadrilateral pyramids, with flat sides that adhere better to food. On top of that, the pyramids are hollowed out, as a cup is, enabling the salt to have the maximum possible contact with the mouth's saliva. Lastly, the salt's unique shape enables it to dissolve three times faster than normal salt. Which, in turn, means that it races to the brain with faster, bigger jolts of salty flavor.

Cargill calls this the "flavor burst" in promoting the kosher salt to food manufacturers, who, of course, are not using these crystals sparingly. The kosher variety is sold by the truckload to food companies, in 80-pound bags stacked thirty to a pallet, and comes in the usual range of grades to meet the industry's needs: "Flake" for cheese and cured meats, "Special Flake" for crackers and breadsticks, "Fine Flake Improved" for icings and soups, and "Shur-Flo Fine Flour Salt" with three additives—sodium fer-

---

* Most salts are kosher in the sense of complying with the guidelines for food as written in the Torah. This salt's designation as kosher was derived from its usefulness in making kosher meats; its unique crystalline structure is adept at soaking up the surface blood.

rocyanide, sodium silicoaluminate, and glycerin—to ensure constant flow and prevent factory dust.

The flavor that salt imparts to food is just one of the attributes that manufacturers rely on. For them, salt is nothing less than a miracle worker in processed foods. It makes sugar taste sweeter. It adds crunch to crackers and frozen waffles. It delays spoilage so that the products can sit longer on the shelf. And, just as importantly, it masks the otherwise bitter or dull taste that hounds so many processed foods before salt is added.

Given the many ways that salt facilitates the making of processed food, it is fitting that Cargill became the industry's leading supplier. In all of its operations, the company prides itself not only on the goods that it sells but also on the service it provides. Being the industry's friend in need helped make Cargill one the richest companies in the world, with salt a small part of its scope. Its revenue climbed 12 percent in 2012, to $133.9 billion, with profits of nearly $1.2 billion.

If you're tempted to rush out and buy some of the company's stock, don't bother. There isn't any to be had. Cargill is privately held, controlled for the most part by the one hundred descendants of the man who founded the company in 1865, William Wallace Cargill. The son of a Scottish sea captain, he started with a single warehouse for grain in Conover, Iowa, strategically placed at the end of the McGregor & Western Railroad line. To this day, Cargill doesn't farm. It doesn't even own any land. Cargill makes its money by being of exquisite utility to the agricultural industry. It supplies farmers with everything they need to make a profit, from chemical fertilizers to Wall Street swap options that hedge their financial risk. It moves the grain and the sugar beets that farmers grow around the world faster and more efficiently than anyone else. Indeed, Cargill isn't just a cog in the global food chain. With grain silos in far-flung locales like Romania, shipping terminals in big sugar producers like Brazil, 140,000 employees in sixty-five countries, and 350 chartered cargo vessels calling on 6,000 ports, Cargill *is* the global food chain.

Above all, the company has a $50 billion trade in food ingredients that makes it extremely likely that whatever you eat or drink today, it will contain something from Cargill. Cargill mills flour for baking, makes malt for brewing, dries corn for cereals and snacks, extracts chocolate from cocoa beans. But most importantly for its customers, Cargill supplies all three pillars of processed food: salt, sugar, and fat. Each day, it produces roughly 4.8 million pounds of food-grade salt alone. As with salt, it fashions its sugar and fat into dozens of formulations that are crafted and honed to meet the industry's precise needs. It has oils and shortenings for frying, icing and whipping; corn syrups for sodas; and five configurations of beet and cane sugars for powdered drinks, candy, condiments, cereal, meats, dairy, and baked goods.

Because of its massive status in the business, Cargill also has the smarts to move urgently—and offer solutions—when concerns about health causes trouble for their customers. In recent years, it introduced Truvia, a zero-calorie sweetener made from leaves of the stevia shrub grown in Latin America; Clear Valley Omega-3 Oil, an unsaturated fat that has been touted for its healthy heart benefits; and Barlív, a fiber made from barley to reduce cholesterol—or as the name would imply, to extend your life.

In 2005, when salt came under fire from regulators and consumer activists, causing food manufacturers to cringe, Cargill was there with one of its most clever solutions yet.

Salt has been a significant part of Cargill's profit stream since 1955, when one of its managers had a clever idea. For many years, the company's barges had been carrying grain down the Mississippi River from the Midwest to New Orleans for shipping overseas and returning empty, to pick up another load. Instead of sending the barges back up the river empty, he suggested, what if they were filled with salt from a vast salt mine in southern Louisiana and then sold at a profit back in the Midwest. Today, with several salt-making facilities, Cargill turns out 1.7 *billion* pounds of the stuff each year for use in food.*

When Cargill first started peddling salt, its sales crews would regale their customers with stories about those first barge trips and the mineral's rich history. They stressed its rarity and value. The raw rock, they would explain, is mined at depths of between 650 and 2,500 feet below the surface of the earth in one of two ways: It is either dug out with machines, or water is pumped into the mine to turn the salt into a brine that is then extracted and left to dry. The other way salt is produced is from seawater, which is pooled into shallow ponds and allowed to lie around until evaporation leaves only the salt behind. Lest anyone grumble about the company's prices, it was helpful for the Cargill sales crews to point out that salt was once so precious that it precipitated wars and in turn became a target in wars, as it did in our own country's civil war. The Union deployed 471 ships and 2,455 guns to stop the 350 tons of salt that had been arriving at New Orleans every day on British ships, and whenever they could, the Union soldiers seized or destroyed salt mines throughout the South. At the time, salt was critical not only for preserving meat; it was also used to disinfect the wounds of the injured. In fact, American history is steeped in salt: The Jamestown colonists made their own salt in 1614 when they got tired of buying it from Britain, setting up wooden evaporation ponds on Smith Island. There was even a time when people, for instance Roman soldiers, were paid their wages in salt. Hence the word *salary*, a derivative of salt.

Starting in 2005, Cargill saw the need to edit its sales pitch. That was the year the federal government's Dietary Guidelines advisory committee first set a maximum limit for sodium of 2,300 milligrams a day in their nutrition recommendations. The limit was particularly onerous for young men, who were averaging twice that sum, approximately two teaspoons a day. But the stakes were high for everybody, the panel said. If people could

---

* Cargill declined to say how much salt it produces, so this figure is an estimate gleaned from federal data and interviews with industry experts. Its closest rival is Morton Salt, best known for salt used at home.

go only part of the way in reaching the 2,300 goal, by reducing their intake of salt by even half a teaspoon a day, this alone would prevent 92,000 heart attacks, 59,000 strokes, and 81,000 deaths, saving the country $20 billion in health care and other costs.

While some scientists quibbled with these numbers, Cargill began telling its customers that it accepted the basic premise that too much salt was bad for you. One Cargill official who regularly makes presentations to the company's customers, Kristen Dammann, took me through her current deck of PowerPoint slides, saying, "Excessive intake has been linked to high blood pressure, and high blood pressure is a risk factor for heart disease. So the idea is that reducing sodium can reduce the risk for hypertension and the risk for heart disease."

As if this wasn't enough—having salt linked to heart attacks by the biggest *seller* of salt—Cargill had more bad news for its food industry customers. In England, government authorities were not just setting vague overall limits on sodium or dithering around with the saltshaker, like the American authorities did back in the 1980s. The British knew well that most of the salt in everyone's diet came from the food industry, so starting in 2003, the Food Standards Agency in London developed a scheme to hold the manufacturers accountable. It set targets for how much sodium they could add to their products—crafting limits for dozens of foods, from bread to cookies to frozen meals. The system was voluntary, but the authorities pressed the industry to meet these targets, and, for companies who were used to heaping as much salt into their products as they wanted, the details were alarming. Soups had to lose 30 percent of their salt, breads 16 percent, meats 10 percent, and so on.

Many of these foods were being made by companies based in the United States, where consumer advocates were turning up the pressure on salt. In 2005, the Center for Science in the Public Interest came out with a damning report entitled "Salt: The Forgotten Killer . . . and FDA's Failure to Protect the Public's Health." The consumer group had been skeptical when the FDA in 1983 asked manufacturers—in gentle tones—to go easy on the salt. So starting that year, the group began tracking 100 brand-name products, such as Campbell's soups and Kraft's Lunchables, and it found little change in their salt loads. From 1983 to 2003, the salt levels dipped by 5 percent, but since 1993—in the absence of any attention from Washington—these products had actually become *saltier*, gaining 6 percent by 2003. "Despite pleas from government and other health experts over the last quarter century to reduce salt consumption, Americans are consuming more—not less—salt," the report said. "Thousands of packaged foods provide one-fourth or more of a day's maximum recommended intake."

All in all, the food industry was facing trouble with salt that made the public's addiction look mild. Consumers might find themselves acting like some hapless junkie when they first try to cut back on their consumption of salt, but at least we know that they, in time, can get their taste buds back to normal and that these cravings will, in turn, subside. What companies face, on the other hand, is a much harsher mistress. The mere suggestion that they might cut back on salt causes them to panic, and it is not the saltshaker they reach for. They lunge for the salt that arrives at their factories in fifty- and eighty-pound sacks, piled to the ceiling on wooden pallets.

Without salt, processed food companies cease to exist.

Which is where Cargill comes in, with the full force of its service-oriented mission. It hired some smart research scientists, bought them a $750,000 scanning electron microscope and other sophisticated equipment, and put them to work finding ways to reduce the industry's dependence on sodium. To see the fruits of their efforts firsthand, I left the company's office complex where cubicle workers sell salt and visited a nearby facility where the focal point was a large, industrial kitchen, its windows heavily shuttered to keep industrial spies at bay. In the ovens here, one of Cargill's technicians, Jody Mattsen, had baked me some loaves of white bread. She had them sliced and placed on trays for us to taste.

"A lot of people would say, 'Hey, let's just take the salt out,'" she said. "You know, that's contributing the sodium, so let's just take it out. So here is an example on that end of the spectrum." She offered me a slice. "Basically, this is a bread with no salt added."

We ate. We gagged. The bread tasted like tin. Without salt, it didn't even look like the puffy, light bread you buy in the grocery store. It was riddled with big air pockets and had a rough texture, and the loaf's normally burnished brown crust had faded to a wan, sickly tan.

Then she slid a piece toward me that, she said, contained the solution Cargill is now offering its customers. This loaf looked fine and tasted fine, and yet it had 33 percent less sodium than normal bread. Cargill's trick was to replace some of the salt with a chemical compound known as potassium chloride.

White and crystalline, potassium chloride looks and feels a lot like salt, but far more importantly, it acts much like salt, chemically speaking. "It's the closest thing currently that we have of something that functions like salt," Mattsen said. "You remember the periodic table from school? Well, on that chart, potassium, with the symbol K, is right below sodium, Na, which means it has similar properties." The chloride part of potassium chloride, she added, is the same chloride in salt, whose chemical name is sodium chloride.

For the purposes of processed food, potassium chloride was basically salt but without the bad sodium. Same salty taste, but no heart attacks or strokes. Intrigued, I began to question my unscientific efforts to compare the pillars of processed foods to drugs of abuse. Yes, salt might be compared to cocaine, for all the pleasure and longing that both provide, but this salt substitute was something else altogether. It wasn't a drug as much as it was a cure. Maybe this was the methadone for an industry hooked on salt. Something to ease the pain of the companies trying to break their habit on salt—without hurting their sales.

This seemed to be a win-win for everybody. Consumers would get less sodium, food manufacturers would stay in business, and Cargill could make up for the dwindling salt market by selling potassium chloride— which it now does, in a brand called Premier. Just like salt, it comes in multiple grades and 1,800-pound pallets, but there is an added bonus for Cargill: The potassium chloride is priced much higher than salt.

To promote potassium chloride, Cargill has even produced a handy instructional flyer for companies that are serious about getting off salt, which it calls the "the 10-step guide." Its advice ranges from urging these companies to know their competition, to figuring out whether to tell consumers about their efforts to cut back on salt. "Do you decide to make a health claim? Do you mention the reduction at all? Or, do you keep it stealth? The answer will depend on what your identified objectives are, who you are trying to reach and what your testing efforts are telling you," the guide says. "We offer a full portfolio of salt alternatives to meet your needs, while still delivering the same great salty taste your customers crave."

As for the higher cost of potassium chloride, Cargill notes that this and other costs associated with creating healthier foods can be passed on to the consumer: "Options such as potassium chloride and alternative flavor systems are more expensive, so understanding your target consumer and their willingness to pay more for a reduced sodium product will help you weigh the pros and cons."

Alas, the potassium chloride solution does pose some significant problems for food companies, as does getting off salt more generally. For one thing, potassium chloride can be quite bitter, which can ruin a product's taste. Some ingredient companies have begun marketing yet more food additives, specifically designed to mask the bitter taste of the added potassium chloride. For another thing, swapping potassium chloride for salt also messes up the intricate formulas engineered by food technicians, throwing other ingredients—including sugar and fat—out of whack. Most commonly, their strength is diminished, forcing technicians to add more sugar and fat to maintain their allure.

The British, so far ahead of American regulators when it comes to salt, have sought to discourage manufacturers from using potassium chloride at all. They point to research that links large amounts of potassium to kidney problems and claim that kids and the elderly may face the highest risk. More broadly, they worry that potassium chloride will undermine their strategy of lowering the country's intake of sodium—a strategy based on lowering people's liking of salt. As the scientists at Monell discovered, processed foods taste horribly salty after you've been off salt for a while. By contrast, potassium chloride reduces the need for sodium while keeping foods tasting just as salty as they do with salt. That would be fine, except that potassium chloride doesn't work with many foods, and they would need to keep using lots of salt to meet the country's undiminished liking for salt.

In the first six years of the British program, the average person's intake of salt fell by 15 percent, and officials there are hoping for much more. "People are starting to complain that when they go abroad, the food tastes too salty," said Graham MacGregor, a professor of cardiovascular medicine in London and an early proponent of the salt reduction effort. "It has saved 10,000 deaths a year from strokes and heart disease, through a public health policy that has cost virtually nothing."

But food manufacturers are starting to complain that the initial reductions were the easiest ones. They had been adding such huge amounts of salt to their foods that cutting back by 20 percent or even 30 percent posed little problem, consumers barely noticed. Thereafter, however, trouble beset the makers of processed foods as they sought to press on with lower amounts of salts.

To get a better look at this problem, I made the rounds of the largest food companies in America, starting with Kellogg, which had branched out from cereal into all kinds of breakfast foods and snacks. At their research facility in Battle Creek, Kellogg's food scientists prepared for me special versions of some of its most iconic brands—without using any salt at all. Their aim was to show me the difficulties they faced in trying to quit their dependence on salt, and in this, they succeeded grandly. It was, to be blunt, a culinary horror show.

The Corn Flakes tasted like metal filings, the Eggo frozen waffles like straw. Cheez-Its lost their golden yellow hue, turning a sickly yellow, and they went all gummy when chewed. The buttery flavor of the Keebler

Town House Light Buttery Crackers, which contained no actual butter to start with, simply disappeared. "Salt really changes the way that your tongue will taste the product," John Kepplinger, a Kellogg vice president and food scientist, told me as we tasted these salt-free foods. "You make one little change, and something that was a complementary flavor now starts to stand out and become objectionable."

Taste wasn't the only revulsion caused by salt's absence. The manufacturers of processed meats complained about the texture they lost when salt was removed. There was even a measurable point—like the bliss point for sugar, except in reverse—at which their taste testers would spit out the meat.

In 2010, Kraft sent me a series of experimental sliced hams from its Oscar Mayer label, with the salt reduced to varying levels. Typically, three slices of this meat had 820 milligrams of sodium, more than half of the daily maximum intake currently recommended for most American adults.

I unwrapped the ham and tasted it straight, without bread. The version with 37 percent less sodium wasn't too bad; it still reminded me of my schoolboy lunches, even without the mayo and Wonder Bread. But the next version, with an additional 3 percent sodium removed, tasted like rubber. Consumers who tested this version failed it on all the big counts: texture, flavor, and aroma. "We often fall off a cliff, and that's what we did here," said Russell Moroz, a Kraft vice president.

That left Oscar Mayer with ham that, at the reduced level, still had a third or more of the daily maximum for sodium, not all of which was coming from the salt. Its Deli Fresh ham, for example, has sodium lactate, sodium phosphates, sodium diacetate, sodium ascorbate, and sodium nitrite all playing critical roles.

In dealing with the British authorities, Kraft, in 2009, reported a litany of production woes. Its Oreos not only needed salt for their flavor, they also needed sodium bicarbonate to increase the alkalinity of the dough; in trying to cut back on both, Kraft said it ended up with cookies that were off-color and bitter. Same thing with its Ritz Crackers, whose allure was dependent on a savory flavor. Cheese, though, appeared to be the hardest of all. Taking more than a bit of salt out of cheddar destroyed the aroma, Kraft said, and using potassium chloride as a salt substitute left a "soapy, bitter aftertaste." The taste testers complained most loudly when it tried to lower the salt *and* the fat in its cheese. "Have stopped short of any further reduction," Kraft advised the British on its cheese endeavors, "as clear that consumer preference would be severely compromised."

In 2010, New York City set out to emulate the Brits on salt. Led by a city health official who had previously tangled with the tobacco industry over smoking, the city put together a set of goals for the processed food industry, establishing limits for every category. With great optimism, the mayor, Michael Bloomberg, kicked off the scheme with a press conference at City Hall, telling reporters, "If we reach these goals, we will save thousands and thousands of lives in New York and the rest of the country from being lost."

One look at the guidelines, however, made it clear why few manufacturers had signed on to the voluntary program. Breads and rolls being sold in New York and the rest of the country were averaging 139 milligrams of sodium in every ounce, and Bloomberg wanted to get them down to 103 milligrams an ounce. He wanted dry soup to drop from 234 to 163 milligrams, processed cheese to plunge from 398 to 297 milligrams, potato chips to go from 203 to 123 milligrams.

Bloomberg couched his voluntary program as the lesser of two evils: "If you want federal regulation, a good way to get it is to not do something." But in the end, the few manufacturers who did agree to make pledges volunteered only their easiest foods—those that were already so salty that a small drop in salt wouldn't be noticed, and those that formed the smallest part of their revenue. Kraft pledged to reduce the salt in its bacon but not in its cheese. Unilever put its butter spreads up for salt reduction, but not its dry soups or its ice cream, which can have, surprisingly, nearly 100 milligrams of salt in a half-cup serving, along with loads of sugar and fat.

"I have a question," one of the reporters said to a representative from the Mars company who was present. "You're doing this with rice, but really your iconic product is candy. Chocolate bars, Snickers. . . . I don't see any commitment there on the billions of dollars you market in candy." The Mars representative's answer was so evasive that the mayor felt obliged to come to his aid. "If you help people buy their rice," Bloomberg told the reporter, "it may help with the next product line. Other questions?"

Among the companies that didn't sign up was one of biggest, most celebrated American food manufacturers, the Campbell Soup Company, which had declined to enlist any of its products in the mayor's initiative.* So I traveled to the company's headquarters in Camden, New Jersey, where officials agreed to show me the challenge they faced in getting out from under their dependence on salt.

This was not their first run-in with salt. The company's habit, in fact, had given it some trouble over the years. When Campbell, in the late 1980s, sought to promote a new line of lower-fat soups as wholesome, the Federal Trade Commission intervened, accusing it of deceptive advertising, since the soups still had hefty amounts of salt. (The company settled the case by agreeing to disclose the sodium levels in its ads.) Similarly, in 2010, when Campbell began promoting its V8 Vegetable Juice as a substitute for fresh vegetables, the salt in the juice—480 milligrams of sodium in each serving cup—drew fire. The juice should not be described as healthy, a scientific journal reviewer said in rejecting a study the company had funded in hopes of buttressing its vegetables claim. (The ads ran anyway, winning an industry award for boosting sales of the juice by 4 percent.)

In meeting with me, Campbell officials said they were laboring to take as much salt out of their products as they could without hurting sales. Their recent achievements included lowering the sodium in V8 from 480 milligrams to 420 and taking some of its Pepperidge Farm bread from 360 milligrams per serving all the way down to 65. This success, they said, was

---

* Some months later, Campbell did join the salt reduction initiative, with the same strategy of the other companies. It pledged to reduce the salt in some of its foods, including canned chili and hash, but not the biggest part of its portfolio, the soups.

due in large part to a special salt the company had acquired that has 50 percent less sodium than ordinary salt. Campbell declined to provide any details on this salt, citing competitive interests. Nonetheless, the officials stressed that, in their view, there was nothing like salt for making the company's foods attractive to consumers and that, much like the rest of the food industry, they were reaching a limit on salt reduction.

To help me see why, Campbell arranged a tasting of two of its stalwart soups: tomato and vegetable beef. My guide was George Dowdie, senior vice president for global research and development. He had worked nearly a decade for Frito-Lay and another ten years for Seagram's before joining Campbell in 2002; this experience gave him a deep and varied appreciation for flavorings and taste. "The reality is, we have to earn the consumer's trust every day," Dowdie said. "And if you disappoint the consumer, in terms of that experience and that enjoyment, there is no guarantee that they will come back."

We stepped into a room adjoining the company's test kitchens, where the staff brought out a stack of white porcelain bowls and several pots of hot soup. "The question has been, really, why is it so difficult to lower salt?" Dowdie said. "At the end of the day, it's a very, very difficult challenge. If you think about the fundamental tastes, we have savory, which some folks call umami. We have bitter, we have sweet, we have sour, but the most difficult of all these tastes really is the salty taste. It has the least understood mechanisms, and there is no substitute for it. Salt has powerful roles in recipes. Think about at home. Just a pinch of salt will explode the flavor. In our world, the role of salt is to really enhance other flavors and other tastes within the soup or the broth or whatever you are cooking."

That may be, but in our tasting it became clear that salt played significant roles beyond enhancing. For starters, even the soups with lowered levels of salt still had hefty sodium loads. Campbell is most proud of a line called Healthy Request, which has 410 milligrams of sodium in each cup—nearly a third of a day's maximum for Americans at highest risk, if they eat only a cup, which is half a can. But Healthy Request brings in barely 10 percent of the company's soup sales, the company told me. The big sellers, like chicken noodle, range as high as 790 milligrams in each cup.

Dowdie's staff ladled out a version of their tomato soup, which they had made especially for me, doing no more than lowering the sodium from 710 milligrams to 480. Dowdie took a sip. "This is not something people could like and eat a lot of," he said. "It's missing something." But then we tasted a version with the same sodium level—only this time, his staff had added some herbs and spices. Dowdie was more bullish on this one: "You taste a well-balanced tomato flavor, like something you'd make at home."

Campbell had figured out that the way to reduce salt in soup was not the Cargill route, adding potassium chloride, but rather the trick that my mother, for one, had used to make her soups taste good: adding fresh herbs and spices.

Campbell declined to discuss what spicing it used and how much it cost, but Dowdie made it clear that there were financial constraints to the more-herbs-less-salt formula. Every time the company took the sodium down a notch, replacing it with fresh herbs, the production cost rose. Who was going to pay for this? Relative to the dirt-cheap price of salt, he said, "this is going to cost you more."

Finally, we tasted a vegetable beef soup in which the sodium had been lowered, without any adjustment in spicing. It didn't just taste flat. The soup had some bad tastes, tastes that hovered somewhere between bitter and metallic. These undesirables—what the industry calls "off-notes"— were likely still present in the regular soup, but the salt—in one of its functions—covers them up.

"The salt is masking these off-notes?" I asked Dowdie.

"Yeah, absolutely," he replied. Green beans can taste bitter without salt, he said, but in this case bitterness could be coming from the WOF—the warmed-over-flavor problem caused by oxidation of the reheated meat.

A year after my visit, Campbell would encounter another stumbling block in its efforts to unhook itself from salt, one that has been perhaps even more of a burden to the food industry than WOF: Wall Street. Campbell was having a lousy year. The revenue was flat, the forecast weak, the stock price was down 5 percent, and stock analysts were complaining mightily about the company's financial prospects. So on July 12, 2011, Campbell's incoming CEO, Denise Morrison, announced a plan to spur sales. She assured investors that she knew what was needed, first and foremost, to drive consumption. It was the same thing Dowdie had said about earning the consumer's trust: no salt, no flavor; no flavor, no buy.

She said that the company would be *adding* more salt to some of its soups. Where the sodium had been lowered from 700 to 800 milligrams per serving, down to 480, the CEO said, it would now be raised back up to 650. "Sodium reduction is important," Morrison told the analysts. "But we have to do other things, like taste."

The move involved only the thirty-one soups in its Select Harvest brand, but Wall Street appreciated that Campbell was now going in what it saw as the right direction. The company's stock price closed up 1.3 percent that day. As one Standard & Poor's analyst said, "We look for future results to benefit from an increased emphasis on bolstering sales with tasty soup products."

chapter fourteen

"I Feel So Sorry for the Public"

At a symposium for nutrition scientists in Los Angeles on February 15, 1985, a professor of pharmacology from Helsinki told the remarkable story of Finland's effort to address its salt habit. In the late 1970s, the Finns were consuming huge amounts of sodium, eating on average more than two teaspoons of salt a day. As a result, the country had developed significant issues with high blood pressure, which in turn brought an epidemic of heart attacks and strokes—indeed, men in the eastern part of Finland had the highest rate of cardiovascular disease in the world. Research showed that this plague was not a quirk of genetics or the result of a sedentary lifestyle—it was a matter, simply put, of processed foods. So when Finnish authorities moved to address the problem, they went right after the manufacturers. Every grocery item that was heavy in salt would now have to be marked prominently with the warning "High Salt Content." This, along with an ambitious public education campaign, would have a dramatic effect: By 2007, Finland's per capita consumption of salt had dropped by a third, and this shift was accompanied by an 80 percent decline in the number of deaths from strokes and heart disease.*

Heikki Karppanen's presentation was met with enthusiastic applause, but one man in the crowd seemed particularly moved by the professor's presentation that day. He had been sitting in the front row, and he rose up eagerly out of his seat to intercept Karppanen as he left the stage. Karppanen noticed him right away, struck by how much he stood out in the room full of academics. The professors dressed in a style charitably described as "frumpy classroom," while the man walking toward him was all "slick boardroom." He wore a suit that was expensively tailored, dark and crisp. His shoes were polished, his black hair neatly trimmed. He approached Karppanen and congratulated him on his work. He said that they shared an interest in salt, and he asked Karppanen to join him for dinner so they could delve more deeply into the subject.

Given how the man had dressed, Karppanen wasn't surprised when a stylish car arrived at his hotel to pick him up that evening for dinner. Nor was he surprised by their destination, an elegant restaurant on the Santa Monica Pier, with sweeping views of the Pacific Ocean. Their conversation, however, was not at all what Karppanen was expecting. His host did indeed have an interest in salt, but from quite a different vantage point: The man's name was Robert I-San Lin, and from 1974 to 1982 he had worked for Frito-Lay. This was the $4-billion-a-year manufacturer of blockbuster brands like Lay's, Doritos, Cheetos, and, of course, Fritos, the simple but lusciously fatty chips made with corn, corn oil, and salt.

Lin didn't just work for the company. He was its chief scientist, which meant that it was his job to figure out ways to keep consumers buying these snacks. This had put him at the center of some of the industry's most intriguing scientific inquiries, adventures really, ranging from chips all the way to soft drinks. Frito-Lay (which was, and is, owned by PepsiCo) had

---

* Since this was an effort to reduce the country's dependence on salt and not a scientific trial in which Finnish officials could randomize the participants and control all the variables, exactly how much of the reduced heart disease was due to the lessened salt consumption remains unclear.

engaged Lin's expertise across the whole spectrum of salt, sugar, and fat. In their laboratories near Dallas, Texas, he had honed bliss points for all three of these keystone ingredients.

When it came to his work with salt, however, Lin found himself increasingly at odds with the company over its strategy for dealing with the simmering health concerns that stemmed from America's overconsumption of salt. He was thrust into corporate dealings that he viewed as deeply troubling.

Karppanen had started off gently at dinner that evening by asking a few probing questions, testing Lin's willingness to discuss the world of salt at Frito-Lay. But it didn't take him long to see that Lin was more than willing to speak freely. In fact, he opened up like never before. Karppanen felt like a confessor of sorts, and Lin had a lot he wanted to say.

Lin was working for Frito-Lay when consumer advocates in the United States had launched their first attack on salty foods. Alarmed by the links to high blood pressure and heart disease, they asked federal regulators in 1978 to reclassify salt as a "risky" food additive, which could have subjected it to severe controls. No company took this threat more seriously than Frito-Lay, Lin explained. This was due in part to the salty nature of the company's snacks, but also to its strong (some would say Texan) corporate culture that tolerated no meddling—in the form of regulation—from the fools up in Washington, D.C. The company's top officials took the push against salt personally. Lin found himself caught between corporate and public interests, struggling to reconcile what was best for the company with what was best for its customers. He sketched for Karppanen the barest outlines of a battle in which the company used "experts" to take potshots at studies linking salt to high blood pressure, raised alarms about the health risks of too *little* salt in one's diet, and financed research into finding a cure for the harmful effects of sodium, which Lin viewed as a crass attempt to divert attention from salt. Salt meant the world to Frito-Lay—as much, if not more, than any other ingredient.

Back in his hotel that night, Karppanen got out his personal diary and found that he couldn't stop writing, jotting down many of the salient points of their conversation. "He was very much disturbed by the experience of what money can buy in the U.S.," Karppanen wrote. "He said everything is for sale if you have enough money."

The diary entries he made that night remained tucked away—until the spring of 2010, when Karppanen retrieved them for me. By chance, I had run across a letter that Lin had sent to Karppanen three weeks after their dinner, buried in some files to which I had gained access. I was particularly intrigued by a memo that was attached to the letter, written when Lin was at Frito-Lay, that detailed some of the company's concerted efforts in defending salt. I found Lin in southern California, in the university town of Irvine. There, in his lovely home off of a winding drive, Lin and I spent several days talking about salt and his years at Frito-Lay and going through the internal company memos, strategy papers, and handwritten notes he had kept.

The details that emerged from this record underscored the concern that Lin had for consumers. While at Frito-Lay, Lin and other company scientists spoke openly about the country's excessive consumption of sodium and the fact that, as Lin said to me on more than one occasion, "people get addicted to salt."

But the documents, along with others I would obtain, also pried open the door to another narrative, one that reflects the food industry's uncanny—and highly consequential—ability to turn adversity into advantage. Cornered on salt, Frito-Lay would find other ways to boost the sales of its snacks. And it would wield these tricks, through the 1990s and beyond, at the precise moment when America's dependence on processed food was peaking. High blood pressure was certainly one cause for concern, but more and more, as obesity overtook hypertension as a national health crisis, the danger in overeating the snacks that Frito-Lay so aggressively marketed lay not in their salt content but in their calories.

Thirty-two years had passed since Robert Lin first tangled with Frito-Lay on the health aspect of its chips, but as we sat at his dining room table, sifting through his records, the feelings of regret still played on his face. In his view, three decades had been lost, time that he and a lot of other smart scientists could have spent searching for ways to ease the industry's addiction to salt, sugar, and fat. "I was employed at a time I couldn't do much about it," he told me. "I feel so sorry for the public."

Like many of the people on the research and development side of the processed food industry, the Robert Lin who went to work for Frito-Lay began his career with a pure heart, as a scientist, intent on discovery and bettering mankind. He came to the United States in the late 1960s from Taiwan after winning a prestigious award to study abroad. His clan was a brainy, demanding one. His brother went to work as a nuclear physicist for the federal laboratories at Los Alamos. All four of his own children would obtain PhDs.

Lin was not only bracingly intelligent as a young man; he was driven and self-confident. He defied his mentors in Taiwan, who had expected him to attend Oxford, or, at the least, an Ivy League school. Instead, Lin chose the University of California at Los Angeles for its medical school. There, and later at the California Institute of Technology, Lin dabbled in the latest brain research and worked on recombinant DNA. Eventually, he decided the field where he could make the most lasting contributions was not nuclear medicine or biophysics but nutrition. As he saw it, the food people ate was nothing less than a matter of (long) life or (early) death. "My thinking was that the human body is supported by its nutritional intake," Lin told me. "If I could understand that better, I could make the body last longer."

But in short order, his passion for science gave way to the realities of the industry. He moved East to work for the life sciences unit of the GTE corporation and then joined a gold rush that was under way on the sweet side of processed foods. Washington had just banned the artificial sweetener called sodium cyclamate for having a toxicity risk, creating a void in the burgeoning market of products for diabetics. Lin joined a startup that was racing to turn an African berry into a sugar substitute. "When you chewed it, not much flavor came out," he told me. "But the molecule we *extracted* from the berry, you could put that on your tongue and it would make even vinegar taste sweet." A disagreement among the principals caused the berry venture to collapse, and Lin was forced to look for more stable employment. He flew to Dallas and interviewed with some executives who were enjoying a gold rush of their own, this one on the salty side of processed foods.

The corporate culture at Frito-Lay was a shock to Lin. As chief scientist, he oversaw a division of 150 researchers and developers, each of whom was expected to dress and act like a senior executive. "Navy blue and charcoal gray," Lin said. "Any man who dressed colorfully was not going to get promoted." Lin, at times, was even told to make desk checks at five minutes past eight in the morning to enforce punctuality. The lab work, however, was wildly fun, a series of puzzles to solve. Lin got dragged out of bed one night when thousands of bottles of Pepsi loaded onto a ship and headed to Japan suddenly started popping their tops like champagne corks. A few weeks later, Lin and his team finally nailed the culprit: The trouble had been caused by the new grape pigment Pepsi was using to replace a synthetic dye called No. 6, which, like cyclamates, had been banned. The grape pigment was natural but had quirks of chemistry that obviously needed more careful managing in the factory. Another time, Lin was called upon to rescue the company's potato chips. Frito-Lay had always been vigilant in keeping its chips incredibly fresh; the policy was, if they were not sold in a matter of days, they would be pulled from the shelves. This strict adherence to freshness was a company hallmark that set it apart from its rivals. But in cases where the chips stayed too long on the shelf, they didn't just go stale; the people eating them would feel nauseous. The problem, Lin found, was light. The chips in those days were packed in see-through plastic bags, and the light they let in caused a chemical change in the chips. Lin solved this by switching to an opaque bag that now, of course, has been widely adopted by the industry.

Lin's influence ranged widely across PepsiCo and the Frito-Lay division and even spilled into the marketing side, where officials labored to learn all the reasons why people would, or would not, buy the company's products. Health concerns were an obvious issue with salty or sugary snacks, but Lin put this matter in proper perspective. When a colleague developed a calculation for measuring the pros and cons of snacks, Lin honed it with all the proper mathematical framing. The reputation that snacks had for being bad for one's health (H) was an issue that worked against the company, along with their cost ($), and failures in quality (Q), like breakage. But other factors worked in the company's favor, making it more likely consumers would decide to purchase (P). Its chips and other snacks tasted great (T). They were convenient (C) and utilitarian (U), ready to eat out of the hand or with meals. Lin added some mathematical weighting (A, B), and threw it all into an equation he called the "Model for Ideal Snack," which explained—from a mathematical perspective—why Frito-Lay was making a killing in fatty and salty snacks. "Every time a consumer is making a decision to buy the snack, if Resistance is greater than Reward, there would simply be no Purchase," Lin wrote in a memo to other Frito-Lay officials. "It would be better to express in the following way: $P = A_1T + A_2C + A_3U - B_1\$ - B_2H - B_3Q$."

One of his more expensive investigations at Frito-Lay was the Monkey Project, aimed at refuting the critics who, in the late 1970s, were making a fuss about saturated fat. Frito-Lay maintained that shoppers could do worse than pick up a bag of its chips; bread and butter, for one example, might sound innocuous but in truth was loaded with salt and fat. So the company spent $1.5 million on an experiment that would prove Lay's chips weren't really that bad after all. Monkeys—130 of them—served as the guinea pigs. An animal research center was hired to run the experiment, with Lin overseeing the science. "We fed them a potato chip chow, three times as much as we felt people would eat in a day, and we did this for five years," Lin said. Monkeys breed fast, so there were actually two generations involved in this trial. The findings, although never disclosed publicly, were comforting to Frito-Lay: The chips maybe weren't great for one's health, but they wouldn't *kill* anyone, either. "We wanted to confirm whether saturated fat was really that bad," Lin said. "We were asking, 'How bad is the chip?' We raised the monkeys for two generations and fed them this controlled diet of potato chip chow mixed with a supplement of vitamins and minerals, and one group had increasing amounts of saturated fat. After five years, the only conclusion was that the group with higher saturated fat had higher cholesterol. But birth defects? There were none. Some might have thought we were wasting time, but I thought it was responsible science. It gave everyone peace of mind."

Defending its chips on cholesterol was one thing. Sodium was quite another. Starting in 1978, the salt that Frito-Lay was loading onto its chips would cause it—along with the entire industry—to undertake some deft maneuvering in Washington.

If there was one consumer group the food industry came to fear the most, it was the organization called the Center for Science in the Public Interest, simply because it was so ruthlessly effective. Founded in 1971, this group of activists would grow to have nine hundred thousand subscribers to its nutrition newsletter, giving it serious clout—and not only in Washington. Its formidable legal team, wielding laws aimed at curbing false advertising, could generate such angst in the food industry that companies would often race to cough up reforms even before a lawsuit was filed. Since 2005, the organization has forced Kellogg to limit its advertising to young kids, Sara Lee to make it clear that its "whole-grain bread" is only 30 percent whole grain, and PepsiCo to change the labeling of its Tropicana Peach Papaya Juice to reflect the facts that it has neither peaches nor papaya and is not a juice. "We're open to listening to legitimate concerns, and this seemed like a reasonable concern," a PepsiCo official said in settling the Tropicana case.

The group's executive director, Michael Jacobson, was trained as a microbiologist at MIT, and a few years after the group started up, Jacobson's interest in salt was ignited. He had just finished a project examining the preservatives, colorings, and chemical processing aids being used by food companies in making their products. As scary as some of these might have seemed, he spotted the far more tangible and pressing target of salt. He saw how the country's rates of high blood pressure were spiking, and how research was linking this scourge to sodium. Jacobson came to view salt—along with fat and sugar—as the biggest issues in processed foods. "I realized that conventional ingredients like salt were probably far more harmful" than the additives he had been studying, he told me. In 1978, he petitioned the FDA to reclassify salt from an ingredient, like pepper or vinegar, that posed no health concerns to a food additive that the agency could regulate by mandating limits or warning labels.

At Frito-Lay, Lin viewed the issues Jacobson raised as perfectly reasonable from a scientific perspective. He could quibble with the quality of the research, but he saw the basic premise as logical and agreed that excessive consumption of salt was a public health problem. Moreover, when federal regulators took Jacobson's petition seriously and opened discussions on the possibility of regulating salt, Lin viewed this as anything but a threat to Frito-Lay. He saw this as an opportunity for his company. Frito-Lay's most iconic product, the potato chip, had less salt than many other snack foods, especially pretzels, which clocked in with triple the sodium loads as potato chips. Lin thought the move in Washington to regulate salt could, in fact, give an edge to Frito-Lay. By moving swiftly to reduce its salt loads, he believed that they could capture a bigger share of the market. "Our products are already low in salt," Lin wrote in a 1978 memo to other company officials. "However, since the public is consuming too much sodium from other foods, it would be wise to lower the salt content to enhance sales."

Lin had only to look to Finland as an example of how the federal government could be a friend, not a foe. There, authorities were requiring manufacturers to label their saltiest foods with the "High Salt Content" warning, but they were also, importantly, incentivizing these same companies to produce lower-salt versions of their products. It did this by letting those companies with these healthier items promote them in a powerful way: They could label their boxes and bags with the comforting phrase "Low Salt." This is where Lin wanted Frito-Lay to go.

So Robert Lin hurled his staff at the problem of finding a way to reduce the company's dependence on salt. A handwritten document by his team entitled "Salt Strategy" shows how they pursued this goal from numerous angles, some involving considerable research and study. The initiatives they examined ranged from adjusting the fat content in potato chips in a way that could lower the need for salt to fiddling with the form of the salt crystals themselves in order to heighten their impact.

In this matter of altering the physical shape of salt, there were two competing schools of thought. One argued that larger crystals were the more efficient way to go, since they seemed to hit the tongue with greater force. The other argued for smaller crystals, which meant grinding the salt into a fine powder that created more surface area for the tongue's saliva to interact with the salt and speed the pleasure-inducing signals to the brain. Lin reached out to salt manufacturers, prodding them for details on their varying grinds of salt. Large crystals or small, however, there was one matter, he knew, that Frito-Lay would hold inviolable: People would have to crave Frito-Lay chips for their salty and fatty taste. If this could happen with less salt, fine. But if there was even the slightest drop in allure, any talk about reducing salt loads would be dead on arrival. Lin understood this. "Generally speaking," he told me, "the food that makes you feel good is the food you want to buy more. There is advertising, but the difference it makes is minor. Ninety percent of it is about making you *feel* good, and feeling good means tasting good."

Long before he could test any of these decreased-salt techniques on focus groups, Lin would try to deal with the inefficiencies he saw. He visited a factory floor where Lay's were being made, and as he stood at the salting station, he was struck—for the first time, really—by the utter lack of sophistication of the manufacturing process. The salt was just being dumped from huge bins onto the chips, which moved below on conveyer belts. The salt that didn't stick to the chips simply fell to the floor, accumulating in huge piles, until workers came along to sweep it into garbage bins. Appalled by this waste, Lin started to tinker with a new method that would apply the salt much more judiciously. It used electrostatics to attach the salt to the chips the way a balloon sticks to the wall after it's been rubbed on a shirt. In addition to greatly reducing waste, this technique could allow Frito-Lay to control the amount of salt that went onto the chips. But Lin soon saw the flaw in his plan: No one cared about the wasted salt, not even the bean counters at Frito-Lay. From a purely financial perspective, salt was so cheap—at ten cents a pound—that using less wasn't worth worrying about. Lin shelved his electrostatic idea.

The looming regulation of salt, on the other hand, consumed Lin's bosses. Increasingly, he was called upon not to unhook the company from salt but to defend the company's usage of salt and attack its critics. Some of the company's strategies were easy enough for Lin to fend off. When his colleagues suggested defending potato chips by touting their potassium content, Lin pointed out that the company's chips did not have nearly enough potassium to offset the harmful effects of the sodium. Lin also warned his colleagues against overreaching in their attacks on research linking sodium to high blood pressure. "I advised them, 'Don't ever say salt has nothing to do with hypertension,'" he told me. But very quickly, the company's campaign to push back on salt regulation went far beyond anything he could control.

In 1979, an FDA panel held a hearing in Washington on the proposal to regulate salt, and Frito-Lay turned out in force. As several company vice presidents looked on from the audience, the company's research director, Alan Wohlman, made an impassioned plea on behalf of salt, citing its deep and historical roots in food production and preservation. He was joined by two medical authorities—a New York City cardiologist and a cancer researcher from Buffalo—who spoke on behalf of the Potato Chip and Snack Foods Association. The cardiologist said that the science of hypertension and salt was not clear, while the cancer researcher went much further in challenging the panel. He warned that, should the proposed regulations succeed in lowering the consumption of salt, Americans would face grave danger: People could die. The risks associated with too little salt in the diet, he said, were particularly high among infants and children, diabetics, pregnant women, and women using estrogen-based contraceptives.

Frito-Lay reported on the hearing in an employee newsletter in which the president and CEO, Wayne Calloway, reiterated this warning: "After careful research, and consultations with noted medical authorities, it was clear that the Select Committee failed to consider the substantial risk to the general population if significant dietary restrictions on salt were imposed," he said.

Robert Lin, who had joined in the preparations for the hearing, soon found himself swept up by the company's all-out push to defeat the proposed regulations. With the FDA's decision still pending in early 1982, he joined other Frito-Lay officials in having the company finance research on whether calcium might negate the harmful effects of salt. In a memo detailing these plans, Lin said he doubted that this research would absolve salt, citing other medical experts who felt the same way. But, he wrote, "From a strategic point of view, an effective promotion of 'Calcium Antihypertension Theory' may release the pressure on sodium for the time being." At another point in the memo, he referred to the research as "powerful ammunition."

When I asked Lin about the memo, he characterized the calcium research as a diversionary tactic that typified the company's all-out scramble to defend its usage of salt. "There may be some people who believe calcium might work, but I didn't believe it," he said. "Pepsi is a good company, but they did some things not quite correctly, and one of these things was fighting salt. It was a macho spirit they had, which said, 'Keep your hands off my company.' "

In the end, time was on the food industry's side. The proposed regulation had surfaced during the last half of the Carter administration, which soon became preoccupied by matters like the energy crisis and the Iranian hostage situation. Amid all the bad news for President Carter, food industry lobbyists easily fended off the proposed curbs on television advertising to children. In 1982, federal bureaucrats were crouching in fear of the axe-wielding Reagan administration when the Food and Drug Administration finally responded to Jacobson's petition on salt. The advisory panel that initially took up the matter four years earlier had sided with him, concluding that salt should indeed no longer enjoy its blanket designation as a safe food additive. Normally, the panel's recommendation would have been adopted by the FDA, according to an official who later wrote an analysis of the agency's decision. Indeed, the officials who ran the FDA at the time agreed that reducing salt consumption was a worthy goal. But this was no easy time for them to be aggressive in dealing with corporate America. Imposing government regulations on the food manufacturers was not in the cards. So instead of regulating salt, the FDA announced that it would try to wean the country off of salt through gentler means—by educating consumers on the health hazards.

Sanford Miller, who at the time was the director of the FDA's Center for Food Safety and Applied Nutrition, told me that he and other agency officials were sincerely worried about the health effects of salt but believed that they did not have sufficient data to withstand the relentless attacks from industry lobbyists. "The salt people, especially, were constantly badgering us," Miller said. Another top agency official at the time, William Hubbard, told me that the agency also worried that the public wasn't ready to make the leap on salt. "We were trying to balance the public health need with what we understood to be the public acceptability," he said. "Common sense tells you if you take it down too low and people don't buy, you have not done something good."

A disillusioned Robert Lin left Frito-Lay that year to join another side of the food industry. He went to work for companies that made nutritional supplements. Like other former food company executives I met, he also overhauled his own diet to avoid the very foods he had once worked so hard to perfect. There were few, if any, processed foods in the cupboards he opened for me. For lunch, he served plain oatmeal, with no sugar added, and raw asparagus. It was pretty stark eating for someone like me, who has been known to detour a vacation to visit a potato chip factory open to tourists. Then again, Lin, at age seventy-five, begins each day with an hour-long march up the big hill behind his house at a mean pace. By avoiding processed foods, Lin has slashed the amount of salt he consumes, which gives him mixed feelings. "When I see salty food, I still love to taste it," he told me. "But I will stop at a certain point. Even though I like it, and can crave it, I'm educated. I know that my body is not designed for eating a lot of salt."

His failure to change Frito-Lay aside, Lin's years there were marked by a number of lasting contributions to the salty snack manufacturer. He believed in the power of intellect in problem-solving, and he established a forum where experts from outside the industry—a Shell oil president, a McKinsey & Co. research analyst, genetic engineering experts from universities in Washington and California—were invited to meet with Frito-Lay officials to discuss ways the company could be more creative in making and selling snacks. Lin sought out brilliance, wherever it might be. Among the invitees to a 1981 session was a marketing official from the tobacco company R. J. Reynolds whom Lin brought in to share what he'd learned about targeting consumers by studying every aspect of their wants and desires. This tobacco official, Greg Novak, was pioneering methods for sifting and sorting consumers by their age, gender, and race, the better to target them through specially tailored advertising, and Lin set the tone for this session by quoting an advertising executive who famously said, "Anyone who designs a product—or an advertising appeal—based on what the people *say* they want is an utter fool."

Five years later, with Lin long gone, this notion—that industry knew better what people wanted—would help Frito-Lay sidestep the concerns about salt, as it ushered in a new era of snacking.

The year was 1986, and Frito-Lay was on a rare cold streak. They'd launched a series of high-profile products, only to see them go down in flames. There was Topples, a corn cracker with cheese topping that, true to its name, toppled right into the dumpsters behind the grocery stores. There was Stuffers, a corn shell with a variety of savory fillings, which got stuffed into those same garbage bins, as did Rumbles, a bite-sized granola bar snack that lasted barely a month on the shelves. Worried that they were losing their touch—along with $52 million in production costs—the marketing team brought in a ringer, Dwight Riskey, a budding expert on the cravings that snacks like these were supposed to generate.

Riskey joined Frito-Lay in 1982, just as Robert Lin was leaving. He had been a fellow at the Monell Chemical Senses Center and part of the team that had found that people could beat the salt habit simply by refraining from salty foods long enough for their taste buds to return to a normal level of sensitivity. In his own projects at Monell, Riskey had conducted experiments that found that a person's fondness for certain foods was greatly influenced by whatever else they are eating or drinking at the time. Your taste for a candy bar, for instance, changes when you are also drinking a Coke. This meant that the bliss point for sweet taste was not fixed; it could go up or down, depending on what else you were consuming. This added a somewhat more complicated, real-world factor to the efforts by food technicians to create the maximum appeal for their products. "I would find when you vary things like salt and sugar in a food, there tends to be one formulation that is best," Riskey told me. "But the truth of the matter is, I could move that peak, that bliss point. I could move it up or down, depending on what other foods or beverages I put into the frame of reference."

Bliss points also changed as people aged. This seemed to help explain why Frito-Lay was having so much trouble launching new snacks. America was aging and growing less fond of salty snacks. The largest single block of customers, the baby boomers who were born between 1946 and 1964, had begun hitting middle age. According to the research, this meant that their liking for salty snacks—both in the concentration of salt and how much they ate—was tapering off every year they grew older. Demographically, this would have a profound effect on Frito-Lay's marketing strategy. Along with the rest of the snack food industry, the company anticipated lower sales due to the aging population, and marketing plans were adjusted accordingly to lure new consumers. Advertising that had been aimed at baby boomers when they had been younger was scaled back. The thirty-five-year-old boomer was no longer targeted with ads like he was when he was twenty.

There was only one problem with this strategy, and it was a great problem for the industry to have. Snack sales *didn't* decline as everyone had projected. Through the early 1980s, they went *up*. It was Dwight Riskey who figured out what was going on.

Riskey kept a second office at his home, a few miles from the Frito-Lay offices in Plano, where his desk and floor were papered with the charts, graphs, and printouts of his various marketing projects. Sizing up consumers and plugging them into specific categories was a critical part of marketing, and he put long hours into his work. In looking at the rising snack sales, he was determined to find out who—demographically—was doing all this eating. One Sunday evening in or around 1989, he was at home in his office when the answer suddenly hit him: He and his marketing colleagues had been misreading the data. They had been measuring the snacking habits of different age groups but not the habits of these groups of people *as they aged*. This was an important distinction. The latter method is known in research as a cohort study, because it follows one group of people over time, and only this method could reveal how the habits of a group like the baby boomers were changing over time.

When Riskey called up a new set of the company's sales data and parsed it with the cohort technique, a new, far more encouraging picture emerged. The baby boomers, in fact, were not eating fewer salty snacks as they aged. Quite the contrary. "In fact, as those people aged, their consumption of all those segments—the cookies, the crackers, the candy, the chips—was going up!" Riskey said. "They were not only eating what they ate when they were younger, they were eating *more* of it. And that was what was causing the big success for all the snack food companies all those years."

To be sure, the baby boomers couldn't hold their own against twenty-year-olds, who wolfed down more salty snacks than the boomers could even dream of consuming. But the good news for Frito-Lay was that baby boomers were eating more at age thirty than they had at twenty—and they weren't alone. Everyone in the country, on average, was eating more salty snacks than they used to. When Riskey ran the numbers, he found that the rate of consumption was edging up about one-third of a pound every year, with the average intake of snacks such as chips and cheese crackers pushing past twelve pounds a year.

Riskey had a theory about what had caused this surge in snack eating by the boomers. Eating real meals had become a thing of the past. Baby boomers, especially, seemed to have abandoned the traditional concept of breakfast, lunch, and dinner—or, at least, they were not conducting these rituals as regularly as they once had. They began skipping breakfast when they had early morning meetings. They skipped lunch when their day was lost to those same meetings, and they needed to catch up on work. They skipped dinner when their kids stayed out late for baseball practice or grew up and moved out of the house. The boomers weren't going hungry through all this. When they skipped these meals, they replaced them with convenient snacks—pulled from cupboards, convenience stores, or the office vending machine. "We looked at this behavior, and said, 'Oh my gosh, people were skipping meals right and left,'" Riskey told me. "It was amazing." This led to the next realization, that the baby boomers "was not a category that is mature, with no growth. This is a category that has huge growth potential. So we started working hard to realize that growth."

To Riskey and the other marketing executives at Frito-Lay, this put the Topples and Stuffers in a new light. They didn't fail because aging Americans were growing less fond of snacks likes these. Nor did they fail because people were growing more leery about salt. They failed because Frito-Lay had gotten a bit lax in how hard it had marketed them, which was easy enough to fix.

Thus began the final phase of Frito-Lay's history, when all hands were called to duty and all the stops were pulled out in creating and marketing salty snacks for Americans of all ages. And it didn't hurt that Frito-Lay's owner, PepsiCo, was already battle-tested from its war with Coke.

PepsiCo was a marketing machine. A year after acquiring Frito-Lay in 1965, it had moved its headquarters from Park Avenue in midtown Manhattan to a sprawling campus in Purchase, New York, but no one at PepsiCo got sleepy in the suburbs. They prided themselves on being the aggressor in soft drinks, finding ways to embarrass and outmaneuver the Goliath, Coca-Cola, wherever they could. Dwight Riskey's revelation about baby boomers setting records for consumption came just as Pepsi—which also now owned Kentucky Fried Chicken, Pizza Hut, and Taco Bell—topped $1 billion for the first time in 1990. That same year, PepsiCo put a symbol of its mission—and our growing appetite—on the front of its glossy annual report. The entire cover was taken up by the portrait of a humongous sumo wrestler, in the ready position with his game face on.

A year later, in 1991, PepsiCo installed one of its most prized corporate warriors, Roger Enrico, into the top spot at Frito-Lay. The son of an iron-ore smelting plant foreman, Enrico would go on to run all of PepsiCo from 1996 to 2001 and come to rival Coke's fabled chairman, Robert Woodruff, as a mastermind of marketing. But when he arrived at Frito-Lay, he was already a star of the soft drink division. It was Enrico who convinced Michael Jackson in 1984 to turn his hit song "Thriller" into a commercial for Pepsi's "New Generation" campaign, and it was Enrico who sunk New Coke a year later with the brilliant counteroffensive that touted Coke's reformulation as a victory for Pepsi.*

As the CEO of Frito-Lay, Enrico would deploy the marketing strategy known as "up and down the street," using Pepsi's delivery crews to maximize sales in convenience stores where America's kids were forming their snack food habits. The crews began delivering Frito-Lay's brands along with the company's soda, and Enrico galvanized his snack food managers with exhortations to dominate the convenience stores. Dwight Riskey re-

---

* The Jackson commercial had unbelievable appeal; posted on YouTube two decades later as an historical artifact, it garnered 45 million views.

called one speech that Enrico delivered to company executives in Orlando in which he groused that the beer company, Anheuser-Busch, was stealing some of Frito-Lay's turf in potato chips with its Eagle Snacks brand.

"They had very high quality, and they were getting very good shelf space," Riskey said. At Enrico's urging, Frito-Lay scrambled to improve the crunch and the taste of its chips and lower its prices enough to spur increased sales. "I think we gained three share points a year for eight years in a row after that," Riskey said. "It was an amazing thing to watch the company respond to the challenge that Enrico laid out. The guy was a business genius."

The food technicians at Frito-Lay also stopped worrying about inventing new products like Topples, and instead embraced the industry's most basic—and reliable—method for getting consumers to buy more food: the line extension. They took their existing snacks and spun them into endless varieties. The classic Lay's were joined by Salt & Vinegar, Salt & Pepper, and Cheddar & Sour Cream. They put out Frito's in Barbecue and Chili Cheese varieties, and Cheetos—which had nearly twice as much salt as potato chips—were transformed into twenty-one varieties.

These were no run-of-the-mill extensions. The science corps at Frito-Lay prided itself on quality invention, putting their all into the taste, crunch, mouthfeel, aroma, and overall appeal of each of these items. The ingredients they used weren't extraordinary: fat and salt, along with sugar in some of the brands like Cheetos, as well starch from potatoes or corn and sundry spices. The magic comes in the weaving, and to get a better feel for this, I called on Steven Witherly, the food scientist who had worked on cheese sauces for Nestlé. Witherly has written a deeply fascinating guide for food industry insiders entitled "Why Humans Like Junk Food," and I brought him two shopping bags filled with a variety of chips to taste. He zeroed right in on the Cheetos.

"This . . . is one of the most marvelously constructed foods on the planet, in terms of pure pleasure," he said, ticking off a dozen attributes of the Cheetos that make the brain say *more*. A key one is the puff's uncanny ability to melt in the mouth like chocolate. "It's called vanishing caloric density," Witherly said. "If something melts down quickly, your brain thinks that there's no calories in it, and like popcorn, you can just keep eating it forever." The only thing more spectacular than Cheetos, he said, was another Frito-Lay creation—the Doritos 3D, a puffy, spherical version of the flat chip: "The added dimension increases the surprise factor when you take a bite," he said. And surprise is a very good thing for increasing consumption.

Even without Robert Lin, Frito-Lay had a formidable research complex near Dallas where nearly five hundred chemists, psychologists, and technicians conducted research that cost up to $30 million a year. Their tools included a $40,000 device that simulated a chewing mouth to test and perfect the chips, discovering things like the perfect break point: People like a chip that snaps with about four pounds of pressure per square inch, no more or less. While they worked to hone the product formulas, the company's sales force of ten thousand revolutionized the food industry's supply system by carrying handheld computers that tracked shortfalls and ensured that the bags on the store shelves were always fresh.

To be sure, with stories beginning to appear in newspapers about America's growing waistline, Frito-Lay did not neglect the concern that consumers developed for their nutritional health. As early as 1988, the company began test marketing low-fat chips aimed at nutrition-conscious consumers. "If we can do for our category what light beer did for beer, it would be a tremendous growth opportunity," a company vice president said at the time. The low-fat chips performed poorly, but another creation, Sun Chips—made with whole grains and less saturated fat and salt—proved to be a huge success among people wanting to eat better.

Overall, the company's usage of salt appeared to be following the industry trend: Levels dipped through much of the 1980s and 1990s, but only slightly. When Robert Lin analyzed Frito-Lay's snacks in 1981, he found that they averaged 180 milligrams of sodium per ounce, with potato chips ranging up to 240 milligrams. Three decades later, the basic Lay's potato chip clocked in at 170 milligrams, but it had been joined by flavored chips and other snacks whose sodium reached much higher: Salt & Vinegar chips, 230; Xxtra Flamin' Hot Cheetos, 300; 2nd Degree Burn Fiery Buffalo Doritos, 380. At that level, every handful of the Doritos had one-quarter of the daily maximum limit for the 143 million Americans who faced the highest risks from excessive sodium.

In response to my questions about its salt reduction, Frito-Lay said that it was taking its responsibility seriously. A company spokeswoman said that the initiatives showing the greatest promise included something Robert Lin had been looking at thirty years before: using a finer grade of salt to minimize the amount of salt needed while maximizing the rush. In March 2010, PepsiCo announced that it was launching a program to slash the salt in its products by an average of 25 percent, which was coupled with plans to promote less sugary drinks. This was the same move that had sparked cheers at Coca-Cola, according to Jeffrey Dunn, the former Coke president. He described for me how his current friends at Coke viewed their counterparts at PepsiCo as having a momentary lapse of sanity, which Coca-Cola planned to take advantage of by doubling down on their own efforts to market Coke.

When it came to snacks, however, Frito-Lay's executives took pains to assure Wall Street that they had not lost their minds. In private meetings, out of earshot of nagging consumer advocates, the company's leaders described detail after detail of the latest marketing operations they were launching to make their snacks an even bigger part of every American's life. Frito-Lay's efforts to tout these campaigns reached a crescendo in March 2010, when PepsiCo hosted a two-day meeting with analysts from Goldman Sachs, Deutsche Bank, and other investor powerhouses. The company brought the Wall Street executives to the Legends Room of Yankee Stadium, where they were greeted by one of Pepsi's newest frontmen: Derek Jeter. "We Yankees love to win, and PepsiCo is a winning company," the shortstop said, and the Pepsi and Frito-Lay executives took over from there.

Doritos, an executive vice president for global sales and marketing told the attendees, had already been turned into the biggest selling corn chip in the world "through a relentless focus on teens." But the company wasn't resting on their laurels. Every product and every segment of the population was being pursued as only Frito-Lay knew how.

Another fat target was the millennials, or Generation Y, born in the 1980s and 1990s and numbering 65 million Americans. The challenge with them lay in their widespread underemployment, Frito-Lay said, which increased the competition for their limited funds. "A dollar can also buy a double cheeseburger or a favorite song from iTunes," the chief marketing officer, Ann Mukherjee, noted. "So we need to think about it differently on Doritos, and we call it the 'And Effect,' which is how do we deliver more than just an intense snack?" Thus, the strategy for millennials became "snackable entertainment." The company's chips would be promoted through sporting events like the Super Bowl and games like the Xbox. Already, these efforts had brought double-digit gains in sales.

In another maneuver aimed at the millennial, Frito-Lay had its technicians come up with ways better to compete with the fast food chains, and their first efforts looked like pure magic. They had created a series of compounds they called Flavor Plus, which mimicked not only the taste of fast food but the smell as well. Just that year, Frito-Lay had released a line of tortilla chips called Late Night (230 milligrams of sodium and 150 calories per ounce) in as many of the fast food flavors and aromas the company's food scientists could come up with: cheeseburgers, tacos, jalapeño poppers. All together, the impulsive, late-hour snacking inspired by these chips pushed sales to $50 million in year one.

The boomers weren't being neglected, the Frito-Lay executives hastened to say. At 180 million people in the United States and 1.4 billion worldwide, they remained the fattest target of all. And with them in mind, Frito-Lay had acquired Stacy's Pita Chip Company in 2006, a $60-million-a-year business that had been started by a Massachusetts couple who made food cart sandwiches and started serving pita chips to their customers waiting in line. In Frito-Lay's hands, the pita chips (310 milligrams sodium and 130 calories per ounce, in twelve varieties) were pure gold, Mukherjee explained. They were irresistible to boomers.

"As I mentioned before, they snack a lot," she said. "But what they're looking for is very different. They're looking for new experiences, real food experiences . . . things that they've never tried before. That's what these boomers are looking to snack on."

Even salt and the persistent concern about its health effects were playing perfectly into the company's marketing plans, the Frito-Lay executives said. They told the Wall Street investors of the company's ongoing pursuit of a "designer sodium," which they hoped, in the near future, would take their sodium loads down by 40 percent. No need to worry about lost sales there, the CEO of Frito-Lay, Al Carey, assured the room. The boomers would see less salt as a bright green light giving them the go signal to snack like never before. In explaining the psychology of this phenomenon, Carey used the old industry term *permission* again.

"The big thing that will happen here is removing the barriers for boomers and giving them permission to snack," Carey said in describing the designer salt. "It has great taste. There is no difference. You cannot taste the difference between Lay's today and this product . . . . I mean, a mom could look at this product and feel good about feeding it to her children or eating it herself. And I think this is a difference from the way people viewed the snack food category over the last several years."

The prospects for lower-salt snacks were so amazing, Carey said, that the company had set its sights on using the designer salt to conquer the toughest market of all for snacks: schools. He cited, for example, the school food initiative championed by former president Bill Clinton and the American Heart Association, which had sought to improve the nutrition of school food by limiting their loads of salt, sugar, and fat. "Imagine this," Carey said. "A potato chip that tastes great *and* qualifies for the Clinton AHA alliance for schools . . . . We think we have ways to do all this on a potato chip and imagine getting that product into schools where children can have this product and grow up with it and feel good about eating it and their parents would, too."

. . .

This phrase, "feel good about eating it," sounded familiar to me, so I went and started digging through the file cabinets in which I stored the research materials I had gathered for this book. I finally found it in a confidential memo, from 1957, that I had obtained.

The author was a psychologist named Ernest Dichter, who counted Sigmund Freud among his friends before emigrating from Austria to the United States in 1938. Dichter started a consulting business in the village of Croton-on-Hudson, New York, through which he coached American companies on the art of motivational research. Dichter became famous in industry circles for encouraging food companies to market their products based on the "sex of food"—as in, Rice Krispies for women and Wheaties for men. For Frito-Lay, however, he had something else in mind, aimed at making its salty snacks more acceptable to Americans. He gave his white paper the title "Creative Memo on Lay's Products."

The company's chips, he wrote, were not selling as well as they could for one simple reason: "While people like and enjoy potato chips, they feel guilty about liking them. There is so much fear about the consequences of eating them. Unconsciously, people expect to be punished for 'letting themselves go' and enjoying them." He then quoted a consumer who explained, "I love them but I don't like to have them around, as they're so fattening. You can't stop eating them once you start."

In talking to consumers, Dichter counted up seven "fears and resistances" to the company's chips, which he ticked off in list fashion: "You can't stop eating them; they're fattening; they're not good for you; they're greasy and messy to eat; they're too expensive; it's hard to store the leftovers; and they're bad for children."

On the last point, he quoted a consumer from Schenectady, New York, who sounded a lot like mothers today when she told his researchers, "Children eat too much of that stuff. They shouldn't be eating it at all. I'd like to see them eat carrot sticks, peaches and apples."

This was a problem, Dichter wrote, and he spent the rest of his 24-page memo laying out the solution. There were numerous tactics Frito-Lay could deploy to counteract all this fear and resistance, he wrote. In time, his prescriptions would become widely used not just by Frito-Lay, but the entire industry.

Starting with the bad-for-you issue, Dichter suggested that Frito-Lay avoid using the word *fried* in referring to its chips and adopt instead the term *toasted*. In the most recent incarnation of this strategy, Frito-Lay in 2010 won a coveted award from the advertising industry for a campaign called "Happiness is Simple," which, according to the company's description of the ads, sought to dispel "perceptions it was the poster child for junk food." The ads didn't show potato chips soaking in oil; they depicted a sky full of flying potatoes magically popping into chips, midair.

To counteract the "fear of letting oneself go," Dichter suggested repacking the chips into smaller bags. "The more anxious consumers, the ones who have the deepest fears about their capacity to control their appetite, will tend to sense the function of the new pack and select it," he said. The latest incarnation of this strategy became part of a Frito-Lay campaign called "Only in a Woman's World," for which it won another advertising award in 2010. Frito-Lay divulged its strategy to the awards panel.

"When we found that women were increasingly avoiding the chip aisle—which our company dominates—we faced a serious challenge," the company said. "While women snack more than men, they weren't snacking as much anymore with Frito-Lay." So the company refocused its advertising to promote healthier-sounding versions of its chips, including Baked Lay's and the smaller packs of the chips that contained only 100 calories each. For dieters, these 100-calorie packs—widely used by food manufacturers—have a major drawback. Recent research has shown they do not work; people who tend to eat compulsively simply go from one little bag to the next.

Finally, and perhaps most significantly, Dichter advised Frito-Lay to move its chips out of the realm of between-meals snacking altogether and turn them instead into an ever-present item in the American diet. "The increased use of potato chips and other Lay's products as part of the regular fare served by restaurants and sandwich bars should be encouraged in a concentrated way," Dichter said, citing a string of examples: "potato chips with soup, with fruit or vegetable juice appetizers; potato chips served as a vegetable on the main dish; potato chips with salad; potato chips with egg dishes for breakfast; potato chips with sandwich orders."

When Dichter wrote his memo in 1957, remember, deli sandwiches were served with a pickle, not potato chips. Chips were eaten alone, as a snack and, as Dichter pointed out, with a growing sense of guilt. Today, Frito-Lay is not only marketing the chips to restaurants. Taking a cue from the dairy and beef industry, Frito-Lay is promoting its snacks for creative uses at home, *as ingredients* in other foods. Its website has a battery of recipes, neatly divided by the snack—Cheetos, Lay's, Stacy's, Doritos; by the time of day—breakfast, dinner, dessert; and by the dish—casserole, poultry dishes, salads. It also has an online cookbook entitled "Tastes from Home with Frito-Lay."

The recipes range from Corn Chowder made with potato chips to Frito Chili Pie to Frito's Ranch Chicken Delight with four cups of corn chips and half a pound of cheese, and, for dessert, Peanut Butter Parfait with Stacy's Cinnamon Sugar Pita Chips for dipping.

Ernest Dichter died in 1991, so I couldn't ask him if he had known back in 1957 just how prescient he was, having convinced the snack industry to weave chips into the fabric of American cuisine. One person, however, working thirty-five miles south in Manhattan, would rival Dichter's genius. His name was Len Holton, and he coined one of the most famous advertising slogans of all time.

Holton had passed away as well, but one of his colleagues, Alvin Hampel, told me the story. It was 1963, and the crew at the ad agency Young & Rubicam were racking their brains to come up with a new slogan for Frito-Lay. Holton was the senior copywriter, already elderly at the time, a stoop-shouldered gentleman who shuffled quietly around the office. While his young colleagues went through their antics, Holton simply took a seat and jotted down a phrase. When he passed it around, his colleagues were dumbstruck by its obviousness. "It was just waiting there to be plucked," Hampel said.

The slogan that Holton came up with, of course, was, "Betcha Can't Eat Just One."

Those five words captured the essence of the potato chip far better than anyone at Frito-Lay could have imagined. In 1986, as obesity rates in America started their climb, a massive multiyear study began that tracked the eating habits of Americans. The study was hardly representative of all Americans. The subjects all worked in the health field, with a professionalism that lent itself to accurate self-reporting. But if anything, these men and women were also likely to be more conscious about the nutritional aspect of the foods they ate, so the findings might well understate the overall American trend. The study followed 120,877 women and men. The researchers excluded people who were already overweight and monitored everything that they ate as well as their physical activity and smoking. In the ongoing study, the participants have been surveyed every four years.

In 2011, the *New England Journal of Medicine* published the latest results. Every four years since 1986, the participants had exercised less, watched TV more, and gained an average of 3.35 pounds. The researchers wanted to know what foods were causing the largest share of the weight gain, so they parsed the data by the caloric content of the foods being eaten. The top contributors to the weight gain included red meat and processed meats, sugar-sweetened beverages, and potatoes, including mashed and French fries. But far and away, the largest weight-inducing food, outstripping all others, was the potato chip.

The chip, at about 160 calories an ounce, led to a 1.69-pound gain in weight in each of the four-year study periods. By comparison, sweets and desserts accounted for less than half a pound.

When the data was published, observers pointed out just how irresistible the chip was, including the way they were packaged. The portion size stated on the chip bag—usually one ounce, or 28 grams—was completely irrelevant to how many chips a person might eat. "People generally don't take one or two chips," said obesity expert Dr. F. Xavier Pi-Sunyer of the St. Luke's–Roosevelt Hospital Center in New York. "They have a whole bag."

But that was only half the story. The chip's ingredients were likely just as effective, if not more so, in leading people to overeat. This starts with the coating of salt, which the tongue hits first, but there is much more inside the chip. They are loaded with fat, which gives them most of their calories. It also delivers the sensation called mouthfeel the moment they are chewed. As food scientists know, fat in the mouth is not like oil on the hand; it is a marvelous sensation, which the brain rewards with instant feelings of pleasure.

There is still more: Potato chips are also loaded with sugar. Not the kind of sugar you will find on the label, though some chip makers do add sugar to their potato chips to meet the cravings of kids. No. The sugar in regular chips is the kind of sugar that the body gets from the starch in the potatoes. Starch is considered a carbohydrate, but more precisely, it is made of glucose, the same kind of glucose you have in your blood. Potatoes don't taste sweet, but the glucose starts working on you like sugar the moment you bite into it, said Eric Rimm, an associate professor of epidemiology and nutrition at the Harvard School of Public Health and one of the study's authors. "The starch is readily absorbed," he told me. "More quickly even than a similar amount of sugar. The starch, in turn, causes the glucose levels in the blood to spike, and this is a concern, in relation to obesity."

These surges in blood glucose are highly problematic for anyone watching their weight. Recent research suggests glucose spikes will cause people to crave more food, as long as four hours after they've eaten whatever caused the blood glucose to spike. Eat chips one hour, crave more the next.

In this regard, potato chips are not the poster child for junk food, as Frito-Lay executives once warned. They are the epitome of processed foods generally, which use salt, sugar, and fat, sometimes interchangeably, to maximize their appeal to consumers. Frito-Lay could take all the salt out of its chips it wanted to create whatever aura of health it wanted. As long as the chips remain alluring—through their fat, their crunch, their salty flavor from salt substitutes—and the marketing campaigns give you psychological permission to eat as many as you like, they will continue to deliver calories. And that, after all, is the ultimate cause of obesity.

"We're Hooked on Inexpensive Food"

The sun was just starting to peek through the clouds when I landed in Switzerland on a Monday morning in May 2011. I was bound for the northern edge of Lake Geneva, where the food giant Nestlé had its research labs and headquarters. The hour was early, the week promising. For months, I had been hearing about the extraordinary and innovative work Nestlé was doing in nutritional science, so I came here to see what the future might hold for salt, sugar, and fat.

Nestlé was certainly in the best position to lead the industry toward making some changes. In the past couple of years, it had eclipsed Kraft to become the largest food manufacturer in the United States—indeed, in the world. Founded in 1866 as an infant-formula maker, Nestlé now competed in almost every part of the grocery store, from drinks (Juicy Juice and Nesquik) to frozen (DiGiorno and Stouffer's) to the checkout lanes (Butterfinger, Baby Ruth, the iconic Crunch). Twenty-nine of its product lines accounted for more than $1 billion in revenue a year each—the "Billionaire Brands Treasury," as Nestlé called them. Its annual sales had pushed past $100 billion each year, with profits in excess of $10 billion, giving Nestlé an accumulation of wealth so profound that one of its former scientists, Steven Witherly, cautioned me against thinking of it as a food manufacturer. "Nestlé," he said, "is a Swiss bank that prints food."

More important, Nestlé was also running the industry's most ambitious and opulent research operation, making it perhaps the company most capable of leading the way on change. Tucked into the hills above the town of Lausanne—with satellite centers in Beijing, Tokyo, Santiago, and St. Louis—the Nestlé research arm had a staff of 700, including 350 scientists. Each year, they conducted more than 70 clinical trials, published 200 peer-reviewed papers, filed for 80 patents, and undertook 300 collaborations with universities, suppliers, and private research institutions. Nestlé was attracting top talent from every corner of science, including the field of brain imaging, which allowed the company to perform nifty experiments like wiring the scalps of its human test subjects to EEG machines in order to see how, say, Dreyer's ice cream (another Billionaire Brand) excites the brain's neurology.

Touring the sprawling, shiny complex at Lausanne was a bit like stepping into the fictional Willy Wonka chocolate factory. (Nestlé, naturally, bought the real-life Wonka factory and brand in 1988, Gobstoppers and all.) Technological wonders abounded, but one of the highlights of the visit was room GR26, known as the "emulsions lab." There, with an electron microscope towering over them, Emmanuel Heinrich and Laurent Sagalowicz showed me how they were tracking fat as it made its way from the mouth to the small intestines. Nestlé, I learned, has developed the means to improve the distribution of fat droplets in ice cream in order to fool people into thinking it is fattier than it really is. Through another sensory trick, it is also trying to keep people from noticing when saturated fat is replaced with healthier oils. To this end, Heinrich was putting the finishing touches on a remarkable invention called "encapsulated oil." In this sleight of hand, a healthier oil—like sunflower or canola—is encased by sugar or protein molecules and then dried into a powder; when used in cookies, crackers, and cakes, this encapsulated oil can mimic saturated fat's ability to generate the alluring sensation known as mouthfeel, but with less risk of heart disease. The upshot: same pleasure for the brain, less saturated fat for the body.

Nestlé also sells food for pets—Purina being yet another one of its Billionaire Brands—and its scientists have done compelling work on that front, too. Teaming up with researchers at Cargill, they corralled a group of compounds called isoflavones—derived from soy germ meal—into a new product called Fit & Trim. The aim is to make dogs more frisky or at least to speed up their metabolism enough to fight an emerging health crisis among canines. "Obesity is not just for humans," as Nestlé said in a report. "Up to 40 percent of dogs in developed countries are overweight or obese."

The research center was all very impressive and state-of-the-art, down to the coffee bar with sleek machines serving Nespresso (the biggest Billionaire Brand of all), but ultimately it was disappointing. By the end of my visit, I came to realize that if Nestlé was going to save the world from obesity or any of the other ill effects of processed foods, it wasn't going to be in our lifetimes. The food that people bought in the grocery store was so perfectly engineered to compel overconsumption that Nestlé's scientists, for all their spectacular technology and deep knowledge of food science, were finding it impossible to come up with viable solutions.

Chief among the disappointments I saw at Nestlé was the quest to turn fiber into a cure for overeating. In its "digestion lab," Nestlé has a refrigerator-sized masticator machine that simulates chewing and digesting—tubes running every which way and computer programming to replicate the gastrointestinal tracts of children, adults, even dogs. One of the lab's scientists, Alfrun Erkner, walked me through their efforts to create the illusion of satiety, the sensation of feeling full. Nestlé has been laboring to create a yogurt that makes you feel full, with minimal calories. But to generate this feeling, the scientists have to stuff this yogurt with so much fiber that even the masticator on its highest setting had trouble getting it down. "People want a magic bullet," Erkner told me. "And it would be nice if we had a pill that would let people eat as much as they want, without putting on weight. But that's not what we can do."

Nestlé had also stumbled in pursuing an even more coveted industry holy grail—a food that would cause you to *lose* weight, not just avoid getting fat. It was a drink called Enviga, and it was produced in collaboration with another formidable player in processed foods, Coca-Cola. Released in 2007, Enviga combined green tea, caffeine, and two artificial sweeteners and was billed, on its label, as a "calorie burner." The more Enviga you drank, the more weight you would lose. In fact, the drink was a sitting duck for the activist lawyers at the Center for Science in the Public Interest. They took one look at the underlying science and hauled Nestlé and Coca-Cola to court for deceptive business practices. Using Nestlé's own data, the consumer group estimated that you would need to drink nearly 180 cans in order to lose one pound. And that was the best-case scenario. Some of the people in the study actually burned calories *more slowly* after drinking Enviga, which would appear to cause them to *gain* weight, not lose it.

An outcry arose from nutrition experts, sales collapsed, and in 2009 Nestlé and Coke settled a separate advertising case brought by two dozen states by agreeing to halt any weight-loss claims. Two years later, Nestlé officials were still sheepish about that venture, although they maintained that, technically speaking, in the best circumstances, the drink *did* speed up the human metabolism, if only a little. "We were a bit premature on Enviga," the company's chief technology officer, Werner Bauer, told me. "We should have first discussed, more publicly, the concept of energy burning. We put it on the market almost as a surprise. People didn't believe it."

As challenging as the science of nutrition might be, the future of salt, sugar, and fat in Nestlé's hands started looking disconcerting when I moved further down the shore of Lake Geneva, to the town of Vevey, where Nestlé has its corporate headquarters. On clear days, the lobby frames the spectacular lake with the majestic Alps in the background, and a grand staircase rises through the building in a double-helix shape, like a strand of DNA. Here, Nestlé was not waiting for its researchers to cue up another miracle drink or fibrous wonder. It was hard at work contradicting itself on the most critical issue of all: obesity.

Here, Nestlé was marketing food products that fatten us up—and then selling other food products that treat those of us who go too far.

On one side of the spectrum, Nestlé was churning out epic quantities of a food that was arguably one of the unhealthiest items in the grocery store—and a major contributor to the obesity epidemic. It's a frozen, microwavable snack called the Hot Pocket, which Nestlé acquired in 2002 for $2.6 billion and now counts as a prestigious member of its Billionaire Brands Treasury. In its promotional literature, Nestlé describes the Hot Pocket as a "fully enrobed sandwich that allows you to eat on the go with no mess!" But it's food on the go that comes with a price. The Pepperoni & Three Cheese Calzone version of the Hot Pocket that I picked up at my local grocery store, for instance, contained well over one hundred ingredients, including salt, sugar, and fat in several configurations along with six permutations of cheese, from "imitation mozzarella" to "imitation cheddar." A single, eight-ounce calzone delivered 10 grams of saturated fat and 1,500 milligrams of sodium—close to my daily limit for each. It also had nearly six teaspoons of sugar, 600 calories, and, for the retailer's convenience, enough preservatives for a shelf life of 420 days.* Nestlé, in response to my questions, said it had acquired Hot Pockets to meet the needs of millennials, especially young males, "as they led the way towards more casual, less formal meals"; that it was improving the product's nutritional profile and planned to discontinue the calzone; and that it now offered a dozen versions of its alternative brand, Lean Pockets, with whole grain crusts and lighter loads of salt, sugar, and fat.

But on the other end of the spectrum, Nestlé was busy covering its bases in a way not even I could have imagined. In 2007, the company acquired the medical nutrition business developed by the pharmaceutical

---

* The nutrition facts on the label divide these numbers in half, defining a serving as one half of the calzone.

firm Novartis, giving Nestlé the means to pursue a solution to one of the grimmest aspects of overeating. Every year, two hundred thousand obese people in the United States—including kids as young as nine—have their stomachs surgically shrunk to help them cut back on eating. Known as gastric bypass surgery, the procedure itself has inherent surgical risks, but the darkest aspect comes later, when the patients are back home—and find, of course, that the cravings for the rich processed foods that led them to overeat in the first place have not gone away. In the most dire cases, people keep eating so much they burst the surgical bands and require emergency care. But even under the best circumstances, they struggle to get enough of the nutrients we need to survive.

This is where Nestlé comes in. It has begun marketing a line of liquid foods, including a product called Peptamen, which is ingested through a tube, and another, called Optifast, that the surgical patients can drink in coping with their smaller stomachs. "Many of these people are malnourished," said Hilary Green, a Nestlé scientist. "Their nutrients are not balanced. And they crave food. By nature, they tend to be more hungry, more often. So the challenge is satisfying that without burdening the stomach."

On my last day at Nestlé, I had lunch with the president of the company's new health science unit, Luis Cantarell. We started off talking about the lack of obesity in Switzerland, which he attributed in part to the country's fondness for outdoor activity, which segued into a discussion about his own personal strategy to stay fit: He resists eating too much pasta, works hard on getting more vegetables, never has meat in the evening, and prefers fish as a source of protein. He told me that the only indulgence he permits himself is a glass of wine.

Quickly, however, our conversation turned to the company's line of formula foods for overeaters, like Peptamen. As bleak as these products might seem, Cantarell said, they are paving the way for a grand merging of food and pharmacy in the not-too-distant future. He envisions—quite excitedly—the prospect of drug-like foods, or food-like drugs, that could upend the traditional approach to medical care, in which expensive drugs are used to treat the scourges of overeating: diabetes, obesity, high blood pressure. "Health care costs are going through the roof, and pharmacological drugs are not the most efficient solutions for chronic medical diseases," he said. "We have the possibility of developing personalized nutrition in a scientific approach, using clinical trials and all the things pharma people do when it comes to developing drugs. Nestlé, with its long tradition, could be an actor in breaking the paradigm."

On my way back to the airport in Geneva, I couldn't shake the image of teenagers gorging on Hot Pockets, only to end up drinking Peptamen through a tube for the rest of their lives. But to be fair, Nestlé had taken some bold steps to reduce the loads of salt, sugar, and fat across its portfolio of foods. Additionally, like other manufacturers, it sold slimmed-down, lower-salt, lower-fat versions of its mainline products, for people with the discipline to curb their intake of calories. Even at that, however, Nestlé is not the World Health Organization—which, as it happens, is headquartered just down the road in Geneva. It's a company, doing what companies do: making money.

It had taken me three and a half years of prying into the food industry's operations to come to terms with the full range of institutional forces that compel even the best companies to churn out foods that undermine a healthy diet. Most critical, of course, is the deep dependence the industry has on salt, sugar, and fat. Almost every one of the hundreds of people I interviewed in the course of writing this book—bench chemists, nutrition scientists, behavioral biologists, food technicians, marketing executives, package designers, chief executives, lobbyists—made the point that companies won't be giving these three up, in any real way, without a major fight. Salt, sugar, and fat are the foundation of processed food, and the overriding question the companies have in determining the formulations of their products is how much they need of each to achieve the maximum allure.

It's simply not in the nature of these companies to care about the consumer in an empathetic way. They are preoccupied with other matters, like crushing their rivals, beating them to the punch. The most amazing thing about the secret 1999 meeting of food company CEOs to discuss obesity was that they got together at all. The grocery store, after all, is littered with the results of their war to outsell one another by arming their products with more salt, sugar, and fat. Witness what happened when Post started coating its cereal with sugar: Rivals came out with versions that went as high as 70 percent. Or look at what happened when Hershey introduced its mega-chocolate cookie in 2003: Kraft responded by rolling out a slew of fattier, sweeter Oreos.

Besides being fiercely competitive, food companies are also deeply obligated toward their shareholders. When companies like Campbell say they will not compromise on taste in lowering the salt, sugar, or fat content of their products, they're not thinking about the consumer's welfare; they're thinking about consumption and sales. As well they should, if they're going to survive. Making money is the sole reason they exist—or so says Wall Street, which is there, at every turn, to remind them of this. Indeed, some experts believe that Wall Street was one of the chief causes of the obesity epidemic when, in the early 1980s, investors shifted their money from stodgy blue chip companies to the high-flying technology industry and other sectors that promised quicker returns. "This put special pressures on food companies," said Marion Nestle, author and former nutrition advisor in the Department of Health and Human Services. "They were already trying to sell their products in an environment in which there were twice as many calories as anybody needed. Now, they had to grow their profits every ninety days. The result was that food companies had to seek new ways to market their foods. And they did that by making larger portions, by making food available absolutely everywhere, by making food as convenient as it could be, and by creating a social environment in which it was okay to eat all day long, in more places, in larger portions."

There is one final factor in the food industry's single-minded pursuit of sales above consumer welfare. In the heat of competition, they look past the health impact of their products. The soda industry has been particularly adept in the department of willful blindness. In 2012, I invited myself to its annual confab with Wall Street investors, where the main topic was the ongoing downturn in sales of soda and how companies were mitigating this by promoting other drinks. Among the new drinks generating excitement: Pure Leaf, a healthy-sounding tea with four teaspoons of sugar per serving; and Crave, a chocolate milk with ten teaspoons of sugar per serving, along with a half-day's quotient of saturated fat. The meeting started off with the chief financial officer of the Dr Pepper Snapple Group, Martin Ellen, who was asked about New York City mayor Michael Bloomberg's proposal to ban the sale of mega-sized soft drinks, which he had labeled a menace to public health. Ellen drew laughs when he started off by calling the initiative "*Your* mayor's proposal"—the hundred or so attendees knew that his company was based in Texas, where no one elected to office would dream of floating such an idea. "If we put aside the matter of choice, and the government's role in our lives, and focus just on the issue of obesity and the soft drink industry, the data doesn't support it," he continued. "Ninety-three percent of our caloric intake comes from foods and drinks other than sugary beverages. And while the industry has been making some inroads over the years, obesity has been going up. Less soft drinks are being consumed, but we are not getting healthier. It is unfair to demonize this industry."

Nutritionists, of course, beg to differ on that.

But so does Jeffrey Dunn, who used to attend these meetings as Coke's president for North and South America. When Dunn looks at the data, he sees soda as a leading cause of obesity. The trend lines, in fact, are a perfect match. Soda consumption took off in the 1980s, and while it has dropped in recent years, the intake of other sugary drinks, like sports ades and vitamin waters and chocolate milk, has risen sharply. By that measure, no one should expect that people—as Dr Pepper's Ellen put it—would be "getting healthier."

Given these proclivities on the part of food companies—competitive, beholden to Wall Street, and in utter denial about their culpability—an intervention by Washington would certainly seem to be in order. Oddly enough, one of the industry people I met who was receptive to federal regulation was the former CEO of Philip Morris, Geoffrey Bible. "I feel like a bit of a wimp on this," he began. "I don't like regulation, because I don't like big government. I think we all should be allowed within reason to exercise our rights and freedom of judgment." But then we discussed how the growing public anger toward tobacco companies caused Philip Morris to embrace regulation, and how his food managers at Kraft in 2003 unilaterally launched a set of anti-obesity initiatives only to face increased competition from their rivals. If nothing else, placing some federal limits on salt, sugar, and fat would put the food manufacturers in the same boat. "Regulation may well be the best way," Bible said, finally. "You would get industry unity on some of these issues, which is very important. But it has to be reasonable."

Some regulatory ideas have cropped up in the last few years, but most of them do not seem reasonable or terribly smart. Like the bill introduced in the Florida legislature by a Republican state senator that would bar people from spending food stamps on items like candy, chips, and soda. That's all America needs: more division based on wealth. Others have pushed for a "fat tax" on soda, but again, why punish the consumer? It would be more sensible to tax salt, sugar, and fat *before* they're added to processed foods. Except for one problem: The companies would surely just pass the cost on to consumers. The bigger challenge lies in closing the price gap between processed and fresh foods so that blueberries could better compete, as a quick snack, with a Snickers bar.

The industry has a different view of food economics: It is their products that make eating affordable. In 2012, an industry group launched a publicity campaign that raises the specter of a planet with nine billion people to argue for a continued reliance on processed foods. In this scenario, salt, sugar, and fat are not demons, but rather safe, reliable, and cheap ways to deliver necessary calories. But even some industry insiders have an alternative view: They argue that the low cost of processed foods has been thwarting the development of healthier ways of feeding the world.

"We're hooked on inexpensive food, just like we're hooked on cheap energy," said James Behnke, the former Pillsbury executive. "The real question is this price sensitivity and, unfortunately, the growing disparity of income between the haves and have-nots. It costs more money to eat fresher, healthier foods. And so, there is a huge economic issue involved in the obesity problem. It falls most heavily on those who have the fewest resources and probably the least understanding or knowledge of what they are doing."

That industry veterans would talk, in this fashion, was one of the more striking revelations in my research for this book. Indeed, I met many intelligent, well-intentioned people—former and current insiders—who are working to beat their industry at its own game. On a personal level, I found that many of the executives I talked to go out of their way to avoid their own products. It got so that I couldn't resist asking everyone I spoke with about their eating habits: John Ruff from Kraft, who gave up sweet drinks and fatty snacks; Luis Cantarell from Nestlé, who eats fish for dinner; Bob Lin from Frito-Lay, who avoids potato chips, along with most everything that is heavily processed; Howard Moskowitz, the soft drink engineering whiz who declines to drink soda. Geoffrey Bible not only stopped smoking his company's cigarettes; when he oversaw Kraft, he worked just as hard at avoiding anything that would send his cholesterol surging. "I was a bit of a fitness freak," he told me. "Played squash, ran fifteen to twenty miles a week."

But most of us can't simply stop eating processed foods. We are still scrambling to get out the door in the morning in one piece, or to please picky eaters, or to put a decent dinner on the table without getting fired for leaving the office early. Many of us have taste buds that are still jacked up for big doses of salt, sugar, and fat. For pleasure or convenience, we need our Frosted Mini-Wheats and our salt and vinegar potato chips, not to mention a few Oreos, to get us through the day.

This dependency poses varying levels of difficulty when it comes to identifying and fending off all of the tricks—in formulation and marketing—that companies use to draw us in. To give me a sense of some of the most extreme struggles that people have, a food company marketing executive invited me to a meeting of her local chapter of Overeaters Anonymous, and it was startling to hear the attendees talk about sugar like it was heroin. Their cars would be littered with food wrappers—just on the drive home from the supermarket. They felt incapable of resisting the treats they bought, so their survival strategy was to avoid all sugar, an approach that struck me as extreme until I sat down with one of our nation's foremost experts on addictive behavior, Nora Volkow, who directs the National Institute on Drug Abuse. A research psychiatrist and scientist, she pioneered the use of brain imaging in finding parallels between food and narcotics, and she became convinced that for some people, overeating is as difficult to overcome as some drug addictions. "Clearly, processed sugar in certain individuals can produce compulsive patterns of intake," she told me. "And in those situations I would recommend they just stay away. Don't try to limit yourself to two Oreo cookies because if the reward is very potent, no matter how good your intentions, you are not going to be able to control them—which is the same message we have for people addicted to drugs."

One of the most promising experiments in resisting the sirens of overeating is taking place in Philadelphia, where a professor of clinical psychology at Drexel University, Michael Lowe, is trying to overcome another root cause of obesity. Besides the influence of Wall Street and the aggressive marketing by soda companies, he points to a tear in the social fabric that first appeared in the early 1980s, as the obesity rates started to surge. "When a lot of us grew up," he told me, "there were three meals a day, and maybe a planned snack at bedtime—and that was it. You never ate outside of those times because you would spoil your appetite. That changed. People began eating everywhere, in meetings or walking down the street. There's no place where food isn't acceptable now, and people are so busy they don't make time to sit down for meals. We have to work to encourage families to eat together, and that used to be automatic."

Lowe has a program under way in which the participants are completely reorienting themselves to processed foods. They're avoiding the worst products, buying healthier substitutes, and dividing the massive serving sizes into reasonable portions so that they will be less tempted to overeat. Steve Comess, a health care executive, went from 232 pounds to 177, and while it took him two years, he said he finally felt in control of his shopping and eating. "It's behavioral," he told me. "I started by reading the labels, so I was making better choices, with better control of my food environment. I'm maximizing the use of fresh foods, to control not only calories, but the fat, salt, and sugar. It's not being perfect; it's keeping within a sustainable range."

This notion of seizing control in order to ward off an unhealthy dependence on processed food may be the best recourse we have in the short term. Consumer advocates are pushing the government to compel the food industry to undertake a wide range of changes in their formulations and marketing, including large reductions in their loads of salt, sugar, and unhealthy fats, restrictions on what foods can be sold through school vending machines, and redesigns of labels to make their nutritional information easier to read. But if the government or industry resists, these changes could take many years. In the meantime, only we can save us.

I made several trips to Philadelphia in the course of reporting this book, drawn to a small neighborhood on the north side of the city that couldn't be more different from the cushy environs of Nestlé in Switzerland. It is called Strawberry Mansion, and the kids here weren't climbing any mountains to stay fit; they could hardly step outside to play on the cracked sidewalks in front of their homes, for fear of the violent crime.

There was, however, plenty to eat. The neighborhood was riddled with corner stores, each with its devastatingly clever layout: soft drinks by the door, followed by rows of sweet cakes graduating into salty snacks and a jackpot of candy at the register. The average kid who walked through the doors of these stores, researchers had found, scooped up chips, candy, and a sugary drink that came to 360 calories—all for just $1.06. With the tiniest bit of spending money from their parents, these kids would often hit the corner store for breakfast on the way to school and then again for a snack on their way back home. The store owners called these times their "rush hours," but in truth the traffic kept up all day and through the late evenings.

I spent hours observing the Strawberry Mansion convenience stores, but it didn't take long before I saw an endless stream of soda and snack trucks making their rounds—practicing their "up and down the street" marketing as they filled up the racks and coolers with Coke and Pepsi, Cheetos and Lay's, Hostess and the locally produced sweets called TastyKake. I'd heard about a group of concerned parents banding together, vigilante-style, with walkie-talkies and battle plans for hitting the stores around one of the neighborhood's schools. So on one trip to the city I caught the first day of their intervention. It was the winter of 2010, bitter cold, but the parents were setting themselves up on the sidewalks outside, blowing into their bare hands, aiming to keep the kids from going in.

This group had had been organized by an ambitious school principal named Amelia Brown who was fed up with the jittery nerves, rising obesity, short attention spans, and all-around declining health of her students, which she blamed, in large part, on the food these stores sold to her kids. She had decided she needed to work on their health, just as she needed to work on boosting their grades. Inside the William D. Kelley School, a spectacular, homegrown effort was under way to teach the students healthier eating. Where posters once hung on the wall warning the kids about drugs, there now were posters warning the kids about salt, sugar, and fat, with their own drawings of the ideal dinner plate. The gym teacher, Beverly Griffin, used replicas of the food pyramid, songs, and games—like dashing around the gym picking up plastic replicas of foods: The team with the most fruits and vegetables won; those with more meat and grains lost. "It's like somebody is saying, 'let's let all those kids get fat, get obese and die,' " said Griffin. Efforts are under way to replicate programs like this, and they shouldn't stop until every elementary school in the country, and the world, has a Beverly Griffin, and every high school delivers basic skills in healthy shopping and cooking.

Principal Brown, however, knew she also had to do something about the corner stores that ring her school. At a meeting held in the school auditorium, she told the volunteer parents, "I need you to go to those stores and say, 'Look, can you not sell to our kids between 8:15 and 8:30? We don't want them to eat sugary items. There is a breakfast program right here. And if you don't do this, we're going to have to boycott for a while.' "

She herself had called on the stores that previous summer, only to realize that her students brought the owners much of the income they needed to pay their bills, including the money they had borrowed to open their stores. So she recruited the parents—not to boycott the stores per se but rather to try to steer her students away. The parents received tactical training from a local community group that used to teach citizens how to fight crack dens, in the 1980s and 1990s, back when cocaine was ravaging this same neighborhood. It wasn't a coincidence that the soda and chips these kids were buying had come to be known on the street as "crack snacks."

On the first day of the operation, one of the parents, McKinley Harris, positioned himself outside the Oxford Food Shop and tried to dissuade kids from going in. They came by in groups, walking themselves to school. Some complied; many did not. "Candy?" he said, shaking his head and peering into the bag held by one of the kids who came dashing out of the shop. "That's not food." He didn't try to confiscate it. He was trying to get the kid to think about his choices. I met later with shop owner Gladys Tejada, who said she empathized with the parents but didn't hold out much hope for their success. *She* certainly couldn't prevent the kids from buying whatever they want. "They like it sweet," she said. "And they like it cheap."

The real heartbreaking moment, however, came a few minutes later when McKinley's wife, Jamaica, came rushing down the street with their kids in tow. She and her husband had been working hard to improve their own family's diet, which required taking taxis to reach supermarkets where they could buy fresh, wholesome food. But this morning had been frenetic, getting the kids ready for school. They still needed breakfast, so she ran into the store to get something for them. The Oxford didn't sell fresh fruit, not even bananas, so she came out a minute later with a healthy-sounding alternative: "fruit and yogurt" breakfast bars for her kids. Reading the front of the label, she said with a measure of pride, "It has calcium." But the fine print on the back told a different story. The bars, in truth, compared poorly with the candy her husband was trying to block. The "healthy" bars had more sugar, and less fiber, than Oreos.

I was overcome by this scene. Here they were, these people of Strawberry Mansion, sick of their kids getting the jitters and stomachaches from the corner-store food, trying to rehabilitate their own eating habits, and getting snookered into buying a "healthy" item that was no healthier than candy. This persistent tactic by food companies to promote one good ingredient, hoping that consumers will overlook the rest, was one of the oldest tricks in the book, going back to the 1920s and 1930s, when companies began adding vitamins to their cereal, touting these healthy additives on the front of the boxes—decades before they had to disclose the sugar content in the fine print on the back. But today, this ploy seems even more pernicious, as more and more people are trying to do the right thing by their eating habits. With all of life's distractions, reading and understanding the *entire* food label is as critical as it is hard to pull off.

If nothing else, this book is intended as a wake-up call to the issues and tactics at play in the food industry, to the fact that we are not helpless in facing them down. We have choices, particularly when it comes to grocery shopping, and I saw this book, on its most basic level, as a tool for defending ourselves when we walk through those doors. Some of the tricks being used to seduce us are subtle, and awareness is key: the gentle canned music; the in-store bakery aromas; the soft drink coolers by the checkout lanes; the placement of some of the most profitable but worst-for-you foods at eye level, with healthier staples like whole wheat flour or plain oats on the lowest shelf and the fresh fruits and vegetables way off on one side of the store.

But there is nothing subtle about the products themselves. They are knowingly designed—*engineered* is the better word—to maximize their allure. Their packaging is tailored to excite our kids. Their advertising uses every psychological trick to overcome any logical arguments we might have for passing the product by. Their taste is so powerful, we remember it from the last time we walked down the aisle and succumbed, snatching them up. And above all else, their formulas are calculated and perfected by scientists who know very well what they are doing. The most crucial point to know is that there is nothing accidental in the grocery store. All of this is done with a purpose.

It is, perhaps, not unreasonable in this scenario to think of the grocery store as a battlefield, dotted with landmines itching to go off. And if you accept this, then it becomes all the more apparent why the food industry is so reliant on salt, sugar, and fat. They are cheap. They are interchangeable. They are huge, powerful forces of nature in unnatural food. And yet, for us, knowing all this can be empowering. You can walk through the grocery store and, while the brightly colored packaging and empty promises are still mesmerizing, you can see the products for what they are. You can also see everything that goes on behind the image they project on the shelf: the formulas, the psychology, and the marketing that compels us to toss them into the cart. They may have salt, sugar, and fat on their side, but we, ultimately, have the power to make choices. After all, we decide what to buy. We decide how much to eat.

acknowledgments

The reporting that led to this book stemmed from three fabulous meals, starting with the crackling hot mess of catfish that Ben Cawthon and I wolfed down at Marilyn's Deli, a roadhouse on State Route 52 in southern Alabama. Ben is a goodhearted civil-rights brawler in the nearby town of Blakely, Georgia, where a deadly outbreak of salmonella in peanuts first drew my attention to food manufacturers. He showed me that the factories that turn out America's food—hardly the fortresses I imagined—are staffed with principled workers quite willing to hold their employers accountable at the risk of their own livelihoods. I'm honored to know Ben, and wish him all the best in his ongoing civic pursuits.

The second meal was lunch at a Washington hotel, where it wasn't the burger that opened my eyes, but how it was ordered. My guest was Dennis Johnson, a soft-spoken lobbyist for the beef industry who is said, in an obvious stretch of the truth, to own the U.S. Department of Agriculture. What he does have, for sure, is a keen insider's view of the health risk in eating ground beef that is undercooked. "I'd like mine *well done*," Dennis instructed the waiter, which got me started asking food company officials about their own eating habits when it comes to salt, sugar, and fat.

And for the third meal, a cookout on the shore of Lake Washington, north of Seattle, the mere act of grocery shopping with Mansour Samadpour was enough to send me reaching for the hand sanitizer. One of the smartest scientists I know, Mansour provides pathogen testing and controls for the country's largest slaughterhouses, not to mention leafy green farms, and he used plastic bags from the produce section to pick up the packaged meat we bought, lest he get any pathogens on his hands. It wasn't just microbes on the beef that worried Mansour, however. He was the first to suggest that I look at what companies *intentionally* add to their products, like salt, and I thank him deeply for this guidance. Among the other experts on meat I'm indebted to are Carl Custer, Jeffrey Bender, Gerald Zirnstein, Loren Lange, Craig Wilson, Ken Peterson, Kirk Smith, James Marsden, Felicia Nestor, Dave Theno, Charles Tant, Michael Doyle—and Bill Marler, the country's dominant and passionate litigator on behalf of people who are sickened by food, and who opened some huge doors for my reporting. One of his clients, Stephanie Smith, is the bravest person I know.

The great meals—and the great company—didn't stop there. In Philadelphia, Leslie Stein showed me to a Korean hot pot shop as we discussed the Monell Chemical Senses Center, where she and other scientists were hugely generous with their time. I thank, especially, Julie Mennella for the look inside the bliss point of kids, and Marcia Pelchat, Danielle Reed, Karen Teff, Michael Tordoff, Paul Breslin, Robert Margolskee, and Gary Beauchamp, their fearless leader, as well as two center alumni who went on to be stars in the world of food science, Dwight Riskey and Richard Mattes. At other institutions, Anthony Sclafani and Adam Drewnowski were fantastically helpful and patient.

Nothing quite matched the Cheez-Its that Kellogg cooked up to impress upon me how reliant it is on salt, and I thank its technicians, as well as those at Kraft, Campbell, and Cargill who prepared similar salt-less gems for me to gag on. There were many, many other industry scientists and marketers who were incredibly generous with their time, but I wish to especially thank Al Clausi, Howard Moskowitz, Michele Reisner, Jeffrey Dunn, Bob Drane, Bob Lin, Jim Behnke, Jerry Fingerman, John Ruff, Daryl Brewster, Steven Witherly, Parke Wilde, and Edward Martin. None were more encouraging than Deb Olson Linday, a marketing genius who pioneered some of the earliest efforts to boost the consumption of cheese, but developed deep qualms about that enterprise. "I wish you Godspeed in writing your book," she wrote in one note after we dined on Pad Thai north of Chicago. "Give 'em hell."

I met Andy Ward of Random House over more noodles in midtown Manhattan, and knew right away he was an editor who could inspire writers to walk through walls. But it feels awkward thanking him. From the conception, to the refining, to the untangling of sentences by his amazingly skilled hands, *Salt Sugar Fat* became his book as much as it is mine, so it's with great admiration—as a partner—that I hope to be lucky enough someday to embark on another adventure with him. Who I *can* deeply thank at Random House is Susan Kamil, for her unwavering support, as well as Tom Perry, Gina Centrello, Avideh Bashirrad, Erika Greber, Sally Marvin, Sonya Safro, Amelia Zalcman, Crystal Velasquez, and Kaela Myers—peerless pros, one and all. I also wish to thank Anton Ioukhnovets for the brilliant cover illustration, and Martin Schneider for his first-rate copyediting.

Scott Moyers, Andrew Wylie, and James Pullen at the Wylie Agency lent their aid and comfort at all the right moments, and I couldn't have dreamt up a more effective team. When Scott returned to publishing, Andrew was there for me, instantly, whenever I needed, and I'm grateful for that.

This book would never have materialized without my editors and colleagues at *The New York Times*, starting with Christine Kay, who first suggested—up in the *Times'* cafeteria, of course—that I do some reporting on peanuts, and then, much later, helped me think through the organization of this book and applied her exquisite editing hands to some early and rough copy. As always, I'm deeply indebted to Matt Purdy, the paper's brilliant investigations editor, for his friendship, encouragement, and giving me unpressured time away from his clutches. I'm also grateful to the paper's editor, Jill Abramson, who first suggested writing a book about food, and to her predecessor, Bill Keller, who warned me it would take longer than I anticipated, which, of course, it did. I'm humbled and grateful to know Gabe Johnson, one of the finest video journalists in the business who joined me in the early reporting, bringing his talent and passion and eye for good food on the road. I'd also like to thank my hero in food writing, Kim Severson, and Barry Meier, whose work at the paper leaves me in awe. Thanks, too, to colleagues Tim Golden, Walt Bogdanich, Stephanie Saul, Debbie Sontag, Paul Fishleder, David McGraw, Andrew Martin, Andrea Elliott, Jim Rutenberg, Jim Glanz, Louise Story, Ginger Thompson, Mike McIntyre, Michael Luo, Jo Becker, David Barstow, Nancy Weinstock, Tony Cenicola, Jessica Kourkounis, Joel Lovell, Mark Bittman, Tara Parker-Pope, Jason Stallman, Debbie Leiderman, and the fabulous writer Charles Duhigg, my guide on all matters in publishing to whom I am deeply indebted. Beyond the paper, I want to thank David Rohde and Kristen Mulvihill, Kevin and Ruth McCoy for their friendship and meals, Laurie Fitch for her Wall Street introductions, Ellen Pollock for cluing me into the power of Stacy's Pita Chips, and the chef/writer Tamar Adler for cooking a luscious meal that showed me how salt in the kitchen was a good thing for healthy eating. I also thank the indomitable Laura Dodd and Cynthia Colonna for research and other assistance, Kristen Courtney and Julia Mecke for squaring away the homefront, and my neighbor Gordon Pradl for a meticulous and thoughtful reading of chapters.

Lee Ellen and Clyde, my parents, taught me to love every food in the world, except liver and stewed okra, and I miss them dearly. This book is for them, and for Oma Bruch, Leah Heyn, Herman Heyn, Phyllis Weber, Frank and Thomas, Kenny and Dominique, Penelope and Emile, Myra and Buzzy Hettleman, Sally and John, Charlotte, Clyde and Gabrielle, Melchior, Bob and Sonya, Andrej, Stella and Robë Felicia and Rafael, and Mal. My wife, Eve Heyn, was there for me from start to the finish, working through reporting puzzles, taking her own fine editing hand to the copy, and granting her unconditional love. I admire and respect and love her dearly. My boy Aren, at thirteen, had my back the whole way, with encouragement and some good ideas, and my other boy Will, though just eight, couldn't be fooled at the dinner table when I stopped talking about *E. coli* in one of his (formerly) favorite foods, hamburgers, and started chatting about Oreo cookies: "Dad! You're *not* going to write about sugar now!" I did, Will. Sorry.

September 2012

a note on sources

This narrative has been drawn from a multitude of sources, including hundreds of interviews with individuals who have been closely associated with advancing or critiquing the activities of the processed food industry and more than one thousand papers and studies that examine the science of making processed foods as well as the health implications of their consumption. Many of these primary sources are cited in the notes that follow, but there are several that warrant a fuller description, in part to assist those who might wish to pursue their own examinations of the industry.

One of the most valuable sources of highly confidential records that provide a view of the inner workings of the food industry is entirely a matter of happenstance. This trove of records stems from the legal war waged over tobacco. Lawsuits brought by four states in 1994 to secure reimbursement for health care expenditures related to tobacco-related illnesses resulted in a 1998 settlement that required the largest tobacco manufacturers to release the internal records produced for the case. These records are being archived at the Legacy Tobacco Documents Library (LT) at the University of California, San Francisco, and number—as of September 2012—81 million pages in 14 million documents. The relevance to this book comes in the corporate affiliations. While the collection's focus is on tobacco, the archives include the records of Philip Morris relating to its ownership of three of the largest food companies: Kraft, General Foods, and Nabisco. I'm grateful to the library archivists for guiding me through their search mechanism that enabled me to ferret out the food-related documents. The records archived thus far span the years 1985 through 2002—the most critical period for examining the health issues relating to processed food—and include memos, meeting minutes, strategy papers, internal speeches, and sales data relating to the manufacturing, advertising, marketing, sales, and scientific research activities of the food companies. In the course of researching this book, I found only one news report that made use of the archive's food-related records: a January 29, 2006, report in the *Chicago Tribune* entitled "Where There's Smoke, There Might Be Food Research, Too," which referenced several memos in which scientists from the food and tobacco divisions of Philip Morris discussed potential collaborations on flavorings and other sensory issues. The Legacy Library is currently acquiring more documents produced in a civil lawsuit brought by the Department of Justice against the nation's top tobacco companies, including Philip Morris, following a 2006 federal judicial decision that the companies violated the Racketeer Influenced and Corrupt Organizations Act (RICO) by misleading the public about the health hazards of smoking, which the companies have appealed.

Another little-known archive of food company records is kept by the Council of Better Business Bureaus. One of its units, the National Advertising Division, provides an arbitration service for companies that allows them to settle disputes with each other out of court. These disputes typically involve challenges to the validity of advertising claims but also include cases that stem from the NAD's own inquiries. I'm indebted to Linda Bean of the Better Business Bureau for sending me copies of dozens of cases involving Coca-Cola, Kellogg, Kraft, General Mills, among others, many of which contain details of the companies' advertising strategies and marketing analysis—highly insightful information that is typically not made public even by the government's consumer watchdog on issues relating to advertising, the Federal Trade Commission.

The marketing divisions of food companies release other confidential information through yet another forum that is more public than they likely appreciate. Each year, advertising campaigns for food and other consumer goods are chosen for recognition by an organization called the Effie Awards, which was created in 1968 and was originally run by the American Marketing Association. The winners must show that they succeeded in boosting sales, so the food companies and their advertising agencies prepare case studies of their marketing campaigns that include details on the product's financial history as well as the consumer targeting strategies they used to achieve the increased sales. I was able to obtain and review dozens of these case studies, which were posted online by the awards organization.

The food scientists who design the thousands of new products created each year have several forums through which they discuss and share the details of their work, including the Institute of Food Technologists. Founded in 1939, the IFT holds an annual meeting and food expo, and I am grateful to the organization for allowing me to attend its 2010 meeting in Chicago. More than twenty-one thousand food industry personnel turned out for this five-day event, which included nine hundred exhibitors and several hundred workshops on a wide range of topics, from adjusting food formulations in order to target the emotional needs of consumers, to controlling pathogens in food, to designing environmentally friendly packaging. Importantly, the IFT also produces a compilation of scientific papers, in abstract form, relating to the design of foods, and I am indebted to the organization for providing me with a copy of 2010 Book of Abstracts. Its 1,400 entries provided me with numerous industry contacts and leads on the most current scientific undertakings in the production of processed foods. Another scientific group, the Association for Chemoreception Sciences, produces its own annual collection of hundreds of abstracts, which I found immensely useful.

On the consumer side, the Center for Science in the Public Interest, based in Washington, has been at the forefront of major challenges to the food industry since its founding in 1971. I am grateful to the organization's director, Michael Jacobson, as well as its senior staffers on nutrition, Bonnie Liebman and Margo Wootan, for opening its files to me. The organization also has a deep archive of reports and studies that it makes publicly available through its website.

The shroud behind which the food industry conducts much of its business extends to the nutritional profiles of its products. Even today, there is only limited public disclosure of the ingredients they use in their products; they are required to list the ingredients on their packages in the order of their relative amounts, with largest ingredients first, but do not need to specify the actual amounts. More significantly, the product formulations are in constant flux. For nutritional information such as calories and the total amounts of sugar, fat, and sodium, I have relied on the companies' own websites whenever possible. I have also relied on the online service Calorie Count, which is owned by *The New York Times*. It posts the nutritional information for products, as well as a grade, from A to F, based on the nutritional scores.

Finally, the enterprise of manufacturing and marketing of foods is, at its most basic level, about sales. Companies are typically loath to provide details on specific products or brands. In numerous instances, I was able to obtain sales data from SymphonyIRI, a market research group, based in Chicago, and I am grateful for their assistance.

Michael Moss, Brooklyn, New York

notes

Prologue: "The Company Jewels"

xi **These eleven men**   The 1999 meeting of food company CEOs was organized by the International Life Sciences Institute, an industry group formed in 1978 to study the safety concerns related to caffeine as a food additive. Since then, the ILSI has broadened its focus to include numerous issues of public health, nutrition, and food safety, with activities geared mainly toward the scientists and technicians at food companies. I'm grateful to Michael Shirreffs, the organization's communications director, for information about the ILSI's history and programs.

xii **"We were very concerned"**   James Behnke to author.

xii **Just that year**   General Mills' share of cereal sales edged past Kellogg briefly that year and then settled into a virtual tie at about 32 percent, followed by Post at 16 percent. See, for example, the trade journal *Food and Beverage Packaging,* which on April 1, 2009, profiled General Mills as the "Packaging Innovator of the Decade." A consulting firm, Innosight, has a revealing profile of Go-Gurt on its website. The Harvard Business School case studies include a 2008 profile of General Mills and its former CEO, Stephen Sanger.

xiii **twice as much sugar**   The image of yogurt as a health food is even further diminished by another comparison. The leading brands, including the regular versions of Yoplait, have nearly twice the sugar of ice cream, per serving.

xv **Kraft's CEO, Bob Eckert, would tell a reporter**   This quotation comes from the unpublished transcript of an interview that Eckert gave to a *Business Week* reporter in August 1999. The transcript is contained in the Philip Morris records provided to the Legacy Tobacco Documents Library (LT).

xvi **"I very much appreciate"**   Michael Mudd's presentation to the CEOs is archived in the Philip Morris records at the LT. Mudd was joined on stage by James Hill, a professor of pediatrics and medicine at the University of Colorado School of Medicine in Denver, where he also directs the Colorado Nutrition Obesity Research Center. Hill presented the health data on obesity and discussed efforts to combat the epidemic. I am grateful to Hill for his recollections of the meeting and for providing me with a copy of the slides he and Mudd presented to the CEOs.

xx **Sanger had been sitting**   Steve Sanger's presence at the 1999 dinner meeting is documented by the attendance lists and seating charts kept by the ILSI, and by interviews with four attendees. Sanger, who is retired from General Mills and declined to be interviewed, said in an email that he could not recall the meeting and stressed that he had had a deep commitment to nutrition. "During my tenure as CEO, the company consistently placed a high priority on improving the nutritional properties of its product line through the addition of whole grains, fiber, and nutrients and the reduction of fat, salt, sugar, and calories. We set corporate objectives for nutritional improvement, invested in R&D to achieve them, tracked progress, and built those metrics into our management incentive systems. As a result, General Mills introduced a steady stream of new and reformulated products offering those nutritional properties including light yogurt, light cake and frosting, light soups, reduced-sugar versions of our most popular pre-sweetened cereals, lower-fat and nonfat yogurts, reduced-salt soups, increased fiber cereals and cereal bars, whole grain cereals, and many others. We also invested heavily in advertising those nutritional improvements to consumers. Some of those products were successful; others were not. In general, consumers proved very responsive to nutritional improvements only if they did not have to sacrifice taste to get them." Tom Forsythe, a spokesman for General Mills, said the company's efforts to produce lower-sugar cereals that still tasted good were hit and miss, and entailed trying to market reduced-sugar versions of popular brands, until 2007, when a breakthrough in formulation allowed it to launch an across-the-board sugar-lowering effort for all of its cereals, which resulted in an average 14 percent reduction. "We used health to drive performance," Forsythe told me. "It's not the only strategy, and as I said, you can't sell healthy products that don't taste good. We have tried and we have failures to prove it."

xxi **effectively ended the meeting**   James Behnke said one or two other company officials spoke after Mudd's presentation, but, "the one we all remember now is Steve. He was the most vocal. At dinner, the reaction was mixed, depending on what table you sat at. But the steam had come out."

xxi **"I don't think anything ever came"**   John Cady to author. The organizers of the CEO meeting later regrouped to weigh their options, which were outlined in a memo entitled, "ILSI CEO Dinner Follow-up Planning." They planned for Mudd to give a 30-minute "recap of the CEO presentation" to lower level company officials, "so the attendees know exactly what their CEOs were exposed to." Discouraged by the CEO response, they decided in pressing forward to ask for less than the $15 million they originally sought from the CEOs, and to suggest only incremental efforts, starting with "items that no one would disagree are things that need to be done." Eventually, Mudd and the other proponents of the industry-wide effort were forced to settle for a single initiative: encouraging kids to get more exercise. Several million dollars raised from

Kraft and others were used to produce educational materials that focused on physical activity as one of the solutions to obesity.

xxi **Publicly, there would be some overtures** For example, see the December 9, 2009, press release from General Mills announcing its sugar reduction, which is posted on the company's website. Tom Forsythe, the company's spokesman, told me the effort was undertaken "because of the attention to sugar." General Mills has continued to staunchly defend the nutritional profile of its cereals, as it did at an American Heart Association conference on sugar, held in Washington, D.C., on May 5, 2010. In a presentation, the company argued that cereal contributes far less sugar than other food items, such as drinks and desserts; that cereal has the fewest calories among popular breakfasts, including bagels with cream cheese, or bacon and eggs; and that Cheerios, with 1 gram of sugar per serving, compares well with Lucky Charms, at 11 grams, in providing whole grains and other nutrients. "From a calorie and nutrient standpoint, both are a good breakfast choice," the company said.

A number of other companies, including Nestlé, are in the process of reducing the levels of salt, sugar, and fat in their products, and in 2010 a group of food retailers and manufacturers called the Healthy Weight Commitment Foundation pledged to trim 1.5 trillion calories from food products by 2015. See chapter 11 for more on this pledge and Kraft's anti-obesity initiatives.

xxiii **"put us in one of those"** Daryl Brewster to author.

xxiii **Children had become especially vulnerable** For data on obesity rates and other food-related health issues, I have relied on the Centers for Disease Control and Prevention in Atlanta. See, for example, Cynthia Ogden et al., CDC, "Prevalence of Obesity among Children and Adolescents: United States, Trends 1963–1965 Through 2007–2008," and U.S. Public Health Service, "The Surgeon General's Call to Action to Prevent and Decrease Overweight and Obesity 2001."

xxiv **outbreak of salmonella** Michael Moss, "Peanut Case Shows Holes in Food Safety Net," *The New York Times*, February 9, 2009.

xxiv **Food manufacturers like Kellogg** Since the salmonella tragedy, Kellogg has made changes to keep better track of the state of its staggering number of suppliers. "In the wake of this unfortunate situation, we took several immediate steps, including establishing new cross-functional Kellogg audit teams to audit suppliers of high-risk ingredients," Kellogg spokeswoman Kris Charles told me. "Our food safety systems include internal teams that audit our suppliers of microbiologically sensitive, high-risk ingredients, such as nuts and seeds, dried fruits and vegetables, and dairy products. These auditors visit each sensitive-ingredient supplier globally to ensure they are maintaining our high standards. Recently, we have been expanding these internal audit teams with a goal of evaluating all ingredient suppliers. More than 900 ingredient supplier locations (representing more than 50 percent of total supplier locations) around the world were audited in 2011."

xxiv **relied on a private inspector** Michael Moss, "Food Safety Problems Elude Private Inspectors," *The New York Times*, March 6, 2009.

xxiv **shipment of hamburger** Michael Moss, "The Burger That Shattered Her Life," *The New York Times*, October 4, 2009.

xxv **until it was mixed together** Cargill said it has a number of alternative safeguards in place to reduce the risk of pathogens, including the imposition of testing procedures on its meat suppliers. Cargill also tests samples of its finished hamburger for pathogens and reports any positive findings "to all the potentially implicated suppliers."

xxviii **"The tobacco wars are coming"** Philip Morris records, LT.

xxix **The industry's dependence** Author visits to the research laboratories of Kellogg and other companies.

xxix **"We are doubling down"** Jeffrey Dunn to author.

Chapter 1: "Exploiting the Biology of the Child"

3 **Forget what we learned** Author interviews with scientists at the Monell Chemical Senses Center in Philadelphia, including David Margolskee, Gary Beauchamp, Danielle Reed, and Paul Breslin. Credit for this discovery goes to Virginia Collings, "Human Taste Response as a Function of Locus of Stimulation on the Tongue and Soft Palate," *Perception and Psychophysics* 16, no. 1 (1974): 169–174. For a discussion of the tongue map misinterpretation, see Linda Bartoshuk, "The Biological Basis of Food Perception and Acceptance," *Food Quality and Preference* 4 (1993): 21–32.

4 **On average, we consume** The average sugar consumption of 22 teaspoons a day is based on the National Health and Nutrition Examination Survey, as reported by the American Heart Association in advocating a reduction of sugar consumption. Rachel Johnson et al., "Dietary Sugars Intake and Cardiovascular Health; a Scientific Statement from the American Heart Association," *Circulation*, September 15, 2009. The figure is for sugar that is added to foods during processing or preparation. In reporting on food consumption, I have also relied on the Economic Research Service of the U.S. Department of Agriculture, whose data can be accessed through the agency's website. However, the agency generally reports figures that are based on the amount of sugar or other commodities made "available" to consumers, also known as "disappearance data." The agency has efforts under way to determine the extent to which this data overestimates the actual consumption by overlooking the food that is spoiled or thrown away.

4 **The highlights start with** Sidney W. Mintz, *Sweetness and Power: The Place of Sugar in Modern History* (New York: Penguin, 1986).

5 **our consumption of sugar-sweetened soda** I'm indebted to John Sicher, the editor and publisher of *Beverage Digest*, for providing me with data that distinguishes between caloric and noncaloric soda consumption as well as data for other sugar-sweetened soft drinks.

5 **That all changed in the late 1960s** Anthony Sclafani to author. Anthony Sclafani and Deleri Springer, "Dietary Obesity in Adult Rats: Similarities to Hypothalamic and Human Obesity Syndromes," *Psychology and Behavior* 17 (1976): 461–471; Anthony Sclafani et al., "Gut T1R3 Sweet Taste Receptors Do Not Mediate Sucrose-Conditioned Flavor Preferences in Mice," *American Journal of Physiology—Regulatory, Integrative, and Comparative Physiology* 299 (2010).

6 **except for "Eddy"** Arlene Love, the sculptor, to author.

6 **Getting buzzed through** I made several visits to the Monell Center for interviews and research. I am grateful to the scientists and support staff for being generous with their time. The center has an extensive guide to its scientists and their work on its website.

7 **they identified the actual protein** Several teams of researchers deserve credit for this discovery. Corie Lok, "Sweet Tooth Gene Found," *Nature*, April 23, 2001; M. Max, "Tas1r3, Encoding a New Candidate Taste Receptor, Is Allelic to the Sweet Responsiveness Locus Sac.," *Nature Genetics* 28, no. 1 (2001): 58–63.

7 **They have even solved** Ryuske Yoshida et al., "Endocannabinoids Selectively Enhance Sweet Taste," *Proceedings of the National Academy of Sciences* 107, no. 2 (2010): 935–939.

8 **This tension between** J. Desor and Lawrence Greene, "Preferences for Sweet and Salty in 9- to 15-Year-Old and Adult Humans," *Science* 1990 (1975): 686–687. For a more recent analysis of taste preferences by age and race, see Julie Mennella et al., "Evaluation of the Monell Forced-Choice, Paired-Comparison Tracking Procedure for Determining Sweet Taste Preferences Across the Lifespan," *Chemical Senses* 36 (2011): 345–355. This study, in addition to assessing the sweet preferences of 356 younger children, evaluated the same in 169 adolescents and 424 adults.

10 **their "bliss point" for sugar** For more reporting on the genesis of the term *bliss point*, see chapter 2.

10 **the group was called ARISE**   Philip Morris records in LT.

12 **an adorable six-year-old girl**   Tatyana Gray's mother was present for the experiment and Tatyana's interviews with me, and I thank them both for letting me write about Tatyana's experience. Thanks also to Susana Finkbeiner of Monell, who prepared the puddings for her tasting.

17 **"I testified that"**   In the early 1990s, Mark Hegsted provided an account of his involvement with the Senate Select Committee on Nutrition and Human Needs, which I obtained from the University of Minnesota School of Public Health's collection of historical documents.

17 **On top of that**   For more on Jacobson's sugar petition, see chapter 14.

17 **The headlines from these**   Ellen Wartella, "Examination of Front-of-Package Nutrition Rating Systems and Symbols Phase 1 Report," *Institute of Medicine*, 2010.

17 **"It was coming from"**   Al Clausi to author. I met with Clausi on several occasions to discuss his work on behalf of the food industry, and I am grateful to him for being generous with his time and sharing his records with me. I obtained other records on Monell's interaction with the Flavor Benefits Committee from the LT.

19 **Much of the work on soda**   Michael Tordoff and Annette Alleva, "Effect of Drinking Soda Sweetened with Aspartame or High-Fructose Corn Syrup on Food Intake and Body Weight," *American Journal of Clinical Nutrition* 51 (1990): 963–969.

20 **"For three weeks we gave them"**   Michael Tordoff to author.

21 **Another of their colleagues**   Karen Teff et al., "48-h Glucose Infusion in Humans: Effect on Hormonal Responses, Hunger, and Food Intake," *Physiology and Behavior* 5 (2007): 733–743; Karen Teff, "Dietary Fructose Reduces Circulating Insulin and Leptin, Attenuates Postprandial Suppression of Ghrelin, and Increases Triglycerides in Women," *Journal of Clinical Endocrinology and Metabolism* 89, no. 6 (2004): 2963–2972;

Karen Teff, "Prolonged Mild Hyperglycemia Induces Vagally Mediated Compensatory Increase in C-Peptide Secretion in Humans," *Journal of Clinical Endocrinology and Metabolism* 89, no. 11 (2004): 5606–5613.

21 **"I'm still shocked"** Karen Teff to author.

23 **This time, however, food companies** The American Heart Association's statement on sugar and records of its "Added Sugars Conference" in May 2010 are available on the organization's website. The records include presentations by the National Cancer Institute, Coca-Cola, the American Institute of Baking International, the National Confectioners Association, and General Mills.

23 **"Let's get practical"** Eyal Shimoni, associate professor, biotechnology and food engineering, Technion—Israel Institute of Technology, in his presentation to the conference and to author.

Chapter 2: "How Do You Get People to Crave?"

25 **What they all wanted** John Lennon's affection for Dr Pepper was recorded by his girlfriend, May Pang, in her biography, *Instamatic Karma* (New York: St. Martin's, 2008); the preferences of the other pop stars were ferreted out by the *Smoking Gun* website. Hillary Clinton relates her experiences with Dr Pepper on the road in her autobiography, *Living History* (New York: Scribner's, 2004). These and other Dr Pepper trivia have been compiled in an online digest run by Christopher Flaherty, *The Highly Unofficial Dr Pepper FAQ*.

26 **Dr Pepper began to slip** "Top-10 Carbonated Soft Drink Companies and Brands for 2002," *Beverage Digest*, February 24, 2003.

26 **"If we are to re-establish"** "Dr Pepper President: Red Fusion Designed to Add 'Excitement' and Appeal to Non–Dr Pepper Users," *Beverage Digest*, May 24, 2002.

27 **He boosted sales**   Howard R. Moskowitz and Alex Gofman, *Selling Blue Elephants* (Upper Saddle River, NJ: Wharton School Publishing, 2007).

27 **as many as sixty thousand**   The Food Marketing Institute, a grocers trade association, says the number of items in grocery stores ranges from 15,000 to 60,000 depending on the store's size, with an average of 38,718.

28 **Supermarket real estate**   Herb Sorensen, *Inside the Mind of the Shopper* (Upper Saddle River, NJ: Wharton School Publishing, 2009).

29 **"I've optimized soups"**   Howard Moskowitz to author.

30 **They devised sixty-one**   Interviews with Moskowitz and Michele Reisner, along with Dr Pepper project records.

31 **"If all of a sudden"**   Howard Moskowitz to author. Michael Moss, "The Hard Sell On Salt," *The New York Times*, May 30, 2010.

32 **As he told a gathering**   Howard Moskowitz, Institute of Food Technologists (IFT) 2010 meeting, Chicago.

32 **The military has long been**   The reporting on Natick was greatly assisted by interviews with several Natick officials, including Jeannette Kennedy, project officer for research on MREs. The military's field rations program is also detailed in the document, "Operational Rations of the Department of Defense," Natick, May 2010.

32 **"The problem in the military"**   Herb Meiselman to author.

33 **Sensory-specific satiety**   Steven Witherly, *Why Humans Like Junk Food: The Inside Story on Why You Like Your Favorite Foods, the Cuisine Secrets of Top Chefs, and How to Improve Your Own Cooking Without a Recipe!* (Lincoln, NE: iUniverse, 2007); Barbara Rolls, "Sensory Specific Satiety in Man," *Physiological Behavior* 27 (1981): 137–142; Marjatta Salmenkallio-Marttila et al., "Satiety, Weight Management, and Foods: Literature Review," VTT Technical Research Center of Finland, Esbo, Finland.

34 **This colleague**   Author correspondence with Balintfy's son, Joseph, a spokesman for the National Institutes of Health. Among other instances, Balintfy cited the term *bliss point* in a 1979 presentation to the Society for the Advancement of Food Service Research.

35 **The company, plagued by bureaucracy**   See especially the Harvard Business School critique Toby E. Stuart, *Kraft General Foods: The Merger.*

35 **"one of the great ho-hummers"**   Ibid.

35 **Maxwell House**   This reporting benefited greatly from interviews with Howard Moskowitz and John Ruff, a General Foods research and development official in the coffee division. Moskowitz, *Selling Blue Elephants.*

40 **The precise ingredients**   Dr Pepper declined to discuss specific ingredients beyond those that are listed on the package, calling the formula proprietary.

43 **By 2006, the company's CEO**   Transcript of the February 23, 2006, presentation by CEO Todd Stitzer to the Consumer Analyst Group of New York.

Chapter 3: "Convenience with a Capital 'C' "

45 **In the spring of 1946**   Al Clausi to author.

46 **coined the phrase**   Al Clausi recalled hearing Mortimer use the expression "convenience foods" in a speech to employees in the early 1950s that Clausi believes may be the first time the phrase was used. "He said, 'General Foods is not just a packaged food company, General Foods is the convenience foods company,' " Clausi told me. "And that signal went out to everybody, in marketing, in technical. That we now need to look at what we're doing and ask, 'How can we make it more convenient?' That was the beginning of the era of instant this, instant that, powdered this, powdered that."

47 **This one took years** Clausi to author. His creation of instant Jell-O pudding is also memorialized in the beautifully illustrated large-format book published by Kraft Foods, *The Greatest Thing Since Sliced Cheese*, which draws on company records and interviews to chronicle the role of food technicians and scientists in creating many of the company's iconic products while steering clear of the more controversial aspects. The impetus for creating this book came from John Ruff, a former Kraft senior vice president, who wished to honor the oft-overlooked labors of food technicians, and I am grateful to him for providing me with a copy. Anne Bucher and Melanie Villines, *The Greatest Thing Since Sliced Cheese: Stories of Kraft Food Inventors and their Inventions* (Kraft Food Holdings, Northfield, Il. 2005).

48 **A competitor, National Brands** National Brands obtained two patents relevant to the production of instant pudding, the first in 1952, patent no. 2,607,692, and the second in 1958, patent no. 2,829,978. Clausi's own patent was issued in 1957, patent no. 2,801,924. The U.S. Patent and Trademark Office has an online database where patents can be retrieved using various search criteria, including the patent number, the name of the inventor, and the company to whom the patent is assigned.

51 **"Quick! Easy!"** Bucher and Villines, *Greatest Thing Since Sliced Cheese*.

51 **When Mortimer emerged** Charles Mortimer to the dinner session of the Conference Board's Third Annual Marketing Conference, New York City, September 22, 1955.

52 **Post introduced a string** This reporting on the development of sugar-coated cereals benefited greatly from Scott Bruce, *Cerealizing America: The Unsweetened Story of American Breakfast Cereal* (Boston: Faber & Faber, 1995), a delightful and well-researched account of the cereal industry pioneers. See also Kenneth Corts, "The Ready-To-Eat Breakfast Cereal Industry in 1994" (Cambridge, MA: Harvard Business School, 1995); and Raymond Gilmartin, *General Mills.*

53 **General Foods at the time**   Stuart, *Kraft General Foods*; "Modern Living: Just Heat and Serve," *Time Magazine*, December 7, 1959; Bucher and Villines, *Greatest Thing Since Sliced Cheese*; "A Chronological History of Kraft General Foods," KGF Archives Department, Glenview, Illinois; "General Foods Plans to Buy Oscar Mayer," *The New York Times*, February 5, 1981; "General Foods Corporation: List of Deals," Lehman Brothers Collection, Harvard Business School; "At General Foods, Did Success Breed Failure?" *The New York Times*, June 11, 1972.

54 **"We thought it would be attractive"**   Al Clausi to author.

54 **"They would drive"**   Al Clausi to author.

55 **As a child**   "Modern Living," *Time Magazine*, December 7, 1959. Charles Mortimer, "Purposeful Pursuit of Profits and Growth in Business," McKinsey Foundation Lectures; "Expert Offers Marketing Tips," *The New York Times*, May 14, 1959; "General Foods Chief Describes 'Benign Revolution in Kitchen,' " *The New York Times*, September 12, 1962.

55 **"Today, consumer expectations"**   Charles Mortimer to the dinner session of the Conference Board's Third Annual Marketing Conference, New York City, September 22, 1955.

56 **"Who says the only food"**   As recounted by Al Clausi to author.

56 **"My daughter"**   As recounted by Al Clausi to author.

56 **"That was a mind spreader"**   Al Clausi to author.

57 **The Tang project had started**   Al Clausi to author.

57 **"Are you working on anything"**   Bucher and Villines, *Greatest Thing Since Sliced Cheese*; Al Clausi and Domenic DeFelice to author.

58 **Bloomquist said that people**   Al Clausi to author.

58 **"We started in Beijing"**   Al Clausi to author.

59 **"low-residue" food**   Bucher and Villines, *Greatest Thing Since Sliced Cheese*.

59 **"Tell NASA we're honored"**   Ibid.

59 **as much as 19 grams**   The amount of sugar in a teaspoon is most commonly estimated at 4.2 grams per teaspoon. Thus, 19 grams of sugar is 4.5 teaspoons.

60 **When sales flattened out**   Kellogg's advertising unit and its agency provided a case study of the 2003 Pop-Tarts campaign to the Effie Awards, which bestowed the company with a gold award in 2004.

60 **"The 30 million tweens"**   Kellogg Effie Award case study.

62 **"It was teaching the basics"**   Betty Dickson to author.

62 **Dickson belonged to**   Digitized copies of the American Home Economics Association publication *Bulletin of American Home Economics Association*, later renamed *The Journal of Home Economics*, are available through the Mann Library at Cornell University. Starting in 1914, they provide insightful reading not only of the association's endeavors but also the social history of meal preparation as it evolved.

63 **the food industry undertook**   *The Journal of Home Economics*, volumes in 1956 and 1957. See for example, vol. 49, no. 3 (March 1957), which includes an announcement by General Foods that its Consumer Service Department was being renamed "General Foods Kitchens." This growing division of the company had six test kitchens where it prepared newly developed products and created recipes for using them. The kitchens were backed by a small army of photographers, writers, and correspondents who answered the thousands of letters General Foods started getting from homemakers, as well as food publicists, who delivered products to newspaper food writers and editors.

63 **"You will find that"**   Susan Marks, *Finding Betty Crocker* (New York: Simon and Schuster, 2005).

64 **In 1957 alone**   *Journal of Home Economics* 49, no. 3 (March 1957): 246.

65 **"When I joined General Mills"**   Marcia Copeland to author.

65 **she was praised** *Journal of Home Economics* 72, no. 4 (Winter 1980): 13. Her students included both boys and girls in the 10th, 11th, and 12th grades, with the foods curriculum described as "using small appliances for food preparation; developing shopping skills; and studying development of food habits."

65 **"Almost every bite"** "Modern Living: Just Heat and Serve," *Time Magazine*, December 7, 1959.

66 **"We taught skills"** Betty Dickson to author.

67 **"Convenience is still"** Al Clausi to author.

67 **Kellogg has gone so far down the road** In interviews and public statements, Kellogg staunchly defends the nutritional profile of its cereals. Acknowledging that some of its brands remain quite sweet, the company said it has numerous others with lesser amounts of sugar, and that an ongoing effort has succeeded in reducing the sugar in its cereals marketed to kids by 16%.

Chapter 4: "Is It Cereal or Candy?"

68 **John Harvey Kellogg** "J. H. Kellogg Dies; Health Expert, 91," *New York Times*, December 16, 1943; "Dr. John Harvey Kellogg," Battle Creek Historical Society; Dr. John Harvey Kellogg, "The Simple Life in a Nutshell," available from Lifestylelaboratory.com; John Kellogg, *The Living Temple* (Battle Creek, MI: Good Health Publishing, 1903); Bruce, *Cerealizing America*; "One Hundred Years: An Overview," Kellogg Company.

69 **a younger brother named Will** "Our Founder," W. K. Kellogg Foundation; "Our History," Kellogg Company; "The Good Old Days," *Promo Magazine*, September 1, 2003; Rachel Epstein, *W. K. Kellogg: Generous Genius* (Danbury, CT: Children's Press, 2000); "A 'Flakey' Patent Case," *Stereoscope*, Historical Society of the U.S. District Court for the Western District of Michigan, vol. 1, no. 3 (Fall 2003).

70 **a marketing whiz** Kraft spun off the Post cereals brand in 2007 in a merger with Ralcorp Holdings, and in 2011 Ralcorp spun off Post Foods into a company. "Post Heritage," Post Foods Company, Battle Creek, Michigan; Bruce, *Cerealizing America*; Nancy Rubin Stuart, *American Empress: The Life and Times of Marjorie Merriweather Post* (Bloomington, IN: iUniverse, 2004).

71 *Collier's* **magazine accused** Bruce, *Cerealizing America*.

72 **By 1970, the Big Three** Corts, *Ready-to-Eat Breakfast Cereal Industry*.

72 **they so completely controlled** "Not Enough Competition in Cereal Industry, Report Says," Associated Press, October 2, 1980; "Cerealmakers Call Federal Study 'Inadequate,' " Associated Press, February 13, 1980; "Bill Could Cripple FTC's Case on Cereal Companies," *Washington Post*, March 5, 1981, F. M. Scherer, "The Welfare Economics of Product Variety: An Application to the Ready-to-Eat Cereals Industry," *Journal of Industrial Economics* (December 1979).

73 **An enterprising dentist** Ira Shannon, "Sucrose and Glucose in Dry Breakfast Cereals," *Journal of Dentistry for Children* (September–October 1974). This study by Shannon, an Air Force dentist, generated newspaper articles throughout the country. See, for example, "Sugar in Breakfast Cereal," *Chicago Tribune*, October 30, 1977. He later wrote a book on his expanded research: Ira Shannon, *The Brand Name Guide to Sugar: Sucrose Content of Over 1,000 Common Foods and Beverages* (Chicago: Nelson-Hall, 1977).

74 **what made Mayer an industry threat** Jean Mayer, "Obesity: Physiologic Considerations," *American Journal of Clinical Nutrition* 9 (September–October 1961); "How to Eat Right and Live Longer," *U.S. News & World Report*, August 9, 1976; "Jean Mayer; Tufts Chancellor, Adviser on U.S. Nutrition," *Los Angeles Times*, January 3, 1993.

75 **"I contend that these cereals"** Jean Mayer, "Sweet Cereals Raise Labeling Issue," *Chicago Tribune*–New York News Syndicate, December 17, 1975.

75 **Sugar took center stage**   Marian Burros, "And Now a Word from Industry," *The Washington Post*, October 20, 1977.

75 **"We never said"**   Ibid.

76 **The battle in Washington**   Arthur Applbaum, "Mike Pertschuk and the Federal Trade Commission," John F. Kennedy School of Government, Harvard University, 1981; Arthur Applbaum, "Mike Pertschuk and the Federal Trade Commission: Sequel," John F. Kennedy School of Government, Harvard University, 1981; Howard Beales, "Advertising to Kids and the FTC: A Regulatory Retrospective that Advises the Present," Federal Trade Commission, speeches.

77 **"As with cigarette advertising"**   Applbaum, "Mike Pertschuk and the Federal Trade Commission."

77 **"If you take on the advertisers"**   Ibid.

78 **formidable team of lobbyists**   Ibid.

78 **Until then, the editorial board**   "The FTC as National Nanny," *The Washington Post*, March 1, 1976.

78 **Thirty-five years later**   "A Ban Too Far," *The New York Times*, May 31, 2012.

79 **the FTC itself nearly capsized**   "Curbing the FTC," *The MacNeil/Lehrer Report*, March 18, 1982; "FTC Ends Consideration of Rule on TV Ads for Children," Associated Press, September 30, 1981; "Regulating the FTC," *Newsweek*, October 15, 1979.

79 **"It became a pivotal moment"**   Bruce Silverglade to author.

79 **"They have suppressed"**   "Pertschuk Exits FTC with Guns Blazing," *The Washington Post*, September 26, 1984.

79 **"I don't make any bones"**   Ibid.; "New Head at FTC, New Era for Kid Ads," *The Washington Post*, October 1, 1981; "FTC Chief Changes Role of 'Nation's Nanny,' " *Christian Science Monitor*, December 6, 1983.

80 **The report ran 340 pages** "FTC Staff Report on Television Advertising to Children," Federal Trade Commission, February 1978.

81 **Dubbed "kidvid"** Jane Brody, "Personal Health," *New York Times*, March 13, 1985; Dale Kunkel and Walter Gantz, "Assessing Compliance with Industry Self-Regulation of Television Advertising to Children," *Journal of Applied Communication Research* 2 (1993).

82 **"It's a marketing tool"** Lisa Belkin, "Food Labels: How Much They Do, And Don't, Say," *The New York Times*, September 18, 1985.

82 **They began selling** Corts, *Ready-to-Eat Breakfast Cereal Industry*; "The Battle for the Cereal Bowl," *Food Processing*, 2009; "Topher's Breakfast Cereal Character Guide," Topher's Castle, LavaSurfer.com, 1998; "1991 Food Processor of the Year: General Mills," *Prepared Foods*, September 1, 1991; Li Li et al., "The Breakfast Cereal Industry," Cornell University, April 20, 2011.

82 **General Mills broke** Corts, *Ready-to-Eat Breakfast Cereal Industry*.

83 **"Sanger pushed"** Fingerman to author.

83 **General Mills jumped out** "Repositioning Cereals as Snacks?" *Brand-Packaging*, March 2000.

83 **"Getting a 0.5 percent share"** Karen Hoggan, "Kellogg, a Cereal Killing?" *Marketing*, October 31, 1991.

84 **These rules, at one time** Bruce, *Cerealizing America*.

85 **"You know how"** Edward Martin to author.

87 **Launched in 1993** Corts, *Ready-to-Eat Breakfast Cereal Industry*.

87 **advertising specialists from Leo Burnett** George Lazarus, "Burnett Drama Still a 'How Done It?' " *Chicago Tribune*, March 28, 1997; "Leo Burnett USA: The Most Effective Agency in America," *Market Wire*, June 8, 2007.

88 **"When you pour"** Case No. 4453, Children's Advertising Review Unit, Council of Better Business Bureaus, February 14, 2006.

88 **"I was used to cooking"** William Thilly to author.

89 **Jenness was no ordinary** "Clients Talk about Burnett," *Advertising Age*, July 31, 1995; "Former Ad Exec to Run Kellogg," *Chicago Tribune*, November 30, 2004; "Getting Settled in Battle Creek," *Grand Rapid Press*, December 26, 2004.

89 **"With the game we're in"** Jenny Rode, "Aggressive But Steady Sells the Cereal," *Battle Creek Enquirer*, March 7, 2006.

90 **Post had reversed** Details on this advertising campaign are disclosed in the case study Kraft and its advertising agency submitted to the Effie Awards in 2006.

90 **In an analysis** Likewise, Kellogg discussed its strategy in a 2007 submission to the Effie Awards for its Frosted Mini-Wheats campaign.

90 **"Help your kids earn an A"** Kellogg announcement, March 12, 2008, included as exhibit in FTC complaint against Kellogg.

90 **The scene was a classroom** FTC complaint against Kellogg, July 27, 2009.

91 **These were the findings** Ibid.

92 **plodded for more than a year** The FTC told me it needed the time to investigate and handle the case, and that its actions were prudent, given the agency's limited powers. "While many companies will voluntarily choose to stop running ads during the pendency of an investigation, the FTC has no legal basis to demand that they do so," Mary Engle, director of the agency's Division of Advertising Practices in the Bureau of Consumer Protection, said in an email. "And, of course, in most instances a company will strongly defend its advertising, and persuading it to sign a settlement can be difficult. We typically only seek preliminary relief from the federal courts in cases we view as clear-cut fraud. Otherwise, negotiating a consent order under which the company agrees to stop making the challenged claims is the most efficient way to proceed."

93 **A resounding 51 percent**   Case No. 4866, National Advertising Division, Council of Better Business Bureaus, June 17, 2008.

Chapter 5: "I Want to See a Lot of Body Bags"

95 **"We were always"**   Jeffrey Dunn to author.

97 **"There will never be"**   Constance L. Hays, *The Real Thing: Truth and Power at the Coca-Cola Company* (New York: Random House, 2004).

97 **The man who instilled**   Ibid.

98 **"The story they always tell"**   Jeffrey Dunn to author.

99 **By 1995, two in three kids**   Soda consumption rates are parsed in various ways. U.S. Secretary of Agriculture Dan Glickman, at the October 1998 symposium "Childhood Obesity: Causes and Prevention," stated that two-thirds of teenage boys were drinking three cans or more of soda a day, and two-thirds of girls were drinking two cans a day.

99 **They talked about "heavy users"**   Jeffrey Dunn to author.

99 **Dunn rose nearly to the top**   Jim Lovel, "Coke's a Big Part of His Life," *Atlanta Business Chronicle*, November 19, 2001.

99 **"At Coke, I do think"**   Jeffrey Dunn to author.

101 **He was put in charge**   "Former Coke Executive Walter Dunn Dead at 86," *Atlanta Business Chronicle*, June 22, 2009.

101 **"He took his job very seriously"**   Jeffrey Dunn to author.

102 **"He was up in first class"**   Ibid.

104 **PepsiCo pulled off**   Roger Enrico and Jesse Kornbluth, *The Other Guy Blinked: How Pepsi Won the Cola Wars* (New York: Bantam Books, 1986).

104 **was 4 percent sweeter**   Ibid.

104 **Coke crushed Pepsi**   Hays, *Real Thing*; Edward Hess, *The Coca-Cola Company*, Harvard Business School, 2008; Michael Watkins, *The Coca-Cola Company: The Rise and Fall of M. Douglas Ivester*, Harvard Business School, 2007; David Yoffie, *Cola Wars Continue: Coke and Pepsi in 2006*, Harvard Business School, 2006.

106 **"They said what's fascinating"**   Jeffrey Dunn to author.

107 **Studies have found**   Jennifer Breneiser and Sarah Allen, "Taste Preference for Brand Name Versus Store Brand Sodas," *North American Journal of Psychology*, vol. 13, no. 2 (2011).

108 **"We were no longer in a battle"**   Sergio Zyman, *The End of Marketing as We Know It* (New York: HarperCollins, 1999).

109 **With diet sodas**   *Beverage Digest* editor John Sicher to author.

110 **"Your heavy-user base"**   Jeffrey Dunn to author. The term *heavy user* also slipped into the conversations Coke had with Wall Street executives. For instance, on December 12, 2003, Doug Daft, the company's chairman and CEO, revealed to investors that Coke was producing a new half-liter bottle, saying, "It's fundamentally about giving people an opportunity who aren't heavy users, heavy drinkers, to seriously consider the opportunity." Four months later, on April 28, 2004, Coke told investors in a conference call that it was introducing a product called C2, which was formulated with half the calories of regular Coke in response to the ever-popular low-carbohydrate Atkins diet; David Van Houten, the chief operating officer said, "We believe that this product will appeal to heavy sugar cola users, and, in total, believe that it will get the total Coke trademark growing again."

110 **said he was astonished**   Todd Putman spoke at a June 2012 conference on soda organized by the Center for Science in the Public Interest, and was interviewed by several media outlets. Coke, in response, said that Putman had worked for the company for only a brief time and that one of the strategies he cited, known as "share of stomach," replacing other

beverages Americans that drank with Coke, was no longer the company's goal. Rather, Coke said, it was responding to health concerns by developing a host of new low- or no-calorie products, which now totaled 41% of the company's lineup, compared with 32% in 1999.

110 **"It was a mind-bending paradigm"** "Former Coke Executive Slams 'Share of Stomach' Marketing Campaign," *The Washington Post*, June 7, 2012.

111 **The advertising policy** Jeffrey Dunn to author.

111 **"If you think in terms"** Ibid.

111 **"Magically, when they would turn"** "Former Coke Executive Slams."

112 **Coke left nothing to chance** Coca-Cola, in 1978, founded an entity called the Coca-Cola Retailing Research Council to address issues of concern to retailers. Coke points out that while it supports the council by funding the research projects, the council's leadership is made up of grocery store executives who make independent decisions in using the research. Coke makes this research available to retailers through a service called Coke Solutions, which provides a wide range of assistance to grocers, from consumer trend analysis to customized marketing materials. One of the council's early endeavors was a 103-page study, "Social Trends and Food Retailing," produced for Coca-Cola in 1980 by SRI International. It noted the increasing numbers of working women with more money but less time on their hands, a trend favoring convenience foods (page 57). Increasing levels of stress would be driving consumers toward "mood foods" (71), the study said. It also divided Americans into four categories: "Belonger Consumers," "Achiever Consumers," "Inner-Directed Consumers," and "Need-Driven Consumers." The latter, comprised of economically challenged Americans, "are likely to buy more saturated fats such as pork, fatty hamburger, ham hocks, etc., and will purchase 'stretch,' 'fill-up,' foods, especially starches (bread, potatoes, spaghetti, noodles, rice, powdered and concentrated milk, etc.)" and are

"heavily inclined to eat processed foods" (86–87). Coca-Cola, nowadays, continues to present its research studies at various industry forums, generating considerable interest from the grocery and convenience stores. "Coca-Cola Bubbling With Ideas," *SCP Daily News*, October, 13, 2006; "Using Shopper Research to Grow Sales," *States News Service*, April 5, 2012. At a trade show in Dallas on April 30, 2012, Coke presented a study on checkout lanes that encouraged grocers to capitalize on "impulse buying" by increasing the use of beverage coolers. Soda, candy, and other items at checkout lanes currently total $5.5 billion in annual revenue but could grow to $7.2 billion with some simple improvements, the report said.

115 **"Coke was doing it"**   Jeffrey Dunn to author.

115 **In 2005, the research arm**   This report, "Convenience Teens: Building Loyalty with the Next Generation," is offered to retailers through Coke's marketing service on a highly restricted basis. The 41-page report, which I obtained a copy of, was copyrighted by the Coca-Cola Company in 2005. In conclusion, the report says of teens, "The social aspects of shopping are extremely important to them—namely, whether or not they feel welcome and like they belong. About technology: teens love it for what it can do for them, because it's novel. They expect to refuel their devices the same way older shoppers expect to refuel their vehicles. Watch Out! Teens purchase the same items from other retailers that they buy at c-stores. For teens, convenience isn't a store; it's everywhere."

116 **a book arrived**   H. Leighton Stewart et al., *Sugar Busters!* (London: Vermilion, 1998).

117 **The company's strategy**   Jeffrey Dunn to author; "Coca-Cola's Marketing Challenges in Brazil: The Tubainas War," Thunderbird School of Global Management; Yoffie, *Cola Wars Continue*; "Successful Retail Innovation in Emerging Markets: Latin American Companies Translate Smart Ideas into Profitable Businesses," Coca-Cola Retailing Research Council, 2006. More recently, Coke announced that it would invest $7.6

billion in Brazil through 2016, adding three new factories for a total of fifty; its focus on Brazil exceeds even its interest in China, where Coke plans to invest $4 billion. Trefis Team, "Coca-Cola Pours into Brazil and China, Pushes PepsiCo Aside in the U.S.," *Forbes*, April 10, 2012. Trefis, an analyst firm, estimates that Coke far outpaces the company's other products, such as Diet Coke and Dasani water, as a measure of the value it brings to the company's stock price. In second place, and surging, was Powerade, a sugar-sweetened sports drink.

117 **wrote a letter**   Jeffrey Dunn to author.

118 **underwent a restructuring**   In public forums and correspondence with the author, Coca-Cola has said that its strategies have embraced much of what Dunn was fighting for, including the marketing of water and a reduced emphasis on sodas in schools. "The world is changing, and we are too," the company said at the Added Sugars Conference sponsored by the American Heart Association on May 5, 2010. Coke said it was expanding its lineup of no- and low-calorie products, improving its labeling with front-side calorie disclosures, and working to promote active, healthy lifestyles. Coke is also driving to put its products in the context of overall diet. "Misperception: Craving sweets is bad," Coke says on its website. "You are literally born with it. Just remember: You may need to control your sweet tooth. Good health depends on a balance between calories you consume and calories you burn through physical activity. There is no such thing as a 'bad' food or beverage. If you love chocolate, ice cream or beverages that contain sugar, you can still include these in your diet—in moderation." That said, Coca-Cola continues to come under fire from health advocates who contend that its tactics aimed at kids have evolved to emphasize social media. For a detailed critique, see Jeff Chester and Kathryn Montgomery, *Interactive Food and Beverage Marketing: Targeting Children and Youth in the Digital Age*, Berkeley Media Studies Group, 2007. At the same time, Coke continues to receive praise from grocers for being aggressive in marketing products like Sprite to kids, such as with TV ads during the 2012 Olympics. "Sprite Targets Teens

with 'Intense' Campaign," *Convenience Store News,* July 30, 2012. "Sprite has a very specific teen target, so we're looking for a crisp articulation," a Coke marketing director explained. In its private discussions with marketers, Coke also continues to voice a strategy of driving consumption through various tactics. It has a program called "My Coke," where kids can send out pictures of a polar bear holding a bottle of Coke through Facebook, where Coke's own page has 47 million "likes." Coke also has a rewards program called My Coke Rewards, which links consumption to free merchandise and donations to schools. Launched in 2006, the program is viewed as a resounding success. "We see a positive volume swing," the program's director said in the September 10, 2009, issue of *Colloquy,* a marketing trade publication. "My Coke Rewards members in general consume two to three times more than the typical U.S. household." Perhaps the single most eye-catching item on Coke's website today is a running tally of how many Coca-Cola drinks people have consumed in the day thus far. The number increases by some 25,000 *each second.* The benchmark, Coke says, is from 2010: "1.7 billion servings daily."

118 **"You really don't want them mad"**   Ibid.

119 **in his presentation**   Jeffrey Dunn to author. I'm grateful to Dunn for sharing with me a copy of the presentation he made to the Madison Dearborn executives.

120 **already agreed to buy**   In July 2012, Madison Dearborn Partners announced it was selling the carrot farming operation, Bolthouse Farms, to the Campbell Soup Company for $1.55 billion.

Chapter 6: "A Burst of Fruity Aroma"

121 **twelve of the most senior**   The reporting on this and other Philip Morris meetings benefited greatly from the records the company has provided to the Legacy Tobacco Documents Library (LT) at the University of California, San Francisco. These records range from the mundane—

mailed invitations to attendees, payment vouchers, and memos on room preparation—to the deeply insightful—meeting agendas, minutes, and presentations. For a description of the building, see "It's Open House at Last at Altria's Midtown Home," *The New York Times*, September 9, 2008.

122 **He was joined by** "Joseph F. Cullman 3rd, Who Made Philip Morris a Tobacco Power, Dies at 92," *The New York Times*, May 1, 2004; "George Weissman, Leader at Philip Morris and in the Arts in New York, Dies at 90," *The New York Times*, July 27, 2009.

122 **When it finished merging** Stuart, *Kraft General Foods*; "Contents for Briefing Book Annual Meeting 1992," LT. The briefing book contains a fount of confidential information about Philip Morris's income and expenditures that year: the portion of its revenue derived from food (50%, compared with 42% for tobacco), its advertising expenditure ($2.4 billion), the cost of operating its fifteen corporate aircraft ($32 million), the sum it spent on lobbying fees ($4.8 million), and the R&D expenditures ($396 million).

124 **"Cigarettes are much the same"** Geoffrey Bible to author.

125 **a Nebraska man named Edwin Perkins** "Edwin Perkins and the Kool-Aid Story," *Historical News*, vol. 31, no. 4, Adams County Historical Society, 1998; Bucher and Villines, *Greatest Thing Since Sliced Cheese*; Jean Sanders, "Edwin E. Perkins: Inventor and Entrepreneur, Kool-Aid King," Nebraska State Education Association, 2008. Credit for Kool-Aid's early success also goes to one of his salesmen. "Bob Maclean, Marketing Expert Who 'Put Kool-Aid on the Map,' " *San Jose Mercury News*, February 21, 1994.

126 **Americans would stir up** Kraft presentation to Philip Morris, June 18, 1996, in LT.

127 **by not using promotional materials** For a discussion of the industry's practices, see "Hearing on the 'Targeting' of Blacks, Hispanics, Other Racial Groups, and Women by Alcohol and Tobacco Company Advertis-

ing," House Committee on Energy and Commerce, Transportation and Hazardous Materials Subcommittee, March 1, 1990.

127 *Adventures of Kool-Aid Man*   See Comic Vine, a comic book retailer.

127 **"Gain kid demand"**   Kraft presentation to Philip Morris, February 26, 1990, in LT.

127 **a mere 5 percent**   Ibid.

127 **won a coveted award**   Philip Morris Quarterly Director's Report, June 1992, marked "confidential," in LT. The award was an Effie.

127 **the company had trademarked**   U.S. Patent and Trademark Office, registration no. 1,646,512, May 28, 1991.

128 **"four clever ways"**   The Tang ad was reported by the Center on Science in the Public Interest in its newsletter, 1990.

128 **"To kids 6–12"**   Kraft presentation to Philip Morris, February 26, 1990, in LT.

128 **a few thoughts of their own**   "Minutes, Corporate Products Committee Meeting, February 26, 1990," in LT.

128 **showing "excellent" results**   Transcript, Philip Morris Annual Meeting of Stockholders, April 23, 1992, in LT.

129 **Each of the major brands**   Al Clausi interviews with author. The technical center is described in detail in a pamphlet, "Welcome to the General Foods Technical Center 20th Anniversary Open House," General Foods, November 11, 1977.

130 **fructose is much sweeter**   Various Kraft and other food scientists to author. For a technical discussion of fructose and specifics on Kraft's experimentation, see U.S. Patent No. 5,102,682, filed on April 7, 1992, Maurice Nasrallah, et al., on behalf of Kraft General Foods.

130 **true power of fructose**   John White, "The Role of Sugars in Foods:

Why Are They Added?" Added Sugars Conference, American Heart Association, May 2010.

131 **"Fructose Team"**   Philip Morris Product Development Symposium, December 5, 1990, in LT.

131 **known as the "Patent King"**   Fouad Saleeb to author; Bucher and Villines, *Greatest Thing Since Sliced Cheese.*

131 **estimated that this move alone**   Toni Nasrallah, "The Development of Taste/Cost Optimized Dry Mix Beverages," Philip Morris Product Development Symposium, December 5, 1990, in LT.

132 **Yale study made headlines**   Jane Brody, "New Data on Sugar and Child Behavior," *The New York Times*, May 10, 1990.

132 **World Health Organization**   I am grateful to Marion Nestle of New York University for being generous with her extensive files on this and other issues relating to nutrition policy and science. There was also widespread media coverage of the WHO proposal. "Commodities: WHO Proposal Worries Sugar Producers," *Inter Press Service*, April 26, 1990.

132 **He gave them a drug**   Adam Drewnowski et al., "Naloxone, an Opiate Blocker, Reduced the Consumption of Sweet High-Fat Foods in Obese and Lean Female Binge Eaters," *American Journal of Clinical Nutrition* 61 (1995): 1206–1212.

132 **experts now agree**   Marion Nestle to author. For a fair-minded and detailed perspective from an industry consultant, see John White, "Straight Talk about High-Fructose Corn Syrup: What It Is and What It Ain't," *American Journal of Clinical Nutrition* 88 (2008): 1716S–1721S; John White, "Misconceptions about High-Fructose Corn Syrup: Is It Uniquely Responsible for Obesity, Reactive Dicarbonyl Compounds, and Advanced Glycation Endproducts?" *Journal of Nutrition*, April 22, 2009.

133 **pure fructose might be**   K. L. Stanhope et al., "Consumption of Fructose and High Fructose Corn Syrup Increases Postprandial Triglycerides,

LDL-Cholesterol, and Apolipoprotein-B in Young Men and Women," *Journal of Clinical Endocrinology and Metabolism* 96, no. 10 (2011): 1596–1605.

134 **for $155 million**   "Contents for Briefing Book Annual Meeting 1992," in LT. The document notes, "We agreed not to disclose the purchase price ($155,000,000)."

134 **"staggering"**   "A World of Growth in Store," Philip Morris, 1995 annual report.

135 **"Yes, you could"**   Paul Halladay to author.

135 **Eighteen days later**   Kraft news release, January 26, 2007, and company officials to author.

135 **sent consumption soaring**   In its submission to the Effie Awards, Kraft said, "Capri Sun's profit increased well beyond the 17.6% consumption increase, thanks to the double whammy of penetration and buy rate increases during a price hike." Kraft won an Effie Award for this campaign.

136 **Only two of the thirty-five**   Stuart, *Kraft General Foods.*

137 **had some strategies of its own**   "Marketing Synergy," 1989, in LT.

137 **Bible told Kraft managers**   Philip Morris Product Development Symposium, December 5, 1990, in LT.

137 **they were back in front**   Kraft Beverage Division presentation to Corporate Products Committee, June 24, 1996, in LT.

138 **"The Beverage division"**   "Minutes, Corporate Products Committee Meeting, June 24, 1996," in LT.

138 **"received extremely high scores"**   Kraft Beverage Division presentation to Corporate Products Committee, June 24, 1996, in LT.

138 **"revealed that African Americans"**   Ibid.

139 **"Consumers in these stores"** Ibid.

140 **"Diabetics already represent"** Ibid.

140 **Kraft went after a younger set** In response to my questions about this presentation, the company said, "Kraft is constantly evaluating the taste preferences of our consumers in order to deliver products that meet their varying preferences. As for advertising to tweens, we agree that food and beverage companies should voluntarily limit what they advertise to kids. That's why, in 2005, we were the first company to change what we advertised to children under the age of 12. We stopped advertising to kids many of the foods and drinks they love, including Tang. And we were thrilled that many others in the industry followed our lead. Today, we advertise very few brands to children." See chapter 11 for more on Kraft's efforts on nutrition.

140 **"For Tang"** "Minutes, Corporate Products Committee Meeting, June 24, 1996," in LT.

140 **"an all-day affair"** Memos and agenda records, in LT.

Chapter 7: "That Gooey, Sticky Mouthfeel"

146 **The entry rules for this group** Richard Mattes, "Is There a Fatty Acid Taste?" *Annual Review of Nutrition* 29 (2009): 305–327; Jean-Pierre Montmayeur and Johannes Le Coutre, *Fat Detection: Taste, Texture, and Post-Ingestive Effects* (Boca Raton, FL: CRC Press, 2010).

148 **results from an experiment** Ivan Araujo and Edmund Rolls, "Representation in the Human Brain of Food Texture and Oral Fat," *Journal of Neuroscience* 24 (2004): 3086–3093.

149 **Brookhaven National Laboratory** Gene-Jack Wang et al., "Enhanced Resting Activity of the Oral Somatosensory Cortex in Obese Subjects," *NeuroReport* 13, no. 9 (2002); Gene-Jack Wang et al., "Exposure to Ap-

petitive Food Stimuli Markedly Activates the Human Brain," *Neuro-Image* 21 (2004): 1790–1797; Gene-Jack Wang et al., "Imaging of Brain Dopamine Pathways: Implications for Understanding Obesity," *Journal of Addiction Medicine* 3, no. 1 (2009): 8–18; Gene-Jack Wang et al., "Brain Dopamine and Obesity," *The Lancet* 357 (2001): 354–357.

149 **He recruited a dozen** Araujo and Rolls, "Representation in the Human Brain."

149 **"Fat and sugar both produce"** Edmund Rolls correspondence with author.

150 **described its operations** Francis McGlone to author.

150 **"I went there to build"** Ibid.

150 **role that odor plays** Dana Small et al. "Separable Substrates for Anticipatory and Consummatory Chemosensation," *Neuron* 57, no. 5 (2008): 786–797.

150 **the power of hearing** Massimiliano Zampini and Charles Spence, "The Role of Auditory Cues in Modulating the Perceived Crispiness and Staleness of Potato Chips," *Journal of Sensory Studies* 19, no. 5 (2004): 347–363.

151 **McGlone had a conversation** Francis McGlone to author.

151 **too many variables** McGlone posted a description of the experiment on his website, NeuroSci, entitled "Ice Cream Makes You Happy."

151 **"Just one spoonful"** "Ice Cream Makes You Happy, Say Unilever Scientists," *FoodNavigator*, May 4, 2005.

151 **Cargill is one of the world's largest** "An Unmatched Breadth of Ingredients for Creating Superior Products: Ingredient Portfolio," Cargill, 2007.

153 **Consumer groups who urge** See especially the Center for Science in

the Public Interest, "Promoting Consumption of Low-Fat Milk: The 1% or Less Social Marketing Campaign," Center for Health Improvement.

154 **describe the textures** Alina Szczesniak et al., "Consumer Texture Profile Technique," *Journal of Food Science* 40 (1970): 1253–1256.

154 **long list of terms** Ibid.

155 **"We were always trying"** Steve Witherly to author.

155 **showed them pictures** Montmayeur and Le Coutre, *Fat Detection*.

156 **"Why is fat so tasty?"** Ibid.

156 **"I want to know"** Adam Drewnowski to author.

157 **devised an experiment** Adam Drewnowski and M. R. C. Greenwood, "Cream and Sugar: Human Preferences for High-Fat Foods," *Physiology and Behavior* 30 (1983): 629–633.

158 **published his study** A. Drewnowski and M. Schwartz, "Invisible Fats: Sensory Assessment of Sugar/Fat Mixtures," *Appetite* 14 (1990): 203–217.

159 **"A dish or a drink"** Adam Drewnowski to author.

Chapter 8: "Liquid Gold"

161 **"We used it on toast"** Dean Southworth to author.

161 **something of a horror** The online guide to nutrition in grocery products, Calorie Count, a division of *The New York Times*, awards nutrition grades to products on a scale of A to F. The "original" version of Cheez Whiz was graded a D; other versions ranged between C and F, with one version, a "light" version, scoring a B.

161 **"Cheese treats QUICK"** Bucher and Villines, *Greatest Thing Since Sliced Cheese*.

162 **"We made adjustments"**   Kraft correspondence with author.

162 **"I imagine it's a marketing"**   Dean Southworth to author.

163 **Day in and day out**   *Report of the Dietary Guidelines Advisory Committee on the Dietary Guidelines for Americans, 2010,* U.S. Departments of Agriculture and Health and Human Services, 2010.

164 **found his calling**   Bucher and Villines, *Greatest Thing Since Sliced Cheese.* See also James Kraft's patent, no. 1,186,524.

165 **"Made up loss-and-gain account"**   Ibid.

165 **caustic descriptors**   Curt Wohleber, "From Cheese to Cheese Food: Kraft Persuaded Americans to Accept Cheese by Divorcing It from Its Microbe-laden Origins," *Invention and Technology* 17, no. 1 (2001).

166 **replaced by sodium phosphate**   In 2009, Kraft said the emulsifying salts sodium phosphate and sodium citrate were added "to create texture of melt properties of process cheese" and represented 40% to 45% of the sodium in processed cheese. Todd Abraham, "Sodium Reduction: Opportunities and Challenges," Kraft Foods, March 30, 2009.

167 **"Forget about the way"**   Bucher and Villines, *Greatest Thing Since Sliced Cheese.*

167 **"Milk in, cheese out"**   Ibid.

168 **In the old days**   Don Blayney, "The Changing Landscape of U.S. Milk Production," Economic Research Service, U.S. Department of Agriculture, 2002; Carl Coppock, "Selected Features of the U.S. Dairy Industry from 1900 to 2000," Coppock Nutritional Services, San Antonio, Texas; Carl Coppock to author; Comptroller General, "Effects and Administration of the 1984 Milk Diversion Program," U.S. General Accounting Office, Washington, D.C., 1985; Alden Manchester and Don Blayney, "Milk Pricing in the United States," Economic Research Service, U.S. Department of Agriculture, 2001; Charles Nicholson and Mark Stephen-

son, "Analysis of Proposed Programs to Mitigate Price Volatility in the U.S. Dairy Industry," Unpublished report to a consortium of dairy industry organizations, with author affiliation with California Polytechnic State University and the University of Wisconsin, 2010; "Overview of the United States Dairy Industry," National Agricultural Statistics Service, USDA, September 22, 2010; John Brouillette et al., "Cow Comfort and the Effects on Productivity and Profitability," *Hudson Valley Agricultural Newsletter.*

169 **"Deep beneath the ground"**　Ward Sinclair, "Under Missouri: A Monument to the Output of the American Cow," *The Washington Post*, December 21, 1981.

170 **discovered the cheese vaults**　John Block to author.

170 **"Some of us were aggravated"**　Sinclair, "Under Missouri."

170 **to make less milk**　Comptroller General, "Effects and Administration."

171 **"They made everything cheaper"**　Ulfert Broockmann to author.

172 **made three hundred thousand pounds**　Kraft presentation on Philadelphia Cream Cheese to the Philip Morris Corporate Products Committee, June 1989, in LT.

173 **"The introduction of new forms"**　Ibid.

173 **"Now, I don't mean to pick"**　Philip Morris Product Development Symposium, December 5, 1990, in LT.

174 **"Media selection will be skewed"**　Kraft presentation on Crockery Spreadable Cheese Snack to the Philip Morris Corporate Products Committee, June 1989, in LT.

175 **"There exists an opportunity"**　"Natural and Specialty Cheeses: The U.S. Market and a Global Perspective," Packaged Facts, 2010.

176 **"Competition is intensifying"** "Kraft USA 1993 Strategic Plan," in LT. At the same time, Kraft recognized the nutritional and other concerns

about cheese, and in its public statements the company emphasized that it was laboring hard to produce numerous low-fat varieties. In an internal report entitled "Contents for Briefing Book Annual Meeting 1992," Kraft anticipated a number of questions about cheese from stockholders: "Is Kraft worried about cholesterol in its cheese products? While dairy products contain both fat and cholesterol, eating them as part of a balanced diet remains a good practice for the vast majority of consumers. Do artificial foods like Velveeta hurt the sales of our other products? The texture and flavor of these products meet unique consumer needs and have generated sizable businesses for Kraft."

176 **kept a close watch on cheese** See consumption data, Economic Research Service, USDA.

177 **"We couldn't win"** Kraft submission to the Effie Awards.

177 **"was happy to be"** Ibid.

179 **Every week for four months** Ibid.

179 **Sales of Philadelphia Cream Cheese surged** Ibid.

180 **"We don't have to eliminate"** Walter Willett to author. In response to my questions about its efforts to increase the consumption of cheese, the company said, "Kraft believes that eating the foods you love and living a healthier lifestyle can, and should, co-exist. Cheese eaten in moderation can be part of a healthy lifestyle. We provide clear, consistent information so consumers can make informed choices as part of a balanced lifestyle. Kraft is proud to market many of which are lower in fat. We also offer Light, Reduced Fat, and Fat Free varieties of Philadelphia Cream Cheese, Kraft Singles and many of the other brands in our portfolio."

180 **Dutch researchers conducted** Mirre Viskaale-van Dongen, "Hidden Fat Facilitates Passive Overconsumption," *Journal of Nutrition* 139 (2009): 394–399.

180 **"The products we used"** Mirre Viskaal-van Dongen to author.

182 **where 1,800 workers** Joe Jerzewski, president and business manager of United Food and Commerce Local 536 to author.

182 **Behind the workers** Photographs of assembly line taken on or near the first day's run.

183 **dubbed the "Food Playground"** Stephen Quickert and Donna Rentschler, "Developing and Optimizing the Lunchables Concept," Philip Morris Product Development Symposium, December 5, 1990, in LT.

183 **In the great churn** Estimates from various grocery retailing experts.

184 **hitting $217 million** Bob Drane to author.

184 **A net loss of $20 million** Ibid.

185 **walked Maxwell through** With Bob Drane at this meeting was Jim McVey, CEO of the Oscar Mayer unit, who shared his recollections with me. "The nice thing about working with Philip Morris is, if you had something that had real potential, they were glad to take funds from their other products and put it behind the product that was moving," McVey told me.

185 **Maxwell turned to Drane** Jim McVey and Bob Drane to author.

186 **The founders were two Bavarian** "Oscar Mayer Foods Co.," *International Directory of Company Histories*, vol. 12, St. James Press, 1996; Bucher and Villines, *Greatest Thing Since Sliced Cheese*.

187 **horrors that were later exposed** Upton Sinclair, *The Jungle* (New York: Doubleday, 1906).

187 **has 3.5 grams of saturated fat** Data from Calorie Count.

187 **red meat consumption fell** Oscar Mayer to Philip Morris, 1991, in LT.

187 **"From 1986 to 1988"** Philip Morris Product Development Symposium, December 5, 1990, in LT.

188 **On a scale of 1 to 10**   Bob Eckert, president of the Oscar Mayer unit, to Philip Morris Corporate Products Committee, October 20, 1995, in LT.

188 **"Talent Search"**   Ibid.

188 **"We completed over"**   Ibid.

191 **To keep their discussions lively**   Bob Drane, "Developing and Optimizing the Lunchables Concept," project presentation, Oscar Mayer.

192 **puns and catchwords**   Ibid.

194 **Philip Morris had all but cornered**   Richard Kluger, *Ashes to Ashes: America's Hundred-Year Cigarette War, the Public Health, and the Unabashed Triumph of Philip Morris* (New York: Knopf, 1996).

194 **"a lovely business"**   Ibid.

194 **One Kraft executive**   John Ruff to author.

195 **But it had paid dearly**   Stuart, *Kraft General Foods.*

195 **"Hamish Maxwell was a brilliant"**   Geoffrey Bible to author.

195 **"I never really worried"**   Ibid.

197 **Philip Morris didn't accomplish this**   John Tindall to Philip Morris Product Development Symposium, December 5, 1990, in LT.

197 **"Suddenly, because of the smoking"**   Ibid.

197 **"Obviously, there was concern"**   Ibid.

198 **"which I fought like crazy"**   Bob Drane to author.

198 **"Lunchables with Dessert"**   Clark Murray, senior product manager, to Philip Morris Corporate Products Committee, January 24, 1991, in LT.

199 **"Our processed meat categories"**   Bob Eckert to Philip Morris Corporate Products Committee, October 20, 1995, in LT.

200 **"You bet"** Geoffrey Bible to author.

200 **"People could point to these things"** Ibid.

201 **"Bob was very keen"** Ibid.

201 **experimented with fresh carrots** Bob Drane to author.

203 **"This is not some big"** *Los Angeles Times*, February 8, 1994.

203 **"We went through"** Bob Drane to author.

205 **"The box was there"** Ibid.

205 **"Lunchables aren't about lunch"** Transcript of Bob Eckert, CEO of Kraft, to Business Week, in LT.

205 **"Kids like to build things"** Bob Drane to author.

207 **The group, called the Cancer Project, that examined** "The Five Worst Packaged Lunchbox Meals," the Cancer Project, Physicians Committee for Responsible Medicine, Spring 2009.

207 **Under pressure from attacks** "Oscar Mayer Lunchables Lunch Combinations Expand Wholesome Product Line," Kraft, August 16, 2010.

207 **"All things started to become clear"** Bob Drane to author.

209 **"People who work"** Ibid.

210 **Drane has also prepared** Bob Drane, "What Role Can the Food Industry Play in Addressing Obesity?" unpublished manuscript.

210 **"Plenty of guilt"** Ibid.

Chapter 10: "The Message the Government Conveys"

212 **President Abraham Lincoln created** Wayne D. Rasmussen, "Lincoln's Agricultural Legacy," Agricultural History Branch, USDA.

212 **two buildings that form** National Registry of Historic Places.

213 **$90 billion trade in snack foods** In keeping with the theme of this chapter, a good place to learn more about the snack trade is a white paper prepared by Dairy Management, an entity overseen by the Secretary of Agriculture whose goal is to increase consumption of cheese and other dairy products. "Snacking: Identifying a World of Opportunity for Diary," Dairy Management Inc., April 2010.

214 **center's annual budget** Center for Nutrition Policy and Promotion correspondence with author.

214 **policies on nutrition** "Dietary Guidelines for Americans," Center for Nutrition Policy and Promotion, USDA. Oversight of the panel of experts chosen to develop the guidelines every five years alternates between the Department of Agriculture and the Department of Health and Human Services.

215 **kids between one to three years** Dietary Guidelines Advisory Committee, *Report of the Dietary Guidelines Advisory Committee on the Dietary Guidelines for Americans, 2010* (Washington, D.C.: U.S. Departments of Agriculture and Health and Human Services, 2010), D2–12.

215 **Topping the list** Ibid, pages D3–13.

216 **blunt in urging people** Walter Willett to author. The Harvard School of Medicine has developed its own versions of the food pyramid and My Plate graphics that differ in significant ways. The protein portion of Harvard's ideal meal, for instance, advises, "Choose fish, poultry, beans and nuts; limit red meat; avoid bacon, cold cuts and other processed meats." And instead of encouraging people to drink milk, the Harvard nutrition scientists emphasize water, with limited milk and juice: "Avoid sugary drinks."

216 **buried the information** The USDA released an abridged version of the expert panel's report, which put the sources of saturated fat on page 25 of this 59-page summary.

217 **"If you really want people"** *The Diane Rehm Show*, February 1, 2011.

217 **"The idea isn't to eliminate"** Ibid.

218 **finding it in the grocery store** R. Post et al., "A Guide to Federal Food Labeling Requirements for Meat and Poultry Products," Labeling and Consumer Protection Staff, USDA, August 2007.

219 **USDA required this information** "Nutrition Labeling of Single Ingredient Products and Ground or Chopped Meat and Poultry Products," Food and Safety Inspection Service, USDA.

219 **"to include expertise"** Craig Henry, Grocery Manufacturers Association, letter to Carole Davis, Center for Nutrition Policy and Promotion, USDA, May 23, 2008.

220 **consumer's view was voiced** This and other comments submitted on the dietary guidelines are available through a database created by the USDA, which can be found at the Center for Nutrition Policy and Promotion's website.

222 **"I am concerned"** Transcript, Conference Report on the Food Security Act of 1985, U.S. Senate, December 18, 1985.

223 **It created two marketing programs** "Federally Authorized Commodity Research and Promotion Programs," U.S. General Accounting Office (now called the U.S. Government Accountability Office), December 1993; "Federal Farm Promotion ('Check-Off') Programs," Congressional Research Service, October 20, 2008; "Understanding Your Beef Checkoff Program," Cattlemen's Beef Board.

223 **yearly consumption of red meat** Carrie Daniel et al., "Trends in Meat Consumption in the United States," *Public Health Nutrition* 14, no. 4 (2011): 575–583. Consumer worries about fat are cited as a reason for decreased consumption in the beef-industry supported study "U.S. Beef Demand Drivers and Enhancement Opportunities," Kansas State University Agricultural Experiment Station and Cooperative Extension Service, June 2009.

224 **"I thought it was a dumb idea"** Mark Thomas to author.

225 **"We've done a lot of research"** Steve Wald, director of new product development, National Cattlemen's Beef Association, in video released by the association, January 8, 2008.

225 **promote more fast food sales** For a summary of some of these product innovations, see "Cattlemen's Beef Board Introduces New Staff, Snack," Cattlemen's Beef Board, February 25, 2008.

225 **Twenty-nine cuts of beef** At my request, the National Cattlemen's Beef Association examined national retail data and found that while a mere 20% of ground beef being sold was lean or leaner, two-thirds of the whole muscle cuts sold in 2012 were of the lean variety.

226 **Worries have arisen** "Background Information for Letter to Secretary Vilsack on Mechanically Tenderized (MT) Beef Products," Safe Food Coalition, June 12, 2009. For a critical perspective on tenderized meat, I'm grateful to Carol Tucker-Forman, a former assistant secretary of agriculture and now a fellow with the Consumer Federation of America.

226 **"lean finely textured beef"** The term has changed over the years, with producers and the USDA arguing for various permutations. For a basic description of the product, see H. Ying and J. G. Sebranek, "Finely Textured Lean Beef as an Ingredient for Processed Meats," Iowa State University, 1997.

227 **It was 15 percent cheaper** From various USDA and industry records obtained through the Freedom of Information Act and sources. Michael Moss, "The Burger That Shattered Her Life," *The New York Times*, October 4, 2009.

227 **The largest producer** Michael Moss, "Company Record on Treatment of Beef Called into Question," *The New York Times*, December 31, 2009.

227 **"It was frozen"** Charles Tant to author.

228 **"I do not consider the stuff"**   Gerald Zirnstein in USDA memo, obtained by author. Additionally, I am grateful to him for discussing this memo and his dealings on the product with me.

228 **first published**   Moss, "Company Record on Treatment."

229 **"That's one of the reasons"**   Video of press conference, Des Moines, Iowa, March 28, 2012.

229 **"a staple of the school lunch program"**   I am indebted to various officials of the USDA school lunch program for sharing their memos, data, and experiences on this matter with me. See also Moss, "Company Record on Treatment."

229 **"I think we are going"**   James Haggerty, " 'Pink Slime' Spurs Beef Backlash," (Scranton, Penn.) *Times-Tribune*, April 15, 2012.

230 **studies offered "convincing" evidence**   "Food, Nutrition, Physical Activity, and the Prevention of Cancer: A Global Perspective," World Cancer Research Fund and American Institute for Cancer Research, 2007, 121, 123.

231 **it called the "Cancer Team"**   For an internal analysis of the beef checkoff campaign's work on the cancer report, see "Project Evaluation Audit: World Cancer Research Fund/American Institute of Cancer Research Report," Sound Governance, June 13, 2008.

231 **also retained the services**   Starting on April 10, 2007, the expenditure of these funds was authorized by the National Cattlemen's Beef Association, with approval from the U.S. Secretary of Agriculture, according to records released by the USDA to author. Exponent provides case studies of its work products on its website.

231 **Exponent conducted its own**   Dominik D. Alexander et al., "Red Meat and Processed Meat Consumption and Cancer," National Cattlemen's Beef Association, 2010.

231 **"an emotional and frightening issue"** "Project Evaluation Audit: World Cancer Research Fund/American Institute of Cancer Research Report."

232 **"Cancer risk is not about diet alone"** Ibid.

232 **"Overall, beef checkoff messages"** Ibid.

233 **"The Secretary of Agriculture"** Opinion of the Court, in *Johanns v. Livestock Marketing Association*, U.S. Supreme Court, May 23, 2005. For an analysis of the case by a former FDA official, see Daniel E. Troy, "Do We Have a Beef with the Court? Compelled Commercial Speech Upheld, But It Could Have Been Worse," *Cato Supreme Court Review*, The Cato Institute.

234 **"I resist ranking"** Ruth Bader Ginsburg in separate opinion concurring in the judgment, in *Johanns v. Livestock Marketing Association*, U.S. Supreme Court, May 23, 2005. I am indebted to a former USDA economist, Parke Wilde, for being generous with his time in discussing his own, similarly critical analysis of the checkoff programs. See, for example, Parke E. Wilde, "Federal Communication About Obesity in the Dietary Guidelines and Checkoff Programs," Discussion Paper No. 27, Tufts University, 2005.

234 **less cheese-laden pizza** A 2006 brochure produced by the USDA, "Your Personal Health: Steps to a Healthier You," has this suggestion for people when they get the urge to eat pizza: "Ask for whole-wheat crust and half the cheese."

234 **"The partnership sells more cheese"** Tom Gallagher, "Checkoff Is Working Hard for You!" *Western Dairy Business*, September 2009.

235 **"In Mexico, a joint promotion with Domino's"** "Report to Congress on the National Dairy Promotion and Research," USDA, July 1, 2002.

237 **"The council will give Kraft"** "Kraft Foods Announces 10 Members of Worldwide Health and Wellness Advisory Council," *Business Wire*, September 3, 2003.

237 **"Both my boys were appalled"** Ellen Wartella to author.

239 **The session started out** I am grateful to various Kraft officials for discussion of the panel's confidential work with me.

239 **"I pointed this out"** Ellen Wartella to author.

240 **sought to refute** Andrea Carlson and Elizabeth Frazao, "Are Health Foods Really More Expensive? It Depends on How You Measure the Price," Economic Information Bulletin No. EIB-96, Economic Research Service, USDA, May 2012.

240 **"Build and defend"** Kraft to Philip Morris Corporate Products Committee, June 24, 1996, in LT.

240 **"We were trying"** Kathleen Spear to author.

241 **"We're a food business"** Ibid.

242 **an advertisement began appearing** Amanda Amos and Margaretha Haglund, "From Social Taboo to 'Torch of Freedom': The Marketing of Cigarettes to Women," *Tobacco Control* 9 (2000): 3–8.

243 **Only internally** "New Product Screening," Philip Morris memo, March 1, 1972, in LT.

243 **"High fat diets may"** Ernst Wynder et al., "Association of Dietary Fat and Lung Cancer," American Health Foundation, New York City, 1986, in LT.

244 **"ranks as one of the great"** Philip Morris Trial Counsel Seminar, La Jolla, California, May 9–12, 1990.

245 **"As new management"** Kraft General Foods Orientation to Management Meeting, July 11–12, 1990, in LT.

246 **"we're helping busy consumers"** "A Powerful Company, Poised for Growth," Presentation to Investment Community, New York City, June 28, 1999.

246 **the company's polling identified it** "Issues Management Q3 Omnibus Survey Key Results," Philip Morris memo, November 7, 2000, in LT.

246 **"Obesity is literally an epidemic"** Jay Poole speech to the Agriculture and Applied Economics Association meeting, 1999, in LT.

247 **1999 strategy paper** "A New Approach to Our Mission: Lessons from the Tobacco Wars," in LT.

248 **"We'd been through a pretty hard time"** Geoffrey Bible to author.

249 **"the right product for consumers"** Ibid.

249 **"He talked about why"** John Ruff to author.

250 **Bible told his food executives** Ibid.

250 **"I used to come home"** Ibid.

253 **from its own research** Kraft presentation to FDA, May 14, 2004.

253 **officials met with the agency** Ibid.

254 **the food industry was discussing** For an analysis of the systems being considered, see Ellen Wartella et al., "Examination of Front-of-Package Nutrition Rating Systems and Symbols," Phase 1 Report, Institute of Medicine, October 13, 2010.

254 **"That was in constant discussion"** John Ruff to author.

256 **"In Capri Sun alone"** Marc Firestone to author.

256 **managed to wrestle** The effort to cut 1.5 trillion calories is being over-

seen by a food industry group and is being monitored by the Robert Wood Johnson Foundation, which in 2012 was working to design a system that could verify and track any changes the industry makes. One challenge in performing this chore, foundation officials told me, would be keeping abreast of the constant flux in grocery products, as new items replace the old; another is ensuring the calorie reductions are not undertaken merely in low-selling versions of the mainline products.

257 **"Do you think"** Transcript, Kraft earnings conference call, July 16, 2003.

257 **Holden gamely replied** Ibid.

257 **removed from her job** Dave Carpenter, "Kraft Demotes Co-CEO Betsy Holden amid Product Setbacks," Associated Press, December 16, 2003.

258 **"The 'Twist, Lick and Dunk' ritual"** Anand Kripalu, Kraft Foods president for South Asia and Indonesia China, *Campaign India*, April 6, 2011.

258 **"A refreshing drink"** Kraft Cadbury announcement, April 14, 2011.

259 **"a broad market change"** Daryl Brewster to author.

260 **"People who otherwise"** Ibid.

260 **The 100-calorie concept** Elaine Wong, "100-Calorie Packs Pack It In," *Brandweek*, May 26, 2009.

260 **found that the small packs** Maura Scott, "The Effects of Reduced Food Size and Package Size on the Consumption Behavior of Restrained and Unrestrained Eaters," *Journal of Consumer Research* 35 (2008): 391–405.

261 **But Hershey wasn't worried** "Hershey Lures Lenny From Kraft," *Chicago Tribune*, March 13, 2001; "Hershey Foods: It's Time to Kiss and Make Up," Mendoza College of Business, University of Notre Dame, March 2003.

261 **"Our desire was to be"**   Daryl Brewster to author.

262 **lineup of Oreo cookies**   "Oreo Enters 100th Year Crossing the $2 Billion Mark; Plans to Reach $1 Billion in Developing Markets in 2012," Kraft announcement, May 3, 2012.

262 **Kraft's big move**   "Cadbury was the final piece of the puzzle," a Kraft vice president, Chris Jakubik, said in a presentation to investors on September 15, 2010, entitled "Hitting Our Sweet Spot." He described Kraft as "shifting from turnaround to growth" and said that the company was poised to lead the industry globally on snacks, with a leading 10.1% share of the market, far ahead of the second-largest snack seller, PepsiCo, at 7.6%.

263 **"My wife saw this"**   Comments on Kraft's website for the cream cheese chocolate product.

Chapter 12: **"People Love Salt"**

268 **more than ten grams**   "Report of the Dietary Guidelines Advisory Committee on the Dietary Guidelines for Americans," 2010, pages D6–17. Table salt is 40% sodium, so ten grams of salt is 4 grams of sodium, or 4,000 milligrams. A teaspoon holds about 6 grams of salt, or 2,300 milligrams of sodium.

268 **published the results**   Richard Mattes, and Diana Donnelly, "Relative Contributions of Dietary Sodium Sources," *Journal of the American College of Nutrition* 10, no. 4 (1991): 383–393.

270 **relied heavily on salt**   Mark Kurlansky, *Salt: A World History* (New York: Walker and Co., 2002).

270 **"People love salt"**   "10-Step Guide to Lowering the Sodium in Food and Beverage Products," Cargill, 2009.

271 **consider the number 2,300**   In examining the health impact of exces-

sive sodium, the Dietary Guideline panel appeared ready to set the recommended maximum at 1,500 milligrams for all Americans, meeting transcripts show. But noting how far above this level most Americans were, the final report retained 2,300 milligrams as a ceiling. The American Heart Association recommends that all adults consume less than 1,500 milligrams per day. Several public health agencies have established sodium limits for children, too, ranging from 1,500 milligrams (ages 1–3 years) to 1,900 (4–8 years) to 2,200 (9–13 years).

271 **lowered this target** "Report of the Dietary Guidelines Advisory Committee on the Dietary Guidelines for Americans, 2010."

271 **These 143 million people** The Centers for Disease Control and Prevention parsed the 2010 Dietary Guidelines for sodium and determined that 57% of American adults meet the criteria for limiting their sodium intake to 1,500 milligrams a day, and that almost all of these people were exceeding the limit. "Usual Sodium Intakes Compared with Current Dietary Guidelines: United States, 2005–2008," Morbidity and Mortality Weekly Report, Centers for Disease Control, October 11, 2011.

271 **turkey dinner from Hungry Man** Owned by the Pinnacle Foods Group, the Hungry Man products have been undergoing reformulations to lower the total sodium content.

272 **"Most of the things we love"** Paul Breslin to author.

273 **"I think the interest in making"** Ibid.

274 **researchers reported the case** L. Wilkins and C. P. Richter, "A Great Craving for Salt by a Child with Corticoadrenal Insufficiency," *Journal of the American Medical Association* 114 (1940): 866–868.

275 **One of Breslin's favorite papers** Stephen Woods, "The Eating Paradox: How We Tolerate Food," *Psychological Review* 98, no. 4 (1991): 488–505.

276 **One of the most intriguing accounts**   Michael Morris et al., "Salt Craving: The Psychobiology of Pathogenic Sodium Intake," *Physiological Behavior* 94, no. 4 (2008): 709–721.

277 **In 2006 a law firm**   Joseph McMenamin and Andrea Tiglio, "Not the Next Tobacco: Defense to Obesity Claims," *Food and Drug Law Journal* 61, no. 3 (2006): 445–518. In April 2012, a forum in Washington hosted by the Grocery Manufacturers Association included a discussion of food addiction moderated by an official from Frito-Lay, and the panelists included a Pennsylvania State University professor of nutrition named Rebecca Corwin who believes the addiction issue should be focused more on the consumer. It is the *way* these foods are being eaten, not the foods themselves, that is problematic, she argues. Highly fat and sugary foods are addictive when people go to extremes and alternate between bingeing and abstaining. Her 2009 paper in the *Journal of Nutrition* elaborates on this: "Even highly palatable food is not addictive in and of itself," she writes. "Rather, it is the manner in which the food is presented (i.e., intermittently), and consumed (i.e., repeated, intermittent 'gorging') that appears to entrain the addiction process." R. L. Corwin and Patricia Grigson, "Symposium Overview: Food Addiction: Fact or Fiction," *Journal of Nutrition* 139, no. 3 (2009): 617–619.

278 **"With few exceptions"**   Paul Breslin to author.

278 **people are drawn**   Howard Moskowitz and Jacquelyn Beckley, "Craving and the Product: Looking at What We Crave and How to Design Products around It," Moskowitz Jacobs Inc., 2001.

278 **"Don't let hunger"**   In 2001, Mars won an Effie Award from the advertising industry for a campaign that used a variation on this theme: "You're Not You When You're Hungry."

279 **This idea that salt**   Leslie Stein et al., "The Development of Salty Taste Acceptance Is Related to Dietary Experience in Human Infants: A Pro-

spective Study," *American Journal of Clinical Nutrition* 95, no. 1 (2012): 123–129.

280 **"Our data would suggest"** Anahad O'Connor, "Taste for Salt Is Shaped Early in Life," *The New York Times*, December 21, 2011.

281 **5 billion pounds** The United States Geological Survey estimates that 4 percent of all salt produced is used for food, with chemicals and ice control dividing the lion's share. See Dennis Kostick, "Salt," *2010 Minerals Yearbook*, U.S.G.S.

Chapter 13: "The Same Great Salty Taste Your Customers Crave"

286 **ten cents a pound** Cargill declined to disclose its prices or how much salt it produces. Pricing and production figures cited in this chapter are estimated by the author derived from food industry sources, public disclosures by other salt producers, and the U.S. Geological Survey, which tracks salt production.

287 **"Salt!"** Alton Brown, Cargill salt promotional video.

288 **Its revenue climbed** "Working to Feed the World," 2011 Cargill Annual Report.

288 **350 chartered cargo vessels** David Whitford and Doris Burke, "Cargill: Inside the Quiet Giant That Rules the Food Business," *Fortune Magazine*, October 27, 2011.

289 **4.8 million pounds** Estimate by author derived from U.S. Geological Survey reports and interviews with agency and industry officials. Dennis Kostick, "Salt," Mineral Commodity Summaries, U.S. Geological Survey, January 2012.

289 **a clever idea** Cargill officials to author.

290 **The Union deployed** Kurlansky, *Salt*.

291 **this alone would prevent** *Report of the Dietary Guidelines Advisory Committee on the Dietary Guidelines for Americans, 2010,* D6–16.

291 **"Excessive intake"** Kristen Dammann to author.

291 **The British knew well** Corinne Vaughan, "The U.K. Food Standards Agency's Programme on Salt Reduction," presentation to the Institute of Medicine, March 2009.

292 **"A lot of people"** Jody Mattsen to author.

294 **"Do you decide"** "10-Step Guide to Lowering the Sodium in Food and Beverage Products," Cargill, 2009.

294 **"Options such as potassium chloride"** Ibid.

294 **have sought to discourage** "Guidance on Salt Reduction in Meat Products for Smaller Businesses," British Meat Processors Association, London.

295 **"People are starting to complain"** Graham MacGregor to author. MacGregor chairs an advocacy group, Consensus Action on Salt and Health. See L. A. Wyness et al., "Reducing the Population's Intake: The U.K. Food Standards Agency's Salt Reduction Programme," *Public Health Nutrition* 15, no. 2 (2011): 254–261.

296 **"Salt really changes"** John Kepplinger to author; Michael Moss, "The Hard Sell on Salt," *The New York Times,* May 30, 2010.

296 **Kraft sent me a series** I'm grateful to the dining section staff of *The New York Times,* who joined me in tasting and evaluating this lower-salt ham.

296 **"We often fall off a cliff"** Russell Moroz to author; Moss, "Hard Sell on Salt."

296 **reported a litany** "Proposals to Revise the Voluntary Salt Reduction Targets: Consultation Response Summaries," Food Standards Agency, London.

297 **"Have stopped short"** Ibid. A review of the U.K. salt reduction efforts was undertaken by the consulting firm Leatherhead Food Research, which suggested that numerous manufacturers were hitting some walls in attempting to lower the sodium in their foods. However, consumer advocates, including Graham MacGregor, believe that more reductions will be attainable as the public's preference for salty taste is lowered. Rachel Wilson et al., "Evaluation of Technological Approaches to Salt Reduction," Leatherhead Food Research, 2012.

297 **"If we reach these goals"** Author transcript of press conference.

297 **One look at the guidelines** "National Salt Reduction Initiative Packaged Food Categories and Targets," New York City Health Department.

297 **volunteered only their easiest foods** "NSRI Corporate Commitments and Comments," New York City Health Department.

298 **scientific journal reviewer** These journal reviews are highly confidential, undisclosed even to the study authors being reviewed. I thank the reviewer for sharing these comments with me. In response, Campbell said that the study was unrelated to the sodium content of its juice and that it believed the vegetables claim remained valid.

298 **Their recent achievements** Data supplied by Campbell to author.

299 **"The reality is"** George Dowdie to author.

299 **"The question has been"** Ibid.

301 **"Sodium reduction is important"** Maria Panaritis, "New Campbell's CEO: Just Add Salt," *Philadelphia Inquirer*, July 13, 2011; Martinne Geller, "Campbell Stirs Things Up," Reuters, July 15, 2011. A week later, Campbell said that it remained committed to reducing the sodium in its products. "It's vital we provide people with a choice," Denise Morrison, the incoming CEO, said in the company's public release. "Campbell Continues to Provide Consumers with an Array of Lower-sodium Choices," Business Wire, July 20, 2011.

301 **"We look for future results"**   Martinne Geller, "Campbell Adds Salt to Spur Soup Sales," Reuters, July 12, 2011.

Chapter 14: "I Feel So Sorry for the Public"

302 **men in the eastern part**   Jaakko Tuomilehto et al., "Sodium and Potassium Excretion in a Sample of Normotensive and Hypertensive Persons in Eastern Finland," *Journal of Epidemiology and Community Health* 34 (1980): 174–178.

302 **a dramatic effect**   Heikki Karppanen and Eero Mervaala, "Sodium Intake and Hypertension," *Progress in Cardiovascular Diseases* 49, no. 2 (2006): 59–75. Pirjo Pietinen, "Finland's Experiences in Salt Reduction," National Institute for Health and Welfare, 2009.

305 **"He was very much disturbed"**   Karppanen to author.

305 **"people get addicted"**   Robert Lin to author.

306 **"My thinking was that"**   Ibid.

308 **"Every time a consumer"**   Robert Lin, "Model for Ideal Snack," Frito-Lay memo, February 8, 1979.

308 **"We fed them a potato chip"**   Robert Lin to author.

308 **"We wanted to confirm"**   Ibid.

309 **the organization has forced**   The Center for Science in the Public Interest makes available its legal actions, including company responses and follow-ups, on its website.

309 **"We're open to listening"**   Center for Science in the Public Interest release, August 11, 2005.

310 **"I realized that conventional"**   Michael Jacobson to author; Moss, "Hard Sell on Salt."

310 **"Our products are already low"**   Robert Lin, "Salt," Frito-Lay memo, March 1, 1978.

311 **A handwritten document**   I am grateful to Robert Lin for sharing, and discussing with me, this document, which provides a detailed record of Frito-Lay's scientific activities on salt.

313 **employee newsletter**   *Frito Bandwagon*, undated. The hearings were held by the Select Committee on GRAS (Generally Recognized as Safe) Substances.

313 **"From a strategic point of view"**   Robert Lin, " 'Calcium Anti-Hypertension' Campaign," Frito-Lay memo, January 28, 1982.

313 **finally responded to Jacobson's petition**   "GRAS Safety Review of Sodium Chloride," FDA, June 18, 1982.

314 **Normally, the panel's recommendation**   Michael Taylor, "FDA Regulation of Added Salt under the Food Additives Amendment of 1958: Legal Framework and Options," presented at Information Gathering Workshop, Committee on Strategies to Reduce Sodium Intake, Institute of Medicine, March 30, 2009.

314 **"The salt people, especially"**   Sanford Miller to author; Moss, "Hard Sell on Salt."

314 **"We were trying to balance"**   William Hubbard to author. Ibid.

314 **"When I see salty food"**   Robert Lin to author.

315 **"Anyone who designs a product"**   Robert Lin, "Consumer Research," Frito-Lay memo on agenda for company meeting with Greg Novak of R. J. Reynolds as a speaker, August 12, 1981.

315 **go down in flames**   "Oops! Marketers Blunder Their Way Through the 'Herb Decade,' " *Advertising Age*, February 13, 1989.

317 **"In fact, as those people aged"** Dwight Riskey to author.

318 **eating more salty snacks** Gary Jacobson, "How Frito-Lay Stays in the Chips: Company Profile," *Management Review*, December 1, 1989; Gary Levin, "Boomers Leave a Challenge," *Advertising Age*, July 8, 1991; "Monday Memo," *St. Louis Post-Dispatch*, August 2, 1993.

318 **Stuffers in a new light** Christine Donahue, "Marketers Return to Product Testing," *Adweek*, May 4, 1987.

319 **Enrico who sunk New Coke** Enrico and Kornbluth, *Other Guy Blinked.*

319 **Enrico would deploy** Dwight Riskey to author.

320 **"They had very high quality"** Ibid.

320 **"This . . . is one of the most"** Steven Witherly to author.

321 **formidable research complex** Robert Johnson, "Marketing in the '90s: In the Chips at Frito Lay, the Consumer Is an Obsession," *Wall Street Journal*, March 22, 1991.

321 **"If we can do for our category"** Jacobson, "How Frito-Lay Stays."

321 **chips performed poorly** Jane Dornbusch, "Flavor In, 'lites out; Low-Fat Products Lose Appeal; No Heavy Demand for 'Lite' Foods," *Boston Herald*, June 23, 1993.

321 **Levels dipped** Randolph Schmid, "Group Finds Little Change in Salt Content of Processed Foods," Associated Press, February 12, 1986; "Who Makes the Best Potato Chip?" *Consumer Reports*, June 1991; "Those New Light Snack Foods: When Marketers Call Their Chips 'Light,' They Must Mean Weight, Fat Content Remains High," *Consumer Reports*, September 1991.

321 **he found that they averaged** Lin, "Salt."

322 **When it came to snacks, however** Mike Esterl, and Valerie Bauerlein, "PepsiCo Wakes Up and Smells the Cola: Criticized for Taking Eye Off Ball and Focusing on Healthy Foods, Company Plans Summer Ad Splash," *Wall Street Journal*, June 28, 2011.

322 **a two-day meeting** A transcript of this meeting, which began on March 22, 2010, was provided by Fair Disclosure Wire.

324 **"The big thing that will happen here"** Ibid. In response to my questions about the investor presentation and the company's strategies, a company spokeswoman said, "PepsiCo has a broad portfolio of food and beverage brands consumers love, and our strategy is designed to grow all parts of our business. One of the ways we've always grown our business is by adapting our portfolio to meet the changing needs and desires of consumers. In response to stronger consumer demand for snacks with less sodium and beverages with less sugar, we've developed and launched products that give consumers these options. We've also built an attractive lineup of health and wellness brands in growing categories like dairy, juice, whole grains and sports nutrition. We believe that offering consumers a wide range of choices that provide great taste, convenience and value will continue to drive PepsiCo's success."

325 **famous in industry circles** Many of Dichter's speeches, papers, and other writing are archived at the Hagley Museum and Library, Wilmington, Delaware.

327 **"It was just waiting"** Alvin Hampel to author.

328 **the latest results** Dariush Mozaffarian et al., "Changes in Diet and Lifestyle and Long-Term Weight Gain in Women and Men," *New England Journal of Medicine* 364, no. 25 (2011): 2392–2404.

329 **"The starch is readily absorbed"** Eric Rimm to author.

331 **largest food manufacturer** "Nestlé's Stellar Performance Tops Our Annual Ranking," *Food Processing*, August 3, 2009.

331 **the "Billionaire Brands Treasury"** "Vision, Action, Value Creation," Nestlé Research, 2010, 26.

332 **"is a Swiss bank that prints food"** Steven Witherly to author.

332 **a remarkable invention** See Nestlé's WIPO patent application, No. WO/2012/089676. Citing competitive reasons, the company declined to elaborate on this work.

333 **"Obesity is not just for humans"** "Vision, Action, Value Creation," 29.

333 **so much fiber** Nestlé was able to show that a fiber-enriched yogurt would make one feel fuller than water crackers, which it detailed in the study. E. Almiron-Roig et al., "Impact of Some Isoenergetic Snacks on Satiety and Next Meal Intake in Healthy Adults," *Journal of Human Nutrition and Dietetics* 22 (2009): 469–474. But Erkner and other Nestlé officials emphasized that these findings were limited and should be viewed with caution. They cited the more sobering view of fiber and satiety in another Nestlé-funded study on fiber: Holly Willis et al., "Increasing Doses of Fiber Do Not Influence Short-Term Satiety or Food Intake and Are Inconsistently Linked to Gut Hormone Levels," *Food and Nutrition Research* 54 (2010).

334 **"calorie burner"** "New Enviga Proven to Burn Calories," *BevNet*, October 11, 2006.

334 **They took one look** Center for Science in the Public Interest, letter dated December 4, 2006, to Coca-Cola and Nestlé; "Center for Science in the Public Interest v. The Coca-Cola Company, Nestlé, Beverage Partners Worldwide," U.S. District Court for the District of New Jersey, 1:07cv539, filed February 1, 2007.

335 **arguably one of the unhealthiest** The online nutrition service Calorie Count awards the Pepperoni & Three Cheese Calzone Hot Pocket a D+; most of the varieties receive Cs and Ds.

335 **Nestlé, in response** Nestlé spokeswoman in email to author. "The brand delivered good tasting products in a very convenient and portable manner; we believed this benefit would grow in importance as millennials led the way towards more casual, less formal meals. The brand appealed mostly to males but provided us with a platform to meet evolving needs (we've since added breakfast items, expanded our Lean Pockets range and introduced Hot Pockets Snackers). Consumer research has helped us define what products make sense for this brand. While the core consumer initially is attracted to Hot Pockets, the additional benefits of Lean Pockets make it his choice as he ages. And the younger male in need of a satisfying sandwich is often still reliant on mom, the gatekeeper to the freezer (because she's the shopper). Her longer list of nutritional interests again leads to Lean Pockets."

336 **Every year, two hundred thousand obese** Jonathan Treadwell et al., "Systematic Review and Meta-Analysis of Bariatric Surgery for Pediatric Obesity," *Annals of Surgery* 248, no. 5 (2008): 763–776; Malcolm Robinson, "Surgical Treatment of Obesity: Weighing the Facts," *New England Journal of Medicine* 361 (2009): 520–521.

336 **"Many of these people"** Hillary Green to author.

336 **the only indulgence** Louis Cantarell to author.

338 **"This put special pressures"** Marion Nestle to Gabe Johnson, *The New York Times*, in unpublished video interview.

339 **its annual confab** I am grateful to the conference sponsor, *Beverage Digest*, for allowing me to attend.

340 **"a bit of a wimp"** Geoffrey Bible to author.

340 **"We're hooked on inexpensive food"** James Behnke to author.

342 **"Clearly, processed sugar"**   Nora Volkow to author.

342 **"When a lot of us grew up"**   Michael Lowe to author.

343 **"It's behavioral"**   Steve Comess to author.

343 **riddled with corner stores**   I am grateful to Sandy Sherman and Brianna Almaguer Sandoval of the Food Trust organization for being generous with their time in showing me their ongoing success in encouraging corner store owners in Philadelphia to sell healthier foods, including fresh fruits and vegetables, and to Gary Foster of the Center for Obesity Research and Education, Temple University, Philadelphia, for discussing his research on corner store and school food. See, for example, Gary Foster et al., "A Policy-Based School Intervention to Prevent Overweight and Obesity," *Pediatrics* 121 (2008): e794–e802.

344 **"It's like somebody is saying"**   Gabe Johnson and Michael Moss, "Food Fight," a *New York Times* video, March 27, 2011.

345 **"I need you to go"**   Amelia Brown to author; Gabe Johnson and Michael Moss, "Food Fight." Michael Moss, "Philadelphia School Battles Students' Bad Eating Habits, on Campus and Off," *New York Times*, March 27, 2011.

345 **"Candy?"**   McKinley Harris to author. Ibid.

selected bibliography

Baron, David P. "Obesity and McLawsuits." Stanford, CA: Stanford Graduate School of Business, 2005.

Beghin, John C., and Helen H. Jensen. "Farm Policies and Added Sugars in U.S. Diets." Ames: Center for Agricultural and Rural Development, Iowa State University, 2008.

Beller, Anne Scott. *Fat and Thin: A Natural History of Obesity*. New York: Farrar, Straus, and Giroux, 1977.

Bender, Marilyn. *At The Top*. New York: Doubleday, 1975.

Brownell, Kelly D., and Katherine Battle Horgen. *Food Fight: The Inside Story of the Food Industry, America's Obesity Crisis, and What We Can Do about It*. New York: McGraw-Hill, 2004.

Bruce, Scott, and Bill Crawford. *Cerealizing America: The Unsweetened Story of American Breakfast Cereal*. Winchester, MA: Faber and Faber, 1995.

Bucher, Anne, and Melanie Villines. *The Greatest Thing Since Sliced Cheese*. Northfield, IL: Kraft Foods, 2005.

Congressional Research Service. "Background on Sugar Policy Issues." Washington, DC: Congressional Research Service, 2007.

Corts, Kenneth S. *The Ready-to-Eat Breakfast Cereal Industry in 1994.* Boston: Harvard Business School Publishing, 1995.

Critser, Greg. *Fat Land: How Americans Became the Fattest People in the World.* New York: Houghton Mifflin, 2003.

Dietary Guidelines Advisory Committee. "Report of the Dietary Guidelines Advisory Committee on the Dietary Guidelines for Americans, 2005." Washington, DC: U.S. Departments of Agriculture and Health and Human Services, 2005.

_____. "Report of the Dietary Guidelines Advisory Committee on the Dietary Guidelines for Americans, 2010." Washington, DC: U.S. Departments of Agriculture and Health and Human Services, 2010.

Dolan, Robert J. "Mike Winsor: A Career in Marketing." Boston: Harvard Business School Publishing, 1998.

Enrico, Roger, and Jesse Kornbluth. *The Other Guy Blinked: And Other Dispatches from the Cola Wars.* New York: Bantam, 1986.

Ensminger, Audrey H., et al., eds. *Foods and Nutrition Encyclopedia.* Clovis, CA: Pegus Press, 1983.

Federal Trade Commission. "Marketing Food to Children and Adolescents: A Review of Industry Expenditures, Activities, and Self-Regulation." Washington, DC: Federal Trade Commission, 2008.

Gerson, Ben. *"Taking the Cake."* Boston: Harvard Business Review, 2004.

Gilmartin, Raymond, Marco Iansiti, and Bianca Buccitelli. "General Mills." Boston: Harvard Business School Publishing, 2008.

Hays, Constance L. *The Real Thing: Truth and Power at the Coca-Cola Company.* New York: Random House, 2004.

Hess, Edward. "The Coca-Cola Company." Charlottesville: University of Virginia Darden School Foundation, 2007.

Hightower, Jim. *Eat Your Heart Out: How Food Profiteers Victimize the Consumer.* New York: Crown, 1975.

Hine, Thomas. *The Total Package: The Secret History and Hidden Meanings of Boxes, Bottles, Cans, and Other Persuasive Containers.* New York: Little Brown, 1995.

Horowitz, Roger. *Putting Meat on the American Table: Taste, Technology, Transformation.* Baltimore, MD: Johns Hopkins University Press, 2006.

Imhoff, Daniel, ed. *The CAFO Reader: The Tragedy of Industrial Animal Factories.* London: University of California Press, 2010.

Institute of Medicine. "Alliances for Obesity Prevention: Finding Common Ground—Workshop Summary." Washington, DC: Institute of Medicine, 2012.

_____. "Examination of Front-of-Package Nutrition Rating Systems and Symbols." Washington, DC: Institute of Medicine, 2010.

_____. "Legal Strategies in Childhood Obesity Prevention." Washington, DC: Institute of Medicine, 2011.

_____. "Nutrition Standards for Foods in Schools: Leading the Way toward Healthier Youth." Washington, DC: Institute of Medicine, 2007.

_____. "Preventing Childhood Obesity: Health in the Balance." Washington, DC: Institute of Medicine, 2004.

_____. "Progress in Preventing Childhood Obesity: How Do We Measure Up?" Washington, DC: Institute of Medicine, 2006.

_____. "Strategies to Reduce Sodium Intake in the United States." Washington, DC: Institute of Medicine, 2010.

_____. "Weight Management: State of the Science and Opportunities for Military Programs." Washington, DC: Institute of Medicine, 2003.

Jacobson, Michael F. *Eater's Digest: The Consumer's Factbook of Food Additives.* Garden City, NY: Doubleday, 1972.

Kessler, David. *The End of Overeating: Taking Control of the Insatiable American Appetite.* New York: Rodale, 2009.

_____. *A Question of Intent: A Great American Battle with a Deadly Industry*. New York: Public Affairs, 2001.

Kluger, Richard. *Ashes to Ashes: America's Hundred-Year Cigarette War, the Public Health, and the Unabashed Triumph of Philip Morris*. New York: Alfred A. Knopf, 1996.

Kotchen, Dan, and Robert Drane. "Oscar Mayer: Strategic Marketing Planning." Boston: Harvard Business School Publishing, 1998.

Kurlansky, Mark. *Salt: A World History*. New York: Penguin, 2002.

Levenstein, Harvey. *Paradox of Plenty: A Social History of Eating in Modern America*. London: Oxford University Press, 1993.

Marks, Susan. *Finding Betty Crocker: The Secret Life of America's First Lady of Food*. Minneapolis: University of Minnesota Press, 2007.

Mintz, Sidney W. *Sweetness and Power: The Place of Sugar in Modern History*. New York: Viking Penguin, 1985.

Montmayeur, Jean-Pierre, and Johannes Le Coutre, eds. *Fat Detection: Taste, Texture, and Post Ingestive Effects*. Boca Raton, FL: CRC Press, 2010.

Moskowitz, Howard, and Alex Gofman. *Selling Blue Elephants: How to Make Great Products That People Want Before They Even Know They Want Them*. Upper Saddle River, NJ: Wharton School Publishing, 2007.

Muth, Mary K., et al. "Consumer-Level Food Loss Estimates and Their Use in the ERS Loss-Adjusted Food Availability Data." Washington, DC: U.S. Department of Agriculture, 2011.

Nestle, Marion. *Food Politics: How the Food Industry Influences Nutrition and Health*. Berkeley: University of California Press, 2007.

Nestle, Marion, and Malden Nesheim. *Why Calories Count: From Science to Politics*. London: University of California Press, 2012.

Netzer, Corinne T. *Encyclopedia of Food Values*. New York: Random House, 1992.

Packard, Vance. *The Hidden Persuaders*. New York: Simon and Schuster, 1957.

Pollan, Michael. *In Defense of Food: An Eater's Manifesto*. New York: Penguin, 2009.

_____. *The Omnivore's Dilemma: A Natural History of Four Meals*. New York: Penguin, 2006.

Roberts, Paul. *The End of Food*. New York: Houghton Mifflin Harcourt, 2008.

Sayle, Bart, and Surinder Kumar. *Riding the Blue Train: A Leadership Plan for Explosive Growth*. London: Penguin, 2006.

Schlosser, Eric. *Fast Food Nation*. New York: Houghton Mifflin, 2001.

Severson, Kim. *Spoon Fed: How Eight Cooks Saved My Life*. New York: Penguin, 2010.

Sorensen, Herb. *Inside the Mind of the Shopper: The Science of Retailing*. Upper Saddle River, NJ: Wharton School Publishing, 2009.

Stuart, Toby. "Kraft General Foods: The Merger." Boston: Harvard Business School Publishing, 1991.

Taubes, Gary. *Good Calories, Bad Calories: Fats, Carbs, and the Controversial Science of Diet and Health*. New York: Anchor Books, 2007.

_____. *Why We Get Fat: And What to Do about It*. New York: Alfred A. Knopf, 2011.

Wansink, Brian. *Mindless Eating: Why We Eat More Than We Think*. New York: Bantam Dell, 2006.

Watkins, Michael, Carin-Isabel Knoop, and Cate Reavis. "The Coca-Cola Company: The Rise and Fall of M. Douglas Ivester." Boston: Harvard Business School Publishing, 2000.

White House Task Force on Childhood Obesity. *Solving the Problem of Childhood Obesity within a Generation*. Washington, DC: Executive Office of the President, 2010.

Witherly, Steven A. *Why Humans Like Junk Food*. Lincoln, NE: iUniverse, 2007.

Yoffie, David B. "Cola Wars Continue: Coke and Pepsi in 2006." Boston: Harvard Business School Publishing, 2007.

Zyman, Sergio. *The End of Marketing as We Know It*. New York: HarperCollins, 1999.

index

About the Author

MICHAEL MOSS was awarded the Pulitzer Prize for explanatory reporting in 2010, and was a finalist for the prize in 1999 and 2006. He is also the recipient of a Loeb Award and an Overseas Press Club citation. Before coming to *The New York Times*, he was a reporter for *The Wall Street Journal*, *Newsday*, and *The Atlanta Journal-Constitution*. He lives in Brooklyn with his wife and two sons.

MICHAEL MOSS is available for select readings and lectures. To inquire about a possible appearance, please visit rhspeakers.com or call 212-572-2013.

About the Type

This book was set in Electra, a typeface designed for Linotype by W. A. Dwiggins, the renowned type designer (1880–1956). Electra is a fluid typeface, avoiding the contrasts of thick and thin strokes that are prevalent in most modern typefaces.